A
Random
Walk
Down
Wall Street

A Random Walk Down Wall Street

INCLUDING A LIFE-CYCLE GUIDE
TO PERSONAL INVESTING

Burton G. Malkiel

CHEMICAL BANK CHAIRMAN'S
PROFESSOR OF ECONOMICS
AT PRINCETON UNIVERSITY

W. W. Norton & Company
NEW YORK·LONDON

The text of this book is composed in Vermillion, with the display set in Berling Bold.
Composition and manufacturing by the Haddon Craftsmen, Inc.

Library of Congress Cataloging-in-Publication Data

Malkiel, Burton Gordon.
    A random walk down Wall Street : including a life-cycle guide to personal
investing / Burton G. Malkiel.—6th ed.
        p. cm.
    Includes bibliographical references (p.) and index.
    1. Investments. 2. Stocks. 3. Random walks (Mathematics)
I. Title.
HG4521.M284 1995
332.6—dc20 95-8148

ISBN 0-393-03888-2

W. W. Norton & Company, Inc., 500 Fifth Avenue, New York, N.Y. 10110
W. W. Norton & Company Ltd., 10 Coptic Street, London WC1A 1PU

To Nancy

Contents

8 CONTENTS

Contents

Preface

Over the past twenty-three years we have become accustomed to accepting the rapid pace of technological change in our physical environment. Innovations such as cellular and video telephones, cable TV, compact discs, microwave ovens, laptop computers, the information superhighway and new medical advances from organ transplants and laser surgery to nonsurgical methods of treating kidney stones and unclogging arteries have materially affected the way we live. Financial innovation over the same period has been equally rapid. In 1973, when the first edition of this book appeared, we did not have money market funds, NOW accounts, automatic tellers, index mutual funds, tax-exempt funds, emerging-market funds, floating-rate notes, zero-coupon bonds, S&P index futures and options, and new trading techniques such as "portfolio insurance" and "program trading," just to mention a few of the changes that have occurred in the financial environment. Much of the new material in this book has been included to explain these financial innovations and to show how you as a consumer can benefit from them.

This edition, the sixth, takes a hard look at the basic thesis of earlier editions of *Random Walk*—that the market prices

stocks so efficiently that a blindfolded chimpanzee throwing
darts at the *Wall Street Journal* can select a portfolio that performs as well as those managed by the experts. Through the
past quarter century that thesis has held up remarkably well.
Over two-thirds of professional portfolio managers have been
outperformed by the unmanaged S&P 500-Stock Index. Nevertheless, a number of studies by academics and practitioners,
completed during the 1980s and 1990s, have cast doubts on the
validity of the theory. And the stock market crash of October
1987 raised further questions concerning the vaunted efficiency
of the market. This edition explains the recent controversy and
reexamines the claim that it's possible to "beat the market." I
conclude that while reports of the death of the efficient-market
theory are vastly exaggerated, there do seem to be some techniques of stock selection that may tilt the odds of success in
favor of the individual investor.

The book remains fundamentally a readable investment
guide for individual investors. As I have counseled individuals
and families about financial strategy, it has become increasingly clear to me that one's capacity for risk bearing depends
importantly upon one's age and ability to earn income from
non-investment sources. It is also the case that the risk involved in most investments *decreases* with the length of time
the investment can be held. For these reasons, optimal investment strategies must be age related. Chapter Fourteen entitled
"A Life-Cycle Guide to Investing" should prove very helpful to
people of all ages. This chapter alone is worth the cost of a
high-priced appointment with a personal financial adviser.

During the mid-1990s, dealing in derivatives (futures and
options) was the most dynamic and rapidly growing part of the
securities business. It also was responsible for spectacular
losses suffered by blue-chip companies like Procter and Gamble, blue-chip banks like Barings PLC, and blue-chip counties
such as Orange County, California. A new chapter (Chapter
Eleven) explores in nontechnical terms the mysterious world of
derivative securities. More importantly, it provides sound advice for individuals concerning how to avoid the potentially
enormous risks involved while pointing out a few instances
where the use of derivatives can help some investors achieve
their portfolio objectives.

Finally, the facts and figures in the book have been completely revised and updated. I survey the stock and bond markets in the mid-1990s and present a set of strategies that should successfully carry investors into the twenty-first century.

My debts of gratitude to those mentioned in earlier editions continue. In addition, I must mention the names of a number of people who were particularly helpful in making special contributions to the sixth edition. These include my colleagues at Princeton, James Litvack and Charles Jones as well as Robert A. Frank, Al Clarke, Shang Song, Donald J. Peters, James Stoeffel, Edward J. Mathias, Abby Joseph Cohen, James Riepe, Roger Ibbotson, and Howard Baker. Special thanks go to James Norris, George Sauter, and John Bogle of the Vanguard Group of Investment Companies. Lugene Whitley and Phyllis Durepos made extraordinary contributions in transforming various illegible drafts and dictating tapes into readable text. Patricia Taylor continued her association with the project and made valuable editorial contributions to the sixth edition. I have also been fortunate to have been able to rely on the superb research assistance of Ethan Hugo and Yexiao Xu.

My wife, Nancy Weiss Malkiel, made by far the most important contributions to the successful completion of the past two editions. In addition to providing the most loving encouragement and support, she read carefully through various drafts of the manuscript and made innumerable suggestions that clarified and vastly improved the writing. She even corrected several errors that had eluded me and a variety of proofreaders and editors over the first four editions. Most important, she has brought incredible joy to my life. No one more deserved the dedication of a book than she.

Burton G. Malkiel
Princeton University
March 1995

Acknowledgments from Earlier Editions

M y debts of gratitude to people and institutions who have helped me with the first edition of this book are enormous in both number and degree. My academic colleagues and friends in the financial community who have contributed to various drafts of chapters are too numerous to mention. I must acknowledge explicitly, however, the many who have read through the entire manuscript and offered extremely valuable suggestions and criticisms. These include Peter Asch, Leo Bailey, Jeffrey Balash, William Baumol, G. Gordon Biggar, Jr., Lester Chandler, Barry Feldman, William Grant, Sol Malkiel, Richard Quandt, Michael Rothschild, H. Barton Thomas, and Robert Zenowich. It is particularly appropriate that I emphasize the usual *caveat* that the above-named individuals are blameless for any errors of fact or judgment in these pages. Many have warned me patiently and repeatedly about the madness of my heresies, and the above list includes several who disagree sharply with my position.

Many research assistants have labored long in compiling information for this book. Especially useful contributions were made by Barry Feldman, Paul Messaris, Barry Schwartz, Greg Smolanek, Ray Soldavin, and Elizabeth Woods. Helen Talar and Phyllis Durepos not only faithfully and accurately typed several drafts of the manuscript, but also offered extremely valuable research assistance as well. Elvira Giaimo provided most helpful computer programming. Many of the supporting studies for this book were conducted at Princeton's Financial Research Center.

A vital contribution was made by Patricia Taylor, a professional writer and editor. She read through two complete drafts of the book and made innumerable contributions to the style, organization, and content of the manuscript. She deserves much of the credit for whatever lucid writing can be found in these pages.

I am also grateful to Arthur Lipper Corporation for permission to use their mutual fund rankings, Wiesenberger Investment Services for the use of their data in many of my tables, Moody's Investors Service for permission to reproduce several of their stock charts, Consumers Union for their estimates of life insurance costs, College Retirement Equities Fund for making available to me James Farrell's performance studies, and Smith, Barney & Co., Inc. for allowing me the run of their investment library.

My association with W. W. Norton & Company has been an extremely pleasant one, and I am particularly grateful to my editor, Starling Lawrence, for his invaluable help.

Finally, the contribution of Judith Malkiel was of inestimable importance. She painstakingly edited every page of the manuscript and was helpful in every phase of this undertaking. This acknowledgment of my debt to her is the largest understatement of all.

In later editions I have been fortunate to have been able to continue to count on the help of many of those who assisted in the earlier editions. In addition, I want to express my gratitude for the absolutely essential assistance of John Bogle, Kelly Mingone, Ian MacKinnon, and Melissa McGinnis of the Vanguard Group of Investment Companies; Frank Wisneski and Ed Owens of Wellington Management Company; H. Bradlee Perry of David L. Babson & Co.; George Putnam of Putnam Funds; George S. Johnston of Scudder, Stevens & Clark; Roger Ford of Prudential Insurance; Robert Salomon, Jr., of Salomon Brothers; William Helman of Smith Barney; Douglas Daniels; and George Smith of Baker, Fentress & Company. Steve Feinstein, William Minicozzi, David Banyard, and Deborah Jenkens provided invaluable research assistance, and Linda Wheeler and Patricia Taylor offered exceedingly skillful editorial assistance. Superb typing support was provided by Barbara Johnson, Barbara Mains, Kay Kerr, Pia Ellen, Claire Cabelus, and especially Phyllis Durepos. Donald Lamm, Robert Kehoe, and Deborah Makay continued to make my association with W. W. Norton a most pleasant one. Joan Ryan and Claire Bien were extremely helpful in preparing new and updated charts. Michele Petersen also assisted in many ways. Finally, Rugby was particularly cooperative in agreeing to chew shoes and pillows instead of this manuscript. The first edition of *Random Walk* was dedicated to Jonathan, without whom the original manuscript would have been completed a year earlier. Because of Rugby's essential contributions, she was added to the dedication of the fourth edition.

PART ONE

Stocks
and
Their
Value

1

Firm Foundations
and
Castles in the Air

What is a cynic? A man who knows the price of everything,
and the value of nothing.
                    —Oscar Wilde, *Lady Windermere's Fan*

I n this book I will take you on a random walk
down Wall Street, providing a guided tour of the complex
world of finance and practical advice on investment opportunities and strategies. Many people say that the individual investor has scarcely a chance today against Wall Street's pros.
They point to techniques the pros use such as "program trading," "portfolio insurance," and investment strategies using
complex derivative instruments, and they read news reports of
mammoth takeovers, and the highly profitable (and sometimes
illegal) activities of well-financed arbitrageurs. This suggests
that there is no longer any room for the individual investor in
today's institutionalized markets. Nothing could be further
from the truth. You can do as well as the experts—perhaps
even better. As I'll point out later, it was the steady investors
who kept their heads when the stock market tanked in October
1987, and then saw the value of their holdings eventually recover and continue to produce attractive returns. And many of
the pros lost their shirts during the mid-1990s using derivative
strategies they failed to understand.

This book presents a succinct guide for the individual investor. It covers everything from insurance to income taxes. It

23

gives advice on shopping for the best mortgage and planning an
Individual Retirement Account. It tells you how to buy life insurance and how to avoid getting ripped off by banks and
brokers. It will tell you about the new trading techniques, the
arcane world of derivatives, and explain why so-called portfolio insurance was of little help to the professional investor
who employed it. It will even tell you what to do about gold and
diamonds. But primarily it is a book about common stocks—an
investment medium that not only has provided generous long-
run returns in the past but also appears to represent good possibilities for the years ahead.

What Is a Random Walk?

A random walk is one in which future steps or directions
cannot be predicted on the basis of past actions. When the
term is applied to the stock market, it means that short-run
changes in stock prices cannot be predicted. Investment advisory services, earnings predictions, and complicated chart patterns are useless. On Wall Street, the term "random walk" is an
obscenity. It is an epithet coined by the academic world and
hurled insultingly at the professional soothsayers. Taken to its
logical extreme, it means that a blindfolded monkey throwing
darts at a newspaper's financial pages could select a portfolio
that would do just as well as one carefully selected by the
experts.

Now, financial analysts in pin-striped suits do not like being
compared with bare-assed apes. They retort that academics
are so immersed in equations and Greek symbols (to say nothing of stuffy prose) that they couldn't tell a bull from a bear,
even in a china shop. Market professionals arm themselves
against the academic onslaught with one of two techniques,
called fundamental analysis and technical analysis, which we
will examine in Part Two. Academics parry these tactics by
obfuscating the random-walk theory with three versions (the
"weak," the "semi-strong," and the "strong") and by creating
their own theory, called the "new investment technology." This
last includes a concept called "beta," and I intend to trample

on that a bit. By the early 1990s, even some academics joined
the professionals in arguing that the stock market was at least
somewhat predictable after all. Still, as you can see, there's a
tremendous battle going on, and it's fought with deadly intent.
That's why I think you'll enjoy this random walk down Wall
Street. It has all the ingredients of high drama—fortunes made
and lost—and classic arguments about their cause.

But before we begin, perhaps I should introduce myself and
state my qualifications as guide. In writing this book I have
drawn on three aspects of my background; each provides a
different perspective on the stock market.

First is my employment at the start of my career as a market
professional with one of Wall Street's leading investment
firms. It takes one, after all, to know one. In a sense, I remain a
market professional in that I currently chair the finance committee of an insurance company that invests over $200 billion
in assets and sit on the boards of several of the largest investment companies in the nation. This perspective has been indis-
pensable to me. Some things in life can never fully be appreciated or understood by a virgin. The same might be said of
the stock market.

Second is my current position as an economist. Specializing
in securities markets and investment behavior, I have acquired
detailed knowledge of academic research and findings on investment opportunities. I have relied on many new research
findings in framing recommendations for you.

Last, and certainly not least, I have been a lifelong investor
and successful participant in the market. How successful I cannot say, for it is a peculiarity of the academic world that a
professor is not supposed to make money. A professor may
inherit lots of money, he may marry lots of money, and he may
spend lots of money, but he is never, never supposed to earn
lots of money; it's unacademic. Anyway, teachers are supposed to be "dedicated," or so politicians and administrators
often say—especially when trying to justify the low academic
pay scales. Academics are supposed to be seekers of knowledge, not of financial reward. It is in the former sense, therefore, that I shall tell you of my victories on Wall Street.

This book has a lot of facts and figures. Don't let that worry you. It is specifically intended for the financial layperson—and offers practical, tested investment advice. You need no prior knowledge to follow it. All you need is the interest and the desire to have your investments work for you.

Investing as a Way of Life Today

At this point, it's probably a good idea to explain what I mean by "investing" and how I distinguish this activity from "speculating." I view investing as a method of purchasing assets in order to gain profit in the form of reasonably predictable income (dividends, interest, or rentals) and/or appreciation *over the long term*. It is the definition of the time period for the investment return and the predictability of the returns that often distinguish an investment from a speculation. An excellent analogy from the first *Superman* movie comes to mind. When the evil Luthor bought land in Arizona with the idea that California would soon slide into the ocean, thereby quickly producing far more valuable beach-front property, he was speculating. Had he bought such land as a long-term holding after examining migration patterns, housing-construction trends, and the availability of water supplies, he would probably be regarded as investing—particularly if he viewed the purchase as likely to produce a dependable future stream of cash returns.

Let me make it quite clear that this is not a book for speculators: I am not going to promise you overnight riches. Indeed, a subtitle for this book might well have been *The Get Rich Slowly but Surely Book*. Remember, just to stay even, your investments have to produce a rate of return equal to inflation. If inflation were to proceed at a 4 percent rate—a rate much lower than we had in the 1970s and early 1980s—the effect on our purchasing power would still be devastating. The following table shows what an average 5.1 percent inflation has done over a recent period. My morning newspaper has risen 900 percent. My afternoon Hershey bar has risen even more and it's actually smaller than it was in 1962, when I was in graduate school. If inflation continued at the same rate, today's Hershey bar would cost over one dollar by the year 2000. It is clear that if we are to cope with even a mild inflation, we must undertake investment strategies that maintain our real purchasing power; otherwise, we are doomed to an ever-decreasing standard of living.

Investing requires a lot of work, make no mistake about it. Romantic novels are replete with tales of great family fortunes lost through neglect or lack of knowledge on how to care for money. Who can forget the sounds of the cherry orchard being cut down in Chekhov's great play? Free enterprise, not the Marxist system, caused the downfall of Chekhov's family: They had not worked to keep their money. Even if you trust all your funds to an investment adviser or to a mutual fund, you still have to know which adviser or which fund is most suitable to handle your money. Armed with the information contained in this book, you should find it a bit easier to make your investment decisions.

Most important of all, however, is the fact that investing is *fun.* It's fun to pit your intellect against that of the vast investment community and to find yourself rewarded with an increase in assets. It's exciting to review your investment returns and to see how they are accumulating at a faster rate than your salary. And it's also stimulating to learn about new ideas for

The Bite of Inflation

	Average 1962	Average 1994	Percentage Increase	Compound Annual Rate of Inflation
Consumer price index	30.20	149.00[b]	393.4	5.1%
Hershey bar	$.05	$.75	1,400.0	8.8
New York Times	.05	.60	1,100.0	8.1
First-class postage	.04	.29	625.0	6.4
Gasoline (gallon)	.31	1.19	283.9	4.3
Hamburger (McDonald's double)	.28[a]	1.65	489.3	5.7
Chevrolet (full size)	2,529.00	19,495.00	670.9	6.6
Refrigerator freezer	470.00	700.00	48.9	1.3

Source: *Forbes,* Nov. 1, 1977, for 1962 prices, and various government and private sources for 1994 prices.
[a]1963 data.
[b]CPI for August 1994.

products and services, and innovations in the forms of financial investments. A successful investor is generally a well-rounded individual who puts a natural curiosity and an intellectual interest to work to earn more money.

Investing in Theory

All investment returns—whether from common stocks or exceptional diamonds—are dependent, to varying degrees, on future events. That's what makes the fascination of investing: It's a gamble whose success depends on an ability to predict the future. Traditionally, the pros in the investment community have used one of two approaches to asset valuation—the "firm-foundation theory" or the "castle-in-the-air theory." Millions have been gained and lost on these theories. To add to the drama, they appear to be mutually exclusive. An understanding of these two approaches is essential if you are to make sensible investment decisions. It is also a prerequisite for keeping you safe from serious blunders. During the 1970s, a third theory, born in academia and named the "new investment technology," became popular in "the Street." Later in the book, I will describe that theory and its application to investment analysis.

The Firm-Foundation Theory

The firm-foundation theory argues that each investment instrument, be it a common stock or a piece of real estate, has a firm anchor of something called "intrinsic value," which can be determined by careful analysis of present conditions and future prospects. When market prices fall below (rise above) this firm foundation of intrinsic value, a buying (selling) opportunity arises, because this fluctuation will eventually be corrected—or so the theory goes. Investing then becomes a dull but straightforward matter of comparing something's actual price with its firm foundation of value.

It is difficult to ascribe to any one individual the credit for originating the firm-foundation theory. S. Eliot Guild is often given this distinction, but the classic development of the technique and particularly of the nuances associated with it was worked out by John B. Williams.

In *The Theory of Investment Value,* Williams presented an actual formula for determining the intrinsic value of stock. Williams based his approach on dividend income. In a fiendishly clever attempt to keep things from being simple, he introduced the concept of "discounting" into the process. Discounting basically involves looking at income backwards. Rather than seeing how much money you will have next year (say $1.05 if you put $1 in a savings bank at 5 percent interest), you look at money expected in the future and see how much less it is currently worth (thus, next year's $1 is worth today only about 95¢, which could be invested at 5 percent to produce $1 at that time).

Williams was actually serious about this. He went on to argue that the intrinsic value of a stock was equal to the present (or discounted) value of all its future dividends. Investors were advised to "discount" the value of moneys received later. Because so few people understood it, the term caught on and "discounting" now enjoys popular usage among investment people. It received a further boost under the aegis of Professor Irving Fisher of Yale, a distinguished economist and investor.

The logic of the firm-foundation theory is quite respectable and can be illustrated best with common stocks. The theory stresses that a stock's value ought to be based on the stream of earnings a firm will be able to distribute in the future in the form of dividends. It stands to reason that the greater the present dividends and their rate of increase, the greater the value of the stock. Thus, differences in growth rates are a major factor in stock valuation. And now the slippery little factor of future expectations sneaks in. Security analysts must estimate not only long-term growth rates but also how long an extraordinary growth can be maintained. When the market gets overly enthusiastic about how far in the future growth can continue, it is popularly held on Wall Street that "stocks are discounting not only the future but perhaps even the hereafter." The point is that the firm-foundation theory relies on some tricky forecasts of the extent and duration of future growth. The foundation of intrinsic value may thus be less dependable than is claimed.

The firm-foundation theory is not confined to economists alone. Thanks to a very influential book, Graham and Dodd's *Security Analysis,* a whole generation of Wall Street security analysts was converted to the fold. Sound investment management, the practicing analysts learned, simply consisted of buying securities whose prices were temporarily below intrinsic value and selling ones whose prices were temporarily too high. It was that easy. Of course, instructions for determining intrinsic value were furnished and any analyst worth his salt could calculate it with just a few taps of the calculator or personal computer. Perhaps the most successful disciple of the Graham and Dodd approach was a canny midwesterner named Warren Buffett, who is often called "the sage of Omaha." Buffett has compiled a legendary investment record, allegedly following the approach of the firm-foundation theory.

The Castle-in-the-Air Theory

The castle-in-the-air theory of investing concentrates on psychic values. John Maynard Keynes, a famous economist and outstandingly successful investor, enunciated the theory most lucidly in 1936. It was his opinion that professional investors prefer to devote their energies not to estimating intrinsic values, but rather to analyzing how the crowd of investors is likely to behave in the future and how during periods of optimism they tend to build their hopes into castles in the air. The successful investor tries to beat the gun by estimating what investment situations are most susceptible to public castle-building and then buying before the crowd.

According to Keynes, the firm-foundation theory involves too much work and is of doubtful value. Keynes practiced what he preached. While London's financial men toiled many weary hours in crowded offices, he played the market from his bed for half an hour each morning. This leisurely method of investing earned him several million pounds for his account and a tenfold increase in the market value of the endowment of his college, King's College, Cambridge.

In the depression years in which Keynes gained his fame, most people concentrated on his ideas for stimulating the economy. It was hard for anyone to build castles in the air or to dream that others would. Nevertheless, in his book *The General Theory of Employment, Interest and Money,* he devoted an entire chapter to the stock market and to the importance of investor expectations.

With regard to stocks, Keynes noted that no one knows for sure what will influence future earnings prospects and dividend payments. As a result, Keynes said, most persons are "largely concerned, not with making superior long-term forecasts of the probable yield of an investment over its whole life, but with foreseeing changes in the conventional basis of valuation a short time ahead of the general public." Keynes, in other words, applied psychological principles rather than financial evaluation to the study of the stock market. He wrote, "It is not sensible to pay 25 for an investment of which you believe the prospective yield to justify a value of 30, if you also believe that the market will value it at 20 three months hence."

Keynes described the playing of the stock market in terms readily understandable by his fellow Englishmen: It is analogous to entering a newspaper beauty-judging contest in which you have to select the six prettiest faces out of a hundred photographs, with the prize going to the person whose selections most nearly conform to those of the group as a whole.

The smart player recognizes that personal criteria of beauty are irrelevant in determining the contest winner. A better strategy is to select those faces the other players are likely to fancy. This logic tends to snowball. After all, the other contestants are likely to play the game with at least as keen a perception. Thus, the optimal strategy is not to pick those faces the player thinks are prettiest, or those the other players are likely to fancy, but rather to predict what the average opinion is likely to be about what the average opinion will be, or to proceed even further along this sequence. So much for British beauty contests.

The newspaper-contest analogy represents the ultimate form of the castle-in-the-air theory of price determination. An investment is worth a certain price to a buyer because he expects to sell it to someone else at a higher price. The investment, in other words, holds itself up by its own bootstraps. The new buyer in turn anticipates that future buyers will assign a still-higher value.

In this kind of world, there is a sucker born every minute— and he exists to buy your investments at a higher price than you paid for them. Any price will do as long as others may be willing to pay more. There is no reason, only mass psychology. All the smart investor has to do is to beat the gun—get in at the very beginning. This theory might less charitably be called the "greater-fool" theory. It's perfectly all right to pay three times what something is worth as long as later on you can find some innocent to pay five times what it's worth.

The castle-in-the-air theory has many advocates, in both the financial and the academic communities. Keynes's newspaper contest is the same game played by "Adam Smith" in *The Money Game.* Mr. Smith also espouses the same view of stock price determination. On the academic side, Oskar Morgenstern was a leading champion. The views he expressed in *Theory of Games and Economic Behavior,* of which he was co-author, have had a significant impact not only on economic theory but also on national security decisions and strategic corporate planning. In 1970 he co-authored another book, *Predictability of Stock Market Prices.* Here, he and his colleague, Clive Granger, argued that the search for intrinsic value in stocks is a search for the will-o'-the-wisp. In an exchange economy the value of any asset depends on an actual or prospective transaction. Morgenstern believed that every investor should post the following Latin maxim above his desk:

Res tantum valet quantum vendi potest.
(A thing is worth only what someone else will pay for it.)

How the Random Walk Is to Be Conducted

With this introduction out of the way, come join me for a random walk through the investment woods, with an ultimate stroll down Wall Street. My first task will be to acquaint you with the historical patterns of pricing and how they bear on the two different theories of pricing investments. It was Santayana who warned that if we did not learn the lessons of the past we would be doomed to repeat the same errors. Therefore, in the pages to come I will describe some spectacular crazes—both long past and recently past. Some readers may pooh-pooh the mad public rush to buy tulip bulbs in seventeenth-century Holland and the eighteenth-century South Sea Bubble in England. But no one can disregard the new-issue mania of 1959–61, the conglomerate wave of the middle 1960s, and the "Nifty Fifty" craze of the 1970s. Those who believe that we are too smart to keep repeating the same mistakes will be interested to read of the 1980s versions of a new-issue craze and a boom in concept stocks in fields running the gamut from high-technology genetic engineering to carpet cleaning. The incredible boom in Japanese land and stock prices and the equally spectacular crash of those prices in the early 1990s provide additional warnings that we are not immune from the errors of the past.

These more recent speculative "bubbles" all involved the savvy institutions and investment pros. All too many investors are lazy and careless—a terrifying combination when greed gets control of the market and everyone wants to cash in on the latest craze or fad.

Then I throw in my own two cents' worth of experience. Even in the midst of a period of speculation, I believe, it is possible to find a logical basis for security prices. At the end of Part One I present some rules that should be helpful in giving investors a sense of value and in protecting you from the horrible blunders made by many professional investment managers.

2
The Madness
of
Crowds

Greed run amok has been an essential feature of every spectacular boom in history. In their frenzy for money, market participants throw over firm foundations of value for the dubious but thrilling assumption that they too can make a killing by building castles in the air. Such thinking can, and has, enveloped entire nations.

The psychology of speculation is a veritable theater of the absurd. Several of its plays are presented in this chapter. The castles that were built during the performances were based on Dutch tulip bulbs, English "bubbles," and good old American real estate and blue-chip stocks. In each case, some of the people made some money some of the time, but only a very few emerged unscathed.

History, in this instance, does teach a lesson: While the castle-in-the-air theory can well explain such speculative binges, outguessing the reactions of a fickle crowd is a most dangerous game. "In crowds it is stupidity and not mother-wit that is accumulated," Gustave Le Bon noted in his 1895 classic on crowd psychology. It would appear that not many have read the book. Skyrocketing markets that depend on purely psychic support have invariably succumbed to the financial law of gravitation. Unsustainable prices may persist for years, but eventually they reverse themselves. Such reversals come with the suddenness of an earthquake; and the bigger the binge, the greater the resulting hangover. Few of the reckless builders of castles in the air have been nimble enough to anticipate these reversals perfectly and escape without losing a great deal of money when everything came tumbling down.

The Tulip-Bulb Craze

The tulip-bulb craze was one of the most spectacular get-rich-quick binges in history. Its excesses become even more vivid when one realizes that it happened in staid old Holland in the early seventeenth century. The events leading to this speculative frenzy were set in motion in 1593 when a newly appointed botany professor from Vienna brought to Leyden a collection of unusual plants that had originated in Turkey. The Dutch were fascinated with this new addition to the garden—but not with the professor's asking price (he had hoped to sell the bulbs and make a handsome profit). One night a thief broke into the professor's house and stole the bulbs, which were subsequently sold at a lower price but at greater profit.

Over the next decade or so the tulip became a popular but expensive item in Dutch gardens. Many of these flowers succumbed to a nonfatal virus known as mosaic. It was this mosaic that helped to trigger the wild speculation in tulip bulbs. The virus caused the tulip petals to develop contrasting colored stripes or "flames." The Dutch valued highly these infected bulbs, called "bizarres." In a short time, popular taste dictated that the more bizarre a bulb, the greater the cost of owning it.

Slowly, tulipmania set in. At first, bulb merchants simply tried to predict the most popular variegated style for the coming year, much as clothing manufacturers do in gauging the public's taste in fabric, color, and hemlines. Then they would buy an extra-large stockpile to anticipate a rise in price. Tulip-bulb prices began to rise wildly. The more expensive the bulbs became, the more people viewed them as smart investments. Charles Mackay, who chronicled these events in his book

Memoirs of Extraordinary Popular Delusions, noted that the ordinary industry of the country was dropped in favor of speculation in tulip bulbs: "Nobles, citizens, farmers, mechanics, seamen, footmen, maid-servants, even chimney sweeps and old clotheswomen dabbled in tulips." Everyone imagined that the passion for tulips would last forever and buyers from all over the world would come to Holland and pay whatever prices were asked for them.

People who said the prices could not possibly go higher watched with chagrin as their friends and relatives made enormous profits. The temptation to join them was hard to resist; few Dutchmen did. In the last years of the tulip spree, which lasted approximately from 1634 to early 1637, people started to barter even their personal belongings, such as land, jewels, and furniture, to obtain the bulbs that would make them even wealthier. Bulb prices reached astronomical levels.

Part of the genius of financial markets is that, when there is a real demand for a method to enhance speculative opportunities, the market will surely provide it. The instruments that enabled tulip speculators to get the most action for their money were "call options" similar to those popular today in the stock market.

A call option conferred on the holder the right to buy tulip bulbs (call for their delivery) at a fixed price (usually approximating the current market price) during a specified period. He was charged an amount called the option premium, which might run 15 to 20 percent of the current market price. An option on a tulip bulb currently worth 100 guilders, for example, would cost the buyer only about 20 guilders. If the price moved up to 200 guilders, the option holder would exercise his right; he would buy at 100 and simultaneously sell at the then current price of 200. He then had a profit of 80 guilders (the 100 guilders' appreciation less the 20 guilders he paid for the option). Thus he enjoyed a fourfold increase in his money, whereas an outright purchase would only have doubled his money. By using the call option it was possible to play the market with a much smaller stake as well as get more action out of any money invested. The call is one way to leverage one's investment. Leveraging is any technique that increases the potential rewards (and risks) of an investment. Such devices helped to ensure broad participation in the market. The same is true today.

The history of the period was filled with tragicomic episodes. One such incident concerned a returning sailor who brought news to a wealthy merchant of the arrival of a shipment of new goods. The merchant rewarded him with a breakfast of fine red herring. Seeing what he thought was an onion on the merchant's counter, and no doubt thinking it very much out of place amid silks and velvets, he proceeded to take it as a relish for his herring. Little did he dream that the "onion" would have fed a whole ship's crew for a year. It was a costly Semper Augustus tulip bulb. The sailor paid dearly for his relish—his no longer grateful host had him imprisoned for several months on a felony charge.

Given the current glut of historians, they have a need to make work by reinterpreting the past. This is also the case for those who study financial history. Such historians are called revisionists. Recently, some financial historians have reexamined the evidence about various financial bubbles and have argued that considerable rationality in pricing may have existed after all. One of these revisionist historians, Peter Garber, has suggested that tulip-bulb pricing in seventeenth century Holland was far more rational than is commonly believed.

Garber makes some good points and I do not mean to imply that there was no rationality at all to the structure of bulb prices that existed during the period. The Semper Augustus, for example, was a particularly rare and beautiful bulb and, as Garber reveals, it was valued greatly even in the years before the tulipmania. Moreover, Garber's research indicates that rare individual bulbs commanded high prices even after the general collapse of bulb prices, albeit at levels that were only a fraction of their peak prices. But Garber can find no rational explanation for such phenomena as a twenty-fold increase in tulip-bulb prices during January of 1637 followed by an even larger decline in prices in February. Apparently, as happens in all speculative crazes, prices eventually got so high that some people decided they would be prudent and sell their bulbs. Soon others followed suit. Like a snowball rolling downhill, bulb deflation grew at an increasingly rapid pace, and in no time at all panic reigned.

Government ministers stated officially that there was no reason for tulip bulbs to fall in price—but no one listened. Dealers went bankrupt and refused to honor their commitments to buy tulip bulbs. A government plan to settle all contracts at 10 percent of their face value was frustrated when bulbs fell even below this mark. And prices continued to decline. Down and down they went until most bulbs became almost worthless—selling for no more than the price of a common onion.

And what of those who had sold out early in the game? In the end, they too were engulfed by the tulip craze. For the final chapter of this bizarre story is that the shock generated by the boom and collapse was followed by a prolonged depression in Holland. No one was spared.

The South Sea Bubble

Suppose your broker has called you and recommended that you invest in a new company with no sales or earnings—just great prospects. "What business?" you say. "I'm sorry," your broker explains, "no one must know what the business is, but I can promise you enormous riches." A con game, you say. Right you are, but 300 years ago in England this was one of the hottest new issues of the period. And, just as you guessed, investors got very badly burned. The story illustrates how fraud can make greedy people even more eager to part with their money.

At the time of the South Sea Bubble, the British were ripe for throwing away money. A long period of English prosperity had resulted in fat savings and thin investment outlets. In those days, owning stock was considered something of a privilege. As late as 1693, for example, only 499 souls benefited from ownership of East India stock. They reaped rewards in several ways, not least of which was that their dividends were untaxed. Also, their number included women, for stock represented one of the few forms of property that females could possess in their own right. The South Sea Company, which obligingly filled the need for investment vehicles, had been formed in 1711 to restore faith in the government's ability to meet its obligations. The company took on a government IOU of almost £10 million. As a reward, it was given a monopoly over all trade to the South Seas. The public believed there were immense riches in such trade, and regarded the stock with distinct favor.

From the very beginning, the South Sea Company reaped profits at the expense of others. Holders of the government securities to be assumed by the company simply exchanged their securities for those of the South Sea Company. Those with prior knowledge of the plan quietly bought up government securities selling as low as £55 and then turned them in at par for £100 worth of South Sea stock when the company was incorporated. Not a single director of the company had the slightest experience in South American trade. This did not stop them from quickly outfitting African slave ships (the sale of slaves being one of the most lucrative features of South American trade). But even this venture did not prove profitable, because the mortality rate on the ships was so high.

The directors were, however, wise in the art of public appearance. An impressive house in London was rented, and the boardroom was furnished with thirty black Spanish upholstered chairs whose beechwood frames and gilt nails made them handsome to look at but uncomfortable to sit in. In the meantime, a shipload of company wool that was desperately needed in Vera Cruz was sent instead to Cartagena, where it rotted on the wharf from lack of buyers. Still, the stock of the company held its own and even rose modestly over the next few years despite the dilutive effect of "bonus" stock dividends and a war with Spain which led to a temporary collapse in trading opportunities. John Carswell, the author of an excellent history, *The South Sea Bubble*, wrote of John Blunt, a director and one of the prime promoters of the securities of the South Sea Company, that "he continued to live his life with a prayerbook in his right hand and a prospectus in his left, never letting his right hand know what his left hand was doing."

Across the Channel, another stock company was formed by an exiled Englishman named John Law. Law's great goal in life was to replace metal as money and create more liquidity through a national paper currency backed by the state and controlled through a network of local agencies. To further his purpose, Law acquired a derelict concern called the Mississippi Company and proceeded to build a conglomerate that became one of the largest capital enterprises ever to exist, even to this day.

The Mississippi Company attracted speculators and their money from throughout the Continent. The word "millionaire" was invented at this time, and no wonder: The price of Mississippi stock rose from 100 to 2,000 in just two years, even though there was no logical reason for such an increase. At one time the inflated total market value of the stock of the Mississippi Company in France was more than eighty times that of all the gold and silver in the country.

Meanwhile, back on the English side of the Channel, a bit of jingoism now began to appear in some of the great English houses. Why should all the money be going to the French Mississippi Company? What did England have to counter this? The answer was the South Sea Company, whose prospects were beginning to look a bit better, especially with the December 1719 news that there would be peace with Spain and hence the way to the South American trade would at last be clear. Mexicans supposedly were waiting for the opportunity to empty their gold mines in return for England's abundant supply of cotton and woolen goods. This was free enterprise at its finest.

In 1720, the directors, an avaricious lot, decided to capitalize on their reputation by offering to fund the entire national debt, amounting to £31 million. This was boldness indeed, and the public loved it. When a bill to that effect was introduced in Parliament, the stock promptly rose from £130 to £300.

Various friends and backers who had shown interest in getting the bill passed received as their reward an option with a twist: The individual was granted a certain amount of stock without having to pay for it; it was simply "sold" back to the company when the price went up, and the individual only collected the profit. Among those rewarded were George I's mistress and her "nieces," all of whom bore a startling resemblance to the king.

On April 12, 1720, five days after the bill became law, the

South Sea Company sold a new issue of stock at £300. The issue could be bought on the installment plan—£60 down and the rest in eight easy payments. Even the king could not resist; he subscribed for stock totaling £100,000. Fights broke out among other investors surging to buy. The price had to go up— and the eager buyers were right. It advanced to £340 within a few days. To ease the public appetite, the South Sea directors announced another new issue—this one at £400. But the public was ravenous. Within a month the stock was £550, and it was still rising. On June 15 yet another issue was put forth, and this time the payment plan was even easier—10 percent down and not another payment for a year. The stock hit £800. Half the House of Lords and more than half the House of Commons signed on. Eventually, the price rose to more than £1,000. The speculative craze was in full bloom.

Not even the South Sea Company was capable of handling the demands of all the fools who wanted to be parted from their money. Investors looked for other new ventures where they could get in on the ground floor. Just as speculators today search for the next Intel and the next Microsoft, so in England in the early 1700s they looked for the next South Sea Company. Promoters obliged by organizing and bringing to the market a flood of new issues to meet the insatiable craving for investment.

As the days passed, new financing proposals ranged from ingenious to absurd—from importing a large number of jackasses from Spain (even though there was an abundant supply in England) to making salt water fresh. Increasingly the promotions involved some element of fraud, such as making boards out of sawdust. There were nearly one hundred different projects, each more extravagant and deceptive than the other, but each offering the hope of immense gain. They soon received the name of "bubbles," as appropriate a name as could be devised. Like bubbles, they popped quickly—usually within a week or so.

The public, it seemed, would buy anything. New companies seeking financing during this period were organized for such purposes as: the building of ships against pirates; encouraging the breeding of horses in England (there were two issues for this purpose); trading in human hair; building of hospitals for bastard children; extracting of silver from lead; extracting sunlight from cucumbers; and even for a wheel of perpetual motion.

The prize, however, must surely go to the unknown soul who started "A Company for carrying on an undertaking of great advantage, but nobody to know what it is." The prospectus promised unheard-of rewards. At nine o'clock in the morning, when the subscription books opened, crowds of people from all walks of life practically beat down the door in an effort to subscribe. Within five hours a thousand investors handed over their money for shares in the company. Not being greedy himself, the promoter promptly closed up shop and set off for the Continent. He was never heard from again.

Not all investors in the bubble companies believed in the feasibility of the schemes to which they subscribed. People were "too sensible" for that. They did believe, however, in the "greater-fool" theory—that prices would rise, that buyers would be found, and that they would make money. Thus, most investors considered their actions the height of rationality as, at least for a while, they could sell their shares at a premium in the "after market," that is, the trading market in the shares after their initial issue.

Whom the gods would destroy, they first ridicule. Signs that the end was near were demonstrated with the issuance of a pack of South Sea playing cards. Each card contained a caricature of a bubble company, with an appropriate verse inscribed underneath. One of these, the Puckle Machine Company, was supposed to produce machines discharging both round and square cannonballs and bullets. Puckle claimed that his machine would revolutionize the art of war. The eight of spades, shown on the following page, described it as follows:

> A rare invention to destroy the crowd.
> Of fools at home instead of fools abroad.
> Fear not, my friends, this terrible machine.
> They're only wounded who have shares therein.

Many individual bubbles had been pricked without dampening the speculative enthusiasm, but the deluge came in Au-

Puckle's Machine

A rare invention to Destroy the Crowd ,
Of Fools at Home instead of Foes Abroad :
Fear not my Friend, this terrible Machine ,
They're only Wounded that have Shares therein .

gust with an irreparable puncture to the South Sea Company. This was self-administered by its directors and officers. Realizing that the price of the shares in the market bore no relationship to the real prospects of the company, they sold out in the summer.

The news leaked and the stock fell. Soon the price of the shares collapsed and panic reigned. Government officials tried in vain to restore confidence, and a complete collapse of the public credit was barely averted. Similarly, the price of Mississippi Company shares fell to a pittance as the public realized that an excess of paper currency creates no real wealth, only inflation. Big losers in the South Sea Bubble included Isaac Newton, who exclaimed, "I can calculate the motions of heavenly bodies, but not the madness of people." So much for castles in the air.

To protect the public from further abuses, Parliament passed the Bubble Act, which forbade the issuing of stock certificates by companies. For over a century, until the act was repealed in 1825, there were relatively few share certificates in the British market.

The Florida Real Estate Craze

The bulbs and bubbles are, admittedly, ancient history. Could the same sort of thing happen in sophisticated modern times? Let's turn to more recent and familiar events from our own past and see. America, the land of opportunity, had its turn in the 1920s. And given our emphasis on freedom and growth, we produced two of the most spectacular booms and two of the loudest crashes civilization has ever known.

Conditions could not have been more favorable for speculative crazes. The country had been experiencing unrivaled prosperity. One could not but have faith in American business, and as Calvin Coolidge said, "The business of America is business." Businessmen were likened to religious missionaries and almost deified. Such analogies were even made in the opposite direction. Bruce Barton, of the New York advertising agency Batten, Barton, Durstine and Osborn, wrote in *The Man No-*

body Knows that Jesus was "the first businessman," and his parables were "the most powerful advertisements of all time."

The euphoric mood of optimism and faith in business that prevailed in the twenties led to widespread enthusiasm about real estate and the stock market. It would appear only natural that Americans, having conquered an entire continent, would succumb to real estate booms. One of the greatest centered on Florida in the middle 1920s. The climate was just right. The population was steadily growing and housing was in short supply. Land values began increasing rapidly. Stories of investments doubling and tripling attracted speculators from all over the country. Easy credit terms added fuel to the speculative frenzy. "This market has no downside risk," the land speculators opined, as Dutchmen undoubtedly said to each other about the tulip-bulb market in an earlier time.

There are reports of Palm Beach land bought for $800,000 in 1923, subdivided, and resold in 1924 for $1.5 million. By the following year the same land sold at $4 million. At the top of the boom there were 75,000 real estate agents in Miami, one-third of the entire population of the city.

Inevitably the boom ended, as do all speculative crazes. By 1926 new buyers could no longer be found and prices softened. Then the speculators dumped their holdings on the market and a complete collapse ensued.

Wall Street Lays an Egg

With this Florida experience so recent, one would have thought that investors would avoid a similar misadventure on Wall Street. But Florida was only a regional prelude to what came next. Beginning in 1928, stock-market speculation became a national pastime. From early March 1928 through early September 1929, the market's percentage increase equaled that of the entire period from 1923 through early 1928. The price rises for the major industrial corporations sometimes reached 10 or 15 points per day. The extent of these rises is illustrated in the table on the following page.

Not "everybody" was speculating in the market, as was

commonly assumed. Borrowing to buy stocks (buying on margin) did increase from only $1 billion in 1921 to almost $9 billion in 1929. Nevertheless, only about a million persons owned stocks on margin in 1929. Still, the speculative spirit was at least as widespread as in the previous crazes and was certainly unrivaled in its intensity. More important, stock-market speculation was central to the culture. John Brooks, in *Once in Golconda,** recounted the remarks of a British correspondent newly arrived in New York: "You could talk about Prohibition, or Hemingway, or air conditioning, or music, or horses, but in the end you had to talk about the stock market, and that was when the conversation became serious."

Unfortunately, there were hundreds of smiling operators only too glad to help the public construct castles in the air. Manipulation on the stock exchange set new records for unscrupulousness. No better example can be found than the operation of investment pools. One such undertaking raised the price of RCA stock 61 points in four days. Let me explain how the pools could manipulate the price of a stock.

An investment pool required close cooperation on the one hand and complete disdain for the public on the other. Generally such operations began when a number of traders banded together to manipulate a particular stock. They appointed a pool manager (who justifiably was considered something of an

Security	Opening Price March 3, 1928	High Price September 3, 1929[a]	Percentage Gain in 18 Months
American Telephone & Telegraph	179½	335⅝	87.0
Bethlehem Steel	56⅞	140⅜	146.8
General Electric	128¾	396¼	207.8
Montgomery Ward	132¾	466½	251.4
National Cash Register	50¾	127½	151.2
Radio Corporation of America	94½	505	434.5

[a]Adjusted for stock splits and the value of rights received subsequent to March 3, 1928.

*Golconda, now in ruins, was a city in India. According to legend, everyone who passed through it became rich.

artist) and promised not to doublecross each other through private operations.

The pool manager accumulated a large block of stock through inconspicuous buying over a period of weeks. If possible, he obtained an option to buy a substantial block of stock at the current market price within a stated period of, say, three or six months. Next he tried to enlist the stock's specialist on the exchange floor as an ally.

Pool members were in the swim with the specialist on their side. A stock-exchange specialist functions as a broker's broker. If a stock was trading at $50 a share and you gave your broker an order to buy at $45, the broker typically left that order with the specialist. If and when the stock fell to $45, the specialist then executed the order. All such orders to buy below the market price or sell above it were kept in the specialist's supposedly private "book." Now you see why the specialist could be so valuable to the pool manager. The book gave information about the extent of existing orders to buy and sell at prices below and above the current market. It was always helpful to know as many of the cards of the public players as possible. Now the real fun was ready to begin.

Generally, at this point the pool manager had members of the pool trade between themselves. For example, Haskell sells 200 shares to Sidney at 40, and Sidney sells them back at 40⅛. The process is repeated with 400 shares at prices of 40¼ and 40½. Next comes the sale of a 1,000-share block at 40⅝, followed by another at 40¾. These sales were recorded on ticker tapes across the country and the illusion of activity was conveyed to the thousands of tape watchers who crowded into the brokerage offices of the country. Such activity, generated by so-called wash sales, created the impression that something big was afoot.

Now, tipsheet writers and market commentators under the control of the pool manager would tell of exciting developments in the offing. The pool manager also tried to ensure that the flow of news from the company's management was increasingly favorable—assuming the company management was involved in the operation. If all went well, and in the speculative atmosphere of the 1928–29 period it could hardly miss, the combination of tape activity and managed news would bring the public in.

Once the public came in the free-for-all started and it was time discreetly to "pull the plug." Since the public was doing the buying, the pool did the selling. The pool manager began feeding stock into the market, first slowly and then in larger and larger blocks before the public could collect its senses. At the end of the roller-coaster ride the pool members had netted large profits and the public was left holding the suddenly deflated stock.

But people didn't have to band together to defraud the public. Many individuals, particularly corporate officers and directors, did quite well on their own. Take Albert Wiggin, the head of Chase, the nation's second largest bank at the time. In July 1929 Mr. Wiggin became apprehensive about the dizzy heights to which stocks had climbed and no longer felt comfortable speculating on the bull side of the market. (He is rumored to have made millions in a pool boosting the price of his own bank.) Believing that the prospects for his own bank's stock were particularly dim (perhaps because of his previous speculation), he sold short over 42,000 shares of Chase stock. Selling short is a way to make money if stock prices fall. It involves selling stock you do not presently own in the expectation of buying it back later at a lower price. It's like hoping to buy low and sell high, but in reverse order.

Wiggin's timing was perfect. Immediately after the short sale the price of Chase stock began to fall, and when the crash came in the fall the stock dropped precipitously. When the account was closed in November, he had netted a multimillion-dollar profit from the operation. Conflicts of interest apparently did not trouble Mr. Wiggin. In fairness to Mr. Wiggin, it should be pointed out that he did retain a net ownership position in Chase stock during this period. Nevertheless, the rules in existence today would not allow an insider to make short-swing profits from trading his own stock.

On September 3, 1929, the market averages reached a peak that was not to be surpassed for a quarter of a century. The "endless chain of prosperity" was soon to break; general business activity had already turned down months before. Prices drifted for the next day, and on the following day, September 5, the market suffered a sharp decline known as the "Babson Break."

This was named in honor of Roger Babson, a frail, goateed, pixyish-looking financial adviser from Wellesley, Massachusetts. At a financial luncheon that day he had said, "I repeat what I said at this time last year and the year before, that sooner or later a crash is coming." Wall Street professionals greeted the new pronouncements from the "sage of Wellesley," as he was known, with their usual derision.

As Babson implied in his statement, he had been predicting the crash for several years and he had yet to be proven right. Nevertheless, at two o'clock in the afternoon, when Babson's words were quoted on the "broad" tape (the Dow Jones financial-news tape, which was an essential part of the furniture in every brokerage house across the country), the market went into a nosedive. In the last frantic hour of trading, two million shares changed hands—American Telephone and Telegraph went down 6 points, Westinghouse 7, and U.S. Steel 9 points. It was a prophetic episode, and after the Babson Break the possibility of a crash, which was entirely unthinkable a month before, suddenly became a common subject for discussion.

Confidence faltered. September had many more bad than good days. At times the market fell sharply. Bankers and government officials assured the country that there was no cause for concern. Professor Irving Fisher of Yale, one of the progenitors of the intrinsic-value theory, offered his soon-to-be-immortal opinion that stocks had reached what looked like a "permanently high plateau."

By Monday, October 21, the stage was set for a classic stock-market break. The declines in stock prices had led to calls for more collateral from margin customers. Unable or unwilling to meet the calls, these customers were forced to sell their holdings. This depressed prices and led to more margin calls and finally to a self-sustaining selling wave.

The volume of sales on October 21 zoomed to over 6 million shares. The ticker fell way behind, to the dismay of the tens of thousands of individuals watching the tape from brokerage houses around the country. Nearly an hour and forty minutes

had elapsed after the close of the market before the last transaction was actually recorded on the stock ticker.

The indomitable Fisher dismissed the decline as a "shaking
out of the lunatic fringe that attempts to speculate on margin."
He went on to say that prices of stocks during the boom had not
caught up with their real value and would go higher. Among
other things, the professor believed that the market had not yet
reflected the beneficent effects of Prohibition, which had made
the American worker "more productive and dependable."

On October 24, later called "Black Thursday," the market
volume reached almost 13 million shares. Prices sometimes fell
$5 and $10 on each trade. Many issues dropped 40 and 50 points
during a couple of hours. On the next day, Herbert Hoover
offered his famous diagnosis, "The fundamental business of
the country . . . is on a sound and prosperous basis."

Tuesday, October 29, 1929, was among the most catastrophic days in the history of the New York Stock Exchange.
Only October 19 and 20, 1987, rivaled in intensity the panic on
the Exchange. Over 16.4 million shares were traded on that day
in 1929. (A 16-million-share day in 1929 would be equivalent to
over a billion-share day in 1995 because of the greater number
of shares now listed on the New York Stock Exchange.) Prices
fell almost perpendicularly, and kept on falling, as is illustrated
by the following table, which shows the extent of the decline
during the autumn of 1929 and over the next three years. With
the exception of "safe" AT&T, which lost only three-quarters of
its value, most blue-chip stocks had fallen 95 percent or more
by the time the lows were reached in 1932.

Security	High Price September 3, 1929[a]	Low Price November 13, 1929	Low Price for Year 1932
American Telephone & Telegraph	304	197¼	70¼
Bethlehem Steel	140⅜	78¼	7¼
General Electric	396¼	168⅛	8½
Montgomery Ward	137⅞	49¼	3½
National Cash Register	127½	59	6¼
Radio Corporation of America	101	28	2½

[a]Adjusted for stock splits and the value of rights received subsequent to September 3, 1929.

Perhaps the best summary of the debacle was given by *Variety*, the show-business weekly, which headlined the story, "Wall Street Lays an Egg." The speculative boom was dead and billions of dollars of share values—as well as the dreams of millions—were wiped out. The crash in the stock market was followed by the most devastating depression in the history of the country.

Again, there are revisionist historians who say there was a method to the madness of the stock-market boom of the late 1920s. Harold Bierman Jr., for example, in his book *The Great Myths of 1929*, has suggested that, without perfect foresight, stocks were not obviously overpriced in 1929 because it appeared that the economy would continue to prosper. After all, very intelligent people, such as Irving Fisher and John Maynard Keynes, believed that stocks were reasonably priced.* Bierman goes on to argue that the extreme optimism undergirding the stock market might even have been justified were it not for inappropriate monetary policies. The crash itself, in his view, was precipitated by the Federal Reserve Board's policy of raising interest rates to punish speculators. There are at least small grains of truth in Bierman's arguments, and economists today often blame the severity of the 1930s' depression on the Federal Reserve for allowing the money supply to decline sharply. Nevertheless, history teaches us that very sharp increases in stock prices (as well as in the general level of the prices of goods and services) are seldom followed by a *gradual* return to relative price stability. Even if prosperity had continued into the 1930s, stock prices could never have sustained their advance of the late 1920s.

In addition, the anomalous behavior of closed-end investment company shares (which I will cover in detail in Chapter Fifteen) provides clinching evidence of wide-scale stock-market irrationality during the 1920s. The "fundamental" value of these closed-end funds consists of the market value of the securities they hold. In most periods since 1930, these funds have

---

*By December 1929, however, even Irving Fisher admitted that the previous high prices were explainable "partly because of unreasoning and unintelligent mania for buying."

sold at *discounts* of about 20 percent from their asset values. From January to August 1929, however, the typical closed-end fund sold at a *premium* of 50 percent. Moreover, the premiums for some of the best known funds were astronomical. Goldman, Sachs Trading Corporation sold at twice its net asset value. Tri-Continental Corporation sold at 256 percent of its asset value. That meant that you could go to your broker and buy, say, AT&T at whatever its market price was, or you would purchase it through the fund at 2½ times that market value. The decimals in these examples are not misplaced. Market prices were two or three *times* the (inflated) value of their underlying assets. Clearly, it was irrational speculative enthusiasm that drove the prices of these funds far above the value at which their individual security holdings could be purchased.

An Afterword

Why are memories so short? Why do such speculative crazes seem so isolated from the lessons of history? I have no apt answer to offer, but I am convinced that Bernard Baruch was correct in suggesting that a study of these events can help equip investors for survival. The consistent losers in the market, from my personal experience, are those who are unable to resist being swept up in some kind of tulip-bulb craze. It is not hard, really, to make money in the market. As we shall see later, investors who select stocks by throwing darts at the stock listings in the *Wall Street Journal* can make fairly handsome long-run returns. What is hard to avoid is the alluring temptation to throw your money away on short, get-rich-quick speculative binges.

And yet the melody lingers on. I have a good friend who once built a modest stake into a small fortune. Then along came a stock called Alphanumeric. In addition to offering an exciting name, it also promised to revolutionize the method of feeding data into computers. My friend was hooked.

I begged him to investigate first whether the huge future earnings that were already reflected in the price could possibly be achieved given the likely size of the market. (Of course, the company had no *current* earnings.) He thanked me for my advice but dismissed it by saying that stock prices weren't based on "fundamentals" like earnings and dividends. "They are based on hopes and dreams," he said. "The history of stock valuation bears me out. This Alphanumeric story will have all the tape watchers drooling with excitement and conjuring up visions of castles in the air. Any delay in buying would be self-defeating." And so my friend had to rush in before greater fools would tread.

And rush in he did, buying at $80, which was close to the peak of a craze in that particular stock. The stock plunged to $2, and with it my friend's fortune—which became much more modest than what he originally started out with. The ability to avoid such horrendous mistakes is probably the most important factor in preserving one's capital and allowing it to grow. The lesson is so obvious and yet so easy to ignore.

3

Stock Valuation from the Sixties into the Nineties

> Everything's got a moral if only you can find it.
> —Lewis Carroll, *Alice's Adventures in Wonderland*

The madness of the crowd, as we have just seen, can be truly spectacular. The examples I have just cited, plus a host of others, have convinced more and more people to put their money under the care of a professional—someone who knows what makes the market tick and who can be trusted to act prudently. Thus most of us find that at least a part (and often all) of our investable funds are in the hands of institutional portfolio managers—those who run the large pension and retirement funds, mutual funds, investment counseling organizations, and the like. While the crowd may be mad, the institution is above all that. The institution is, to borrow a phrase from Tennyson, "of loyal nature and of noble mind." Very well, let us then take a look at the sanity of institutions.

The Sanity of Institutions

By 1960, institutions and other professional investors accounted for almost half of the total shares traded on the New York Stock Exchange. Three decades later, institutions such as mutual funds or pension funds had come to dominate the market almost completely. During the mid-1990s, these organizations generally accounted for 90 percent or more of the trading volume on the New York Stock Exchange. Surely, in a market where professional investors dominate trading, the game must have changed. The hard-headed, sharp-penciled reasoning of the pros ought to be a guarantee that the extravagant excesses of the past will be avoided.

And yet in 1983 a company with no annual sales and only a "plan" to manufacture personal robots was prepared for offering to the public at a proposed market capitalization of $100 million—the latter value being obtained by multiplying the number of shares outstanding by the price per share. Throughout the past forty years of institutional domination of the market, prices often gyrated more rapidly and by much greater amounts than could plausibly be explained by apparent changes in their anticipated intrinsic values.

In 1955, for example, General Electric announced that its scientists had created exact duplicates of the diamond. The market became entranced at once, despite the public acknowledgment that these diamonds were not suitable for sale as gems and that they could not be manufactured cheaply enough for industrial use. Within twenty-four hours, the shares of G.E. rose 4¼ points. This increased the total market value of all G.E. shares by almost $400 million, approximately twice the then current value of total worldwide diamond sales and six times the value of all industrial diamond sales. Clearly, the price rise was not due to the worth of the discovery to the company, but rather to the castle-building potential this would hold for prospective buyers. Indeed, speculators rushed in so fast to beat the gun that the entire price rise was accomplished in the first minutes of trading during the day following the announcement.

In 1988, Johnson and Johnson announced that one of its relatively minor prescription skin products, Retin-A, which had been around for years as an acne medication, might have a much broader market than had previously been imagined. Test results had shown that repeated applications of Retin-A to aging skin could actually remove wrinkles. Immediately following the announcement, Johnson and Johnson's common stock jumped up in price by $8 a share, thus increasing the market value of the company by approximately $1.5 billion, an amount that represented a substantial multiple of even the most optimistic forecasts for increased Retin-A sales.

Of course, we should not generalize from isolated instances. Professional investors, however, did participate in several distinct speculative movements from the 1960s through the 1990s. In each case, professional institutions bid actively for stocks not because they felt such stocks were undervalued under the firm-foundation principle, but because they anticipated that some greater fools would take the shares off their hands at even more inflated prices. Since these speculative movements relate to present-day markets, I think you'll find this institutional tour especially useful.

The Soaring Sixties

The New "New Era":
The Growth-Stock/New-Issue Craze

In the 1959–61 period, growth was the magic word. It was the corollary to the Soaring Sixties, the wonderful decade to come. Growth stocks (those issues for which an extraordinary rate of earnings growth was expected), especially those associated with glamorous new technologies like Texas Instruments and Varian Associates, far outdistanced the standard blue-chip stocks. Wall Street was eager to pay good money for space travel, transistors, klystron tubes, optical scanners, and other esoteric things. Backed by this strong enthusiasm, the price of securities in these businesses rose wildly.

By 1959, the traditional rule that stocks should sell at a multiple of 10 to 15 times their earnings had been supplanted by multiples of 50 to 100 times earnings, or even more for the most glamorous issues. For example, in 1961 Control Data sold for over 200 times its previous year's earnings. Even well-established growth companies such as IBM and Texas Instruments sold at price-earnings multiples over 80. (A year later they sold at multiples in the 20s and 30s.)

Growth took on an almost mystical significance, and questioning the propriety of such valuations became, as in the gen-

eration past, almost heretical. These prices could not be justified on firm-foundation principles. But investors firmly believed that later in the wonderful decade of the sixties, buyers
would eagerly come forward to pay even higher prices. Lord
Keynes must have smiled quietly from wherever it is that
economists go when they die.

I had just gone to work on Wall Street during the boom and
recall vividly one of the senior partners of my firm shaking his
head and admitting that he knew of no one over forty, with any
recollection of the 1929–32 crash, who would buy and hold the
high-priced growth stocks. But the young Turks held sway.
Newsweek quoted one broker as saying that speculators have
the idea that anything they buy "will double overnight. The
horrible thing is, it has happened."

More was to come. Promoters, eager to satisfy the insatiable thirst of investors for the space-age stocks of the Soaring
Sixties, created new offerings by the dozens. More new issues
were offered in the 1959–62 period than at any previous time in
history. The new-issue mania rivaled the South Sea Bubble in
its intensity and also, regrettably, in the fraudulent practices
that were revealed.

It was called the "tronics boom," since the stock offerings
often included some garbled version of the word "electronics"
in their title even if the companies had nothing to do with the
electronics industry. Buyers of these issues didn't really care
what the companies made—so long as it sounded electronic,
with a suggestion of the esoteric. For example, American Music
Guild, whose business consisted entirely of the door-to-door
sale of phonograph records and players, changed its name to
Space-Tone before "going public." The shares were sold to the
public at 2, and within a few weeks rose to 14.

The name was the game. There were a host of "trons" such
as Astron, Dutron, Vulcatron, and Transitron, and a number of
"onics" such as Circuitronics, Supronics, Videotronics, and
several Electrosonics companies. Leaving nothing to chance,
one group put together the winning combination Powertron Ul-
trasonics.

Jack Dreyfus, of Dreyfus and Company, commented on the
mania as follows:

Take a nice little company that's been making shoelaces for 40 years and sells at a respectable six times earnings ratio. Change the name from Shoelaces, Inc. to Electronics and Silicon Furth-Burners. In today's market, the words "electronics" and "silicon" are worth 15 times earnings. However, the real play comes from the word "furth-burners," which no one understands. A word that no one understands entitles you to double your entire score. Therefore, we have six times earnings for the shoelace business and 15 times earnings for electronic and silicon, or a total of 21 times earnings. Multiply this by two for furth-burners and we now have a score of 42 times earnings for the new company.

In a later investigation of the new-issue phenomenon, the Securities and Exchange Commission uncovered considerable evidence of fraudulence and market manipulation. For example, some investment bankers, especially those who underwrote the smaller new issues, would often hold a substantial volume of securities off the market. This made the market so "thin" at the start that the price would rise quickly in the after market. In one "hot issue" that almost doubled in price on the first day of trading, the SEC found that a considerable portion of the entire offering was sold to broker-dealers, many of whom held on to their allotments for a period until the shares could be sold at much higher prices. The SEC also found that many underwriters allocated large portions of hot issues to insiders of the firms such as partners, relatives, officers, and other securities dealers to whom a favor was owed. In one instance, 87 percent of a new issue was allocated to "insiders," rather than to the general public, as was proper.

The following table shows some representative new issues of this period and records their price movements after the shares were issued. At least for a while, the new-issue buyers did very well indeed. Large advances over their already inflated initial offering prices were scored for such companies as Boonton Electronics and Geophysics Corporation of America. The speculative fever was so great that even Mother's Cookie could count on a sizable gain. Think of the glory they could have achieved if they had called themselves "Mothertron's Cookitronics." Ten years later, the shares of most of these companies were almost worthless.

Security	Offering Date	Offering Price	Bid Price First Day of Trading	High Bid Price 1961	Low Bid Price 1962
Boonton Electronics Corp.	March 6, 1961	5½ [a]	12¼ [a]	24½ [a]	1⅝ [a]
Geophysics Corp. of America	December 8, 1960	14	27	58	9
Hydro-Space Technology	July 19, 1960	3	7	7	1
Mother's Cookie Corp.	March 8, 1961	15	23	25	7

[a] Per unit of 1 share and 1 warrant.

Where was the Securities and Exchange Commission all this time? Hadn't it changed the rule from "Let the buyer beware" to "Let the seller beware"? Aren't new issuers required to register their offering with the SEC? Can't they (and their underwriters) be punished for false and misleading statements?

Yes to all these questions and yes, the SEC was there, but by law it had to stand by quietly. As long as a company has prepared (and distributed to investors) an adequate prospectus, the SEC can do nothing to save buyers from themselves. For example, many of the prospectuses of the period contained the following type of warning in bold letters on the cover.

WARNING: THIS COMPANY HAS NO ASSETS OR EARN-INGS AND WILL BE UNABLE TO PAY DIVIDENDS IN THE FORESEEABLE FUTURE. THE SHARES ARE HIGHLY RISKY.

But just as the warnings on packs of cigarettes do not prevent many people from smoking, so the warning that this investment may be dangerous to your wealth cannot block a speculator from forking over his money if he is hell-bent on doing so. The SEC can warn a fool but it cannot prevent him from parting with his money. And the buyers of new issues were so convinced the stocks would rise in price (no matter what the company's assets or past record) that the underwriter's problem was not how he could sell the shares but how to allocate them among the frenzied purchasers.

Fraudulence and market manipulation are different matters. Here the SEC can take and has taken strong action. Indeed, many of the little known brokerage houses on the fringes of respectability, which were responsible for most of the new issues and for manipulation of their prices, were suspended for a variety of peculations.

The staff of the SEC is limited, however; the major problem is the attitude of the general public. When investors are infused with a get-rich-quick attitude and are willing to snap up any piece of bait, anything can happen—and usually does. Without public greed, the manipulators would not stand a chance.

The tronics boom came back to earth in 1962. The tailspin started early in the year and exploded in a horrendous selling wave five months later. Growth stocks, even the highest-quality ones, took the brunt of the decline, falling much further than the general market. Yesterday's hot issue became today's cold turkey.

Many professionals refused to accept the fact that they had speculated recklessly. Rather they blamed the decline on President Kennedy's tough stand with the steel industry, which led to a rollback of announced price hikes. Former president Eisenhower blamed the decline on Kennedy's "reckless spending programs," and columnist Walter Lippmann chastised Kennedy for not fulfilling his "promise to bring about something near to the full employment of capital and labor and a rising rate of economic growth."

Others did recognize the speculative mania and said simply that the market (and growth stocks in particular) was "too high" in 1961. As far as steel prices were concerned, with strong foreign competition in steel the price rises would probably have been rescinded anyway. Very few pointed out that it is always easy to look back and say when prices were too high or too low. Fewer still said that no one seems to know the proper price for a stock at any given time.

Synergy Generates Energy:
The Conglomerate Boom

The market shook off its losses and settled down to ponder its next move. It was not too long in coming.

I've said before that part of the genius of the financial market is that if a product is demanded, it is produced. The product that all investors desired was expected growth in earnings per share. And if growth wasn't to be found in a name, it was only to be expected that someone would find another way to produce it. By the mid-sixties, creative entrepreneurs had discovered that growth was a word and that the word was *synergism.*

Synergism is the quality of having 2 plus 2 equal 5. Thus, it seemed quite plausible that two separate companies with an earning power of $2 million each might produce combined earnings of $5 million if the businesses were consolidated. This magical, mystical, surefire profitable new creation was called a conglomerate.

While antitrust laws at that time kept large companies from purchasing firms in the same industry, it was possible for a while to purchase firms in other industries without interference from the Justice Department. The consolidations were carried out in the name of synergism. Ostensibly, mergers would allow the conglomerate to achieve greater financial strength (and thus greater borrowing capabilities at lower rates); to enhance marketing capabilities through the distribution of complementary product lines; to give greater scope to superior managerial talents; and to consolidate, and thus make more efficient, operating services such as personnel and accounting departments. All this led to synergism—a stimulation of sales and earnings for the combined operation that would have been impossible for the independent entities alone.

In fact, the major impetus for the conglomerate wave of the 1960s was that the acquisition process itself could be made to produce growth in earnings per share. Indeed, the managers of conglomerates tended to possess financial expertise rather than the operating skills required to improve the profitability of the acquired companies. By an easy bit of legerdemain, they could put together a group of companies with no basic potential at all and produce steadily rising per-share earnings. The following example shows how this monkey business was performed.

Suppose we have two companies—the Able Circuit Smasher Company, an electronics firm, and Baker Candy Company, which makes chocolate bars. Each has 200,000 shares outstanding. It's 1965 and both companies have earnings of $1 million a year, or $5 per share. Let's assume neither business is growing and that, with or without merger activity, earnings would just continue along at the same level.

The two firms sell at different prices, however. Since Able Circuit Smasher Company is in the electronics business, the market awards it a price-earnings multiple of 20 which, multiplied by its $5 earnings per share, gives it a market price of $100. Baker Candy Company, in a less glamorous business, has its earnings multiplied at only 10 times and, consequently, its $5 per share earnings command a market price of only $50.

The management of Able Circuit would like to become a conglomerate. It offers to absorb Baker by swapping stock at the rate of two for three. The holders of Baker shares would get two shares of Able stock—which have a market value of $200—for every three shares of Baker stock—with a total market value of $150. Clearly this is a tempting proposal, and the stockholders of Baker are likely to accept cheerfully. The merger is approved.

We have a budding conglomerate, newly named Synergon, Inc., which now has 333,333 shares* outstanding and total earnings of $2 million to put against them, or $6 per share. Thus, by 1966 when the merger has been completed, we find that earnings have risen by 20 percent, from $5 to $6, and this growth seems to justify Able's former price-earnings multiple of 20. Consequently, the shares of Synergon (née Able) rise from $100 to $120, everybody's judgment is confirmed, and all go home rich and happy. In addition, the shareholders of Baker who were bought out need not pay any taxes on their profits until they sell their shares of the combined company. The top

*There are 200,000 original shares of Able plus an extra 133,333, which get printed up to exchange for Baker's 200,000 shares according to the terms of the merger.

three lines of the following table illustrate the transaction thus far.

	Company	Earnings Level	Number of Shares Outstanding	Earnings per Share	Price-Earnings Multiple	Price
Before merger 1965	Able	$1,000,000	200,000	$ 5.00	20	$100
	Baker	1,000,000	200,000	5.00	10	50
After first merger 1966	Synergon (Able and Baker combined)	2,000,000	333,333	6.00	20	120
	Charlie	1,000,000	100,000	10.00	10	100
After second merger 1967	Synergon (Able, Baker, and Charlie combined)	3,000,000	433,333	6.92	20	138⅜

A year later, Synergon finds Charlie Company, which earns $10 per share or $1 million with 100,000 shares outstanding. Charlie Company is in the relatively risky military-hardware business so its shares command a multiple of only 10 and sell at $100. Synergon offers to absorb Charlie Company on a share-for-share exchange basis. Charlie's shareholders are delighted to exchange their $100 shares for the conglomerate's $120 shares. By the end of 1967, the combined company has earnings of $3 million, shares outstanding of 433,333, and earnings per share of $6.92.

Here we have a case where the conglomerate has literally manufactured growth. Neither Able, Baker, nor Charlie was growing at all; yet simply by virtue of the fact of their merger, the unwary investor who may finger his *Stock Guide* to see the past record of our conglomerate will find the following figures:

Earnings per Share

	1965	1966	1967
Synergon, Inc.	$5.00	$6.00	$6.92

Clearly, Synergon is a growth stock and its record of extraordinary performance appears to have earned it a high and possibly even an increasing multiple of earnings.

The trick that makes the game work is the ability of the electronics company to swap its high-multiple stock for the stock of another company with a lower multiple. The candy company can only "sell" its earnings at a multiple of 10. But when these earnings are packaged with the electronics company, the total earnings (including those from selling chocolate bars) could be sold at a multiple of 20. And the more acquisitions Synergon could make, the faster earnings per share would grow and thus the more attractive the stock would look to justify its high multiple.

The whole thing was like a chain letter—no one would get hurt as long as the growth of acquisitions proceeded exponentially. Of course, the process could not continue for long, but the possibilities were mind-boggling for those who got in at the start. It seems difficult to believe that Wall Street professionals could be so myopic as to fall for the conglomerate con game, but accept it they did for a period of several years. Or perhaps as subscribers to the castle-in-the-air theory, they only believed that other people would fall for it.

The story of Synergon describes the standard conglomerate earnings "growth" gambit. There were a lot of other monkeyshines practiced. Convertible bonds (or convertible preferred stocks) were often used as a substitute for shares in paying for acquisitions. A convertible bond is an IOU of the company, paying a fixed interest rate, that is convertible at the option of the holder into shares of the firm's common stock. As long as the earnings of the newly acquired subsidiary were greater than the relatively low interest rate that was placed on the convertible bond, it was possible to show even more sharply rising earnings per share than those in the previous illustration. This is because no new common stocks at all had to be issued to consummate the merger, and thus the combined earnings could be divided by a smaller number of shares.

One company was truly creative in financing its acquisition program. It used a convertible preferred stock that paid no cash dividend at all.* Instead, the conversion rate of the security

---

*Convertible preferred stock is similar to a convertible bond in that the preferred dividend is a fixed obligation of the company. But neither the principal nor the pre-

was to be adjusted annually to provide that the preferred stock be convertible into more common shares each year. The older pros in Wall Street shook their heads in disbelief over these shenanigans.

It is hard to believe that investors did not count the dilution potential of the new common stock that would be issued if the bondholders or preferred stockholders were to convert their securities into common stock. Indeed, as a result of such manipulations, corporations are now required to report their earnings on a "fully diluted" basis, to account for the new common shares that must be set aside for potential conversions. But most investors in the middle 1960s ignored such niceties and were satisfied only to see steadily and rapidly rising earnings.

Automatic Sprinkler Corporation (later called A-T-O, Inc. and later still, at the urging of its modest chief executive officer Mr. Figgie, Figgie International) is a good example of how the game of manufacturing growth was actually played during the 1960s. Between 1963 and 1968, the company's sales volume rose by over 1,400 percent. This phenomenal record was due solely to acquisitions. In the middle of 1967, four mergers were completed in a twenty-five-day period. These newly acquired companies were all selling at relatively low price-earnings multiples, and thus helped to produce a sharp growth in earnings per share. The market responded to this "growth" by bidding up the price-earnings multiple to over 50 times earnings in 1967. This boosted the price of the company's stock from about $8 per share in 1963 to $73⅝ in 1967.

Mr. Figgie, the president of Automatic Sprinkler, performed the public relations job necessary to help Wall Street build its castle in the air. He automatically sprinkled his conversations with talismanic phrases about the energy of the free-form company and its interface with change and technology. He was careful to point out that he looked at twenty to thirty deals for each one he bought. Wall Street loved every word of it.

---

ferred dividend is considered a *debt*, so your company can usually skip a payment with greater freedom. Of course, in the example above, the stock paid no cash dividend at all.

Mr. Figgie was not alone in conning Wall Street. Managers of other conglomerates almost invented a new language in the process of dazzling the investment community. They talked about market matrices, core technology fulcrums, modular building blocks, and the nucleus theory of growth. No one from Wall Street really knew what the words meant, but they all got the nice, warm feeling of being in the technological mainstream.

Conglomerate managers also found a new way of describing the businesses they had bought. Their shipbuilding businesses became "marine systems." Zinc mining became the "space minerals division." Steel fabrication plants became the "materials technology division." A lighting fixture or lock company became part of the "protective services division." And if one of the "ungentlemanly" security analysts (somebody from CCNY rather than Harvard Business School) had the nerve to ask how you can get 15 to 20 percent growth from a foundry or a meat packer, the typical conglomerate manager suggested that his efficiency experts had isolated millions of dollars of excess costs; that his marketing research staff had found several fresh, uninhabited markets; and that the target of tripling profit margins could be easily realized within two years. To this add talk of breakfast and Sunday meetings with your staff, and the image of the hardworking, competent, go-go atmosphere is complete.

Instead of going down with merger activity, the price-earnings multiples of conglomerate stocks rose higher and higher. Prices and multiples for a selection of conglomerates in 1967 are shown in the following table.

	1967		1969	
Security	High Price	Price-Earnings Multiple	Low Price	Price-Earnings Multiple
Automatic Sprinkler (A-T-O, Inc.)	73⅝	51.0	10⅞	13.4
Litton Industries	120½	44.1	55	14.4
Teledyne, Inc.	71½[a]	55.8	28¼	14.2
Textron, Inc.	55	24.9	23¼	10.1

[a]Adjusted for subsequent split.

The music slowed drastically for the conglomerates on January 19, 1968. On that day, the granddaddy of the conglomerates, Litton Industries, announced that earnings for the second quarter of that year would be substantially less than had been forecast. It had recorded 20 percent yearly increases for almost an entire decade. The market had so thoroughly come to believe in alchemy that the announcement was greeted with disbelief and shock. In the selling wave that followed, conglomerate stocks declined by roughly 40 percent before a feeble recovery set in.

Worse was to come. In July, the Federal Trade Commission announced that it would make an in-depth investigation of the conglomerate merger movement. Again the stocks went tumbling down. The Securities and Exchange Commission and the accounting profession finally made their move and began to make attempts to clarify the reporting techniques for mergers and acquisitions. Perhaps weak parts do not a strong whole make. The sell orders came flooding in. These were closely followed by new announcements from the SEC and the Assistant Attorney General in charge of antitrust, indicating a strong concern about the accelerating pace of the merger movement.

The aftermath of this speculative phase revealed two disturbing factors. First, conglomerates were mortal and were not always able to control their far-flung empires. Indeed, investors became disenchanted with the conglomerate's new math; 2 plus 2 certainly did not equal 5 and some investors wondered if it even equaled 4. Second, the government and the accounting profession expressed real concern about the pace of mergers and about possible abuses. These two worries on the part of investors reduced—and in many cases eliminated—the premium multiples that had been paid for the anticipation of earnings from the acquisition process alone. This in itself makes the alchemy game almost impossible, for the acquiring company has to have an earnings multiple larger than the acquired company if the ploy is to work at all.

The combination of lower earnings and flattened price-earnings multiples led to a drastic decline in the prices of conglomerates, as the preceding table indicates. It was the professional investors who were hurt the most in the wild scramble for chairs. Few mutual or pension funds were without large holdings of conglomerate stocks. Castles in the air are not reserved as the sole prerogative of individuals; institutional investors can build them, too. An interesting footnote to this episode is that by the 1980s deconglomeration came into fashion. Many of the old conglomerates began to shed their unrelated, poor-performing acquisitions in order to boost their earnings.

Many of these sales were financed through a popular innovation of the 1980s, the leveraged buyout (LBO). Under an LBO the purchaser, often the management of the division assisted by professional deal makers, puts up a very thin margin of equity, borrowing 90 percent or more of the funds needed to complete the transaction. The tax collector helps out by allowing the bought-out entity to increase the value of its depreciable asset base. The combination of high interest payments and larger depreciation charges ensures that taxes for the new entity will remain low or nonexistent for some time. If things go well, the owners can often reap windfall profits. William Simon, a former secretary of the Treasury, made a multimillion-dollar killing on one of the earliest LBOs of the 1980s, Gibson Greeting Cards. A number of the early LBOs of the 1980s proved to be quite successful. Later in the decade, however, as the LBO wave accelerated and the prices paid for the companies tended to increase as did their associated debt levels, fewer of these transactions fulfilled their expectations. As the economy turned less robust in the late 1980s and early 1990s, the high fixed-interest costs of companies in debt up to their eyeballs placed these entities in considerable financial jeopardy. The financial fallout in the early 1990s from the explosion of some of the most poorly considered LBOs injured not only many individual investors, but many banks and life insurance companies as well.

Performance Comes to the Market:
The Bubble in Concept Stocks

Our next speculative mania came into being during the mid-sixties, when there was heightened competition among mutual funds for the customer's dollar. In such an atmosphere, it is obvious that it would be easier to sell a fund with stocks in its portfolio that went up in value faster than the stocks in its competitors' portfolios.

And perform the funds did—at least over short periods of time. Fred Carr's highly publicized Enterprise Fund racked up a 117 percent total return (including both dividends and capital gains) in 1967 and followed this with a 44 percent return in 1968. The corresponding figures for the Standard & Poor's 500-Stock Index were 25 percent and 11 percent, respectively. This performance brought large amounts of new money into the fund, and into other funds that could boast glamorous performances. The public no longer bet on the horse but rather on the jockey.

How did these jockeys do it? They concentrated the portfolio in dynamic stocks, which had a good story to tell, and at the first sign of an even better story, they would quickly switch. For a while the strategy worked well and led to many imitators. The camp followers were quickly given the accolade "go-go" funds, and the fund managers were often called "the youthful gunslingers." "Nothing succeeds so well as success," Talleyrand once observed, and this was certainly true for the performance funds in their early years—the customers' dollars flowed in.

The performance game was not limited to mutual funds. It spread to all kinds of investing institutions. Businessmen who had to make constantly larger contributions to their workers' pension funds to meet retirement obligations began to ask pointedly whether they might be able to reduce their current expenses by switching more of the fund from fixed-income bonds into common stocks with exciting growth possibilities. Even university endowment-fund managers were pressured to strive for performance. McGeorge Bundy of the Ford Foundation chided the portfolio managers of universities:

It is far from clear that trustees have reason to be proud of their performance in making money for their colleges. We recognize the risks of unconventional investing, but the true test of performance in the handling of money is the record of achievement, not the opinion of the respectable. We have the preliminary impression that over the long run caution has cost our colleges and universities much more than imprudence or excessive risk-taking.

And so performance investing took hold of Wall Street in the late 1960s. The commandments for fund managers were simple: Concentrate your holdings in a relatively few stocks and don't hesitate to switch the portfolio around if a more desirable investment appears. And because near-term performance was especially important (investment services began to publish monthly records of mutual-fund performance) it would be best to buy stocks with an exciting concept and a compelling story. You had to be sure the market would recognize the beauty of your stock now—not far into the future. Hence, the birth of the so-called concept stock.

Xerox was a classic example of a concept stock. The concept was that of a new industry where machines would make dry copies by electrostatic transference. The company, Xerox, with its patent protection and its running head start, could look forward to several years of increased earnings. It was a true story—a believable story, one that would quicken the pulse of any good performance manager.

But even if the story were not totally believable, as long as the investment manager was convinced that the average opinion would think that the average opinion would believe the story, that's all that was needed. The youthful gunslingers became disenchanted with normal security analysts who could tell you how many railroad ties Penn Central had, but couldn't tell you when the company was about to go bankrupt. "I don't want to listen to that kind of security analyst," one of Wall Street's gunslingers told me. "I just want a good story or a good concept." The author Martin Mayer quoted one fund manager as saying, "Since we hear stories early, we can figure enough people will be hearing it in the next few days to give the stock a bounce, even if the story doesn't prove out." Many Wall Streeters looked on this as a radical new investment strategy, but John Maynard Keynes had it all spotted in 1936.

Eventually, it reached a point where any concept would do.

Enter Cortess W. Randell. His concept was a youth company for the youth market. He became founder, president, and major stockholder of National Student Marketing. First, he sold an image—one of affluence and success. He owned a personal white Learjet named Snoopy, an apartment in New York's Waldorf Towers, a castle with a mock dungeon in Virginia, and a yacht that slept twelve. Adding to his image was an expensive set of golf clubs propped up by his office door. Apparently the only time the clubs were used was at night when the office cleanup crew drove wads of paper along the carpet.

He spent most of his time visiting the financial community or calling them on the sky phone from his Lear, and sold the concept of NSM in the tradition of a South Sea Bubble promoter. Randell's real métier was evangelism. The concept that Wall Street bought from Randell was that a single company could specialize in servicing the needs of young people. NSM built its early growth via the merger route, just as the ordinary conglomerates of the 1960s had done. The difference was that each of the constituent companies had something to do with the college-age youth market. Subsidiary companies sold magazine subscriptions, books and records, posters, paper dresses, guidebooks for summer jobs, student directories, a computer dating service, youth air fare cards, sweatshirts, live entertainment programs, and a variety of consumer staples. What could be more appealing to a youthful gunslinger than a youth-oriented concept stock—a full-service company to exploit the youth subculture? Youth was in—this one couldn't miss. Glowing press releases issued forth from company headquarters and Randell's earnings projections for the company became increasingly optimistic.

While there were some thistles among such roses (the earnings growth was produced by the old conglomerate gambit with the generous support of some creative accounting), the "concept" investors bought heavily in the company and blithely ignored all questions. When Gerry Tsai's Manhattan Fund bought 120,000 shares for $5 million, it became clear that Randell had obtained the imprimatur of Wall Street's performance investors. Even some of the most august and conservative firms, including Bankers Trust, Morgan Guaranty, and Boston's venerable State Street Fund, bought stock. Pension funds, including United States Trust Company (the country's largest trust company) bought the stock for many of its accounts. University endowment-fund managers, heeding the words of McGeorge Bundy, also bought in the mad scramble for performance. Blocks of NSM were bought by Harvard, Cornell, and the University of Chicago. Bundy himself practiced what he preached, and the previously conservatively managed Ford Foundation Fund also bought a large block.

The following table shows the high prices and enormous price-earnings multiples for National Student Marketing and for a small group of other concept stocks. The number of institutional holders (probably understated) for each security is also shown. Clearly, institutional investors are at least as adept as the general public at building castles in the air.

There were other concepts. Health care, for example, attracted quite a few adherents. Given the increasing numbers of older people and the spread of federal and private health insurance plans, someone was bound to make lots of money. Four Seasons Nursing Centers of America looked just like that someone. The biggest and most aggressive mutual funds bought in. At one point in 1969, institutions owned close to 50 percent of the company's stock.

The company expanded at a feverish pace, financing itself largely through the issuance of debt. These borrowings were sweetened, however, with so-called equity kickers. This meant that attached to each bond were warrants to buy common stock of Four Seasons at fixed prices. Thus, if the stock price continued to go up, the bondholders could exercise their war-

Security	High Price 1968–69	Price-Earnings Multiple at High	Number of Institutional Holders Year-end 1969	Low Price 1970	Percentage Decline
Four Seasons Nursing Centers of America	90¾	113.4	24	0.20	99
National Student Marketing	35¾[a]	111.7	21	⅞	98
Performance Systems	23	∞	13	⅛	99

[a] Adjusted for subsequent stock split.

rants and make additional profits. As the debt mounted up no one seemed to worry much about the old ideas of prudent debt ratios, for this was a new concept and the rules of the game had changed. On June 26, 1970, the company filed a petition for reorganization under Chapter X of the Bankruptcy Act.

Minnie Pearl's concept is our last example of the period. Minnie Pearl was a fast-food franchising firm that was as accommodating as all get-out. To please the financial community, Minnie Pearl's chickens became "Performance Systems." After all, what better name could be chosen for performance-oriented investors? On Wall Street a rose by any other name does not smell as sweet. The ∞ shown in the table under "price-earnings multiple" indicates that the multiple was infinity. Performance Systems had no earnings at all to divide into the stock's price at the time it reached its high in 1968. As the table indicates, Minnie Pearl laid an egg—and a bad one at that. The subsequent performance for this and the other stocks listed was indeed truly remarkable—although not quite what their buyers had anticipated.

Why did the stocks actually perform so badly? One general answer was that their price-earnings multiples were inflated beyond reason. If a multiple of 100 drops to the more normal multiple of 15 for the market as a whole, you have lost 85 percent of your investment right there. But in addition most of the concept companies of the time ran into severe operating difficulties. The reasons were varied: too rapid expansion, too much debt, loss of management control, etc. These companies were run by executives who were primarily promoters, not sharp-penciled operating managers. In addition, fraudulent practices were common. For example, Performance Systems reported profits of $3.2 million in 1969. The SEC claimed that this report was "false and misleading." In 1972 Performance Systems issued a revision of the 1969 report. Apparently a loss of $1.3 million more accurately reflected 1969 operations. Similarly, the management of National Student Marketing was accused of fraud. NSM's Cortess Randell eventually pleaded guilty to stock fraud; he served eight months in prison and was fined.

And so when the 1969–71 bear market came, these concept

stocks went down just as fast as they went up. In the end it was the pros who were conned most of all. While there is nothing wrong with seeking good performance, the mad rush to outgun the competition week by week had disastrous consequences. The cult of performance and the concept of "concept" stocks were henceforth greeted with disdain when mentioned in Wall Street.

The Sour Seventies

The Nifty Fifty

Like generals fighting the last war, Wall Street's pros were planning not to repeat the mistakes of the 1960s in the 1970s. No more would they buy small electronics companies or exciting concept stocks. There was a return to reason and with it a return to "sound principles" that translated to investing in blue-chip companies with proven growth records. These were companies, so the thinking went, that would never come crashing down like the speculative favorites of the 1960s. Nothing could be more prudent than to buy their shares and then relax on the golf course while the long-term rewards materialized.

There were only four dozen or so of these premier growth stocks that so fascinated the institutional investors. The names were very familiar—IBM, Xerox, Avon Products, Kodak, McDonald's, Polaroid, and Disney, to list a few. They were called the "Nifty Fifty." They were "big-capitalization" stocks, which meant that an institution could buy a good-sized position without disturbing the market. And since most pros realized that picking the exact correct time to buy is difficult if not impossible, these stocks seemed to make a great deal of sense. So what if you paid a price that was temporarily too high? Since these stocks were proven growers, sooner or later the price you paid would be justified. In addition, these were stocks which—like the family heirlooms—you would never sell. Hence they were also called "one-decision" stocks. You made a decision to buy them, once, and your portfolio-management problems were over.

These stocks provided security blankets for institutional investors in another way, too. They were so respectable. Your colleagues could never question your prudence in investing in IBM. True, you could lose money if IBM went down, but that was not considered a sign of imprudence (as it would be to lose money in a Performance Systems or a National Student Marketing). Like greyhounds in chase of the mechanical rabbit, big pension funds, insurance companies, and bank trust funds loaded up on the Nifty Fifty one-decision growth stocks. Hard as it is to believe, the institutions had actually started to speculate in blue chips. This was a case of classic insanity. The heights to which the stocks rose were unbelievable. In the table below, I have listed the price-earnings multiples achieved by a handful of these stocks in 1972. For comparison, the price-earnings multiples at the start of the 1980s are listed, too. Institutional managers blithely ignored the fact that no sizable company could ever grow fast enough to justify an earnings multiple of 80 or 90. They once again proved the maxim that stupidity well packaged can sound like wisdom.

Security	Price-Earnings Multiple 1972	Price-Earnings Multiple 1980
Sony	92	17
Polaroid	90	16
McDonald's	83	9
Intl. Flavors	81	12
Walt Disney	76	11
Hewlett-Packard	65	18

Perhaps one might argue that the craze was simply a manifestation of the return of confidence in late 1972. Richard Nixon had been reelected by a landslide, peace was "at hand" in Vietnam, price controls were due to come off, inflation was apparently "under control," and no one knew what OPEC was. But, in fact, the market had already started to decline in early 1972, and when it did the Nifty Fifty mania became even more pathological. For as the market in general collapsed, the Nifty Fifty continued to command record earnings multiples and, on a relative basis, the overpricing greatly increased. There appeared to be a "two-tier" market. *Forbes* magazine commented as follows:

> [The Nifty Fifty appeared to rise up] from the ocean; it was as though all of the U.S. but Nebraska had sunk into the sea. The two tier market really consisted of one tier and a lot of rubble down below.
>
> What held the Nifty Fifty up? The same thing that held up tulip-bulb prices in long-ago Holland—popular delusions and the madness of crowds. The delusion was that these companies were so good that it didn't matter what you paid for them; their inexorable growth would bail you out.

The end was inevitable. The Nifty Fifty craze ended like all other speculative manias. The Nifty Fifty were—in the words of *Forbes* columnist Martin Sosnoff—taken out and shot one by one. The oil embargo and the difficulty of obtaining gasoline hit Disney and its large stake in Disneyland and Disneyworld. Production problems with new cameras hit Polaroid. The stocks sank like stones into the ocean. A critical cover story in widely respected *Forbes* magazine sent Avon Products down almost 50 percent in six months. The real problem was never the particular needle that pricked each individual bubble. The problem was simply that the stocks were ridiculously overpriced. Sooner or later the same money managers who had worshiped the Nifty Fifty decided to make a second decision and sell. In the debacle that followed, the premier growth stocks fell completely from favor.

The Roaring Eighties

The Roaring Eighties had its fair share of speculative excesses, and again unwary investors paid the price for building castles in the air. The decade started with another spectacular new-issue boom.

The Triumphant Return of New Issues

The high-technology new-issue boom of the first half of 1983 was an almost perfect replica of the 1960s episodes with the names altered slightly to include the new fields of biotechnology and microelectronics. The 1983 craze made the promoters of the sixties look like pikers. Fifteen billion dollars' worth of new public offerings were floated, approximately four times the previous record established in 1981 and greater than the cumulative total of new issues for the entire preceding decade. For investors, initial public offerings were the hottest game in town. Just getting a piece of a new issue automatically made you a winner, or so it seemed, as prices often soared in the after market.

Typical of the period was a promising new technology stock, Diasonics, Inc., a manufacturer of medical imaging equipment located in the heartland of technological America, Silicon Valley, south of San Francisco. Diasonics' shares were offered at $22 each. By the end of the first day of trading, Diasonics had spurted over 20 percent to 26¾. Nothing to get excited about there. After all, the market value of Diasonics stock was "only" 10 times the company's total sales for the previous year and 100 times the previous year's earnings. In the feverish new-issue market of 1983, such multiples were commonplace. Arthur Rock, the chairman of Diasonics' executive committee, thought the price was so reasonable that he sold 50,000 of his shares for a total of $3.3 million.

Down the valley from Diasonics, another group was working hard to throw something on the table for investors. They thought a machine should do the dishing up—specifically a personal robot. Was the robot ready for the task? Well, not quite. The company, called Androbot, *planned* to manufacture a line of personal robots. The company's major product, B.O.B. (an acronym for Brains on Board), was *nearly* ready for manufacture; there were just a few small problems. Apparently, product development was not yet complete, and it was not clear that the "significant technological obstacles" mentioned in the prospectus could be overcome. Moreover, software applications had not been developed, and the prospectus suggested that early prototype models were not yet, in the computer vernacular, user friendly. Finally, it was not clear that any of Androbot's products could be mass-produced or that a market for the products existed at the prices that would have to be charged. But the proposed market capitalization of Androbot was less than $100 million (for a company with no sales, earnings, or net assets), and that didn't buy much in the heady new-issue market of 1983. Incidentally, the underwriter for this proposed flotation was not one of the small schlock houses on the fringe of respectability, but the thundering herd itself, Merrill Lynch.

The flood of new issues contained such names as Fortune Systems, Spectravideo, and Whirlyball International. As was true in the earlier new-issue booms, even companies in more mundane businesses were favored in the market. A chain of three restaurants in New Jersey called "Stuff Your Face, Inc." was registered with the SEC. Indeed, the enthusiasm extended to "quality" issues such as Fine Art Acquisitions Ltd. This was not some Philistine outfit peddling discount clothing or making computer hardware. This was a truly aesthetic enterprise. Fine Art Acquisitions, the prospectus tells us, was in the business of acquiring and distributing fine prints and art deco sculpture replicas. One of the company's major assets consisted of a group of nude photographs of Brooke Shields taken about midway between her time in the stroller and her entrance to Princeton. Apparently, there were some potential legal problems, such as a suit by Mom Shields, who had some objection to the exploitation of these pictures of the prepubescent eleven-year-old Brooke. But, after all, this was for "artistic" purposes and obviously this was a class company.

The bubble appears to have burst early in the second half of 1983. The carnage in the small company and new-issue markets was truly catastrophic. It was probably the offering of Muhammed Ali Arcades International that started the debacle.

In a sense, the proposed Muhammed Ali Arcades offering was not particularly remarkable considering all the other garbage that was coming out at the time. But the offering was unique in that it showed that a penny could still buy a lot. The company proposed to offer units of one share and two warrants for the modest price of 1¢. Of course, this was 333 times what insiders had recently paid for their own shares. That wasn't unusual either, but when it was discovered that the champ himself had resisted the temptation to buy any stock in his namesake company, investors began to take a good look at where they were. Most did not like what they saw. The result was a dramatic decline in small company stocks in general and in the market prices of initial public offerings in particular. In the course of a year, many investors lost as much as 80 or 90 percent of their money.

The cover of the prospectus of Muhammed Ali Arcades International featured a picture of the former champ standing over a fallen opponent. In his salad days, Ali used to claim that he could "float like a butterfly and sting like a bee." It turned out that the Ali Arcades offering (as well as the Androbot offering that was scheduled for July 1983) never did get floated. But many others did, particularly stocks of those companies on the bleeding edge of technology. As has been true time and time again, it was the investors who got stung.

Concepts Conquer Again: The Biotechnology Bubble

What electronics was to the 1960s, biotechnology became to the 1980s. This technology promised to produce a group of products whose uses ranged from the treatment of cancer to the growing of food that would be hardier and more nutritious because it had been genetically modified. In its cover story "Biotech Comes of Age" in January 1984, *Business Week* put its imprimatur on the boom. "The fundamental question—'Is the technology real?'—has been settled," the magazine reported. The biotech revolution was likened to that of the computer. The magazine reported that gene-splicing progress "has out-distanced the most optimistic forecasts" and projected dramatic increases in the sales of biotechnology products.

Such optimism was also reflected in the prices of biotech company stocks. Genentech, the most substantial company in the industry, came to market in 1980. During the first twenty minutes of trading, the stock almost tripled in value, as investors anticipated that they were purchasing the next IBM at its initial public offering. Other new issues of biotech companies were eagerly gobbled up by hungry investors who saw a chance to get into a multibillion-dollar new industry on the ground floor. The key product that drove the first wave of the biotech frenzy was Interferon, a cancer-fighting drug. Analysts predicted that sales of Interferon would exceed $1 billion by 1982. (In reality, sales of this successful product were barely $200 million in 1989, but there was no holding back the dreams of castles in the air.) Analysts continuously predicted an explosion of earnings two years out for the biotech companies. Analysts were continuously disappointed. But the technological revolution was real and hope springs eternal. Even weak companies benefited under the umbrella of the technology potential.

Valuation levels of biotechnology stocks reached levels previously unknown to investors even during the most pathological phase of the growth-stock boom of the 1960s. Speculative growth stocks might have sold at 50 times earnings in the 1960s. In the 1980s, some biotech stocks actually sold at 50 times *sales.* As a student of valuation techniques, I was fascinated to read how security analysts rationalized these prices. Since biotech companies typically had no current earnings (and realistically no positive earnings expected for several years) and little sales, new valuation methods had to be devised. My favorite was the "product asset valuation" method recommended by one of Wall Street's leading securities houses. Basically, the method involved the estimation of the value of all the products in the "pipeline" of each biotech company. Even if the planned product involved nothing more than the drawings of a genetic engineer, a potential sales volume and a profit margin were estimated for each product that was even a glint in some scientist's eye. Sales could be estimated by taking the "expected clinical indications" for the future drug, predicting the potential number of patient users, and assuming a generous price tag. The total value of the "product pipeline" would then give the analyst a fair idea of the price at which the company's stock should sell.

None of the potential problems seemed real to the optimists. Perhaps FDA approval would be delayed. (Interferon was delayed for several years.) Would the market bear the fancy drug price tags that were projected? Would patent protection be possible since virtually every product in the biotechnology pipeline was being developed simultaneously by several companies, or were patent clashes inevitable? Would much of the potential profit from a successful drug be siphoned off by the marketing partner of the biotech company, usually one of the major drug companies? In the mid-1980s, none of these potential problems seemed real. Indeed, the biotech stocks were regarded by one analyst as *less risky* than standard drug companies because there were "no old products which need to be offset because of their declining revenues." We had come full circle—having positive sales and earnings was actually considered a drawback because those profits might decline in the future.

From the mid-1980s to the late 1980s, most biotechnology stocks lost three-quarters of their market value. To be sure, the crash of 1987 didn't help. But biotech stocks generally continued heading south even as the market recovered in 1988. Market sentiment had changed from acceptance of an exciting story and multiples in the stratosphere to a desire to stay closer to earth with low-multiple stocks that actually pay dividends. Nor did the fate of the biotechnology industry improve in the 1990s. While the stocks rose early in the decade, they had a severe sinking spell towards the middle of the 1990s, with the popular Biotech Index, which is traded on the American Stock Exchange, falling more than 50 percent from 1992 to 1994. By the mid-1990s, the industry was losing money at a rate of $4 billion per year. One industry professional, Richard M. Beleson of Capital Research, was moved to compose a *Biotech Bear Market Ballad* in 1994. One of the verses went as follows:

> Those were the days my friend.
> We thought they'd never end.
> We'd clone a gene and form a company.
> We'd raise some venture cash
> And do our IPO in a flash.
> Cause selling dreams
> Requires no p-e.

The denouement to the story occurred during one terrible day in the fall of 1994 when the small brokerage firm of David Blech and Company, Wall Street's biggest champion of small biotech

stocks, closed its doors for trading. The top seven percentage
losers on the NASDAQ exchange were biotech stocks for
which Blech was the underwriter and leading market maker.
The average percentage decline for these stocks on that single
day was close to 40 percent. Castles in the air can come crashing down with breathtaking suddenness.

The Chinese Romance with the *Lycoris* Plant

How history does repeat itself. An almost perfect replica of
the tulip-bulb craze occurred in China during the mid-1980s. As
the Chinese government began a process of economic reform,
markets sprang up for all sorts of products including household
plants. A particularly desirable flowering plant was the Jun Zi
Lan plant (literally the "Gentleman Blue" plant) a kind of *Lycoris radiata* belonging to the Clivia family. The plant had originated in Africa and was brought to the city of Changchun in
northern China during the 1930s. Originally, the plant was held
only by the royal family, but soon it became a sign of distinction and taste for prominent families to possess several varie-
ties. Later, the city of Changchun designated the *Lycoris* as the
city flower and, by the start of the 1980s, half of the families in
the city grew this plant.

As news of the flower spread to other parts of northeastern
China, demand for the plant increased substantially. Since it
takes several years for new plants to grow, supplies could not
be increased immediately. And so prices began to rise and
many enterprising Chinese speculators tried to cash in on the
popularity of the plant by buying up all they could find in the
market. As in the tulip-bulb craze, optimism begat more optimism. The speculation spawned technicolor dreams of castles
in the air surrounded by *Lycoris* plants. Prices of the plants
reached dizzying heights. During the early 1980s, a typical
plant sold for about 100 Yuan (about $30). By 1985, prices in-
creased 2,000-fold to 200,000 Yuan (about $60,000) for plants
that were especially desirable. To put this number in perspective, a plant sold for about 300 years salary of the average
college graduate in China.

As has always been the case, the bubble was easily

pricked. Apparently the proximate cause of the collapse was a number of press reports in the summer of 1985 describing the madness of the phenomenon. As soon as it became clear that the party would not continue, an avalanche of selling overtook the market. Prices of *Lycoris* plants plunged 99 percent or more. By the start of 1986, a number of Chinese gentlemen speculators were indeed blue.

Some Other Bubbles of the 1980s

The late 1980s also had its share of spectacular booms and busts in more prosaic companies, whose concepts caught the fancy of Wall Street. Whereas many investors lost 75 percent of their initial purchase price in the biotech boom, others saw well over 90 percent of their investment dollars disappear while chasing these other concepts. Two additional examples will illustrate the point.

Alfin Fragrances   Alfin Fragrances, a cosmetics company, jumped into the spotlight in late 1985 when it announced a new face cream, Glycel, which could slow the aging process and reverse skin damage. Glycel's believability was enhanced by the news that it contained "ingredients developed in Switzerland by Christiaan Barnard," the doctor who pioneered the first successful heart transplant. The image was perfect. Barnard, sixty-three years old at the time, presented himself as a modern-day Ponce de Léon. He was always seen in the presence of his lovely twenty-two-year-old "girlfriend." Even in the hyperbolic world of the cosmetics industry, Barnard's claims that Glycel could penetrate the skin and reverse the aging process seemed excessive. But for a while, both the public and Wall Street were convinced. Introductory $195 kits of the product sold out at Neiman Marcus and other fine department stores. Extraordinary growth seemed assured and the stock price tripled within a month after the announcement of Glycel. Even the prestigious firm of Morgan Stanley joined the bandwagon, "justifying" the stratospheric price-earnings multiple for the stock, and indicating that "the stock will head even higher."

But, unfortunately, Alfin's beauty was only skin deep.

Alfin's claim that Glycel penetrated skin cells to "bring back the memory of the cell" wrinkled a lot of scientific brows. One dermatologist claimed, "It would be like giving someone a blood transfusion by rubbing blood into the skin." The product received a fatal blow from the FDA, which insisted that any product intended to alter a normal bodily function such as aging was a drug, not a cosmetic, and that the agency would require proof of efficacy. Rather than subjecting its product to that kind of scrutiny, Alfin withdrew Glycel from distribution. The stock, which sold near $40 in early 1986, fell to near $2 in 1989. Investors with dreams of castles in the air usually suffer rude awakenings.

ZZZZ Best   My favorite boom and bust of the late 1980s is the story of ZZZZ Best. Here was an incredible Horatio Alger story that captivated investors. In the fast-paced world of entrepreneurs who strike it rich before they can shave, Barry Minkow was a genuine legend of the 1980s. Minkow's career began at age nine. His family could not afford a babysitter so Barry often went to work at the carpet-cleaning shop managed by his mother. There he began soliciting jobs by phone. By age ten he was actually cleaning carpets. Working evenings and summers, he saved $6,000 within the next four years and by the age of fifteen he bought some steam-cleaning equipment and started his own carpet-cleaning business in the garage of the family home. The company was called ZZZZ Best (and pronounced *zeee best*). Still in high school and too young to drive, Minkow hired a crew to pick up and clean carpets while he sat in class fretting over each week's payroll. With Minkow working a punishing schedule (and having friends drive him to appointments), the business flourished. He was proud of the fact that he hired his father and mother to work for the business. By age eighteen, Minkow was a millionaire.

Minkow's insatiable appetite for work extended to self-promotion. He took on all the tangible trappings of success. He drove a red Ferrari and lived in a $700,000 home with a large pool in which a big black Z was painted on the bottom. He also publicly extolled good old-fashioned American virtues. He wrote a book entitled *Making It in America,* in which he claimed that teenagers didn't work hard enough. He gave generously to charities and appeared on anti-drug commercials with the slogan "My act is clean, how's yours?" By this time, ZZZZ Best had 1,300 employees and locations throughout California as well as in Arizona and Nevada.

Was over 100 times earnings too much to pay for a mundane carpet-cleaning company? Of course not, when the company was run by a genius and a spectacularly successful businessman, who could also show his toughness. Minkow's favorite line to his employees was "My way or the highway." And he once boasted that he would fire his own mother if she stepped out of line. When Minkow told Wall Street that his company was better run than IBM and that it was destined to become "the General Motors of carpet cleaning," investors listened with rapt attention. As one security analyst told me at the time, "This one can't miss."

In 1987, Minkow's bubble burst with shocking suddenness. It turned out that ZZZZ Best was cleaning more than carpets— it was also laundering money for the mob. ZZZZ Best was accused of acting as a front for organized-crime figures who would buy equipment for the company with "dirty" money and replace their investment with "clean" cash skimmed from the proceeds of ZZZZ Best's legitimate carpet-cleaning business. But in fact, the spectacular growth of the company was itself mainly an elaborate fiction produced with fictitious contracts, phony credit card charges, and the like. The whole operation was a giant Ponzi scheme where money was recycled from one set of investors to pay off another. In addition, Minkow was charged with skimming millions from the company treasury for his own personal use. Minkow, as well as all the investors in ZZZZ Best, were in wall-to-wall trouble.

The final chapter of the story (after Chapter XI) occurred in 1989 when Minkow, then twenty-three, was convicted of fifty-seven counts of fraud and sentenced to twenty-five years in prison and required to make restitution of $26 million he was accused of stealing from the company. The United States district judge, in rejecting pleas for leniency, told Minkow, "You are dangerous because you have this gift of gab, this ability to communicate." The judge added, "You don't have a conscience." As *Barron's* Alan Abelson, who actually predicted the collapse long in advance, opined, "ZZZZ Best will likely turn out for investors as ZZZZ worst." Most investors who lost their entire stake in the company would certainly agree.

As of the mid-1990s, Minkow would start his day at 3:00 A.M., reporting for duty in the bakery of the Lampoc Federal Prison Camp. In his spare time, he became a born-again Christian, earning a bachelor's and master's correspondence-school degree from Liberty University, founded by Jerry Falwell. He hopes one day to have a ministry of his own and his behavior as a model prisoner may well earn him an early release.

The lessons of market history are clear. Styles and fashions in investors' evaluations of securities can and often do play a critical role in the pricing of securities. The stock market at times conforms well to the castle-in-the-air theory. For this reason, the game of investing can be extremely dangerous.

Another lesson that cries out for attention is that investors should be very wary of purchasing today's hot "new issue." A study by the investment firm of Kidder Peabody examined the performance of over 1,000 initial public offerings (IPOs) of common stock from 1983 through mid-1988. Their remarkable conclusion was that two-thirds of these IPOs actually underperformed the Dow Jones industrial average from their issue date through mid-1988. While it is true that smaller stocks tend to outperform larger ones over long periods of time, that finding applies to established companies that trade in the secondary markets—not to IPOs. With only a one in three chance of outperforming the Dow average, investors would be well advised to treat new issues with a healthy dose of skepticism.

Certainly investors in the past have built many castles in the air with IPOs. Remember that the major sellers of the stock of IPOs are the managers of the companies themselves. They try to time their sales to coincide with a peak in the prosperity of their companies or with the height of investor enthusiasm for some current fad. The biotech IPOs that proliferated during the late 1980s are a good example. In such cases, the urge to get on the bandwagon—even in high-growth industries—produced a profitless prosperity for investors.

The Nervy Nineties

The Japanese Yen for Land and Stocks

Perhaps the most spectacular boom and bust of the late twentieth century involved the Japanese real estate and stock markets. From 1955 to 1990, the value of Japanese real estate increased over 75 times. By 1990, the total value of all Japanese property was estimated at nearly $20 trillion—equal to more than 20 percent of the entire world's wealth and about double the total value of the world's stock markets. America is twenty-five times bigger than Japan in terms of physical acreage, and yet Japan's property in 1990 was appraised to be worth five times as much as all American property. Theoretically, the Japanese could have bought all the property in America by selling off metropolitan Tokyo. Just selling the Imperial Palace and its grounds at their appraised value would have raised the cash to buy all of California. The tulips were even in full bloom around Japan's golf courses. By 1990, the total value of all golf courses in Japan reached $500 billion, an amount double the value of all equities traded on the Australian stock exchange.

The stock market countered by rising like a helium balloon on a windless day. Stock prices increased 100 fold from 1955 to 1990. At their peak in December 1989, Japanese stocks had a total market value of about $4 trillion, almost 1.5 times the value of all U.S. equities and close to 45 percent of the world's equity market capitalization. Firm foundation investors were aghast at such figures. They read with dismay that Japanese stocks sold at over 60 times earnings, almost five times book value and well over 200 times dividends. In contrast, U.S. stocks sold at about 15 times earnings, and London equities sold at 12 times earnings. The high prices of Japanese stocks were even more dramatic on a company by company comparison. The value of NTT Corporation, Japan's telephone giant, which was privatized during the boom, exceeded the value of AT&T, IBM, Exxon, General Electric, and General Motors all put together. Dai Ichi Kangyo Bank sold at 56 times earnings while an equivalent U.S. bank, Citicorp, sold at 5.6 times earnings. Nomura Securities, Japan's largest stock broker, sold at a market value exceeding the total value of all U.S. brokerage firms combined.

Two myths propelled the real estate and stock markets. The first was that land prices could never go down in Japan, and the second was that stock prices could only go up. These myths were fueled by large amounts of cash from the Japanese tradition of almost compulsive saving and by extremely low returns from regular savings accounts, which yielded under one percent. Playing the stock market became a national preoccupation. Almost overnight, Japanese male commuters switched from their usual pornographic comic books to lurid tales of vivid conquests of the stock market. It is said that in Britain there is a betting shop (or turf accountant) on every corner. In Japan, there was a stock broker on every corner. Nomura Securities reached intellectual customers through its ad featuring "Copernicus and Ptolemy." These compared Nomura's perpetually bullish stock outlook with the enlightened Copernican view that the earth and planets revolved around the sun. The naysaying view that stock and real estate markets were dangerously high was compared with Ptolemy's conviction that the sun revolved around the earth. Another sales brochure, put out by a Japanese stockbroker, featured a housewife, a cloud draping her hand, and an arrow about to fly ever upward. This was clearly a time for building castles in the air.

Japanese corporations also played a major role in the market frenzy. Businesses were allowed to set up tax advantaged speculative trading accounts (called *toklein* accounts) to play the market. During the boom, firms often made more money from trading stock than from producing goods. This party was too good to miss. Moreover, with low interest rates, it was possible to borrow money to get more funds to play the market. In fact, corporations began to float bonds in the European markets with interest rates as low as one percent, by offering warrants to buy the companies' stock, which, of course, would become quite valuable if the bull market continued. Optimism continued to breed optimism, and it appeared that the party could go on forever.

Supporters of the stock market had answers to all the logical objections that could be raised. Were price-earnings ratios in the stratosphere? "No" said the sales people at Kabuto-cho (Japan's Wall Street). "Japanese earnings are understated relative to U.S. earnings because depreciation charges are overstated and earnings do not include the earnings of partially owned affiliated firms." P/Es adjusted for these effects would be much lower. Were yields, at well under ½ of one percent, unconscionably low? The answer was that this simply reflected the low interest rates at the time in Japan. Was it dangerous that stock prices were five times the value of assets? Not at all. The book values did not reflect the dramatic appreciation of the land owned by Japanese companies. And the high value of Japanese land was "explained" by both the density of Japanese population and the various regulations and tax laws restricting the use of habitable land.

In fact, none of the "explanations" for the soaring heights of the real estate and stock markets could hold water. Even when earnings and dividends were adjusted, the multiples were still far higher than in other countries and extraordinarily inflated relative to Japan's own history. Moreover, Japanese profitability had been declining and the strong yen was bound to make it more difficult for Japan to export its products. While land was scarce in Japan, its manufacturers, such as its auto makers, were finding abundant land for new plants at attractive prices in foreign lands. And rental income had been rising far more slowly than land values, indicating a falling rate of return on real estate unless prices continued to skyrocket. Finally, the low interest rates that had been underpinning the market had already begun to rise in 1989.

Perhaps the cleverest "explanation" for the runaway Japanese real estate and stock markets was that "Japan was different." Every professional with whom I talked in the late 1980s was convinced that the powerful Ministry of Finance (MoF) would somehow find a way to avoid any unpleasantness. It could restrict land available for development if prices started to fall. It could change a rule here or there, or institute a new regulation to cure any ills in the stock market. The view was widespread in world financial markets that the Japanese market was "rigged" and would continue to be so as part of a government policy to promote lofty stock prices and cheap capital for economic growth. How often we make egregious errors by ignoring history and economic fundamentals and conclude that "this time it's different." And so the bubble grew. Optimism bred more optimism. Speculators used shares as collateral to borrow money to buy property, which could be used to borrow to buy more shares.

Much to the distress of those speculators who had concluded that the fundamental laws of financial gravity were not applicable to Japan, Isaac Newton arrived there in 1990. Interestingly, it was the government itself which dropped the apple. The Bank of Japan (Japan's Federal Reserve) saw the ugly spectre of a general inflation stirring among the borrowing frenzy and the liquidity boom underwriting the rise in land and stock prices. The case for tightening credit *before* a major rise in the general inflation rate rather than afterwards is that the longer the delay, the greater the eventual pain is likely to be in terms of lost economic output and rising unemployment. And so, the central bank restricted credit and engineered a rise in interest rates. The hope was that further rises in property prices would be choked off and the stock market might be eased downwards.

Interest rates, which had already been going up during 1989, rose sharply in 1990. The stock market was not eased down: Instead, it collapsed. The fall was almost as extreme as the U.S. stock-market crash from the end of 1929 to mid-1932. The Japanese (Nikkei) stock-market index reached a high of almost 40,000 on the last trading day of the decade of the 1980s. By mid-August 1992, the index had declined to 14,309, a drop of about 63 percent. In contrast, the Dow Jones industrial average fell 66 percent from December 1929 to its low in the summer of 1932 (although the decline was 77 percent from the September 1929 level). Of course, in 1932 we suffered a serious depression, whereas the Japanese economy kept rolling along in the 1990s with only normal fluctuations. Thus, the decline in Japan represented mainly a revaluation of equities. Moreover, even when interest rates returned to their pre-crash levels, the Japanese market remained near its mid-1992 lows. The chart that follows shows quite dramatically that the rise in stock prices during the

mid- and late-1980s represented a change in valuation relationships. The fall in stock prices from 1990 on simply reflected a
return to the price-book value relationships that were typical in
the early 1980s.

It is more difficult to date and measure the collapse in the
real estate market since property rarely changes hands. Nevertheless, the air also rushed out of the real estate balloon during
the early 1990s. Various measures of land prices and property
values indicate a decline roughly as severe as that of the stock
market. The bursting of the bubble destroyed the myth that
Japan was different and its asset prices would always rise. The
financial laws of gravity know no geographic boundaries.

The Japanese Stock-Market Bubble
Japanese Stock Prices Relative to Book Values 1980–95

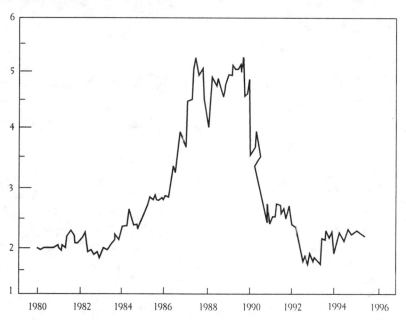

Source: Morgan Stanley Research and author's estimates.

Probably more so than any other chapter in the book, this
review of recent stock valuations seems inconsistent with the
view that the stock market is rational and efficient. But the

lesson, it seems to me, is *not* that markets at times can be irrational and, therefore, that we should abandon the firm-foundation theory. Rather, the clear conclusion is that, in every case, the market did correct itself. The market eventually corrects any irrationality—albeit in its own slow, inexorable fashion. Anomalies are able to crop up, markets can get irrationally optimistic, and often they attract unwary investors. But eventually, true value is recognized by the market, and this is the main lesson investors must heed.

4

The Firm-Foundation
Theory
of Stock Prices

The greatest of all gifts is the power to estimate things at
their true worth.
                    —La Rochefoucauld,
                        Reflexions; ou sentences et maximes morales

Investors can and should learn vicariously
from the stock market. And I hope the historical review in
Chapter Three has provided sufficient warning to save you
from the traps that ensnare builders of castles in the air. Autop-
sies should be as useful in the practice of investment as in
medicine. At the same time, to be forewarned is not to be fore-
armed in the investment world. Investors also need a sense of
justification for market prices—a standard, even if only a very
loose one, with which to compare current market prices. Is
there such a thing? I happen to think so—though I believe it
neither rests on a firm foundation nor floats like a castle in the
air.

The firm-foundation theorists, who include many of Wall
Street's most prosperous and highly paid security analysts,
know full well that purely psychic support for market valuations has proved a most undependable pillar, and skyrocketing
markets have invariably succumbed to the financial laws of
gravity. Therefore, many security analysts devote their energies to estimating a stock's firm foundation of value. Let's see
what lies behind such estimates.

The "Fundamental" Determinants
of Stock Prices

What is it that determines the real or intrinsic value of a share? What are the so-called fundamentals that security analysts look at in estimating a security's firm foundation of value?

I said in the first chapter that firm-foundation theorists view the worth of any share as the present value of all dollar benefits the investor expects to receive from it. Remember that the word "present" indicates that a distinction must be made between dollars expected immediately and those anticipated later on, which must be "discounted." All future income is worth less than money in hand; for if you had the money now you could be earning interest on it. In a very real sense, time is money.

In arriving at their value estimates, firm-foundation theorists usually take the standpoint of a very long-term investor who buys his shares "for keeps." One may buy 100 shares of IBM at $100 per share hoping that someone will come along later to purchase them from you at $150. But far less speculative estimates of value can be made by looking at the long-run flow of IBM dividends. The only benefits a long-term investor receives will come to her if the company pays out some part of its earnings in cash dividends. Thus, the worth of a share to a long-term investor will be the present or discounted value of all the future dividends the firm is expected to pay. As a popular rhyme on Wall Street goes:

> A cow for her milk,
> A hen for her eggs,
> And a stock, by heck,
> For her dividends.

Of course, the price of a common stock is dependent on a number of factors. I will now describe four determinants affecting the value of shares and then give four broad rules for applying these to determine the present (or firm-foundation) value of the stocks you are considering. If you follow these rules consistently, firm-foundation theorists suggest you will find yourself safe from the speculative crazes I have just described.

Determinant 1: The expected growth rate.   Most people don't realize the implications of compound growth on financial decisions. Albert Einstein once described compound interest as the "greatest mathematical discovery of all time." It is often said that the Indian who sold Manhattan Island in 1626 for $24 was rooked by the white man. In fact, he may have been an extremely sharp salesman. Had he put his $24 away at 6 percent interest, compounded semiannually, it would now be worth over $50 billion, and with it his descendants could buy back much of the now-improved land. Such is the magic of compound growth!

Similarly, the implications of various growth rates for the size of future dividends may be surprising to many readers. As the table below shows, growth at a 15 percent rate means that dividends will double every five years.* Alternate rates are also presented.

Growth Rate of Dividends	Present Dividend	Dividend in Five Years	Dividend in Ten Years	Dividend in Twenty-Five Years
5 percent	$1.00	$1.28	$1.63	$ 3.39
15 percent	1.00	2.01	4.05	32.92
25 percent	1.00	3.05	9.31	264.70

The catch (and doesn't there always have to be at least one, if not twenty-two?) is that dividend growth does not go on forever. Corporations and industries have life cycles similar to most living things. There is, for corporations in particular, a high mortality rate at birth. Survivors can look forward to rapid growth, maturity, and then a period of stability. Later in the life cycle, companies eventually decline and either perish or undergo a substantial metamorphosis. Consider the leading corporations in the United States 100 years ago. Such names as Eastern Buggy Whip Company, La Crosse and Minnesota

*A handy rule for calculating how many years it takes dividends to double is to divide 72 by the long-term growth rate. Thus, if dividends grow at 15 percent per year they will double in a bit less than five years (72 ÷ 15).

Steam Packet Company, Lobdell Car Wheel Company, Savanna and St. Paul Steamboat Line, and Hazard Powder Company, the already mature enterprises of the time, would have ranked high in a *"Fortune* Top 500" list of that era. All are now deceased.

Look at the industry record. Railroads, the most dynamic growth industry a century ago, finally matured and enjoyed a long period of prosperity before entering their recent period of decline. The paper and aluminum industries provide more recent examples of the cessation of rapid growth and the start of a more stable, mature period in the life cycle. These industries were the most rapidly growing in the United States during the 1940s and early 1950s. By the 1960s, they were no longer able to grow any faster than the economy as a whole. Similarly, the most rapidly growing industry of the late 1950s and 1960s, electric equipment, had slowed to a crawl by the 1970s.

And even if the natural life cycle doesn't get a company, there's always the fact that it gets harder and harder to grow at the same percentage rate. A company earning $1 million need increase its earnings by only $100,000 to achieve a 10 percent growth rate, whereas a company starting from a base of $10 million in earnings needs $1 million in additional earnings to produce the same record.

The nonsense of relying on very high long-term growth rates is nicely illustrated by working with population projections for the United States. If the populations of the nation and of California continue to grow at their recent rates, 120 percent of the United States population will live in California by the year 2035! Using similar kinds of projections, it can be estimated that at the same time 240 percent of the people in the country with venereal disease will live in California. As one Californian put it on hearing these forecasts, "Only the former projections make the latter one seem at all plausible."

As hazardous as projections may be, share prices must reflect differences in growth prospects if any sense is to be made of market valuations. Also, the probable length of the growth phase is very important. If one company expects to enjoy a rapid 20 percent growth rate for ten years, and another growth company expects to sustain the same rate for only five years, the former company is, other things being equal, more valuable to the investor than the latter. The point is that growth rates are general rather than gospel truths. And this brings us to the firm-foundation theorists' first rule for evaluating securities:

> *Rule 1: A rational investor should be willing to pay a higher price for a share the larger the growth rate of dividends.*

To this is added an important corollary:

> *Corollary to Rule 1: A rational investor should be willing to pay a higher price for a share the longer an extraordinary growth rate is expected to last.*

Determinant 2: The expected dividend payout. The amount of dividends you receive at each payout—as contrasted to their growth rate—is readily understandable as being an important factor in determining a stock's price. The higher the dividend payout, other things being equal, the greater the value of the stock. The catch here is the phrase *other things being equal.* Stocks that pay out a high percentage of earnings in dividends may be poor investments if their growth prospects are unfavorable. Conversely, many companies in their most dynamic growth phase often pay out little or none of their earnings in dividends. But for two companies whose expected growth rates are the same, you are better off with the one whose dividend payout is higher.

Beware of the stock dividend. This provides no benefits whatever. The practice is employed on the pretext that the firm is preserving cash for expansion while providing dividends in the form of additional shares. Stockholders presumably like to receive new pieces of paper—it gives them a warm feeling that the firm's managers are interested in their welfare. Some even think that by some alchemy the stock dividend increases the worth of their holdings.

In actuality, only the printer profits from the stock dividend. To distribute a 100 percent stock dividend, a firm must print one additional share for each share outstanding. But with twice as many shares outstanding, each share represents only half the interest in the company that it formerly did. Earnings per share and all other relevant per-share statistics about the company are now halved. This unit change is the only result of a stock dividend. Stockholders should not greet with any joy the declaration of stock splits or dividends—unless these are accompanied by higher cash dividends or news of higher earnings.

The only conceivable advantage of a stock split (or large stock dividend) is that lowering the price level of the shares might induce more public investors to purchase them. People like to buy in 100-share lots, and if a stock's price is very high many investors will feel excluded. But 2 and 3 percent stock dividends, which are so commonly declared, do no good at all.

The distribution of new certificates for stock dividends brings up the whole concept of actual certificates of ownership. This is an incredibly cumbersome and archaic system and should be eliminated. Records of ownership could easily be kept on the memory disks of large computers. Some bonds are actually recorded that way now. If stockholders could rid themselves of their atavistic longing for pretty embossed certificates, Wall Street could reduce its paperwork burden, commission rates might be reduced, and environmentalists could congratulate themselves on another victory.

Now that I've got that off my chest, let's sum up by printing the second rule:

> *Rule 2: A rational investor should be willing to pay a higher price for a share, other things being equal, the larger the proportion of a company's earnings that is paid out in cash dividends.*

Determinant 3: The degree of risk.   Risk plays an important role in the stock market, no matter what your overeager broker may tell you. There is always a risk—and that's what makes it so fascinating. Risk also affects the valuation of a stock. Some people think risk is the only aspect of a stock to be examined.

The more respectable a stock is—that is, the less risk it has—the higher its quality. Stocks of the so-called blue-chip companies, for example, are said to deserve a quality premium. (Why high-quality stocks are given an appellation derived from the poker tables is a fact known only to Wall Street.) Most investors prefer less risky stocks and, therefore, these stocks can command higher price-earnings multiples than their risky, low-quality counterparts.

While there is general agreement that the compensation for higher risk must be greater future rewards (and thus *lower* current prices), measuring risk is well-nigh impossible. This has not daunted the economist, however. A great deal of attention has been devoted to risk measurement by both academic economists and practitioners. Indeed, risk measurement is so important that an entire part of this book (Part Three) is largely devoted to this subject.

According to one well-known theory, the bigger the swings—relative to the market as a whole—in an individual company's stock prices (or in its total yearly returns, including dividends), the greater the risk. For example, a nonswinger such as AT&T gets the *Good Housekeeping* seal of approval for "widows and orphans." That's because its earnings do not decline much if at all during recessions, and its dividend has never been cut. Therefore, when the market goes down 20 percent, AT&T usually trails with perhaps only a 10 percent decline. AT&T is probably not as safe as it was before the 1983 divestiture and deregulation, which led to increased competition in the telecommunications industry. Nevertheless, the stock still qualifies as one with less than average risk. Amdahl, on the other hand, has a very volatile past record and it characteristically falls by 40 percent or more when the market declines by 20 percent. It is called a "flyer," or an investment that is a "businessman's risk." The investor gambles in owning stock in such a company, particularly if he may be forced to sell out during a time of unfavorable market conditions.

When business is good and the market mounts a sustained upward drive, however, Amdahl can be expected to outdistance AT&T. But if you are like most investors, you value stable returns over speculative hopes, freedom from worry about your portfolio over sleepless nights, and limited loss exposure over the possibility of a downhill roller-coaster ride. You will prefer the more stable security, other things being the same. This leads to a third basic rule of security valuation.

Rule 3: A rational (and risk-averse) investor should be willing to pay a higher price for a share, other things being equal, the less risky the company's stock.

I should warn the reader that a "relative volatility" measure may not fully capture the relevant risk of a company. Part Three will present a thorough discussion of this important risk element in stock valuation.

Determinant 4: The level of market interest rates. The stock market, no matter how much it may think so, does not exist as a world unto itself. Investors should consider how much profit they can obtain elsewhere. Interest rates, if they are high enough, can offer a stable, profitable alternative to the stock market. Consider periods such as the early 1980s when yields on *prime* quality corporate bonds soared to over 15 percent. Long-term bonds of somewhat lower quality were being offered at even higher interest rates. The expected returns from stock prices had trouble matching these bond rates; money flowed into bonds while stock prices fell sharply. Finally, stock prices reached such a low level that a sufficient number of investors were attracted to stem the decline. Again in 1987, interest rates rose substantially, preceding the great stock market crash of October 19. To put it another way, in order to attract investors from high-yielding bonds, stock must offer bargain-basement prices.*

On the other hand, when interest rates are very low, fixed-interest securities provide very little competition for the stock

---

*The point can be made another way by noting that since higher interest rates enable us to earn more now, any deferred income should be "discounted" more heavily. Thus, the present value of any flow of future dividend returns will be lower when current interest rates are relatively high. The relationship between interest rates and stock prices is somewhat more complicated, however, than this discussion may suggest. Suppose investors expect that the rate of inflation will increase from 5 to 10 percent. Such an expectation is likely to drive interest rates up by about 5 percentage points to compensate investors for holding fixed-dollar-obligation bonds whose purchasing power will be adversely affected by greater inflation. Other things being the same, this should make stock prices fall. But with higher expected inflation, investors may reasonably project that corporate earnings and dividends will also increase at a faster rate, causing stock prices to rise. A full discussion of inflation, interest rates, and stock prices is contained in Chapter Thirteen, where it is shown that corporate earnings and dividends do tend to grow with inflation.

market and stock prices tend to be relatively high. During the early 1990s, when bank rates on certificates of deposit fell to three percent, or less, and long-term rates on U.S. Treasury securities fell below six percent, money poured out of the banks and the bond markets and into the stock market. This pushed up stock prices and, thus, the justification for the last rule for the firm-foundation theory:

> *Rule 4: A rational investor should be willing to pay a higher price for a share, other things being equal, the lower are interest rates.*

Two Important Caveats

The four valuation rules imply that a security's firm-foundation value (and its price-earnings multiple) will be higher the larger the company's growth rate and the longer its duration; the larger the dividend payout for the firm; the less risky the company's stock; and the lower the general level of interest rates.

As I indicated earlier, economists have taken rules such as these and expressed in a mathematical formula the exact price (present value) at which shares should sell. In principle, such theories are very useful in suggesting a rational basis for stock prices and in giving investors some standard of value. Of course, the rules must be compared with the facts to see if they conform at all to reality, and I will get to that in a moment. But before we even think of using and testing these rules in a very precise way, there are two important caveats to bear in mind.

Caveat 1: Expectations about the future cannot be proven in the present.   Remember, not even Jeane Dixon can accurately predict all of the future. Yet some people have absolute faith in security analysts' estimates of the long-term growth prospects of a company and the duration of that growth.

Predicting future earnings and dividends is a most hazardous occupation. It requires not only the knowledge and skill of an economist, but also the acumen of a psychologist. On top of that, it is extremely difficult to be objective; wild optimism and extreme pessimism constantly battle for top place. During the early 1960s, when the economy and the world situation were relatively stable, investors had no trouble convincing themselves that the coming decade would be soaring and prosperous. As a result, very high growth rates were projected for a large number of corporations. Years later, in 1980, the economy was suffering from severe "stagflation" and an unstable international situation. The best that investors could do that year was to project modest growth rates for most corporations.

The point to remember is that no matter what formula you use for predicting the future, it always rests in part on the indeterminate premise. Although many Wall Streeters claim to see into the future, they are just as fallible as the rest of us. As Samuel Goldwyn once said, "Forecasts are difficult to make—particularly those about the future."

Caveat 2: Precise figures cannot be calculated from undetermined data.

It stands to reason that you can't obtain precise figures by using indefinite factors. Yet to achieve desired ends, investors and security analysts do this all the time. Here's how it's done.

Take a company that you've heard lots of good things about. You study the company's prospects, and suppose you conclude that it can maintain a high growth rate for a long period. How long? Well, why not ten years?

You then calculate what the stock should be "worth" on the basis of the current dividend payout, the expected future growth rate of dividends, and the general level of interest rates, perhaps making an allowance for the riskiness of the shares.* It turns out to your chagrin that the price the stock is worth is just slightly less than its present market price.

You now have two alternatives. You could regard the stock as overpriced and refuse to buy it, or you could say, "Perhaps this stock could maintain a high growth rate for eleven years rather than ten. After all, the ten was only a guess in the first

*If you actually want to do the calculation, just write out your estimates for the future flow of dividends expected, get hold of a vest-pocket calculator or laptop computer, and perform the whole operation while riding into work on the train.

place, so why not eleven years?" And so you go back to your computer and lo and behold you now come up with a worth for the shares that is larger than the current market price. Armed with this "precise" knowledge, you make your sound purchase.

The reason the game worked is that the longer one projects growth, the greater is the stream of future dividends. Thus, the present value of a share is at the discretion of the calculator. If eleven years was not enough to do the trick, twelve or thirteen might well have sufficed. There is always some combination of growth rate and growth period that will produce any specific price. In this sense, it is intrinsically impossible, given human nature, to calculate the intrinsic value of a share.

J. Peter Williamson, author of an excellent textbook for financial analysts entitled *Investments,* provides another example. In the book, Williamson estimated the present (or firm-foundation) value of IBM shares by using the same general principle of valuation I have described above; that is, by estimating how fast IBM's dividends would grow and for how long. At the time IBM was the premier growth stock in the country, Williamson first made the seemingly sensible assumption that IBM would grow at a fairly high rate for some number of years before falling into a much smaller mature growth rate. When he made his estimate, IBM was selling at a pre-split price of $320 per share.

> I began by forecasting growth in earnings per share at 16%. This was a little under the average for the previous ten years. . . . I forecast at 16% growth rate for 10 years, followed by indefinite growth at . . . 2%. . . . When I put all these numbers into the formula I got an intrinsic value of $172.94, about half of the current market value.

Since the intrinsic value and market value of IBM stock were so far apart, Williamson decided that perhaps his estimates of the future might not be accurate. He experimented further:

> It doesn't really seem sensible to predict only 10 years of above average growth for IBM, so I extended my 16% growth forecast to 20 years. Now the intrinsic value came to $432.66, well above the market.

Had Williamson opted for thirty years of above-average growth, he would be projecting IBM to generate a future sales volume about one-half the then current U.S. national income. In fact, we know that IBM stopped growing in the mid-1980s and that it reported some enormous losses in the early 1990s before a recovery started in 1994 under new management.

The point to remember from such examples is that the mathematical precision of the firm-foundation value formulas is based on treacherous ground: forecasting the future. The major fundamentals for these calculations are never known with certainty; they are only relatively crude estimates—perhaps one should say guesses—about what might happen in the future. And depending on what guesses you make, you can convince yourself to pay any price you want to for a stock.

There is, I believe, a fundamental indeterminateness about the value of common shares even in principle. God Almighty does not know the proper price-earnings multiple for a common stock.

Testing the Rules

With the rules and caveats in mind, let us take a closer look at stock prices and examine whether the rules seem to conform to actual practices. Let's start with Rule 1—the larger the anticipated growth rate, the higher the price of a share.

To begin, we'll reformulate the question in terms of price-earnings (P/E) multiples rather than the market prices themselves. This provides a good yardstick for comparing stocks—which have different prices and earnings—against one another. A stock selling at $100 per share with earnings of $10 per share would have the same P/E multiple (10) as a stock selling at $40 with earnings of $4 per share. It is the P/E multiple, not the dollar price, that really tells you how a stock is valued in the market.

Our reformulated question now reads: Are actual price-earnings multiples higher for stocks where a high growth rate is anticipated? A major study by John Cragg and myself strongly indicates that the answer is yes.

It was easy to collect the first half of the data required. P/E multiples are printed daily in papers such as the *New York Times* and the *Wall Street Journal*. To obtain information on expected long-term growth rates, we surveyed eighteen leading investment firms whose business it is to produce the forecasts upon which buy and sell recommendations are made. (I'll describe later how they make these forecasts.) Estimates were obtained from each firm of the five-year growth rates anticipated for a large sample of stocks.

I will not bore you with the details of the actual statistical study that was performed.* The results are illustrated, however, for a few representative securities in the chart below. It is clear that, just as Rule 1 asserts, high P/E ratios are associated with high expected growth rates. This general pattern

Effect of High Expected Long-Term Growth Rates—Price-Earnings Multiples Pushed Up*

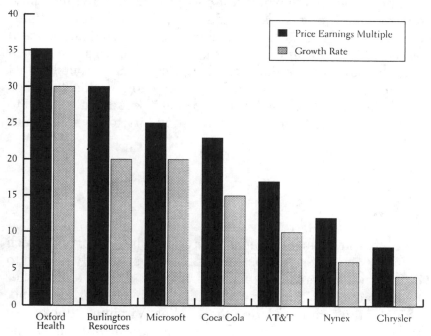

*Data for 1995.

*It is listed among the references for this chapter.

has held up in every year since 1961, when we began the study.

In addition to demonstrating how the market values different growth rates, the chart can also be used as a practical investment guide. Suppose you were considering the purchase of a stock with an anticipated 15 percent growth rate and you knew that, on average, stocks with 15 percent growth sold, like Coca Cola, at 19 times earnings. If the stock you were considering sold at a price-earnings multiple of 25, you might reject the idea of buying the stock in favor of one more reasonably priced in terms of current market norms. If, on the other hand, your stock sold at a multiple below the average in the market for that growth rate, the security is said to represent good value for your money. I'll return to the practical use of such techniques, as well as the pitfalls, at several later points.

How about Rules 2, 3, and 4? Just as we were able to test for a relationship between earnings multiples and anticipated growth rates, it was also possible to collect the necessary data and find the ways in which not only growth, but dividend payout, risk, and interest rates influence price-earnings multiples in the market. The particular techniques used need not concern us. What is important to realize is that there does seem to be a logic to market valuations. Market prices seem to behave just as the four rules developed by the firm-foundation theorists would lead us to expect. It is comforting to know that at least to this extent there is an underlying rationality to the stock market.

One More Caveat

So market prices do seem to have an inherent logic. In each of many recent years, stock prices have been closely related to differential patterns of expected growth as well as to the other "fundamental" valuation influences so important to proponents of the firm-foundation theory. Yes, Virginia, it looks like there may be a firm foundation of value after all, and some jokers in Wall Street actually think you can make money knowing what it is.

***Caveat 3: What's growth for the goose is not always growth
for the gander.*** The difficulty comes with the value the market puts on specific fundamentals. It is always true that the
market values growth, and that higher growth rates and larger
multiples go hand in hand. But the crucial question is: How
much more should you pay for higher growth?

There is no consistent answer. In some periods, as in the
early 1960s and 1970s, when growth was thought to be especially desirable, the market has been willing to pay an enormous price for stocks exhibiting high growth rates. At other
times, such as the late 1980s and early to mid-1990s, high-
growth stocks commanded only a modest premium over the
multiples of common stocks in general.

The point is illustrated in the following table. IBM, during
its rapid growth phase, consistently sold at a much higher multiple than the market. But the differential in multiples has been
quite volatile. IBM's multiple was over three times that of the
market in December 1961. Five months later it was not even
two times as great. At the low points in the market in 1970 and
especially in 1980, IBM sold at only very small premiums over
the general market. While it is true that the growth prospects
for IBM were significantly lower in the 1980s and 1990s than
they were in the 1960s, the big changes in relative valuations
between 1961 and 1962 and between 1968 and 1970 cannot be
explained by changing expectations of IBM's growth prospects.

Price-Earnings Multiples for IBM and for the Market in General[a]

| | P/E Multiples | | Premium: IBM P/E as a % of S&P P/E |
	IBM	S&P Index	
Market peak 1961	64	20	320%
Market low 1962	29	16	181
Market peak 1968	50	18	278
Market low 1970	25	16	156
Market peak 1972	44	17	259
Market low 1980	9	7	129
Market peak 1994	19	17	112

[a]As measured by Standard & Poor's Industrial Index (425-Stock Index through 1972, 400-Stock Index for 1980 and 1994 figures).

A similar way of looking at the changing premiums paid for growth stocks is shown in the following chart, which graphs the premiums for Smith, Barney Index of Emerging Growth Stocks compared with the stocks of Standard & Poor's 500-Stock Index. The chart tells a disappointing story for anyone looking for a consistent long-term valuation relationship. Growth can be as fashionable as tulip bulbs, as investors in growth stocks painfully learned. During the early 1980s, growth stocks reached extremely high valuations relative to the market as a whole. During the late 1980s and early to mid-1990s, the premium for growth was lower than at any time during the preceding twenty years.

From a practical standpoint, the rapid changes in market valuations that have occurred suggest that it would be very dangerous to use any one year's valuation relationships as an

The Premium Paid for Growth
Smith, Barney Emerging Growth Index
P/E Relative to S&P 500

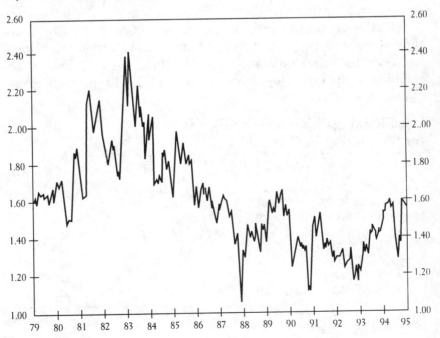

indication of market norms. However, by comparing how growth stocks are currently valued with historical precedent, investors should at least be able to isolate those periods when a touch of the tulip bug has smitten investors. When the first edition of this book was published in 1973, I warned that growth stocks were extremely richly priced and that investors should approach these stocks with extraordinary care. The chart above shows that the earnings multiples of growth stocks are now reasonably modest and thus growth companies appear to offer attractive value for the remainder of the 1990s, relative to the market as a whole.

What's Left of the Firm Foundation?

A renowned rabbi, whose fame for adjudicating disputes had earned him the reputation of a modern-day Solomon, was asked to settle a long-standing argument between two philosophers. The rabbi listened intently as the first disputant vigorously presented his case. The rabbi reflected on the argument and finally pronounced, "Yes, you are correct." Then the second philosopher presented his case with equal vigor and persuasion and argued eloquently that the first philosopher could not be correct. The rabbi nodded his approval and indicated, "You are correct." A bystander, somewhat confused by this performance, accosted the rabbi to complain, "You told both philosophers they were right, but their arguments were totally contradictory. They both can't be correct." The rabbi needed only a moment to formulate his response: "Yes, you are indeed correct."

In adjudicating the dispute between the firm-foundation theorists and those who take a castle-in-the-air view of the stock market, I feel a little like the accommodating rabbi. It seems clear that so-called fundamental considerations do have a profound influence on market prices. We have seen that price-earnings multiples in the market are influenced by expected growth, dividend payouts, risk, and the rate of interest. Higher anticipations of earnings growth and higher dividend payouts tend to increase price-earnings multiples. Higher risk and higher interest rates tend to pull them down. There is a logic to the stock market, just as the firm foundationists assert.

Thus, when all is said and done, it appears that there is a yardstick for value, but one that is a most flexible and undependable instrument. To change the metaphor, stock prices are in a sense anchored to certain "fundamentals" but the anchor is easily pulled up and then dropped in another place. For the standards of value, we have found, are not the fixed and immutable standards that characterize the laws of physics, but rather the more flexible and fickle relationships that are consistent with a marketplace heavily influenced by mass psychology.

Not only does the market change the values it puts on the various fundamental determinants of stock prices, but the most important of these fundamentals are themselves liable to change depending on the state of market psychology. Stocks are bought on expectations—not on facts.

The most important fundamental influence on stock prices is the level and duration of the future growth of corporate earnings and dividends. But, as I pointed out earlier, future earnings growth is not easily estimated, even by market professionals. In times of great optimism, it is very easy for investors to convince themselves that their favorite corporations can enjoy substantial and persistent growth over an extended period of time. By raising his estimates of growth, even the most sober firm-foundation theorist can convince himself to pay any price whatever for a share.

During periods of extreme pessimism, many security analysts will not project any growth that is not "visible" to them over the very short run and hence will estimate only the most modest of growth rates for the corporations they follow. But if expected growth rates themselves and the price the market is willing to pay for this growth can both change rapidly on the basis of market psychology, then it is clear that the concept of a *firm* intrinsic value for shares must be an elusive will-o'-the-wisp. As an old Wall Street proverb runs: No price is too high for a bull or too low for a bear.

Dreams of castles in the air, of getting rich quick, may therefore play an important role in determining actual stock prices. And even investors who believe in the firm-foundation theory might buy a security on the anticipation that eventually the average opinion would expect a larger growth rate for the stock in the future. After all, investors who want to reap extraordinary profits may find that the most profitable course of action is to beat the gun and anticipate future changes in the intrinsic value of shares.

Still, this analysis suggests that the stock market will not be a perpetual tulip-bulb craze. The existence of some generally accepted principles of valuation does serve as a kind of balance wheel. For the castle-in-the-air investor might well consider that if prices get too far out of line with normal valuation standards, the average opinion may soon expect that others will anticipate a reaction. To be sure, these standards of value are extremely loose ones and difficult to estimate. But sooner or later in a skyrocketing market, some investors may begin to compare the growth rates that are implicit in current prices with more reasonable and dispassionate estimates of the growth likely to be achieved.

It seems eminently sensible to me that both views of security pricing tell us something about actual market behavior. But the important investment question is how you can use the theories to develop practically useful investment strategies. More about this in Part Two, where we take a close look at how the professionals use the two theories in their own investing, and in Part Three, where we examine the academic approach to investing.

How the Pros Play the Biggest Game in Town

5

Technical and Fundamental Analysis

A picture is worth ten thousand words.

—Old Chinese proverb

Twice in October 1987, over 600 million shares with a total market value of about $25 billion were traded on the New York Stock Exchange. Exchanges of shares valued at $15 billion are now considered almost routine for a day's trading on the big board. And this is only part of the story. A large volume of trading is also carried out on the American Stock Exchange, on the NASDAQ market, and on a variety of regional exchanges across the country. Professional investment analysts and counselors are involved in what has been called the biggest game in town.

If the stakes are high, so are the rewards. New trainees from the Harvard Business School routinely draw salaries of well over $100,000 per year. Experienced security analysts and successful salesmen, euphemistically called "account executives," make considerably more. At the top of the salary scale are the money managers themselves—the men and women who run the large mutual, pension, and trust funds. "Adam Smith," after writing the best-selling book, *The Money Game,* boasted that he would make a quarter of a million dollars from his book. His Wall Street friends retorted, "You're only going to make as much as a second-rate institutional salesman." Admit-

115

tedly, the depression that hit Wall Street after the crash of 1987 has made such talk appear somewhat overstated. Still, it is fair to conclude that while not the oldest, the profession of high finance is certainly one of the most generously compensated.

Part Two of this book concentrates on the methods and results of the professionals of Wall Street, LaSalle Street, Montgomery Street, and the various road-town financial centers. It then shows how academics in towns like Princeton and Berkeley have analyzed these professional results and have concluded that they are not worth the money you pay for them.

Academicians are a notoriously picayune lot. With their ringing motto, "Publish or perish," they keep themselves busy by preparing papers demolishing other people's theories, defending their own work, or constructing elaborate embellishments to generally accepted ideas.

The random-walk, or efficient-market, theory is a case in point. We now have three versions—the "weak," the "semi-strong," and the "strong." All three espouse the general idea that except for long-run trends, future stock prices are difficult, if not impossible, to predict. The weak says you cannot predict future stock prices on the basis of past stock prices. The semi-strong says you cannot even utilize published information to predict future prices. The strong goes flat out and says that nothing—not even unpublished developments—can be of use in predicting future prices; everything that is known, or even knowable, has already been reflected in present prices. The weak form attacks the underpinnings of technical analysis, and the semi-strong and strong forms argue against many of the beliefs held by those using fundamental analysis.

Technical versus Fundamental Analysis

The attempt to predict accurately the future course of stock prices and thus the appropriate time to buy or sell a stock must rank as one of investors' most persistent endeavors. This search for the golden egg has spawned a variety of methods ranging from the scientific to the occult. There are people today who forecast future stock prices by measuring sunspots, looking at the phases of the moon, or measuring the vibrations along the San Andreas Fault. Most, however, opt for one of two methods: technical or fundamental analysis.

The alternative techniques used by the investment pros are related to the two theories of the stock market I covered in Part One. Technical analysis is the method of predicting the appropriate time to buy or sell a stock used by those believing in the castle-in-the-air view of stock pricing. Fundamental analysis is the technique of applying the tenets of the firm-foundation theory to the selection of individual stocks.

Technical analysis is essentially the making and interpreting of stock charts. Thus its practitioners, a small but abnormally dedicated cult, are called chartists. They study the past—both the movements of common stock prices and the volume of trading—for a clue to the direction of future change. Most chartists believe that the market is only 10 percent logical and 90 percent psychological. They generally subscribe to the castle-in-the-air school and view the investment game as one of anticipating how the other players will behave. Charts, of course, tell only what the other players have been doing in the past. The chartist's hope, however, is that a careful study of what the other players are doing will shed light on what the crowd is likely to do in the future.

Fundamental analysts take the opposite tack, believing the market to be 90 percent logical and only 10 percent psychological. Caring little about the particular pattern of past price movement, fundamentalists seek to determine an issue's proper value. Value in this case is related to growth, dividend payout, interest rates, and risk, according to the rules of the firm-foundation theory outlined in the last chapter. By estimating such factors as growth for each company, the fundamentalist arrives at an estimate of a security's intrinsic value. If this is above the market price, then the investor is advised to buy. Fundamentalists believe that eventually the market will reflect accurately the security's real worth. Perhaps 90 percent of the Wall Street security analysts consider themselves fundamentalists. Many would argue that chartists are lacking in dignity and professionalism.

What Can Charts Tell You?

The first principle of technical analysis is that all information about earnings, dividends, and the future performance of a company is automatically reflected in the company's past market prices. A chart showing these prices and the volume of trading already comprises all the fundamental information, good or bad, that the security analyst can hope to know. The second principle is that prices tend to move in trends: A stock that is rising tends to keep on rising, whereas a stock at rest tends to remain at rest.

A true chartist doesn't even care to know what business or industry a company is in, as long as he can study its stock chart. A chart shaped in the form of an "inverted bowl" or "pennant" means the same for Digital Equipment as it does for MCI. Fundamental information on earnings and dividends is considered at best to be useless—and at worst a positive distraction. It is either of inconsequential importance for the pricing of the stock or, if it is important, it has already been reflected in the market days, weeks, or even months before the news has become public. For this reason, many chartists will not even read the newspaper except to follow the daily price quotations.

One of the original chartists, John Magee, operated from a small office in Springfield, Massachusetts, where even the windows were boarded up to prevent any outside influences from distracting his analysis. Magee was once quoted as saying, "When I come into this office I leave the rest of the world outside to concentrate entirely on my charts. This room is exactly the same in a blizzard as on a moonlit June evening. In here I can't possibly do myself and my clients the disservice of saying 'buy' simply because the sun is out or 'sell' because it is raining."

As shown in the figure opposite, you can easily construct a chart. You simply draw a vertical line whose bottom is the stock's low for the day and whose top is the high. This line is crossed to indicate the closing price for the day. In the figure, the stock had a range of quotations that day between 20 and 21

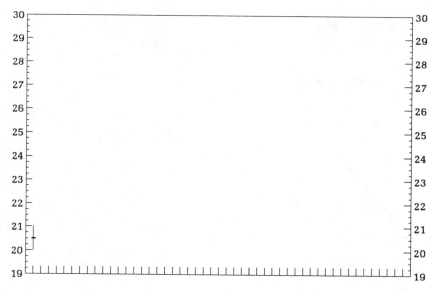

and closed at 20½. The process can be repeated for each trading day. It can be used for individual stocks or for one of the stock averages that you see in the financial pages of most newspapers. Often the chartist will also indicate the volume of shares of stock traded during the day by another vertical line at the bottom of the chart. Gradually, the highs and lows on the chart of the stock in question jiggle up and down sufficiently to produce patterns. To the chartist, these patterns have the same significance as X-ray plates to a surgeon.

One of the first things the chartist looks for is a trend. The figure at the top of the following page shows one in the making. It is the record of price changes for a stock over a number of days—and the prices are obviously on the way up. The chartist draws two lines connecting the tops and bottoms, creating a "channel" to delineate the uptrend. Since the presumption is that momentum in the market will tend to perpetuate itself, the chartist interprets such a pattern as a bullish augury—the stock can be expected to continue to rise. As Magee wrote in the bible of charting, *Technical Analysis of Stock Trends,* "Prices move in trends, and trends tend to continue until something happens to change the supply-demand balance."

Suppose, however, that at about 24, the stock finally runs into trouble and is unable to gain any further ground. This is

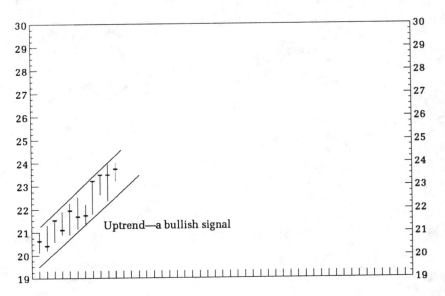

called a resistance level. The stock may wiggle around a bit and then turn downward. One pattern, which chartists claim reveals a clear signal that the market has topped out, is a head-and-shoulders formation. This is shown in the figure below.

The stock first rises and then falls slightly, forming a rounded shoulder. It rises again, going slightly higher, before once more receding, forming a head. Finally the right shoulder

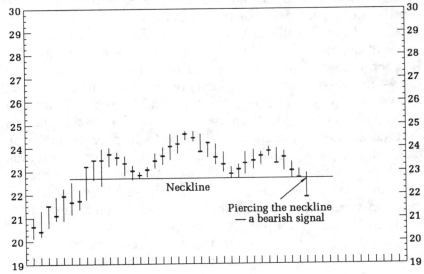

is formed, and chartists wait with bated breath for the sell signal, which sounds loud and clear when the stock "pierces the neckline." With the glee of Count Dracula surveying one of his victims, the chartists are off and selling, anticipating that a prolonged downtrend will follow as it allegedly has in the past. Of course, sometimes the market surprises the chartist. For example, as shown in the following chart, the stock may make an end run up to 30 right after giving a bear signal. This is called a bear trap or, to the chartist, the exception that tests the rule.

It follows from the technique that the chartist is a trader, not a long-term investor. The chartist buys when the auguries look favorable and sells on bad omens. He flirts with stocks just as some flirt with the opposite sex, and his scores are successful in-and-out trades, not rewarding long-term commitments. Indeed, the psychiatrist Don D. Jackson, author with Albert Haas, Jr., of *Bulls, Bears and Dr. Freud,* suggested that such an individual may be playing a game with overt sexual overtones.

When the chartist chooses a stock for potential investment there is typically a period of observation and flirtation before he commits himself, since for the chartist—as in romance and sexual conquest—timing is essential. There is mounting excitement as the stock penetrates the base formation and rises higher. Finally, if the affair has gone well, there is the moment

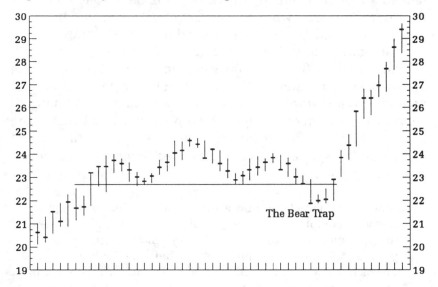

The Bear Trap

of fulfillment—profit-taking, and the release and afterglow that follow. The chartist's vocabulary features such terms as double bottoms, breakthrough, violating the lows, firmed up, big play, ascending peaks, and buying climax. And all this takes place under the pennant of that great symbol of sexuality: the bull.

The Rationale for the Charting Method

Probably the hardest question to answer is: Why is charting supposed to work? Some of my best friends are chartists and I have listened very carefully to their explanations, but I have yet really to understand them. Indeed, many chartists freely admit that *they* don't know why charting should work—history just has a habit of repeating itself. Even Magee, the chartist seer, went so far as to say that we can never hope to know "why" the market behaves as it does, we can only aspire to understand "how."

According to Magee, the situation in the stock market is analogous to that of a pig in a barn. The barn is all closed up on the ground floor, but it has a hayloft above with a large open door. The pig has a harness around his body to which is attached a long pole, the top of which is visible through the hayloft door. Of course, when the pig moves about, so will the pole. Magee supposed that we are perched in a nearby tree observing the motions of the top of the pole, which is all we can see. We must deduce from the pole's movement what is happening below, just as market participants must deduce what is happening in the market from the price movements they can observe. Magee went on to say that it is not important to know the color or size of the pig, or even whether it is a pig at all; it is only important to be able to make predictions about the next movement of the pole.

Some of the watchers who are not comfortable with highly abstract symbols will assign "meanings" to the pole's movements. They will try to "interpret" these movements as corresponding to various assimilative, combative, copulative, etc., actions of the pig. Others [like Magee, the author], who might consider themselves "pure technicians," will watch the pole, and work entirely on the basis of what the pole has done, is doing, or might be expected to do according to trends, repetitive motions, extrapolations, etc.

Yet it is in our nature to ask why. To me, the following explanations of technical analysis appear to be the most plausible. Trends might tend to perpetuate themselves for either of two reasons. First, it has been argued that the crowd instinct of mass psychology makes it so. When investors see the price of a speculative favorite going higher and higher, they want to jump on the bandwagon and join the rise. Indeed, the price rise itself helps fuel the enthusiasm in a self-fulfilling prophecy. Each rise in price just whets the appetite and makes investors expect a further rise.

Second, there may be unequal access to fundamental information about a company. When some favorable piece of news occurs, such as the discovery of a rich mineral deposit, it is alleged that the insiders are the first to know and they act, buying the stock and causing its price to rise. The insiders then tell their friends, who act next. Then the professionals find out the news and the big institutions put blocks of the shares in their portfolios. Finally, the poor slobs like you and me get the information and buy, pushing the price still higher. This process is supposed to result in a rather gradual increase in the price of the stock when the news is good and a decrease when the news is bad. Chartists claim that this scenario is somewhat close to what actually happened in the notorious Texas Gulf Sulphur case, where insiders profited on the basis of nonpublic information. Chartists are convinced that even if they do not have access to this inside information, observation of price movements alone enables them to pick up the scent of the "smart money" and permits them to get in long before the general public.

Chartists believe that another reason their techniques have validity is that people have a nasty habit of remembering what they paid for a stock, or the price they *wish* they had paid. For example, suppose a stock sold for about $50 a share for a long period of time, during which a number of investors bought in. Suppose then that the price drops to $40.

The chartists claim that the public will be anxious to sell

out the shares when they rise back to the price at which they were bought, and thus break even on the trade. Consequently, the price of $50 at which the stock sold initially becomes a "resistance area." Each time the resistance area is reached and the stock turns down again, the theory holds that the resistance level becomes even harder to cross, because more and more investors get the idea that the market or the individual stock in question cannot go any higher.

A similar argument lies behind the notion of "support levels." Chartists say that many investors who failed to buy when the market fluctuated around a relatively low price level will feel they have missed the boat when prices rise. Presumably such investors will jump at the chance to buy when prices drop back to the original low level.

Chartists also believe that investors who sold shares when the market was low and then saw prices rise will be anxious to buy those shares back if they can get them again at the price for which they sold. The argument then is that the original low price level becomes a "support area," since investors will believe that prices will again rise above that level. In chart theory, a "support area" that holds on successive declines becomes stronger and stronger. So if a stock declines to a support area and then begins to rise, the traders will jump in believing the stock is just "coming off the pad." Another bullish signal is flashed when a stock finally breaks through a resistance area. In the lexicon of the chartists, the former resistance area becomes a support area, and the stock should have no trouble gaining further ground.

Why Might Charting Fail to Work?

It is easier for me to present the *logical* arguments against charting. First, it should be noted that the chartist buys in only after price trends have been established, and sells only after they have been broken. Since sharp reversals in the market may occur quite suddenly, the chartist will often miss the boat. By the time an uptrend is signaled, it may already have taken place. Second, such techniques must ultimately be self-defeating. As more and more people use it, the value of any technique depreciates. No buy or sell signal can be worthwhile if everyone tries to act on it simultaneously.

Moreover, traders will tend to anticipate technical signals. If they see a price about to break through a resistance area, they will tend to buy before, not after, it breaks through. If it ever was profitable to use such charting techniques, it will now be possible only for those who anticipate the signals. This suggests that others will try to anticipate the signal still earlier. Of course, the earlier they anticipate, the less certain they are that the signal will occur, and in the scrambling to anticipate signals it is doubtful that any profitable technical trading rules can be developed.

Perhaps the most telling argument against technical methods comes from the logical implications of profit-maximizing behavior on the part of investors. Suppose, for example, that Universal Polymers is selling at around 20 when Sam, the chief research chemist, discovers a new production technique that promises to double the company's earnings and stock price. Now Sam is convinced that the price of Universal will hit 40 when the news of his discovery comes out. Since any purchases below 40 will provide a swift profit, he may well buy up all the stock he can until the price hits 40, a process that could take no longer than a few minutes.

Even if Sam doesn't have enough money to drive up the price himself, surely his friends and the financial institutions do have the funds to move the price so rapidly that no chartist could get into the act before the whole play is gone. The point is that the market may well be a most efficient mechanism. If some people know that the price will go to 40 tomorrow, it will go to 40 today. Of course, if Sam makes a public announcement of his discovery as the law requires, the argument holds with even greater force. Prices may adjust so quickly to new information as to make the whole process of technical analysis a futile exercise. In the next chapter, I'll examine whether the evidence supports such a pessimistic view of charting.

From Chartist to Technician

Though chartists are not held in high repute in Wall Street, their colorful methods, suggesting an easy way to get rich quick, have attracted a wide following. The companies that manufacture and distribute stock charts and charting paper have enjoyed a boom in their sales, and chartists themselves still find excellent employment opportunities with mutual funds and brokerage firms.

In the days before the computer, the laborious task of charting a course through the market was done by hand. Chartists were often viewed as peculiar people, with green eye-shades and carbon on their fingers, who were tucked away in a small closet at the back of the office. Now chartists have the services of a marvelous personal computer, hooked into a variety of data networks and replete with a large display terminal which, at the tap of a finger, can produce any conceivable chart one might want to see. The chartist (now always called a technician) can, with the glee of a little child playing with a new electric train, produce a complete chart of a stock's past performance, including measures of volume, the 200-day moving average (an average of prices over the previous 200 days recalculated each day), the strength of the stock relative to the market and relative to its industry, and literally hundreds of other averages, ratios, oscillators, and indicators.

Once the chart has been thus displayed, another press of the button will make a copy of the entire picture, which may be studied further on the train back to Larchmont and later tacked on one of the bulletin boards around the room. The result is akin to the Pentagon war room. One mutual fund was known to concentrate its technical information in what it called "information central." The computer also adds an aura of mystery and wonder to charting. Even if the chartist's techniques are unscientific, it is difficult to make fun of the computer, and some of the public's awe and admiration for computers has rubbed off on the technical analysts.

The Technique of Fundamental Analysis

Fred Schwed, Jr., in his charming and witty exposé of the financial community in the 1930s, *Where Are the Customers' Yachts?,* tells of a Texas broker who sold some stock to a customer at $760 a share at the moment when it could have been purchased anywhere else at $730. When the outraged customer found out what had happened, he complained bitterly to the broker. The Texan cut him short. "Suh," he boomed, "you-all don't appreciate the policy of this firm. This heah firm selects investments foh its clients not on the basis of Price, but of Value."

In a sense, this story illustrates the difference between the technician and the fundamentalist. The technician is interested only in the record of the stock's price, whereas the fundamentalist's primary concern is with what a stock is really worth. The fundamentalist strives to be relatively immune to the optimism and pessimism of the crowd and makes a sharp distinction between a stock's current price and its true value.

In estimating the firm-foundation value of a security, the fundamentalist's most important job is to estimate the firm's future stream of earnings and dividends. To do this, he or she must estimate the firm's sales level, operating costs, corporate tax rates, depreciation policies, and the sources and costs of its capital requirements.

Basically, the security analyst must be a prophet without the benefit of divine inspiration. As a poor substitute, the analyst turns to a study of the past record of the company, a review of the company's investment plans, and a firsthand visit to and appraisal of the company's management team. This yields a wealth of data. The analyst must then separate the important from the unimportant facts. As Benjamin Graham put it in *The Intelligent Investor,* "Sometimes he reminds us a bit of the erudite major general in 'The Pirates of Penzance,' with his 'many cheerful facts about the square of the hypotenuse.'"

Since the general prospects of a company are strongly influenced by the economic position of its industry, the obvious starting point for the security analyst is a study of industry prospects. Indeed, in almost all professional investment firms, security analysts specialize in particular industry groups. The fundamentalist hopes that a thorough study of industry conditions will produce valuable insights into factors that may be operative in the future but are not yet reflected in market prices.

A brief, but deadly, example will help illustrate the process. It involves a research study undertaken late in 1980 by the investment firm of Smith, Barney & Co. The analysis covered the funeral service industry and the prospects for Service Corporation International.

The report first gave a broad picture of the funeral service industry. Demand for the industry's services is governed by an indisputable fact: We all die. Thanks to the abundance of data gathered by the U.S. census, it is easy to estimate the industry's potential market. You just look at the number of people in various age categories and then multiply by the mortality rate for each age group. The Smith, Barney report presented two tables, based on census data, that showed the mortality rate rising into the twenty-first century. The grim fact is that funeral services is a growth industry. The Smith, Barney report also pointed out that the industry was highly fragmented, consisting of small, family-owned and -operated companies averaging about $150,000 in annual revenues. Because of their small size, most operations could not take advantage of economies of scale and were not well suited to professional management techniques.

The report then turned to an analysis of Service Corporation International, which at the time operated 189 funeral homes. Not only was this the largest organization in the industry, its revenues of $550,000 per unit were more than three times the national average. Management, of course, is key to any firm's profitability, and in this case the executives had decided to make the company an industry leader through selective acquisitions and the introduction of professional management practices. This decision was not being executed with a sledgehammer. Rather, generous financial incentives were used to encourage the principals of all acquired firms to remain. Moreover, each funeral home would keep its local distinctive name and a decentralized management system was put in effect. Service Corporation International believed its advanced managerial approach was unique within the industry, and the Smith, Barney report did not contradict this assumption.

The report went on to note the particular innovations made by Service Corporation's management. Its relatively large size permitted it to take advantage of centralized training, embalming, and purchasing of all its supplies from caskets to floral arrangements. The latter aspect of the business was particularly profitable. Service Corp. opened floral shops in all of its larger funeral homes. Since almost half of all floral sales are funeral related, these shops gave the company a substantial captive market. In addition, the company pioneered in marketing prearranged funeral services where customers make down payments in advance for future funeral services. These "preneed" sales had two important advantages for Service Corp.: (1) They assured continuing volume stability and future revenue growth and (2) they produced interest earnings on the prearranged payments, which became a source of the company's earnings.

For the preceding decade, Service Corp.'s sales and earnings per share had grown at better than a 15 percent rate. The Smith, Barney report projected that future growth would be at least as large, particularly since Service Corp.'s management had positioned the company to increase its share of the market. This, plus the fact that the company's stock was selling at a P/E multiple 40 percent below that of the S&P 500, indicated that the stock's price was below reasonable estimates of its firm foundation of value.

Recall that the first principle of valuation of the firm-foundation theory is that a stock is worth more—should sell at a higher price-earnings multiple—the larger its anticipated rate of growth. In late 1980, Service Corporation International sold at a price-earnings ratio of 5, while the price-earnings multiple for the market as a whole was approximately 9. The expected growth rate of earnings and dividends for the market as a whole in 1980 was less than 10 percent, but Service Corp. was expected to grow at a rate of better than 15 percent; hence, by our first valuation principle, it deserved to sell at a *higher* multiple than that of the market as a whole. Since the stock actually sold at a lower multiple than that of the market (5 versus 9), it could be considered undervalued.

Of course, other principles of valuation mentioned in Chapter Four were also relevant. By the second principle, stocks are worth more to investors, other things being the same, if the company can finance its growth and still pay out a reasonable share of its earnings in dividends. On this score, one could probably justify a bit of a discount for Service Corp., since its dividend yield (based on the estimated dividend for 1980) was only about half of that for the market as a whole. Still, on balance, the extraordinary growth potential of the company had to be the dominant factor for valuation.

The firm-foundation theory also suggests that the riskier a stock, the lower the multiple it should sell at. While it is true that Service Corp. was a small company and thus riskier than some of the more established blue-chip companies, other aspects of its business actually made it less risky than the general market. Service Corp. had a great deal of resistance to economic downturns, since people do not stop dying during recessions. Moreover, it dealt in those markets where the parameters of growth could be relatively precisely defined. Hence, on this score, Service Corp. would deserve a premium multiple to the market.

It is also possible to use the empirical relationships discussed in Chapter Four to argue that Service Corp. represented a good value. In 1980, when the analysis was made, stocks for which a 15 percent rate of growth was expected sold, on average, at over 15 times earnings, and Service Corp.'s multiple was only one-third of that. This further enhanced its appeal and made it an excellent candidate for multiple improvement. For all these reasons, Smith, Barney recommended purchase of Service Corporation International.

The Smith, Barney report represents the technique of fundamental analysis at its finest. People who followed its "buy" advice found that Service Corp. enjoyed much better performance than the market during the 1980s and early 1990s despite suffering some business reverses late in the decade of the 1980s, which necessitated the company taking some large write-offs.

Why Might Fundamental Analysis
Fail to Work?

Despite its plausibility and scientific appearance, there are three potential flaws in this type of analysis. First, the information and analysis may be incorrect. Second, the security analyst's estimate of "value" may be faulty. Third, the market may not correct its "mistake" and the stock price might not converge to its value estimate.

The security analyst traveling from company to company and consulting with industry specialists will receive a great deal of fundamental information. Some critics have suggested that, taken as a whole, this information will be worthless. What investors make on the valid news (assuming it is not yet recognized by the market) they lose on the bad information. Moreover, the analyst wastes considerable effort in collecting the information and investors pay heavy brokerage fees in trying to act on it. To make matters even worse, the security analyst may be unable to translate correct facts into accurate estimates of earnings for several years into the future. A faulty analysis of valid information could throw estimates of the rate of growth of earnings and dividends far wide of the mark.

The second problem is that even if the information is correct and its implications for future growth are properly assessed, the analyst might make a faulty value estimate. We have already seen how difficult it is to translate specific estimates of growth and other valuation factors into a single estimate of intrinsic value. Recall the widely different estimates of the value for IBM shown in Chapter Four. I have suggested earlier that the attempt to obtain a precise measure of intrinsic value may be an unrewarding search for a will-o'-the-wisp. Thus, even if the security analyst's estimates of growth are correct, this information may already be reflected accurately by the market, and any difference between a security's price and value may result simply from an incorrect estimate of value.

The final problem is that even with correct information and value estimates, the stock you buy might still go down. For example, suppose that Biodegradable Bottling Company is selling at 20 times earnings, and the analyst estimates that it can sustain a long-term growth rate of 25 percent. If, on average, stocks with 25 percent anticipated growth rates are selling at 30 times earnings, the fundamentalist might conclude that Biodegradable was a "cheap stock" and recommend purchase.

But suppose, a few months later, stocks with 25 percent growth rates are selling in the market at only 20 times earnings. Even if the analyst was absolutely correct in his growth-rate estimate, his customers might not gain because the market revalued its estimates of what growth stocks in general were worth. The market might correct its "mistake" by revaluing all stocks downward, rather than raising the price for Biodegradable Bottling.

And as the chart in Chapter Four indicated, such changes in valuation are not extraordinary—these are the routine fluctuations in market sentiment that have been experienced in the past. Not only can the average multiple change rapidly for stocks in general but the market can also dramatically change the premium assigned to growth. Both these phenomena were important during the early 1970s. It became apparent that accurately forecasting future earnings and dividend growth provided no guarantees: Even the most successful growth companies of the early 1970s turned in miserable price performances from 1972 on because of the devastating fall in earnings multiples, especially for rapidly growing companies. Clearly, then, one should not take the success of fundamental analysis for granted.

Using Fundamental and Technical Analysis Together

Many analysts use a combination of techniques to judge whether individual stocks are attractive for purchase. One of the most sensible procedures can easily be summarized by the following three rules. The persistent, patient reader will recognize that the rules are based on principles of stock pricing I have developed in the previous chapters.

Rule 1: Buy only companies that are expected to have above-average earnings growth for five or more years. An extraordinary long-run earnings growth rate is the single most important element contributing to the success of most stock investments. Merck, McDonald's, Service Corporation International, and practically all the other really outstanding common stocks of the past were growth stocks. As difficult as the job may be, picking stocks whose earnings grow is the name of the game. Consistent growth not only increases the earnings and dividends of the company but may also increase the multiple that the market is willing to pay for those earnings. Thus, the purchaser of a stock whose earnings begin to grow rapidly has a chance at a *potential* double benefit—both the earnings *and* the multiple may increase.

Rule 2: Never pay more for a stock than its firm foundation of value. While I have argued, and I hope persuasively, that you can never judge the exact intrinsic value of a stock, many analysts feel that you can roughly gauge when a stock seems to be reasonably priced. Generally, the earnings multiple for the market as a whole is a helpful benchmark. Growth stocks selling at multiples in line with or not very much above this multiple often represent good value. Service Corp. in the study just described is a good example. Its multiple was actually below the market's.

There are important advantages to buying growth stocks at very reasonable earnings multiples. If your growth estimate turns out to be correct, you may get the double bonus I mentioned in connection with Rule 1: The price will tend to go up simply because the earnings went up, but also the multiple is likely to expand in recognition of the growth rate that is established. Hence, the double bonus. Suppose, for example, you buy a stock earning $1 per share and selling at $7.50. If the earnings grow to $2 per share and if the price-earnings multiple increases from 7½ to 15 (in recognition that the company now can be considered a growth stock) you don't just double your money—you quadruple it. That's because your $7.50 stock will be worth $30 (15, the multiple, times $2, the earnings).

Now consider the other side of the coin. There are special

risks involved in buying "growth stocks" where the market has already recognized the growth and has bid up the price-earnings multiple to a hefty premium over that accorded more run-of-the-mill stocks. Stocks like International Flavors and Fragrances, Avon Products, and other recognized growth companies had earnings multiples well above 50 when the first edition of *Random Walk* came out. The warning was made very clear that the risks with very-high-multiple stocks were enormously high.

The problem is that the very high multiples may already fully reflect the growth that is anticipated, and if the growth does not materialize and earnings in fact go down (or even grow more slowly than expected), you will take a very unpleasant bath. The double benefits that are possible if the earnings of low-multiple stocks grow can become double damages if the earnings of high-multiple stocks decline. When earnings fall, the multiple is likely to crash as well. But the crash won't be so loud if the multiple wasn't that high in the first place. Reread the grim stories of National Student Marketing or the Nifty Fifty growth stocks or the 1990s crash of Japanese blue-chip stocks in Chapter Three if you want more evidence of the enormous risks involved with very-high-multiple stocks.

What is proposed, then, is a strategy of buying unrecognized growth stocks whose earnings multiples are not at any substantial premium over the market. Of course, it is very hard to predict growth. But even if the growth does not materialize and earnings decline, the damage is likely to be only single if the multiple is low to begin with, while the benefits may double if things do turn out as you expected. This is an extra way to put the odds in your favor.

We can summarize the discussion thus far by restating the first two rules: *Look for growth situations with low price-earnings multiples. If the growth takes place there's often a double bonus—both the earnings and the multiple rise, producing large gains. Beware of very-high-multiple stocks where future growth is already discounted. If growth doesn't materialize, losses are doubly heavy—both the earnings and the multiple drop.*

Rule 3: Look for stocks whose stories of anticipated growth are of the kind on which investors can build castles in the air.
I have stressed the importance of psychological elements in stock price determination. Individual and institutional investors are not computers that calculate warranted price-earnings multiples and print out buy and sell decisions. They are emotional human beings—driven by greed, gambling instincts, hope, and fear in their stock-market decisions. This is why successful investing demands both intellectual and psychological acuteness.

Stocks that produce "good feelings" in the minds of investors can sell at premium multiples for long periods even if the growth rate is only average. Those not so blessed may sell at low multiples for long periods even if their growth rate is above average. To be sure, if a growth rate appears to be established, the stock is almost certain to attract some type of following. The market is not irrational. But stocks are like people—what stimulates one may leave another cold, and the multiple improvement may be smaller and slower to be realized if the story never catches on.

So Rule 3 says to ask yourself whether the story about your stock is one that is likely to catch the fancy of the crowd. Is it a story from which contagious dreams can be generated? Is it a story on which investors can build castles in the air—but castles in the air that really rest on a firm foundation?

You don't have to be a technician to follow Rule 3. You might simply use your intuition or speculative sense to judge whether the "story" on your stock is likely to catch the fancy of the crowd—particularly the notice of institutional investors. Technical analysts, however, would look for some tangible evidence before they could be convinced that the investment idea was, in fact, catching on. This tangible evidence is, of course, the beginning of an uptrend or a technical signal that could "reliably" predict that an uptrend would develop.

While the rules I have outlined seem sensible, the important question is whether they really work. After all, lots of other people are playing the game, and it is by no means obvious that anyone can win consistently.

In the next two chapters, I shall look at the actual record.

Chapter Six asks the question: Does technical analysis work?
Chapter Seven looks at the performance record of fundamentalists. Together they should help us evaluate how well professional investment people do their job and what value we
should put on their advice.

6

Technical Analysis
and the
Random-Walk Theory

Things are seldom what they seem. Skim milk masquerades as cream.

—Gilbert and Sullivan, *H.M.S. Pinafore*

Not earnings, nor dividends, nor risk, nor gloom of high interest rates stay the chartists from their assigned task: studying the price movements of stocks. Such single-minded devotion to numbers has somehow yielded the most colorful theories and has produced much of the folk language of Wall Street:

"Hold the winners, sell the losers."

"Switch into the strong stocks."

"Sell this issue, it's acting poorly."

"Don't fight the tape."

All are popular prescriptions of technical analysts as they cheerfully collect their brokerage fees for churning your account.

Technical analysts build their strategies upon dreams of castles in the air and expect their tools to tell them which castle is being built and how to get in on the ground floor. The question is: Do they work?

Holes in Their Shoes and
Ambiguity in Their Forecasts

University professors are sometimes asked by their students, "If you're so smart, why aren't you rich?" The question usually rankles professors, who think of themselves as passing up worldly riches to engage in such an obviously socially useful occupation as teaching. The same question might more appropriately be addressed to technicians. For, after all, the whole point of technical analysis is to make money, and one would reasonably expect that those who preach it should practice it successfully in their own investments.

On close examination, technicians are often seen with holes in their shoes and frayed shirt collars. I, personally, have never known a successful technician, but I have seen the wrecks of several unsuccessful ones. (This is, of course, in terms of following their own technical advice. Commissions from urging customers to act on their recommendations are very lucrative.) Curiously, however, the broke technician is never apologetic about his method. If anything, he is more enthusiastic than ever. If you commit the social error of asking him why he is broke, he will tell you quite ingenuously that he made the all-too-human error of not believing his own charts. To my great embarrassment, I once choked conspicuously at the dinner table of a chartist friend of mine when he made such a comment. I have since made it a rule never to eat with a chartist. It's bad for digestion.

When Joseph Granville, probably the best known and most followed chartist of the early 1980s, was asked how his "foolproof" system had led him to make some egregious errors during the 1970s, he answered calmly that he was "on drugs" during that period and simply had not paid proper attention to his charts. The "drug" in his case was golf and Granville was convinced that his joining "golfers anonymous" had made him a born-again savior. He believed that he would never again, for the rest of his life, "make a serious mistake on the stock market." When asked why he didn't simply use his system to play the market himself and thereby make a fortune, he exclaimed that his mission in life was to enrich others, not himself: "Everyone I touch I make rich."*

While technicians might not get rich following their own advice, their store of words is precious indeed. Consider this advice offered by one technical service:

> The market's rise after a period of reaccumulation is a bullish sign. Nevertheless, fulcrum characteristics are not yet clearly present and a resistance area exists 40 points higher in the Dow, so it is clearly premature to say the next leg of the bull market is up. If, in the coming weeks, a test of the lows holds and the market breaks out of its flag, a further rise would be indicated. Should the lows be violated, a continuation of the intermediate term downtrend is called for. In view of the current situation, it is a distinct possibility that traders will sit in the wings awaiting a clearer delineation of the trend and the market will move in a narrow trading range.

If you ask me exactly what all this means, I'm afraid I cannot tell you, but I think the technician probably had the following in mind: "If the market does not go up or go down, it will remain unchanged." Even the weather forecaster can do better than that.

Obviously, I'm biased against the chartist. This is not only a personal predilection but a professional one as well. Technical analysis is anathema to the academic world. We love to pick on it. Our bullying tactics are prompted by two considerations: (1) after paying transactions costs, the method does not do better than a buy-and-hold strategy for investors, and (2) it's easy to pick on. And while it may seem a bit unfair to pick on such a sorry target, just remember: It's your money we are trying to save.

While the advent of the computer may have enhanced the standing of the technician for a time, it has ultimately proved to be his undoing. Just as fast as the technician creates charts to show where the market is going, the academic gets busy con-

---

*Granville predicted not only stock tremors, but earth tremors as well. In 1980, he predicted that Los Angeles would be destroyed in May 1981 by an earthquake measuring 8.3 or more on the Richter scale. There was a severe earthquake around Los Angeles 13 years later in 1994, but, fortunately, it failed to destroy the city.

structing charts showing where the technician has been. Since it's so easy to test all the technical trading rules on the computer, it has become a favorite pastime for academics to see if they really work.

Is There Momentum in the Stock Market?

The technician believes that knowledge of a stock's past behavior can help predict its probable future behavior. In other words, the sequence of price changes prior to any given day is important in predicting the price change for that day. This might be called the wallpaper principle. The technical analyst tries to predict future stock prices just as we might predict that the pattern of wallpaper behind the mirror is the same as the pattern above the mirror. The basic premise is that there are repeatable patterns in space and time.

Chartists believe there is momentum in the market. Supposedly, stocks that have been rising will continue to do so, and those that begin falling will go on sinking. Investors should, therefore, buy stocks that start rising and continue to hold their strong stocks. Should the stock begin to fall or "act poorly," investors are advised to sell.

These technical rules have been tested exhaustively by using stock price data on both major exchanges going back as far as the beginning of the twentieth century. The results reveal that past movements in stock prices cannot be used reliably to foretell future movements. The stock market has no memory. The central proposition of charting is absolutely false, and investors who follow its precepts will accomplish nothing but increasing substantially the brokerage charges they pay.*

One set of tests, perhaps the simplest of all, compares the price change for a stock in a given period with the price change in a subsequent period. For example, technical lore has it that if the price of a stock rose yesterday it is more likely to rise today. It turns out that the correlation of past price movements with present and future price movements is close to zero. Last

---

*References to all the studies cited may be found in the bibliography.

week's price change bears little relationship to the price change this week, and so forth. Whatever slight dependencies have been found between stock price movements in different time periods are extremely small and economically insignificant. While there is some short-term momentum in the stock market, as will be described more fully in Chapter Eight, any investor who pays transactions costs cannot benefit from it.

Economists have also examined the technician's thesis that there are often sequences of price changes in the same direction over several days (or several weeks or months). Stocks are likened to fullbacks who, once having gained some momentum, can be expected to carry on for a long gain. It turns out that this is simply not the case. Sometimes one gets positive price changes (rising prices) for several days in a row; but sometimes when you are flipping a fair coin you also get a long string of "heads" in a row, and you get sequences of positive (or negative) price changes no more frequently than you can expect random sequences of heads or tails in a row. What are often called "persistent patterns" in the stock market occur no more frequently than the runs of luck in the fortunes of any gambler playing a game of chance. This is what economists mean when they say that stock prices behave like a random walk.

Just What Exactly Is a Random Walk?

To many people this appears to be arrant nonsense. Even the most casual reader of the financial pages can easily spot patterns in the market. For example, look at the stock chart on the following page.

The chart seems to display some obvious patterns. After an initial rise the stock turned down, and once the decline got under way the stock headed persistently downhill. Happily for the bulls, the decline was arrested and the stock had another sustained upward move. One cannot look at a stock chart like this without realizing the self-evidence of these statements. How can the economist be so myopic that he cannot see what is so plainly visible to the naked eye?

The persistence of this belief in repetitive patterns in the

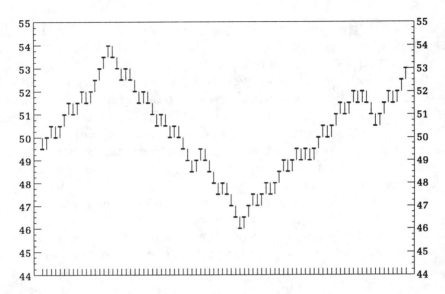

stock market is due to statistical illusion. To illustrate, let me describe an experiment in which I asked my students to participate. The students were asked to construct a normal stock chart showing the movements of a hypothetical stock initially selling at $50 per share. For each successive trading day, the closing stock price would be determined by the flip of a fair coin. If the toss was a head, the students assumed that the stock closed ½ point higher than the preceding close. If the flip was a tail, the price was assumed to be down by ½. The chart displayed above was actually the hypothetical stock chart derived from one of these experiments.

The chart derived from random coin tossings looks remarkably like a normal stock price chart and even appears to display cycles. Of course, the pronounced "cycles" that we seem to observe in coin tossings do not occur at regular intervals as true cycles do, but neither do the ups and downs in the stock market.

It is this lack of regularity that is crucial. The "cycles" in the stock charts are no more true cycles than the runs of luck or misfortune of the ordinary gambler. And the fact that stocks seem to be in an uptrend, which looks just like the upward move in some earlier period, provides no useful information on the dependability or duration of the current uptrend. Yes, history does tend to repeat itself in the stock market, but in an infinitely surprising variety of ways that confound any attempts to profit from a knowledge of past price patterns.

In other simulated stock charts derived through student coin tossings, there were head-and-shoulders formations, triple tops and bottoms, and other more esoteric chart patterns. One of the charts showed a beautiful upward breakout from an inverted head and shoulders (a very bullish formation). I showed it to a chartist friend of mine who practically jumped out of his skin. "What is this company?" he exclaimed. "We've got to buy immediately. This pattern's a classic. There's no question the stock will be up 15 points next week." He did not respond kindly to me when I told him the chart had been produced by flipping a coin. Chartists have no sense of humor. I got my comeuppance when *Business Week* hired a technician, who was adept at hatchet work, to review the first edition of this book.

My students used a completely random process to produce their stock charts. With each toss, as long as the coins used were fair, there was a 50 percent chance of heads, implying an upward move in the price of the stock, and a 50 percent chance of tails and a downward move. Even if they flip ten heads in a row, the chance of getting a head on the next toss is still 50 percent. Mathematicians call a sequence of numbers produced by a random process (such as those on our simulated stock chart) a random walk. The next move on the chart is completely unpredictable on the basis of what has happened before.

To a mathematician, the sequence of numbers recorded on a stock chart behaves no differently from that in the simulated stock charts—with one clear exception. There is a long-run uptrend in most averages of stock prices in line with the long-run growth of earnings and dividends. After adjusting for this trend, there is essentially no difference. The next move in a series of stock prices is largely unpredictable on the basis of past price behavior. No matter what wiggle or wobble the prices have made in the past, tomorrow starts out roughly fifty-fifty. The next price change is no more predictable than the flip of a coin.

Now, in fact, the stock market does not quite measure up to the mathematician's ideal of the complete independence of present price movements from those in the past. There have been some dependencies found, as will be explained more fully in Chapter Eight. But any systematic relationships that exist are so small that they are not useful for an investor. The brokerage charges involved in trying to take advantage of these dependencies are far greater than any advantage that might be obtained. Thus, an accurate statement of the "weak" form of the random-walk hypothesis goes as follows:

> The history of stock price movements contains no useful information that will enable an investor consistently to outperform a buy-and-hold strategy in managing a portfolio.

If the weak form of the random-walk hypothesis is a valid description of the stock market, then, as my colleague Richard Quandt says, "Technical analysis is akin to astrology and every bit as scientific."

I am *not* saying that technical strategies never make money. They very often do make profits. The point is rather that a simple "buy-and-hold" strategy (that is, buying a stock or group of stocks and holding on for a long period of time) typically makes as much or more money.

When scientists want to test the efficacy of some new drug they usually run an experiment where two groups of patients are administered pills—one containing the drug in question, the other a worthless placebo (a sugar pill). The results of the administration to the two groups are compared and the drug is deemed effective only if the group receiving the drug did better than the group getting the placebo. Obviously, if both groups got better in the same period of time the drug should not be given the credit, even if the patients did recover.

In the stock-market experiments, the placebo with which the technical strategies are compared is the buy-and-hold strategy. Technical schemes often do make profits for their users, but so does a buy-and-hold strategy. Indeed, as we shall see later, a naïve buy-and-hold strategy using a dart-board-selected portfolio has provided investors with an average annual rate of return of approximately 10 percent over the past seventy years. Only if technical schemes produce better returns than the market can they be judged effective. To date, none has consistently passed the test.

Some More Elaborate Technical Systems

Devotees of technical analysis may argue with some justification that I have been unfair. The simple tests I have just described do not do justice to the "richness" of technical analysis. Unfortunately for the technician, even some of his more elaborate trading rules have been subjected to scientific testing. Since many of the systems tested are very popular, let's briefly examine a few in detail.

The Filter System

Under the popular "filter" system a stock that has reached a low point and has moved up, say 5 percent (or any other percent you wish to name here and throughout this discussion), is said to be in an uptrend. A stock that has reached a peak and has moved down 5 percent is said to be in a downtrend. You're supposed to buy any stock that has moved up 5 percent from its low and hold it until the price moves down 5 percent from a subsequent high, at which time you sell the stock and, perhaps, even sell short. The short position is maintained until the price rises at least 5 percent from a subsequent low.

This scheme is very popular with brokers, and forms of it have been recommended in a variety of investment books. Indeed, the filter method is what lies behind the popular "stop-loss" order favored by brokers, where the client is advised to sell his stock if it falls 5 percent below his purchase price to "limit his potential losses." The argument is that presumably a stock that falls by 5 percent will be going into a downtrend anyway.

Exhaustive testing of various filter rules based on past price changes has been undertaken. The percentage drop or rise that filters out buy and sell candidates has been allowed to vary from 1 percent to 50 percent. The tests covered different time periods from 1897 to the present and involved individual stocks as well as assorted stock averages. Again, the results are remarkably consistent. When the higher brokerage commissions incurred under the filter rules are taken into consideration, these techniques cannot consistently beat a policy of simply buying the individual stock (or the stock average in question) and holding it over the period during which the test is performed. The individual investor would do well to avoid employing any filter rule and, I might add, any broker who recommends it.

The Dow Theory

The Dow theory is a great tug-of-war between resistance and support. When the market tops out and moves down, that previous peak defines a resistance area, since people who missed selling at the top will be anxious to do so if given another opportunity. If the market then rises again and nears the previous peak, it is said to be "testing" the resistance area. Now comes the moment of truth. If the market breaks through the resistance area, it is likely to keep going up for a while and the previous resistance area becomes a support area. If, on the other hand, the market "fails to penetrate the resistance area" and instead falls through the preceding low where there was previous support, a bear-market signal is given and the investor is advised to sell.

The basic Dow principle implies a strategy of buying when the market goes higher than the last peak and selling when it sinks through the preceding valley. There are various wrinkles to the theory, such as penetration of a double or triple top being especially bullish, but the basic idea is followed by many chartists and is part of the gospel of charting.

Unhappily, the signals generated by the Dow mechanism have no significance for predicting future price movements. The market's performance after *sell* signals is no different from its performance after *buy* signals. Relative to simply buying and holding the representative list of stocks in the market averages, the Dow follower actually comes out a little behind, since the strategy entails a number of extra brokerage costs as the investor buys and sells when the strategy decrees.

The Relative-Strength System

Here an investor buys and holds those stocks that are acting well, that is, outperforming the general market indices in the recent past. Conversely, the stocks that are acting poorly relative to the market should be avoided or, perhaps, even sold short. While there do seem to be some time periods when a relative-strength strategy would have outperformed a buy-and-hold strategy, there is no evidence that it can do so consistently. As indicated earlier, there is some evidence of momentum in the stock market. Nevertheless, a computer test of relative-strength rules over a twenty-five-year period suggests that such rules do not, after accounting for brokerage charges, outperform the placebo of a buy-and-hold investment strategy.

Price-Volume Systems

These strategies suggest that when a stock (or the general market) rises on large or increasing volume, there is an unsatisfied excess of buying interest and the stock can be expected to continue its rise. Conversely, when a stock drops on large volume, selling pressure is indicated and a sell signal is given.

Again, the investor following such a system is likely to be disappointed in the results. The buy and sell signals generated by the strategy contain no information useful for predicting future price movements. As with all technical strategies, however, the investor is obliged to do a great deal of in-and-out trading, and thus his brokerage costs are far in excess of those necessitated in a buy-and-hold strategy. After accounting for these brokerage charges, the investor does worse than he would by simply buying and holding a diversified group of stocks.

Reading Chart Patterns

Perhaps some of the more complicated chart patterns, such as were described in the preceding chapter, are able to reveal the future course of stock prices. For example, is the downward penetration of a head-and-shoulders formation a reliable bearish omen? As one of the gospels of charting, *Technical Analy-*

sis, puts it, "One does not bring instantly to a stop a heavy car moving at seventy miles per hour and, all within the same split second, turn it around and get it moving back down the road in the opposite direction." Before the stock turns around, its price movements are supposed to form one of a number of extensive reversal patterns as the smart-money traders slowly "distribute" their shares to the "public." Of course, we know some stocks do reverse directions in quite a hurry (this is called an unfortunate V formation), but perhaps these reversal patterns and other chart configurations can, like the Roman soothsayers, accurately foretell the future. Alas, the computer has even tested these more arcane charting techniques, and the technician's tool (magician's wand) has again betrayed him.

In one elaborate study, the computer was programmed to draw charts for 548 stocks traded on the New York Stock Exchange over a five-year period. It was instructed to scan all the charts and identify any one of thirty-two of the most popularly followed chart patterns. The computer was told to be on the lookout for heads and shoulders, triple tops and bottoms, channels, wedges, diamonds, and so forth. Since the machine is a very thorough (though rather dull) worker, we can be sure that it did not miss any significant chart patterns.

Whenever the machine found that one of the bearish chart patterns such as a head and shoulders was followed by a downward move through the neckline toward décolletage (a most bearish omen), it recorded a sell signal. If, on the other hand, a triple bottom was followed by an upside breakout (a most favorable augury), a buy signal was recorded. The computer then followed the performance of the stocks for which buy and sell signals were given and compared them with the performance record of the general market.

Again, there seemed to be no relationship between the technical signal and subsequent performance. If you had bought only those stocks with buy signals, and sold on a sell signal, your performance after brokerage costs would have been no better than that achieved with a buy-and-hold strategy. Indeed, the strategy that came closest to producing above-average returns (not accounting for brokerage costs) was to buy right after one of the bear signals.

Randomness Is Hard to Accept

Human nature likes order; people find it hard to accept the notion of randomness. No matter what the laws of chance might tell us, we search for patterns among random events wherever they might occur—not only in the stock market but even in interpreting sporting phenomena.

In describing an outstanding performance by a basketball player, reporters and spectators alike commonly use expressions such as "Shaquille O'Neal has the hot hand" or "Reggie Miller is a streak shooter." Those who play, coach, or otherwise follow basketball are almost universally convinced that if a player has successfully made his last shot, or last few shots, he is more likely to make his next shot. A 1980s study by a group of psychologists, however, suggests that the "hot-hand" phenomenon is a myth.

The psychologists did a detailed study of every shot taken by the Philadelphia 76ers over a full season and a half. They found no evidence of any positive correlation between the outcomes of successive shots. Indeed, they found that a hit by a player followed by a miss was actually a bit likelier than the case of making two baskets in a row. Moreover, the researchers looked at sequences of more than two shots. Again, they found that the number of long streaks (that is, hitting of several baskets in a row) was no greater than could have been expected in a random set of data (such as flipping coins where every event was independent of its predecessor). While the event of making one's last two or three shots clearly influenced the player's perception of whether he would make his next shot, the hard evidence was that there was no effect. The researchers then confirmed their study by examining the free-throw records of the Boston Celtics and by conducting controlled shooting experiments with the men and women of the Cornell University varsity basketball teams. The outcomes of previous shots influenced players' predictions but not their performance.

These findings do not imply that basketball is a game of chance rather than skill. Obviously there are players who are more adept at making baskets and free-throws than others. The point is, however, that the probability of making a shot is independent of the outcome of previous shots. The psychologists conjecture that the persistent belief in the hot hand could be due to memory bias. If long sequences of hits or misses are more memorable than alternating sequences, observers are likely to overestimate the correlation between successive shots. When events sometimes do come in clusters and streaks, people look for explanations and patterns. They refuse to believe that they are random even though such clusters and streaks do occur frequently in random data such as are derived from the tossing of a coin. So it is in the stock market as well.

A Gaggle of Other Technical Theories to Help You Lose Money

Once the academic world polished off most of the standard technical trading rules, it turned its august attention toward some of the more fanciful schemes. The world of financial analysis would be much quieter and duller without the chartists, as the following techniques amply demonstrate.

The Hemline Indicator

Not content with price movements, some technical analysts have broadened their investigations to include other movements as well. One of the most charming of these schemes has been called by Ira Cobleigh the "bull markets and bare knees" theory. Check the hemlines of women's dresses in any given year and you'll have an idea of the level of stock prices. There does seem to be a loose tendency for bull markets to be associated with bare knees, and depressed markets to be associated with bear markets for girl watchers, as the chart on the next page reveals.

For example, in the late nineteenth and early part of the twentieth centuries, the stock market was rather dull, and so were hemlines. But then came rising hemlines and the great bull market of the twenties, to be followed by long skirts and the crash of the thirties. (Actually, the chart cheats a bit: Hem-

The Hemline Indicator

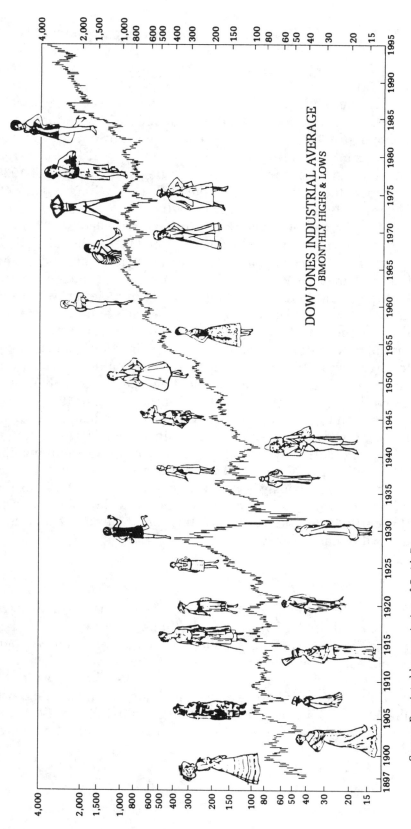

DOW JONES INDUSTRIAL AVERAGE
BMONTHLY HIGHS & LOWS

Source: Reprinted by permission of Smith Barney.

lines fell in 1927, prior to the most dynamic phase of the bull market.)

Unfortunately, things do not work out as well in the post–World War II period. The market declined sharply during the summer of 1946, well in advance of the introduction of the "New Look" featuring longer skirt lengths in 1947. Similarly, the sharp stock-market decline that began at the end of 1968 preceded the introduction of the midi-skirt, which was high fashion in 1969 and especially in 1970.

How did the theory work out during the crash of 1987? Looking at the chart, you might think the hemline indicator failed. After all, in the spring of 1987, when designers began shipping their fall lines, very short skirts were decreed as the fashion for the time. But along about the beginning of October, when the first chill winds began blowing across the country, a strange thing happened: Most women decided that mini-skirts were not for them. As women went back to long skirts, designers quickly followed suit. "Short skirts now look ridiculous to me," declared Bill Blass. The rest is stock-market history. Now we know the real culprit for the stock-market crash of 1987.

But don't get too optimistic about using the hemline indicator to give you a leg up on market timing. There is a problem for those who seriously would try to project these relationships into the future. While there is no theoretical ceiling on stock prices, there obviously is a ceiling on dress heights. Perhaps the advent of fanny-high micro-mini-skirts and hot pants during the early 1970s indicated that this stock-market theory had gone about as far as it could.

The Super Bowl Indicator

Why did the market go up in 1993? That's easy to answer for a technical analyst who uses the Super Bowl indicator. The Super Bowl indicator forecasts how the stock market will perform based on which team wins the Super Bowl. A victory by an NFL team predicts a bull market in stocks whereas a victory by an AFL team is bad news for stock-market investors. Since the Dallas Cowboys defeated the Buffalo Bills in 1993, the auguries for a stock-market rise were good; again, the market responded correctly by rising smartly during the first half of the year. In the twenty-five years following the first Super Bowl, this indicator has only been wrong once or twice. It failed in 1970 when the Kansas City Chiefs' (AFL) victory was followed by a bull market in stocks and in 1987 when a victory by the New York Giants (NFL) was followed by the stock-market crash (although the market did end 1987 higher than it started so the indicator was not technically wrong). Naturally, it makes no sense that the results of the Super Bowl should be useful as a market forecaster. Nevertheless, chance correlations will always pop up. The success of the Super Bowl indicator simply illustrates nothing more than the fact that it's sometimes possible to correlate two completely unrelated events.

The Odd-Lot Theory

This theory holds that except for the investor who is always right, no person can contribute more to successful investment strategy than an investor who is known to be invariably wrong. The "odd-lotter," according to popular superstition, is precisely that kind of person. Thus, success is assured by buying when the odd-lotter sells and selling when the odd-lotter buys.

Odd-lotters are the people who trade stocks in less than 100-share lots (called round lots). Most amateurs in the stock market cannot afford the $5,000 investment to buy a round lot (100 shares) of stock selling at $50 a share. They are more likely to buy, say, ten shares for a more modest investment of $500.

By examining the ratio of odd-lot purchases (the number of shares these amateurs bought during a particular day) to odd-lot sales (the number of shares they sold) and by looking at what particular stocks odd-lotters buy and sell, one can supposedly make money. These uninformed amateurs, presumably acting solely out of emotion and not with professional insight, are lambs in the street being led to slaughter. They are, according to legend, invariably wrong.

It turns out that the odd-lotter isn't such a stupendous dodo after all. A little stupid? Maybe. There is some indication that the performance of odd-lotters might be slightly worse than the stock averages. However, the available evidence (which admittedly does not match what has been accumulated in testing many of the other technical strategies) indicates that knowledge of his actions is not useful for the formulation of investment strategies.

One of the available studies examines the theory that an investor can make use of data on odd-lot sales and odd-lot purchases in selecting stocks. Supposedly, a switch from net odd-lot buying (where odd-lot shares purchased exceed odd-lot shares sold) to net odd-lot selling (odd-lot sales greater than odd-lot purchases) should be taken as a "buy" signal, since the boobs who sell odd-lots obviously don't know what they're doing. The data did not support this contention. Indeed, the rule failed to indicate the major turning points for individual stocks or for the market as a whole. Moreover, the odd-lot index was a very volatile one, switching back and forth from net sales to net purchases quite frequently. This suggests that an investor who followed the strategy would incur very heavy brokerage charges, which would eat substantially into his capital.

With the exception of a few technicians who sell their services to the public, few professional investment people believe in the odd-lot theory anymore. Indeed, some professional investors have seriously suggested that a new odd-lot theory is applicable to today's institutionally dominated market. Instead of looking at the behavior of the little guy in the market, it is suggested that the yo-yos who run the big mutual funds and pension funds are the odd-lotters of today, and that investors should look at what they are doing and then do the opposite.

A Few More Systems

To continue this review of technical schemes would soon generate rapidly diminishing returns. Probably few people seriously believe that the sunspot theory of stock-market movements can make money for them. But do you believe that by following the ratio of advancing to declining stocks on the New York Stock Exchange you can find a reliable leading indicator of general stock-market peaks? A careful computer study says no. Do you think that a rise in short interest (the number of shares of a stock sold short] is a bullish signal (since eventually the stock will be repurchased by the short seller to cover his position)? Exhaustive testing indicates no relationship either for the stock market as a whole or for individual issues. Do you think that a moving-average system (for example, buy a stock if its price goes higher than its average price over the past 200 days and sell it if it goes below the average) can lead you to extraordinary stock-market profits? Not if you have to pay commissions to buy and sell!

Technical Market Gurus

I mentioned earlier that Joseph Granville was one of the most widely followed forecasters of the early 1980s. His record had been good for a time in the late 1970s, and at his heyday he had the power to move markets. At 6:30 P.M. on January 6, 1981, Granville sent word to his 3,000 investor-subscribers around the world, "Sell the market—sell everything." The next morning brokerage houses were deluged with sell orders, and the Dow Jones industrial average dropped 24 points, representing some $40 billion in paper losses, three times the dollar amount lost on Black Thursday in 1929. Granville's buy recommendation the previous April had sent the Dow up 30 points in one day and his sell signal in September 1981 touched off near panic on world financial markets. Think of the ego satisfaction. Public adulation for Granville resembled that accorded rock stars. His traveling seminars were always oversubscribed. Asked at one seminar how he stayed close to the market when traveling, he dropped his pants to reveal various stock quotes printed on his shorts. When Joseph Granville talked, investors really did listen—at least for a while.

Unfortunately for Granville, his forecast accuracy during the 1980s left much to be desired. The Granville market letter warned of stock-market disaster throughout the early 1980s. Indeed, with the Dow Jones industrial average at 800, Granville told subscribers we were in a stock-market crash. He opined that investors should not only sell all their stock, but sell short as well, to take advantage of the coming financial Armageddon. The market responded by rising to the 1,200 level. "The bull market has been just a bubble," Granville remarked in 1984, continuing to warn a somewhat smaller number of listeners that the crash was near at hand. Granville's followers missed the spectacular bull market of the 1980s. His reputation as a seer and a mover of markets had been severely damaged.

During the 1980s, Granville was succeeded as the most influential market guru by Robert Prechter. Prechter became interested in the parallels between social psychology and the stock market while a Yale undergraduate. After college, while Granville was making his reputation, Prechter spent four years playing drums in a rock band, after which he joined Merrill Lynch as a junior technical analyst. There Prechter stumbled upon the work of an obscure accountant, R. N. Elliott, who had devised an arcane theory which he modestly entitled the "Elliott wave theory." Elliott's premise was that there were predictable waves of investor psychology and that they steered the market with natural ebbs and flows. By watching them, Elliott believed one could call major shifts in the market. Prechter was so excited about this discovery that he quit Merrill Lynch in 1979 to write an investor newsletter from the unlikely location of Gainesville, Georgia.

Prechter's initial predictions were uncannily accurate. Early in the 1980s, he predicted a major bull market with the Dow expected to rise to the 3,600 level, after an interim stop at 2,700. Just when Granville's predictions were shown to be flat-out wrong, Prechter was the golden knight of the day by keeping his followers fully invested through October of 1987.

Tarnish set in after October 1987. To Prechter's credit, he did say that there was "a 50/50 risk of a 10% decline" in the market on October 5, 1987, when the Dow was still selling above the 2,600 level, and he advised traders and investors with a short-term outlook to sell. Institutional investors were advised, however, to hang on for the ultimate target of 3,686 in the Dow. After the crash, with the Dow near 2,000, Prechter turned bearish for the long term and recommended holding Treasury bills. He predicted that "the great bull market is probably over" and that by the early 1990s the Dow Jones industrial average would plunge below 400. By not advising repurchase,

Prechter missed out on a blue-chip stock rally, which two years later pushed the Dow well above its prior peak. This was a mortal wound for a golden guru.

Prechter was succeeded by Elaine Garzarelli, an executive vice-president of the investment firm of Lehman Brothers. Garzarelli was not a one-indicator woman. She plunged into the ocean of financial data and used no fewer than thirteen different indicators to predict the course of the market. Garzarelli always liked to study vital details. As a child, she would get animal organs from the local butcher and dissect them.

Garzarelli was the Roger Babson of the 1987 crash. Turning bearish in August, she was recommending by September 1 that her clients get completely out of the stock market. By October 11, she was almost certain that a crash was imminent. Two days later, in a forecast almost frighteningly prescient, she told *USA Today* that a drop of more than 500 points in the Dow Jones averages was coming. Within a week, her predictions were realized.

But the crash was Garzarelli's last hurrah. Just as the media were coronating her as the "Guru of Black Monday," and as adulatory articles appeared in magazines from *Cosmopolitan* to *Fortune,* she drowned in her prescience—or her notoriety. After the crash she said she wouldn't touch the market and predicted that the Dow would fall another 200 to 400 points. Thus, Garzarelli missed the bounce-back in the market. Moveover, those who put money in her hands were sadly disappointed. The mutual fund that was launched in the summer of 1987 to capitalize on her fame and talent had a terrific start. From 1988 on, however, she badly underperformed the market each year until she left the management of the fund in 1994. In explaining her lack of consistency, she gave the time-honored explanation of technicians: "I failed to believe my own charts." Later in 1994, Garzarelli and Lehman parted company.

The moral to the story is obvious. With large numbers of people predicting the market, there will always be some who have called the last turn or even the last few turns, but none will be consistently accurate. To paraphrase the biblical warning, "He who looks back at the predictions of market gurus dies of remorse."

Why Are Technicians Still Hired?

It seems very clear that under scientific scrutiny chart-reading must share a pedestal with alchemy. There has been a remarkable uniformity in the conclusions of studies done on all forms of technical analysis. Not one has consistently outperformed the placebo of a buy-and-hold strategy. Technical methods cannot be used to make useful investment strategies. This is the fundamental conclusion of the random-walk theory.

A former colleague of mine, who believed that the capitalist system would be sure to weed out all useless growths such as the flourishing technicians, was convinced that the technical cult was just a passing fad. "The days of these modern-day soothsayers on Wall Street are numbered," he would say. "Brokers will soon learn they can easily do without the technicians' services."

The chartist's durability, and the fact that over the years he has been hired in increasing numbers, suggests that the capitalist system may garden like most of the rest of us. We like to see our best plants grow, but as summer wears on somehow the weeds often manage to get the best of us. And as I often tell my wife when she remarks about the abundance of weeds in our lawn, "At least they're green."

The point is, the technicians often play an important role in the greening of the brokers. Chartists recommend trades—almost every technical system involves some degree of in-and-out trading. Trading generates commissions, and commissions are the lifeblood of the brokerage business. The technicians do not help produce yachts for the customers, but they do help generate the trading that provides yachts for the brokers. Until the public catches on to this bit of trickery, technicians will continue to flourish.

Appraising the Counterattack

As you might imagine, the random-walk theory's dismissal of charting is not altogether popular among technicians. Academic proponents of the theory are greeted in some Wall Street quarters with as much enthusiasm as Saddam Hussein addressing a meeting of the B'nai Brith. Technical analysts consider the theory and its implications to be, in the words of one veteran professional, "just plain academic drivel." Let us pause, then, and appraise the counterattack by beleaguered technicians.

Perhaps the most common complaint about the weakness of the random-walk theory is based on a distrust of mathematics and a misconception of what the theory means. "The market isn't random," the complaint goes, "and no mathematician is going to convince me it is." Even so astute a commentator on the Wall Street scene as "Adam Smith" displays this misconception when he writes:

> I suspect that even if the random walkers announced a perfect mathematic proof of randomness I would go on believing that in the long run future earnings influence present value, and that in the short run the dominant factor is the elusive *Australopithecus*, the temper of the crowd.

Of course earnings and dividends influence market prices, and so does the temper of the crowd. We saw ample evidence of this in earlier chapters of the book. But, even if markets were dominated during certain periods by irrational crowd behavior, the stock market might still well be approximated by a random walk. The original illustrative analogy of a random walk concerned a drunken man staggering around an empty field. He is not rational, but he's not predictable either.

Moreover, new fundamental information about a company (a big mineral strike, the death of the president, etc.) is also unpredictable. It will occur randomly over time. Indeed, successive appearances of news items must be random. If an item of news were not random, that is, if it were *dependent* on an earlier item of news, then it wouldn't be news at all. The weak form of the random-walk theory says only that stock prices cannot be predicted on the basis of past stock prices. Thus, criticisms of the type quoted above are not valid.

The technical analyst will also cite chapter and verse that the academic world has certainly not tested every technical scheme that has been devised. That is quite correct. No economist or mathematician, however skillful, can prove conclusively that technical methods can never work. All that can be said is that the small amount of information contained in stock-market pricing patterns has not been shown to be sufficient to overcome the brokerage costs involved in acting on that information. Consequently, I have received a flood of letters condemning me for not mentioning, in my earlier editions of this book, a pet technical scheme that the writer is convinced actually works.

Being somewhat incautious, I will climb out on a limb and argue that no technical scheme whatever could work for any length of time. I suggest first that methods which people are convinced "really work" have not been adequately tested; and second, that even if they did work, the schemes would be bound to destroy themselves.

Each year a number of eager people visit the gambling parlors of Las Vegas and Atlantic City and examine the last several hundred numbers of the roulette wheel in search of some repeating pattern. Usually they find one. And so they stay until they lose everything because they do not retest the pattern.* The same thing is true for technicians.

If you examine past stock prices in any given period, you can almost always find some kind of system that would have worked in a given period. If enough different criteria for selecting stocks are tried, one will eventually be found that selects the best ones of that period.

Let me illustrate. Suppose we examine the record of stock prices and volume over the five-year period 1991 through 1995 in search of technical trading rules that would have worked during that period. After the fact, it is always possible to find a technical rule that works. For example, it might be that you should have bought all stocks whose names began with the letters X or D, whose volume was at least 3,000 shares a day, and whose earnings grew at a rate of 10 percent or more during

*Edward O. Thorp actually did find a method to win at blackjack. Thorp wrote it all up in *Beat the Dealer*. Since then casinos switched to the use of several decks of cards in order to make it more difficult for card counters, and as a last resort, they banish the counters from the gaming tables.

the preceding five-year period. The point is that it is obviously possible to describe, after the fact, which categories of stocks had the best performance. The real problem is, of course, whether the scheme works in a different time period. What most advocates of technical analysis usually fail to do is to test their schemes with market data derived from periods other than those during which the scheme was developed.

Even if the technician follows my advice, tests his scheme in many different time periods, and finds it a reliable predictor of stock prices, I still believe that technical analysis must ultimately be worthless. For the sake of argument, suppose the technician had found that there was a reliable year-end rally, that is, every year stock prices rose between Christmas and New Year's Day. The problem is that once such a regularity is known to market participants, people will act in a way that prevents it from happening in the future.*

Any successful technical scheme must ultimately be self-defeating. The moment I realize that prices will be higher after New Year's Day than they are before Christmas, I will start buying before Christmas ever comes around. If people know a stock will go up *tomorrow,* you can be sure it will go up *today.* Any regularity in the stock market that can be discovered and acted upon profitably is bound to destroy itself. This is the fundamental reason why I am convinced that no one will be successful in employing technical methods to get above-average returns in the stock market.

Implications for Investors

The past history of stock prices cannot be used to predict the future in any meaningful way. Technical strategies are usually amusing, often comforting, but of no real value. This is the weak form of the random-walk theory, and it is the consistent conclusion of research done at universities such as Chicago,

---

*If such a regularity was known to only one individual, he would simply practice the technique until he had collected a large share of the marbles. He surely would have no incentive to share a truly useful scheme by making it available to others.

M.I.T., Yale, Princeton, and Stanford. It has been published mainly in investment journals, but also in more esoteric ones such as *Kyklos* and *Econometrica*. Technical theories enrich only the people preparing and marketing the technical service or the brokerage firms who hire technicians in the hope that their analyses may help encourage investors to do more in-and-out trading and thus generate commission business for the brokerage firm.

Using technical analysis for market timing is especially dangerous. Since there is a long-term uptrend in the stock market, it can be very risky to be in cash. An investor who frequently carries a large cash position to avoid periods of market decline is very likely to be out of the market during some periods where it rallies smartly. During the decade of the 1980s, the Standard & Poor's 500 Index provided a very handsome total return (including dividends and capital changes) of 17.6 percent. But, an investor who happened to be out of the market and missed just the ten best days of the decade—out of a total of 2,528 trading days—was up only 12.6 percent. The point is that market timers risk missing the infrequent large sprints that are the big contributors to performance.

The implications of this analysis are simple. If past prices contain little or no useful information for the prediction of future prices, there is no point in following any technical trading rule for timing the purchases and sales of securities. A simple policy of buying and holding will be at least as good as any technical procedure. Discontinue your subscriptions to worthless technical services, and eschew brokers who read charts and are continually recommending the purchase or sale of securities.

There is another major advantage to a buy-and-hold strategy that I have not yet mentioned. Buying and selling, to the extent that it is profitable at all, tends to generate capital gains, which are subject to tax. Buying and holding enables you to postpone or avoid gains taxes. By following any technical strategy, you are likely to realize most of your capital gains and pay larger taxes (as well as paying them sooner) than you would under a buy-and-hold strategy. Thus, simply buying and holding a diversified portfolio suited to your objectives will enable you to save on investment expense, brokerage charges, and taxes; and, at the same time, to achieve an overall performance record at least as good as that obtainable using technical methods.

7

How Good Is
Fundamental
Analysis?

How could I have been so mistaken as to have trusted the
experts?   —John F. Kennedy (after the Bay of Pigs fiasco)

In the beginning he was a statistician. He wore
a white, starched shirt and threadbare blue suit. He quietly put
on his green eyeshade, sat down at his desk, and recorded
meticulously the historical financial information about the
companies he followed. The result: writer's cramp. Automation
meant using a slide rule.

But then a metamorphosis began to set in. He rose from his
desk, bought blue button-down shirts and gray flannel suits,
threw away his eyeshade, and began to make field trips to visit
the companies that previously he had known only as a collection of financial statistics. His title now became security analyst.

As time went on, the security analyst's stature continued to
grow, and increasingly women joined the profession's ranks as
full participants. Portfolio managers began to rely on analysts'
reports and recommendations in deciding which stocks should
be bought or sold. Eventually, analysts reached the pinnacle of
professionalism and came to be called bona-fide *chartered financial analysts.*

The Views from Wall Street and Academia

Some of Wall Street's portfolio managers actually invest on the basis of the charts and various technical schemes described in the last chapter. But even on Wall Street, technicians are considered a rather strange cult, and little faith is put in their recommendations. Thus, the studies casting doubt on the efficacy of technical analysis would not be considered surprising by most professionals. At heart, the Wall Street pros are fundamentalists. The really important question is whether fundamental analysis is any good.

Two extreme views have been taken about the efficacy of fundamental analysis. The view of many on Wall Street is that fundamental analysis is becoming more powerful and skillful all the time. The individual investor has scarcely a chance against the professional portfolio manager and a team of fundamental analysts.

An opposite-extreme view is taken by much of the academic community. Some academicians have gone so far as to suggest that a blindfolded monkey throwing darts at the *Wall Street Journal* can select stocks with as much success as professional portfolio managers. They have argued that fund managers and their fundamental analysts can do no better at picking stocks than a rank amateur. Many have concluded that the value of professional investment advice is nil.

My own view of the matter is somewhat less extreme than that taken by many of my academic colleagues. Nevertheless, an understanding of the large body of research on these questions is essential for any intelligent investor. This chapter will recount the major battle in an ongoing war between academics and market professionals that has shaken Wall Street to its bedrock. Current field reports have the academics claiming victory and the professionals screaming "Foul."

Are Security Analysts
Fundamentally Clairvoyant?

Forecasting future earnings is the security analysts' *raison d'être*. As a top Wall Street professional put it in his fraternity magazine, *Institutional Investor:* "Expectation of future earnings is still the most important single factor affecting stock prices." As we have seen, growth (in earnings and therefore in the ability to pay dividends) is the key element needed to estimate a stock's firm foundation of value. The analyst who can make accurate forecasts of the future will be richly rewarded. "If he is wrong," *Institutional Investor* puts it, "a stock can act precipitously, as has been demonstrated time and time again. Earnings are the name of the game and always will be."

To predict future directions, analysts generally start by looking at past wanderings. "A proven score of past performance in earnings growth is," one analyst told me, "a most reliable indicator of future earnings growth." If management is really skillful, there is no reason to think it will lose its Midas touch in the future. If the same adroit management team remains at the helm, the course of future earnings growth should continue as it has in the past, or so the argument goes.

Such thinking flunks in the academic world. Calculations of past earnings growth are no help in predicting future growth. If you had known the growth rates of all companies during, say, the 1975–1985 period, this would not have helped you at all in predicting what growth they would achieve in the 1985–1995 period. And knowing the fast growers of the eighties and nineties will not help analysts find the fast growers of the early twenty-first century. This startling result was first reported by British researchers for companies in the United Kingdom in an article charmingly titled "Higgledy Piggledy Growth." Learned academicians at Princeton and Harvard applied the British study to U.S. companies—and, surprise, the same was true here!

"IBM," the cry immediately went up. "Remember IBM." I do remember IBM: a steady high grower for decades. For a while it was a glaring exception. But after the mid-1980s, even the mighty IBM failed to continue its dependable growth pattern. I also remember Polaroid and dozens of other firms that chalked up consistent large growth rates until the roof fell in. I hope you remember *not* the exception but rather the rule: There is no reliable pattern that can be discerned from past records to aid the analyst in predicting future growth.

A good analyst will argue, however, that there's much more to predicting than just examining the past record. Rather than measure every factor that goes into the actual forecasting process, John Cragg and I decided to concentrate on the end result: the prediction itself.

Donning our cloak of academic detachment, we wrote to nineteen major Wall Street firms engaged in fundamental analysis. The nineteen firms, which asked to remain anonymous, included some of the major brokerage firms, mutual-fund management companies, investment advisory firms, and banks engaged in trust management. They are among the most respected names in the investment business.

We requested—and received—past earnings predictions on how these firms felt earnings for specific companies would behave over both a one-year and a five-year period. These estimates, made at several different times, were then compared with actual results to see how well the analysts forecast short-run and long-run earnings changes. The results were surprising.

Bluntly stated, the careful estimates of security analysts (based on industry studies, plant visits, etc.) do very little better than those that would be obtained by simple extrapolation of past trends, which we have already seen are no help at all. Indeed, when compared with actual earnings growth rates, the five-year estimates of security analysts were actually worse than the predictions from several naïve forecasting models.

For example, one placebo with which the analysts' estimates were compared was the assumption that every company in the economy would enjoy a growth in earnings approximating the long-run rate of growth of the national income. It often turned out that if you used this naïve forecasting model, you would make smaller errors in forecasting long-run earnings growth than by using the professional forecasts of the analysts.

Our method of determining the efficacy of the security analyst's diagnoses of his companies is exactly the same as was used before in evaluating the technicians' medicine. We compared the results obtained by following the experts with the results from some naïve mechanism involving no expertise at all. Sometimes these naïve predictors work very well. For example, if you want to forecast the weather tomorrow you will do a pretty good job by predicting that it will be exactly the same as today. It turns out that while this system misses every one of the turning points in the weather, for most days it is quite reliable. How many weather forecasters do you suppose do any better?

When confronted with the poor record of their five-year growth estimates, the security analysts honestly, if sheepishly, admitted that five years ahead is really too far in advance to make reliable projections. They protested that while long-term projections are admittedly important, they really ought to be judged on their ability to project earnings changes one year ahead.

Believe it or not, it turned out that their one-year forecasts were even worse than their five-year projections. It was actually harder for them to forecast one year ahead than to estimate long-run changes.

The analysts fought back gamely. They complained that it was unfair to judge their performance on a wide cross section of industries, since earnings for electronics firms and various "cyclical" companies are notoriously hard to forecast. "Try us on utilities," one analyst confidently asserted. So we tried it, and they didn't like it. Even the forecasts for the stable utilities were far off the mark. Those the analysts confidently touted as high growers turned out to perform much the same as the utilities for which only low or moderate growth was predicted. This led to the second major finding of our study: There is not one industry that is easy to predict.

Moreover, no analysts proved consistently superior to the others. Of course, in each year some analysts did much better than average, but there was no consistency in their pattern of performance. Analysts who did better than average one year were no more likely than the others to make superior forecasts in the next year.

My findings with Cragg have been confirmed by several other researchers. For example, Michael Sandretto of Harvard and Sudhir Milkrishnamurthi of M.I.T. completed a massive study of the one-year forecasts of the most widely followed companies between 1977 and 1981. The number of companies monitored was about 1,000 each year, and, in general, estimates were available from five or six analysts for each company. All estimates were made for the then current year, so that 1981 estimates had been made early in 1981. The staggering conclusion of the study was that the average annual error of the analysts was 31.3 percent over the five-year period. The error rates each year were remarkably consistent—the lowest error rate was 27.6 percent in 1978, the highest 33.5 percent in 1981. Financial forecasting appears to be a science that makes astrology look respectable.

Amidst all these accusations and counterassertions, there is a deadly serious message. It is this: Security analysts have enormous difficulty in performing their basic function of forecasting earnings prospects for the companies they follow. Investors who put blind faith in such forecasts in making their investment selections are in for some rude disappointments.

Why the Crystal Ball Is Clouded

It is always somewhat disturbing to learn that a group of highly trained and well-paid professionals may not be terribly skillful at their calling. Unfortunately, this is hardly unusual. Similar types of findings could be made for most groups of professionals. There is, for example, a classic example in medicine. At a time when tonsillectomies were very fashionable, the American Child Health Association surveyed a group of 1,000 children, eleven years of age, from the public schools of New York City, and found that 611 of these had had their tonsils removed. The remaining 389 were then examined by a group of physicians, who selected 174 of these for tonsillectomy and declared the rest had no tonsil problem. The remaining 215 were reexamined by another group of doctors, who recommended 99 of these for tonsillectomy. When the 116 "healthy" children were examined a third time, a similar percentage were told their tonsils had to be removed. After three examinations, only 65 children remained who had not been recommended for tonsillectomy. These remaining children were not examined further because the supply of examining physicians ran out.

Numerous other studies have shown similar results. Radiologists have failed to recognize the presence of lung disease in about 30 percent of the X-ray plates they read, despite the clear presence of the disease on the X-ray film. Another experiment proved that professional staffs in psychiatric hospitals could not tell the sane from the insane. The point is that we should not take for granted the reliability and accuracy of any judge, no matter how expert. When one considers the low reliability of so many kinds of judgments, it does not seem too surprising that security analysts, with their particularly difficult forecasting job, should be no exception.

There are, I believe, four factors that help explain why security analysts have such difficulty in predicting the future. These are: (1) the influence of random events; (2) the creation of dubious reported earnings through "creative" accounting procedures; (3) the basic incompetence of many of the analysts themselves; and (4) the loss of the best analysts to the sales desk or to portfolio management. Each factor deserves some discussion.

1. The Influence of Random Events

A company is not an entity unto itself. Many of the most important changes that affect the basic prospects for corporate earnings are essentially random, that is, unpredictable.

Take the utility industry, to which I referred earlier. Presumably it is one of the most stable and dependable groups of companies. During the early 1960s, almost every utility analyst expected Florida Power and Light to be the fastest-growing utility. The analysts saw a continued high population growth, increased demands for electric power among existing customers, and a favorable regulatory climate.

Everything turned out exactly as forecast except for one small detail. The favorable Florida regulatory climate turned distinctly unfavorable as the sixties progressed. The Florida Public Utilities Commission ordered Florida Power and Light to make several substantial rate cuts and the utility was not able to translate the rapid growth in demand for electric power into higher profits. As a result, the company closed the decade with a mediocre growth record, far below the ebullient forecasts. In the 1970s, similar kinds of mistakes were made as analysts failed to predict the increased fuel costs resulting from the tenfold increase in the international price of oil. In the early 1980s, analysts failed to appreciate the effect of the 1979 accident at Three Mile Island on the later performance of utilities with uncompleted nuclear power plants. And in the first half of the 1990s, analysts failed to appreciate the extent to which competition would reduce the profit margins of the telephone utilities. Thus, even the "stable" utility industry has proved extraordinarily difficult to predict.

U.S. government budgetary, contract, and regulatory decisions can have enormous implications for the fortunes of individual companies. So can the incapacitation of key members of management, the discovery of a major new product, the finding of defects in a current product, a major oil spill, industrial accidents, natural disasters such as floods and hurricanes, etc. The stories of unpredictable events affecting earnings are endless.

2. The Creation of Dubious Reported Earnings through "Creative" Accounting Procedures

A firm's income statement may be likened to a bikini—what it reveals is interesting but what it conceals is vital. National Student Marketing, one of the concept stocks I mentioned in Chapter Three, led the beauty parade in this regard. Andrew Tobias described it all in *The Funny Money Game.*

In its fiscal 1969 report, National Student Marketing made generous use of terms such as "deferred new product development and start-up costs." These were moneys actually spent during 1969 but not charged against earnings in that year. "Unamortized costs of prepaid sales programs" carried the ploy even further. These were advertising expenses that were not charged against earnings on the flimsy excuse that they would produce sales in the future. Subsidiary losses were easily handled: The companies were simply sold, removing their unfavorable results from the consolidated accounting statement. Actually, it wasn't quite that simple, because the sales were consummated after the close of the fiscal year—but the accountants had no difficulty in arranging for the sale retroactively.

Since expenses were uncounted, why not count unearnings? No sooner said than done. These were duly noted in the sales column as unbilled receivables, on the justification that the actual billing of the sales could be expected to materialize in the future. Finally came "the $3,754,103 footnote." Almost $4 million was added to net income in the form of earnings from companies whose acquisitions were "agreed to in principle and closed subsequent" to the end of fiscal 1969.

It turned out that even accepting the rest of the creative accounting, if you didn't count the earnings of companies that were not legally part of National Student Marketing in 1969, the company barely broke even. Of course, the imprimatur of a prestigious accounting firm was affixed to the bottom of a statement assuring the public that the accounts were prepared in accordance with "generally accepted accounting principles."*

Similarly, in Chapter Three I described how Barry Minkow's late 1980s carpet-cleaning empire, ZZZZ Best, was built on a mosaic of phony credit card holdings and fictitious contracts. These two are admittedly extreme examples, but the general problem is not uncommon. Seeming miracles can be accomplished with depreciation; the peculiarities of conglomerate accounting; the franchise accounting game; and the special features of the reports of land-sales companies, computer-leasing companies, and insurance companies. It is small wonder that security analysts have trouble estimating reported future earnings.

*In 1972, the Securities and Exchange Commission charged National Student Marketing Corp., its auditors, two law firms, and fifteen individuals with violations of federal securities laws. Included in the SEC suit was a charge that the company had issued "materially false and misleading" financial statements. Cortess Randell, the company's chief executive officer, served a prison sentence. A partner of the accounting firm of Peat, Marwick, Mitchell & Co. was convicted of having made false and misleading statements.

3. The Basic Incompetence of Many of the Analysts Themselves

The overall performance of analysts in many respects reflects the limit of their abilities. Their record with regard to STP Corporation is certainly a good example.

In the early 1970s, racing car driver Andy Granatelli's STP was the darling of the Wall Street fraternity. Report after report indicated why it was likely to enjoy a large, long-term growth rate. Analysts pointed to its consistent pattern of growth over ten years. On the argument that the future would be more of the same, and that STP could continue to create its destiny through its marvelously successful advertising campaign, the Wall Street fraternity gave STP an estimated 20 percent growth rate for earnings in future years. As STP's stock price rose, analysts recommended the shares with greater and greater enthusiasm. Needless to say, but said nevertheless, STP management actively encouraged this enthusiasm.

Few analysts bothered to ask about the company's major product, STP oil treatment, which apparently accounted for three-quarters of the firm's revenues and earnings. What did the product really do? Could one really believe that STP helped cars start faster in winter and made engines run longer, quieter, and cooler in summer?

Admittedly, some analysts had a queasy feeling, but this was carefully reasoned away. For example, in the May 17, 1971, issue of the *Wall Street Transcript,* one analyst was quoted as saying: "The risk is that it is difficult to prove what exactly the product accomplishes, and people fear that the FTC might attack the company on an efficacy basis. We feel there is a very low probability of that happening and in the meantime consumers think the product works and that's the important thing. It is sort of a 'cosmetic company' for the car." If ever there was a castle in the air, STP certainly qualified.

While the above analyst was being quoted, *Consumer Reports* was completing its report on STP. This was published in July 1971 and stated that STP was a worthless oil thickener, not a panacea that would make ailing engines healthy again. Indeed, the consumer magazine reported that "STP can change the viscosity of a new car's oil to a considerably thicker grade than certain auto manufacturers recommend." The magazine went on to say that the major auto manufacturers positively discouraged the practice of using such additives, and suggested that STP might modify the properties of a car's engine oil so much that the new-car warranty terms might be affected.

The stock fell abruptly and the company's consistent record of past earnings growth came to an untimely end. As one analyst confided after the debacle, "I guess we just didn't ask the right questions."

To be perfectly blunt, many security analysts are not particularly perceptive, critical, or competent. I learned this early in the game as a young Wall Street trainee. In attempting to learn the techniques of the pros, I tried to duplicate some analytic work done by a metals specialist named Louie. Louie had figured that for each 1¢ increase in the price of copper, the earnings for a particular copper producer would increase by $1 per share. Since he expected a 5¢ increase in the price of copper, he reasoned that this particular stock was "an unusually attractive purchase candidate."

In redoing the calculation, I found that Louie had misplaced a decimal point. A penny increase in the price of copper would increase earnings by 10¢, not by $1. When I pointed this out to Louie (feeling sure he would want to put out a correction immediately) he simply shrugged his shoulders and declared, "Well, the recommendation sounds more convincing if we leave the report as is." Attention to detail was clearly not the forte of this particular analyst. From then on, I referred to him as Sloppy Louie (not to denigrate the excellent fish restaurant of the same name in South Street Seaport near the New York financial district).

To balance this inattention to detail and careful work, we have those who glory in it. Take Railroad Roger, for example. Roger will accurately recount every conceivable statistic on track miles and freight carloadings for hours on end. But Roger does not have the faintest clue what the rails will earn next year, or which should be favored for purchase. Oil analyst Doyle performs in a similar manner. His knowledge concerning refinery capacity is encyclopedic, but he lacks the critical acumen to translate this into judgments useful for investment decision-making.

Many analysts, however, emulate Louie. Generally too lazy to make their own earnings projections, they prefer to copy the forecasts of other analysts or to swallow the ones released by corporate managements without even chewing. Then it's very easy to know whom to blame if something goes wrong. "That ***!!! treasurer gave me the wrong dope." And it's much easier to be wrong when your professional colleagues all agreed with you. As Keynes put it, "Worldly wisdom teaches that it is better for reputation to fail conventionally than to succeed unconventionally."

Corporate management goes out of its way to ease the forecasting task of the analyst. Let me give you a personal example: A two-day field trip was arranged by a major corporation to brief a whole set of Wall Street security analysts on its operations and future programs.

We were picked up in the morning by the company's private plane for visits and briefings at three of the company's plants. In the evening, we were given first-class accommodations and royally wined and dined. After two more plant visits the next day, we had a briefing, replete with slide show, indicating a "most conservative five-year forecast" of robustly growing earnings.

At each stop, we were showered with gifts—and not only the usual souvenir mock-ups of the company's major products. We also received a variety of desk accessories for the office, a pen and pencil set, leather billfold, tie bar, cuff links, and a tasteful piece of jewelry to "take home to the wife or mistress, as the case may be." Throughout each day liquor and wine flowed in abundance. As one bleary-eyed analyst confided at the end of the trip, "It's very hard not to have a warm feeling for this company."

I do not mean to imply that most Wall Street analysts typically receive payola for touting particular stocks. Indeed, from my own experience, I would judge that the standards of ethics in Wall Street are very high. Sure, there are crooks, but I would guess far fewer than in other professions, despite the celebrated insider trading cases of the late 1980s and early 1990s.

I do imply that the *average* analyst is just that—a well-paid and usually highly intelligent person who has an extraordinarily difficult job and does it in a rather mediocre fashion. Analysts are often misguided, sometimes sloppy, perhaps self-important, and at times susceptible to the same pressures as other people. In short, they are really very human beings.

4. The Loss of the Best Analysts to the Sales Desk or to Portfolio Management

My fourth argument against the profession is a paradoxical one: Many of the best security analysts are not paid to analyze securities. They are either very high-powered institutional salespeople or efficient new-business getters, successful in bringing new underwriting business to their firms; or they get promoted to be prestigious portfolio managers.

Brokerage houses that pride themselves on their research prowess project an aura of respectability by sending a security analyst to chaperone the regular salesperson on a call to a financial institution. Institutional investors like to hear about a new investment idea right from the horse's mouth, and so the regular salesperson usually sits back and lets the analyst do the talking. Thus, most of the articulate analysts find their time is spent with institutional clients, not with financial reports and corporate treasurers. They also find that their monetary rewards are heavily dependent upon their ability to bring commission business to the firm.

Another magnet pulling analysts away from the study of stocks is the ability of some to attract to their firm profitable underwriting clients, that is, companies who need to borrow money or sell new common stock to raise funds for expansion. The analyst on a field trip who is looking for new, small, expanding companies as potential investment recommendations may put a great deal of effort into selling her firm's investment banking services. I have seen many a security analyst make her reputation by her ability to attract such clients to the firm. She may not come up with good earnings forecasts or select the right stocks for investment, but she brings the bacon home to her firm and that is the name of the game.

Finally, both the compensation and prestige structures within the securities industry induce many analysts away from research work into portfolio management. It's far more exciting and remunerative to "run money" in the line position of portfolio manager than only to advise in the staff position of security analyst. Small wonder that many of the best-respected security analysts do not remain long in their jobs.

Do Security Analysts Pick Winners?
The Performance of the Mutual Funds

I can almost hear the chorus in the background as I write these words. It goes something like this: The real test of the analyst lies in the performance of the stocks he recommends. Maybe Sloppy Louie, the copper analyst, did mess up his earnings forecast with a misplaced decimal point; but if the stocks he recommended made money for his clients, his lack of attention to detail can surely be forgiven. "Analyze investment performance," the chorus is saying, "not earnings forecasts."

Fortunately, the records of one group of professionals—the mutual funds—are publicly available. Better still for my argument, many of the men and women at the funds are the best and highest-paid analysts and portfolio managers in the business. They stand at the pinnacle of the investment profession.

They allegedly are the first to learn and act on any new fundamental information that becomes available. By their own admission they can clearly make above-average returns. As one investment manager recently put it: "It will take many years before the general level of competence rises enough to overshadow the startling advantage of today's aggressive investment manager." "Adam Smith" echoes a similar statement:

All the players in the Game are getting rapidly more professional. . . . The true professionals in the Game—the professional portfolio managers—grow more skilled all the time. They are human and they make mistakes, but if you have your money managed by a truly alert mutual fund or even by one of the better banks, you will have a better job done for you than probably at any time in the past.

Statements like these were just too tempting to the lofty-minded in the academic world. Given the wealth of available data, the time available to conduct such research, and the overwhelming desire to prove academic superiority in such matters, it was only natural that academia would zero in on mutual-fund performance.

Again, the evidence from several studies is remarkably uniform. Investors have done no better with the average mutual fund than they could have done by purchasing and holding an unmanaged broad stock index. In other words, over long periods of time mutual-fund portfolios have not outperformed randomly selected groups of stocks. While funds may have very good records for certain short time periods, there is generally no consistency to superior performance.

The table below shows the returns from the average general-equity mutual fund over the ten-year period from the mid-1980s to the mid-1990s. As a comparison, the Standard & Poor's 500-Stock Index is used to represent the market. The table shows that the average mutual fund *underperformed* the S & P index by over two percentage points per year. Similar results have been found for different time periods and for pension-fund managers as well as mutual-fund managers. Simply buying and holding the stocks in a broad-market index is a strategy that is very hard for the professional portfolio manager to beat.

In addition to the scientific evidence that has been accumulated, several less formal tests have verified this finding. In June 1967, the editors of *Forbes* magazine, for example, intrigued with the results of academic studies, chose a portfolio of common stocks by throwing darts at the stock-market page of the *New York Times.* They struck 28 names and constructed

Mutual Funds vs The Market Index

| | TOTAL RETURN Ten Years Ended December 31, 1994 | |
	Cumulative	Annual Rate
Standard & Poor's 500 Index	+281.65%	+14.33%
Average general equity fund	+214.80%	+12.15%

a simulated portfolio consisting of a $1,000 investment in each stock. Seventeen years later, in mid-1984, that $28,000 portfolio (with all dividends reinvested) was worth $131,697.61. The 370 percent gain easily beat the broad market indices. Moreover, the 9.5 percent annual compounded rate of return has been exceeded only by a minuscule number of professional money managers. In the early 1990s, the *Wall Street Journal* started a dartboard contest where each month the selections of four experts were pitted against the selections of four darts. The *Journal* kindly let me throw the darts for the first contest. By the mid-1990s, the experts appeared to be somewhat ahead of the darts. If, however, the performance of the experts was measured from the day after their selections and their attendant publicity was announced in the *Journal,* the darts were actually slightly ahead. Does this mean that the wrist is mightier than the brain? Perhaps not, but I think that the *Forbes* editors raised a very valid question when they wrote: "It would seem that a combination of luck and sloth beats brains."*

How can this be? Every year one can read the performance rankings of mutual funds. These *always* show many funds beating the averages—some by significant amounts. The problem is that there is no consistency to the performances, at least during the 1980s and early 1990s. A manager who has been better than average one year has only a 50 percent chance of doing better than average the next year. Just as past earnings growth cannot predict future earnings, neither can past fund performance predict future results. Fund managements are also subject to random events—they may grow fat, become lazy, or break up. An investment approach that works very well for one period can easily turn sour the next. One is tempted to conclude that a very important factor in determining performance ranking is our old friend Lady Luck.

To shed further light on this issue, the table on the following page shows the top ten funds of 1968 (as well as fund number nineteen) and then follows their record over the next six years.

---

*Forbes retired the dart-board fund in 1984 because "the merger and takeover waves eliminated too many of its stocks; only 15% of the original 28 companies remain."

Some Results of the Performance Derby

1968 Rank	Fund	1969 Rank[a]	1970 Rank[a]	1971 Rank[a]	1972 Rank[a]	1973 Rank[a]	1974 Rank[a]	1968 Net Asset Value[b] per Share	1974 Net Asset Value per Share
1	Mates Investment Fund	312	424	512	465	531	400	15.51	1.12
2	Neuwirth Fund	263	360	104	477	397	232	15.29	6.24
3	Gibraltar Growth Fund[c]	172	456	481				17.27	
4	Insurance Investors Fund[c]	77	106	317	417	224		7.45	
5	Pennsylvania Mutual	333	459	480	486	519	521	11.92	1.09
6	Puerto Rican Investors Fund[c]	30	308	387	435			19.34	
7	Crown Western-Dallas	283	438	207	244	330	133	13.86	4.66
8	Franklin Dynatech Series	342	363	112	120	453	453	14.47	4.56
9	First Participating Fund	49	283	106	27	220	310	19.25	13.47
10	Connecticut Western Mutual Fund[c]	5	202					127.27	
19	Templeton Growth Fund	1	241	163	1	81	84	4.00	6.23

Source: Lipper Analytical Division, Lipper Analytical Services, Inc.
[a]Out of 381 funds surveyed in 1969, 463 in 1970, 526 in 1971, 537 in 1972, 536 in 1973, and 527 in 1974.
[b]The net asset values for 1968 have been adjusted for all subsequent splits.
[c]No longer surveyed by Lipper.

I mentioned in Part One that performance investing was a product of the 1960s and became especially prominent during the 1967–68 strong bull market. Capital preservation had given way to capital productivity. The fund managers who turned in the best results for the period were written up in the financial press like sports celebrities. When the performance rankings were published in 1967 and 1968, the go-go funds with their youthful gunslingers as managers and concept stocks as investments were right at the top of the pack, outgunning all the competition by a wide margin.

The game ended unceremoniously with the bear market that commenced in 1969 and continued until 1971. The go-go funds suddenly went into reserve. It was fly now and pay later for the performance funds. Their portfolios of volatile concept stocks were no exception to the financial law of gravitation. They went down just as sharply as they had gone up. The legendary brilliance of the fund managers turned out to be mainly a legend of their own creation. The top funds of 1968 had a perfectly disastrous performance in the ensuing years (I was not able to extend my table beyond 1974 because by 1975 many of the funds were no longer in business).

The Mates Fund, for example, was number one in 1968. At the end of 1974, the Mates Fund sold at about one-fourteenth of its 1968 value and Mates finally threw in the towel. He then left the investment community to enter a business catering to a new fad. In New York City he started a singles' bar, appropriately named "Mates."

It seems clear that one cannot count on consistency of performance. Unlike Steffi Graf, portfolio managers do not *consistently* outdistance their rivals. (In fact, sometimes even Steffi loses.) But I must be fair: There are exceptions to the rule. Note portfolio manager number nineteen. The Templeton Growth Fund has been a superior performer not only during the period covered in the table but in other periods as well. It is an excellent counterexample to the rule—but such examples are very rare.

The illustration from the late 1960s appeared in the first edition of this book. Similar examples can be found for subsequent years. The table on page 183 presents the 1980 to 1990 ranking for the twenty top funds of the 1970 to 1980 period. Again, there is no consistency. Many of the top funds ranked close to the bottom over the next decade. While the top 20 funds almost doubled the average fund return during the 1970s (19.0 percent versus 10.4 percent), those same funds did worse than average (11.1 percent versus 11.7 percent) over the next decade. Again, however, there is one striking exception. The number ten fund of the 1970s was the number one fund of the 1980s. That fund was the Magellan Fund managed by the legendary Peter Lynch. If you want to rush out and buy Magellan Fund today, I must warn you that Lynch retired in 1990 at the ripe old age of 46. By quitting at the peak of his performance, he has guaranteed himself membership in the portfolio managers "Hall of Fame." Unfortunately, individual investors can no longer bet on Lynch to continue to beat the Street.

In any activity in which large numbers of people are engaged, while the average is likely to predominate, the unexpected is bound to happen. The very small number of really good performers we find in the investment management business actually is not at all inconsistent with the laws of chance. Indeed, as I mentioned earlier, the fact that good past performance of a mutual fund is generally no help in predicting future performance only serves to emphasize this point. The preceding tables show just how inconsistent fund performance can be.

Perhaps the laws of chance should be illustrated. Let's engage in a coin-tossing contest. Those who can consistently flip heads will be declared winners. The contest begins and 1,000 contestants flip coins. Just as would be expected by chance, 500 of them flip heads and these winners are allowed to advance to the second stage of the contest and flip again. As might be expected, 250 flip heads. Operating under the laws of chance, there will be 125 winners in the third round, 63 in the fourth, 31 in the fifth, 16 in the sixth, and 8 in the seventh.

By this time, crowds start to gather to witness the surprising ability of these expert coin-tossers. The winners are overwhelmed with adulation. They are celebrated as geniuses in the art of coin-tossing—their biographies are written and people urgently seek their advice. After all, there were 1,000 con-

How the Top 20 Equity Funds of the 1970s Performed During the 1980s

Fund Name	Rank 1970–1980	Rank 1980–1990
Twentieth Century Growth	1	176
Templeton Growth	2	126
Quasar Associates	3	186
44 Wall Street	4	309
Pioneer II	5	136
Twentieth Century Select	6	20
Security Ultra	7	296
Mutual Shares Corp.	8	35
Charter Fund	9	119
Magellan Fund	10	1
Over-the-Counter Securities	11	242
American Capital Growth	12	239
American Capital Venture	13	161
Putnam Voyager	14	78
Janus Fund	15	21
Weingarten Equity	16	36
Hartwell Leverage Fund	17	259
Pace Fund	18	60
Acorn Fund	19	172
Stein Roe Special Fund	20	57
Average annual return:		
Top 20 funds	+19.0%	+11.1%
All funds	+10.4%	+11.7%
Number of funds	177	309

testants and only 8 could consistently flip heads. The game continues and there are even those who eventually flip heads nine and ten times in a row.* The point of this analogy is not to indicate that investment-fund managers can or should make their decisions by flipping coins, but that the laws of chance do operate and they can explain some amazing success stories.

As long as there are averages, some people will beat them. With large numbers of players in the money game, chance will—and does—explain some super performance records. The very great publicity given occasional success in stock selection

*If we had let the losers continue to play (as mutual-fund managers do, even after a bad year), we would have found several more contestants who flipped eight or nine heads out of ten and were therefore regarded as expert tossers.

reminds me of the story of the doctor who claimed he had developed a cure for cancer in chickens. He proudly announced that in 33 percent of the cases tested remarkable improvement was noted. In another third of the cases, he admitted, there seemed to be no change in condition. He then rather sheepishly added, "And I'm afraid the third chicken ran away."

While the preceding discussion has focused on mutual funds, it should not be assumed that the funds are simply the worst of the whole lot of investment managers. In fact, the mutual funds have had a somewhat *better* performance record than many other professional investors. The records of life insurance companies, property and casualty insurance companies, pension funds, foundations, college endowments, state and local trust funds, personal trusts administered by banks, and individual discretionary accounts handled by investment advisers have all been studied. This research suggests that there are no sizable differences in investment performance among these professional investors or between these groups and the market as a whole. As in the case of the mutual funds, there are some exceptions, but again they are very rare. *No scientific evidence has yet been assembled to indicate that the investment performance of professionally managed portfolios as a group has been any better than that of randomly selected portfolios.*

Many people ask me how this thesis—first published in 1973—has held up. The answer is, "Very well indeed." While there continue to be some exceptions to the thesis, as I freely admitted in 1973, history has been very kind to random walkers. In the twenty-year period to 1994, over two-thirds of the professionals who manage mutual-fund common-stock portfolios were outperformed by the unmanaged Standard & Poor's 500-Stock Index.

Can Any Fundamental System Pick Winners?

Research has also been done on whether above-average returns can be earned by employing trading systems based on press announcements of new fundamental information. The answer seems to be a clear no.

Systems have been devised in which a news event such as the announcement of an unexpectedly large increase in earnings or a stock split triggers a *buy* signal. But the evidence points mainly toward the efficiency of the market in adjusting so rapidly to new information that it is impossible to devise successful trading strategies on the basis of such news announcements.* Research indicates that, on average, stock prices react well in advance of unexpectedly good or unexpectedly bad earnings reports. In other words, the market is usually sufficiently efficient at anticipating published earnings announcements that investment strategies involving purchases or sales of stocks after the publication of those announcements do not appear to offer any help to the general investor. While it is true that some studies have found that stock price reactions to earnings announcements are not always complete, whatever abnormalities exist do not occur *consistently* over time and have been small enough that only a professional broker-dealer would have earned abnormal profits.

Similarly, no new information is obtained from announcements of stock splits. While it is true that companies announcing stock splits have generally enjoyed rising stock prices in the period prior to the announcement of the splits, the relative performance of the stocks after the announcement turns out to be precisely in line with that of the general market. The research indicates that splits are a consequence, not a cause, of rising stock prices and that no useful investment strategy can be undertaken on the basis of news of impending stock splits. These studies lend support to the old Wall Street maxim, "A pie doesn't grow through its slicing."

There has also been a good deal of research on the usefulness of dividend increases as a basis for selecting stocks that will give above-average performance. The argument is that an increase in a stock's dividend is a signal by management that it anticipates strong future earnings. Dividend increases, in fact, are usually an accurate indicator of increases in future earn-

---

*These tests are often referred to as tests of the "semi-strong" form of the random-walk hypothesis. As mentioned earlier, the "weak" form asserts that past price information cannot be exploited to develop successful trading strategies. The "semi-strong" form says that no publicly announced news event can be exploited by investors to obtain above-average returns.

ings. There is also some tendency for a strong price performance to follow the dividend announcement. However, any rise
in price resulting from the dividend increase, while perhaps not
immediately reflected in the price of stock, was reflected reasonably completely by the end of the announcement month.

The Verdict on Market Timing

Many professional investors move money from cash to
equities or to long-term bonds based on their forecasts of fundamental economic conditions. Indeed, several institutional
investors now sell their services as "asset allocators" or "market timers." The words of John Bogle, chairman of the Vanguard Group of Investment Companies, are closest to my views
on the subject of market timing. Bogle said: "In 30 years in this
business, I do not know anybody who has done it successfully
and consistently, nor anybody who *knows* anybody who has
done it successfully and consistently. Indeed, my impression is
that trying to do market timing is likely, not only *not* to add
value to your investment program, but to be counterproduc-
tive."

Bogle's point may be very well illustrated by an examination of the chart on the following page. The chart shows the
percentage of total assets held in cash of all equity mutual
funds from 1970 to 1994. It shows that mutual-fund managers
have been incorrect in their allocation of assets into cash in
essentially every market cycle during the seventies and eighties. Note that caution on the part of mutual-fund managers (as
represented by a very high cash allocation) coincides almost
perfectly with troughs in the market. Peaks in mutual funds'
cash positions have coincided with market troughs during 1970,
1974, 1982, and the end of 1987 after the great stock-market
crash. Another peak in cash positions occurred in late 1990,
just before the market rallied during 1991. Conversely, the allocation to cash of mutual-fund managers was almost invariably
at a low during peak periods in the market. Clearly the ability
of mutual-fund managers to time the market has been egregiously poor.

Obviously being "out of the stock market" during a period

Equity Mutual Funds' Cash to Total Assets Ratio and the S&P 400

Ratio %

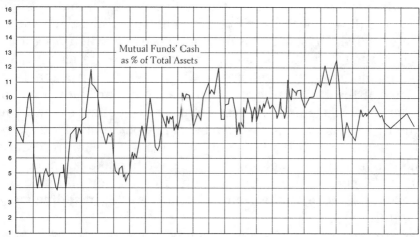
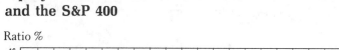
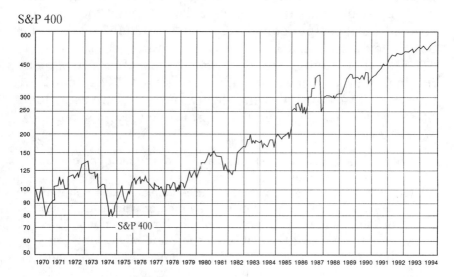

S&P 400

Source: Goldman, Sachs & Co.

of sharp decline, such as October 1987, would have saved you a lot of grief and money. We all hear of those "astute" few who "knew" the market was too high in early October and sold out. But unless those timers got back into the market right after the lows were hit, they were not more successful than investors who followed a "buy-and-hold" strategy. And the facts suggest that successful market timing is extraordinarily difficult to achieve.

Remember, over the past forty-five years the market has risen in thirty years, been even in three years, and declined in only twelve. Thus, the odds of being successful when you are in cash rather than stocks are almost three to one against you. An academic study by Professors Richard Woodward and Jess Chua of the University of Calgary shows that holding on to your stocks as long-term investments works better than market timing because your gains from being in stocks during bull markets far outweigh the losses in bear markets. The professors conclude that a market timer would have to make correct decisions 70 percent of the time to outperform a buy-and-hold investor. I've never met anyone who can bat .700 in calling market turns.

Another example of the difficulty of market timing is provided by two covers from *BusinessWeek,* one of the most respected business periodicals. On August 13, 1979, when the S&P Index stood at 105, *BusinessWeek* ran a cover story on "The Death of Equities," and on May 9, 1983, after a 60 percent rise in the market, they ran another cover story, "The Rebirth of Equities." The economist and highly successful investor John Maynard Keynes rendered the appropriate verdict some sixty years ago:

> We have not proved able to take much advantage of a general systematic movement out of and into ordinary shares as a whole at different phases of the trade cycle. . . . As a result of these experiences I am clear that the idea of wholesale shifts is for various reasons impracticable and indeed undesirable. Most of those who attempt it sell too late and buy too late, and do both too often, incurring heavy expenses and developing too unsettled and speculative a state of mind, which, if it is widespread, has besides the grave social disadvantage of aggravating the scale of the fluctuations.

The Semi-strong and Strong Forms of the Random-Walk Theory

The academic community had rendered its judgment. Fundamental analysis is no better than technical analysis in enabling investors to capture above-average returns. Nevertheless, given its propensity for splitting hairs, the academic community soon fell to quarreling over the precise definition of fundamental information. Some said it was what is known now; others said it extended to the hereafter. It was at this point that what began as the strong form of the random-walk theory split into two. As we have seen, the "semi-strong" form says that no published information will help the analyst to select undervalued securities. The argument here is that the structure of market prices already takes into account any public information that may be contained in balance sheets, income statements, dividend declarations, etc.; professional analyses of these data will at best be useless. The "strong" form says that absolutely nothing that is known or even knowable about a company will benefit the fundamental analyst. Not only all the news that is public but also all the information that it is possible to know about the company has already been reflected in the price of the stock. According to the strong form of the theory not even "inside" information can help the investors.

The strong form of the theory is obviously an overstatement if it does not admit the possibility of gaining from inside information. Nathan Rothschild made millions in the market when his carrier pigeons brought him the first news of Wellington's victory at Waterloo before other traders were aware of the victory. But today, the information superhighway carries news far more swiftly than carrier pigeons. On the morning after the first bombing of Iraq in January 1991 and the clear indication that victory would be achieved quickly, the Dow Jones industrial average opened 80 points over the previous day's close. The adjustment of market prices was immediate. Moreover, insiders who do profit from trading on the basis of nonpublic information are breaking the law. Therefore, corporate managements make every effort to announce promptly any major event that might have a significant impact on their stock prices.

The basic problem, both forms of the theory say, is that security analysts are very good at interpreting whatever new information does become available and acting on it quickly. Information is disseminated rapidly today, and it gets reflected almost immediately in market prices. The fact that they all react so quickly makes it extremely difficult for the analysts to realize a significant profit in the stock market on the basis of fundamental analysis.*

Nobel laureate Paul Samuelson sums up the situation as follows:

> If intelligent people are constantly shopping around for good value, selling those stocks they think will turn out to be over-valued and buying those they expect are now undervalued, the result of this action by intelligent investors will be to have existing stock prices already have discounted in them an al-lowance for their future prospects. Hence, to the passive in-vestor, who does not himself search out for under- and over-valued situations, there will be presented a pattern of stock prices that makes one stock about as good or bad a buy as another. To that passive investor, chance alone would be as good a method of selection as anything else.

This is a statement of the random-walk, or efficient-market, theory. The "narrow" (weak) form of the theory says that tech-nical analysis—looking at past stock prices—could not help investors. The "broad" (semi-strong and strong) forms state that fundamental analysis is not helpful either: All that is known concerning the expected growth of the company's earn-ings and dividends, all of the possible favorable and unfavor-able developments affecting the company that might be studied by the fundamental analyst, is already reflected in the price of the company's stock. Thus, throwing darts at the financial page will produce a portfolio that can be expected to do as well as

---

*It might actually be very inconvenient for professional analysts if it could be shown that they did get above-average returns. This would imply that some other group (presumably the public) was earning below-average returns. Think of the reform-ers who would press to restrict the pros' activities so as to protect the public.

any managed by professional security analysts. In a nutshell, the broad form of the random-walk theory states:

> Fundamental analysis cannot produce investment recommen- dations that will enable an investor consistently to outper- form a buy-and-hold strategy in managing a portfolio.

The random-walk theory does not, as some critics have pro- claimed, state that stock prices move aimlessly and erratically and are insensitive to changes in fundamental information. On the contrary, the point of the random-walk theory is just the opposite: The market is so efficient—prices move so quickly when new information does arise—that no one can consis- tently buy or sell quickly enough to benefit.

Even the legendary Benjamin Graham, heralded as the fa- ther of fundamental security analysis, reluctantly came to the conclusion that fundamental security analysis could no longer be counted on to produce superior investment returns. Shortly before he died in 1976, he was quoted in an interview in the *Financial Analysts Journal* as follows:

> . . . I am no longer an advocate of elaborate techniques of security analysis in order to find superior value opportunities. This was a rewarding activity, say, 40 years ago, when Gra- ham and Dodd was first published; but the situation has changed. . . . [Today] I doubt whether such extensive efforts will generate sufficiently superior selections to justify their cost. . . . I'm on the side of the "efficient market" school of thought. . . .

And Peter Lynch, just after he retired from managing the Ma- gellan Fund, admitted that most investors would be better off in an index fund rather than investing in an actively managed equity mutual fund.

The Middle of the Road: A Personal Viewpoint

Let's first briefly recap the diametrically opposed view- points about the functioning of the stock market. The view of most investment managers is that professionals certainly outperform all amateur and casual investors in managing money. Much of the academic community, on the other hand, believes that professionally managed investment portfolios cannot outperform randomly selected portfolios of stocks with equivalent risk characteristics. Random walkers claim that the stock market adjusts so quickly and perfectly to new information that amateurs buying at current prices can do just as well as the pros. Thus, the value of professional investment advice is nil—at least insofar as it concerns choosing a stock portfolio.

I walk a middle road. I believe that investors might reconsider their faith in professional advisers, but I am not as ready as many of my academic colleagues to damn the entire field. While it is abundantly clear that the pros do not consistently beat the averages, I must admit that there are exceptions to the rule of the efficient market. Well, a few. While the preponderance of statistical evidence supports the view that market efficiency is high, some gremlins are lurking about that harry the efficient-market theory and make it impossible for anyone to state that the theory is conclusively demonstrated. Finding inconsistencies in the efficient-market theory became such a cottage industry during the late 1980s and 1990s that I will devote the next chapter to an analysis of the market anomalies that have been uncovered.

Moreover, I worry about accepting all the tenets of the efficient-market theory, in part because the theory rests on several fragile assumptions. The first is that perfect pricing exists. As the quote from Paul Samuelson indicates, the theory holds that, at any time, stocks sell at the best estimates of their intrinsic values. Thus, uninformed investors buying at the existing prices are really getting full value for their money, whatever securities they purchase.

This line of reasoning is uncomfortably close to that of the "greater-fool" theory. We have seen ample evidence in Part One that stocks sometimes do not sell on the basis of anyone's estimate of value (as hard as this is to measure)—that purchasers are often swept up in waves of frenzy. The market pros were largely responsible for several speculative waves from the 1960s through the 1990s. The existence of these broader influences on market prices at least raises the possibility that investors may not want to accept the current tableau of market prices as being the best reflection of intrinsic values.

Another fragile assumption is that news travels instantaneously. I doubt that there will ever be a time when all useful inside information is immediately disclosed to everybody. Indeed, even if it can be argued that all relevant news for the major stocks followed by institutional investors is quickly reflected in their prices, it may well be that this is not the case for all the thousands of small companies that are not closely followed by the pros. Moreover, the efficient-market theory implies that no one possesses monopolistic power over the market and that stock recommendations based on unfounded beliefs do not lead to large buying. But brokerage firms specializing in research services to institutions wield considerable power in the market and can direct tremendous money flows in and out of stocks. In this environment, it is quite possible that erroneous beliefs about a stock by some professionals can for a considerable time be self-fulfilling.

Finally, there is the enormous difficulty of translating known information about a stock into an estimate of true value. We have seen that the major determinants of a stock's value concern the extent and duration of its growth path far into the future. Estimating this is extraordinarily difficult, and there is considerable scope for an individual with superior intellect and judgment to turn in a superior performance.

But while I believe in the possibility of superior professional investment performance, I must emphasize that the evidence we have thus far does not support the view that such competence exists; and while I may be excommunicated from some academic sects because of my only lukewarm endorsement of the semi-strong and particularly the strong form of the efficient-market theory, I make no effort to disguise my heresy in the financial church. It is clear that if there are exceptional financial managers, they are very rare. This is a fact of life with which both individual and institutional investors have to deal.

8

A More Deliberate Walk
Down Wall Street:
Is the Stock Market
Predictable After All?

It is difference of opinion that makes horse races.
—Mark Twain, *Pudd'nhead Wilson*

Even a dart-throwing chimpanzee can select a portfolio that performs as well as one carefully selected by the experts. This, in essence, is the practical application of the theory of efficient markets that has been presented in Part Two. The theory holds that the market appears to adjust so quickly to information about individual stocks and the economy as a whole that no technique of selecting a portfolio—neither technical nor fundamental analysis—can *consistently* outperform a strategy of simply buying and holding a diversified group of securities such as those that make up the popular market averages.

The broad acceptance of this thinking by financial economists and market practitioners became evident as the 1980s progressed. More and more, individual and institutional investors threw in the stock-picking towel and opted for indexing—that is, simply buying and holding one or more of the broad market indexes such as the Standard & Poor's 500-Stock Index, the Wilshire 5,000 Index, an index that contains an additional 4,500 smaller companies, the Morgan Stanley Capital (EAFE) Index of European, Australian and Pacific Rim Securities, and perhaps additional indexes of stocks from a variety of emerging markets. By the mid-1990s, literally hundreds of billions of dollars of pension-fund, endowment, and individual portfolios were invested in a variety of indexed products.

But the 1980s also spawned, both within and outside the academic community, new doubters about market efficiency and renewed attacks to batter the theory down. With easy access to large-scale computers and with financial and stock price data of all sorts available both to practitioners and to academicians, the search was on to make one's fortune and/or academic reputation by proving the efficient-market theory wrong and demonstrating that market prices were, in fact, predictable. It is much easier to get published by reporting a startling new finding that future returns can be accurately forecast than by providing another confirmation of market efficiency. An academic battle of epic proportions was under way as a new generation of financial economists tried to make their reputation (and gain tenure at prestigious universities) by attempting to tear down, or at least rebuild, the efficient-market temple of their elders.

And then, in the midst of it all, the stock market crashed with such ferocity that the thundering herd was buried under the debris for months to come. Early in October 1987, the most popular stock-market index in the United States, the Dow Jones average of 30 major industrial corporations, sold at approximately the 2,600 level. After October 19, a day in which this index fell by over 500 points on unprecedented trading volume, the market traded under the 1,800 level—a drop of approximately one-third within a single month. This is efficient? To many observers, such an event stretches the credibility of the efficient-market theory beyond the breaking point. Did the stock market really accurately reflect all relevant information about individual stocks and the economy when it sold at 2,600 early in October? Had fundamental information about the economic prospects of U.S. corporations changed that much in the following two weeks to justify a drop in share valuations of almost one-third? The financial press was unambiguous in its judgment. Just after the crash, the *Wall Street Journal* opined that the efficient-market theory was "the most remarkable error in the history of economic theory." A bit later, *Business Week* described the theory as a "failure."

Some academic economists came to similar conclusions.

Lawrence Summers claimed that "the stock in the efficient market hypothesis . . . crashed along with the rest of the market on October 19, 1987." Robert Shiller concluded from a longer history of stock-market fluctuations that stock prices show far "too much variability" to be explained by an efficient-market theory of pricing, and one must look to behavioral considerations and to crowd psychology to explain the actual process of price determination in the stock market. This view was obviously shared by thousands of investors who left the stock market in disgust. No amount of esoteric academic evidence could convince them that the market was an efficient and hospitable place in which to invest.

This chapter presents an ivy-tower view of the debate and the new evidence uncovered during the 1980s and 1990s. I will review all the recent research proclaiming the demise of the efficient-market theory and purporting to show that market prices are, in fact, predictable. My conclusion is that such obituaries are greatly exaggerated and the extent to which the stock market is usefully predictable has been vastly overstated. I'll also refer back to the underlying rational model of stock valuation that was suggested in Part One and describe the "fundamental" events that could provide a rational explanation for the October 1987 crash. We will see that while the stock market may not be perfect in its assimilation of knowledge, it still does seem to do a quite creditable job.

While I will present all research results in nontechnical terms, the reader should be warned that the material which follows is a bit tougher than was the case in earlier chapters. But don't skip these pages! Some of the statistical findings suggest potentially useful investment strategies for individual investors.

Predictable Patterns in the Behavior of Stock Prices

Recall that the weak form of the efficient-market hypothesis (the random-walk notion) says simply that the technical analysis of past price patterns to predict the future is useless because any information from such an analysis will already have been incorporated in current market prices. If today's direction—up or down, forward or backward—does indeed predict tomorrow's step, then you will act on it today rather than tomorrow. Thus, if market participants were confident that the price of any security would double next week, the price would not reach that level over five working days. Why wait? Indeed, unless the price adjusted immediately, a profitable arbitrage opportunity would exist and would be expected to be exploited immediately in an efficient market. The arbitrageur (or "arb" as these players are now known on Wall Street) would simply buy today and then sell out at a big profit next week. If the flow of information is unimpeded, then tomorrow's price change in speculative markets will reflect only tomorrow's "news" and will be independent of the price change today. But "news" by definition is unpredictable and thus the resulting price changes must also be unpredictable and random.

A "random walk" would characterize a price series where all subsequent price changes represent random departures from previous prices. More formally, the random-walk model states that investment returns are serially independent, and that their probability distributions are constant through time. As was noted in Chapter Six, the earliest empirical work on the random-walk hypothesis generally found that stock price changes from time to time were essentially independent of (or unrelated to) each other. While some of these studies found that there was some slight correlation between successive price changes, researchers concluded that profitable investment strategies could not be formulated on the basis of the extremely small dependencies found.

More recent work, however, indicated that the random-walk model does not strictly hold. As will be noted below, some consistent patterns of correlations, inconsistent with the model, have been uncovered. Nevertheless, it is less clear that violations exist of the weak form of the efficient-market hypothesis, which states only that unexploited trading opportunities should not persist in any efficient market.

1. Stocks do sometimes get on one-way streets.   Several studies completed during the 1980s have been inconsistent with the pure random-walk model. They show that price changes measured over short periods of time do tend to persist. For example, researchers Andrew Lo and A. Craig MacKinlay found that for the two decades ending in the mid-1980s, broad portfolio stock returns for weekly and monthly holding periods showed positive serial correlation. In other words, a positive return in one week is more likely than not to be followed by a positive return in the next week.

Well, that looks like interesting news to an investor. However, this rejection of the random-walk model is due largely to the behavior of small stocks in the portfolios, which are less frequently traded than larger capitalization stocks. In part, such serial correlation may be induced by new information about the market being incorporated into large capitalization stocks first and then into the smaller stocks with a lag. Thus, positive news for the market as a whole can produce a series of positive portfolio moves since the good news gets incorporated into the prices of smaller stocks only later in some instances, when the small stocks are finally traded. In any event, the research findings do not necessarily imply any inefficiencies in stock price formation. It is not clear that an investor who pays commission costs can formulate a trading strategy to exploit the small correlations that have been found.

2. But eventually stock prices do change direction and hence stockholder returns tend to reverse themselves. Buying stocks that performed poorly during the past two years or so is likely to give you above-average returns over the next two years. This is the finding of research carried out by Eugene Fama and Kenneth French as well as by James Poterba and Lawrence Summers and by Werner De Bondt and Richard Thaler. In research jargon, they say that while stock returns over short horizons such as a week or a month may be positively correlated, stock returns over longer horizons, such as a year or more, display negative serial correlation. Richard Quandt, Zsuzsanna Fluck, and I have confirmed that this result continued to hold into the 1990s. Thus, a contrarian investment strategy—that is, buying those stocks that have had relatively poor recent performance—might be expected to outperform a strategy of buying those stocks that recently produced superior returns. The implicit advice to investors is to shun recently fashionable stocks and concentrate one's buying on those stocks that are currently out of favor.

Of all the anomalies that have been uncovered or alleged, this one strikes me not only as one of the most believable but also as potentially most beneficial for investors. Certainly, the evidence in Part One of this book shows clearly that fads and fashions can play a role in stock pricing. At times, growth stocks have been all the rage; at other periods electronics stocks or biotechnology securities have caught investors' fancies. No matter what the fad, all carried stock prices to extremes and led to severe losses for investors who purchased at the apex. If investors could avoid buying at the top of an unwarranted "bubble," serious investment mistakes could be avoided. Similarly, if those stocks that were overly popular turn out to be poor investments, perhaps the stocks that have recently been shunned by investors—the ugly ducklings of the investment world—will eventually come out from under their cloud. Particularly when such a contrarian approach is wedded to a fundamental-value approach (to avoid buying stocks simply because they are unpopular), investors may well benefit from such a strategy.

The psychological explanation for such reversals in realized stock returns suggests the dominance of "castle-in-the-air" builders among investment decision-makers. If stock prices were always influenced by fads and fashions which tended to arise and then decay over time, such reversals in security returns would be expected. Hence, many investigators have concluded that the evidence concerning reversals in returns is inconsistent with the efficient-market hypothesis. Well—maybe yes, but maybe no. There are both logical and statistical reasons to continue to stand by the theory of efficient markets.

Return reversals over different time periods are often rooted in solid economic facts rather than psychological swings. The volatility of interest rates constitutes a prime economic influence on share prices. Since bonds—the frontline reflectors of interest-rate direction—compete with stocks for the investor's dollars, one should logically expect systematic relationships between interest rates and stock prices. Specifically, when interest rates go up, share prices should fall, other things being the same, so as to provide larger expected stock returns in the future. Only if this happens will stocks be competitive with higher-yielding bonds. Similarly, when interest rates fall, stocks should tend to rise, since they can promise a lower total return and still be competitive with lower-yielding bonds.

It's easy to see how fluctuations in interest rates can produce return reversals in stocks. Suppose interest rates go up. This causes both bond and stock prices to fall and tends to produce low and often negative rates of return over the time periods when the interest rates rose. Suppose now that interest rates fall back to their original level. This causes bond and stock prices to rise and tends to produce very high returns for stockholders. Thus, over a cycle of interest-rate fluctuations, we will tend to see relatively large stock returns following low stock returns—that is, exactly the kinds of return reversals found by investigators. The point is that such return reversals need not be due to fads that decay over time. They can also result from the very *logical* and *efficient* reaction of stock-market participants to fluctuations in interest rates.

Obviously, in any given period there are many influences on stock prices apart from interest rates so one should not expect to find a perfect correspondence between movements of interest rates and stock prices. Nevertheless, the *tendency* of interest rates to influence stock prices could account for the sorts of return reversals that have been found historically, and such a relationship is perfectly consistent with the existence of highly efficient markets.

Statistically, there are also reasons to doubt the "robustness" of this finding concerning return reversals. It turns out that correlations of returns over time are much lower in the period since 1940 than they were in the period before 1940. Thus, the employment of simple contrarian investment strategies is no guarantee of success. And even if fads are partially responsible for some return reversals (as when a particular group of stocks comes in and out of favor), fads don't occur all the time.

Finally, it should be noted that it may not be possible to profit from the tendency for individual stocks to exhibit patterns of return reversals. While such reversals may be statistically significant, they may only represent reversion to the mean rather than predictable opportunities to earn above-average returns. Zsuzsanna Fluck, Richard Quandt, and I simulated an investment strategy of buying stocks which had experienced relatively poor recent two- or three-year performance. We found that during the 1980s and early 1990s, those stocks did enjoy improved returns in the next period of time, but they recovered only to the average stock-market performance. Thus, there was a statistically strong pattern of return reversal, but not one that you could make money on. And even if the recent "losers" did produce extraordinary subsequent returns, this does not imply that stock prices systematically "overshoot" their appropriate levels. Stocks that have gone down sharply after some unfavorable business reversals exhibit heightened uncertainty and volatility and, therefore, greater risk for investors. Since investors require higher returns for bearing greater risk, a finding that future returns in these stocks are relatively generous is quite consistent with the efficient functioning of markets. Suspicion that there is no evidence of systematic price overreactions is reinforced by the failure to find significant price reversals following sharp runups in prices.

So what's an investor to do? As the careful reader knows, I believe the stock market is fundamentally logical. I also recognize that the market does get carried away with popular fads or fashions. Similarly, pessimism can often be overdone. Thus, "value" investors operating on the firm-foundation theory will often find that stocks which have produced very poor recent returns may provide very generous returns in the future. Knowing that careful statistical work also supports this tendency, at least to some extent, should give investors an additional measure of comfort in undertaking a contrarian investment strategy coupled with a firm-foundation approach. But remember that the statistical relationship is a loose one and that some unpopular stocks may be justly unpopular and undoubtedly somewhat riskier. Certainly some companies that have been going downhill may continue to go "down the tubes." The relationships are sufficiently loose and uncertain that one should be very wary of expecting sure success from any simple contrarian strategy.

3. Stocks are subject to seasonal moodiness, especially at the beginning of the year and the end of the week.   Discoveries of several apparently predictable stock patterns indicate that a walk down Wall Street may not be perfectly random. Investigators have documented a "January effect," where stock returns are abnormally higher during the first few days of January. The effect appears to be particularly strong for smaller firms. Even after adjusting for risk, small firms appear to offer investors abnormally generous returns—with the excess returns being largely produced during the first few days of the year. Such an effect has also been documented for several foreign stock markets. This led to one book being published during the 1980s with the provocative title *The Incredible January Effect.* Investors and especially stockbrokers, with visions of large commissions dancing around in their heads, designed strategies to capitalize on this "anomaly" believed to be so dependable.

One possible explanation for a "January effect" is that tax effects are at work. Some investors may sell securities at the end of the calendar year to establish short-term capital losses for income-tax purposes. If this selling pressure depresses stock prices prior to the end of the year, it would seem reasonable that the bounce-back during the first week in January could create abnormal returns during that period. While this effect could be applicable for all stocks, it would be larger for small firms because stocks of small companies are more volatile and less likely to be in the portfolios of tax-exempt institutional investors and pension funds. One might suppose that traders would take advantage of any excess returns during this period. Unfortunately, however, the transactions costs of trading in the stocks of small companies are substantially higher than for larger companies (because of the higher bid-asked spreads) and there appears to be no way a commission-paying ordinary investor could exploit this anomaly.

Other investigators have also documented a so-called weekend effect, where average stock returns are negative from the close of trading on Friday to the close of trading on Monday. In other words, there is some justification for the expression "blue Monday on Wall Street." According to this line of thinking, you should buy your stocks on Monday afternoon at the close, not on Friday afternoon or Monday morning, when they tend to be selling at slightly higher prices.

The general problem with these anomalies is that they are typically small relative to the transactions costs required to exploit them and they are not always dependable in that they often fail soon after being discovered. The "small firm effect" is a good example. No sooner had it been discovered in the early 1980s than it failed to work: Small stocks were relatively poor performers throughout much of the bull market of the 1980s. Moreover, during January of some years, small stocks would often underperform larger issues.

Even if the "small firm effect" were to persist (and the data do suggest that higher returns have been earned from small company stocks over very long periods of history), it's not at all clear that such a finding would violate market efficiency. A finding that small company stocks outperform the stocks of larger companies on a risk-adjusted basis depends importantly on how one measures risk. We will see in Part Three that beta (relative volatility), the risk measure typically used in the studies that have found anomalies, may be a very poor measure of risk. Thus, it is impossible to distinguish if the abnormal returns are truly the result of inefficiencies or result instead because of inadequacies in our measure of risk. The higher returns for smaller companies may simply be the requisite reward owed to investors for assuming a greater risk of disappointment in the investment returns they expect, just as larger returns are achieved over the long run from investing in relatively volatile long-term bonds than from more predictable short-term Treasury bills. Finally, it is also possible that the small firm effect is simply a result of what is called "survivorship bias" in currently available computer tapes of past returns. Today's list of companies include only small firms that have survived—not the small firms that later went bankrupt.

In conclusion, serious questions remain concerning the adjustment for risk involved in documenting the "January/small firm effect." Moreover, the dependability of the phenomenon is open to question. Finally, the magnitudes of the "start-of-the-year" and "end-of-the-week" effects are very small relative to the transactions costs involved for the individual investor to exploit them. Consequently, I am not prepared to admit that important violations of weak-form market efficiency have been uncovered.

Predictable Relationships Between Certain "Fundamental" Variables and Future Stock Prices

Academics and financial analysts in the semi-strong school of market efficiency believe that all public information about a company is always reflected in the stock's price. Thus, they are skeptical about the ability of "fundamental" security analysts to pore over data concerning a company's earnings and dividends in an effort to find "undervalued" stocks, which represent particularly good "value" for investors. Anomalies given considerable attention in the 1980s and 1990s are quantifications of some value techniques of security analysts: Look for securities that sell (1) at low multiples compared with their earnings, (2) low prices relative to the value of their assets, and (3) with high dividends compared with their market prices. Has this new scientific evidence proved that the Wall Street security analysts were right all the time?

4. There is some evidence that stocks with low price-earnings multiples outperform those with high multiples. We have come to another potential anomaly with which I have considerable intellectual sympathy. One of my cardinal rules of stock selection is to look for companies with reasonable growth prospects that have yet to be discovered by the stock market and thus are selling at relatively low earnings multiples. I have also warned investors repeatedly about the dangers of very-high-multiple stocks that may be the current favorites of the investment community. Particularly since earnings growth is so hard to forecast, it's far better to be in low-multiple stocks; if growth does materialize, both the earnings and the earnings multiple will likely increase, giving the investor a double benefit. Buying a high-multiple stock whose earnings growth fails to material-ize subjects investors to a double whammy. Both the earnings *and* the multiple can fall.

There is some evidence that a portfolio of stocks with rela-tively low earnings multiples has often produced above-aver-age rates of return even after adjusting for risk. For example, the following figure shows the returns during the 1980s from ten equal-sized groups of exchange-traded (NYSE, ASE, or NAS-DAQ) stocks, ranked by their P/E ratios. Group 1 had the low-est P/Es, Group 2 the second lowest, etc. The figure shows that as the P/E of a group of stocks increased, the return decreased. To some extent this phenomenon is related to the "small firm effect" referenced above. But again, as with the small firm ef-fect, the "P/E effect" appears to vary over time—it is certainly not dependable over every specific investment period. More-over, even if it can be shown to persist on average over a long period of time, one can never be sure if the excess returns are due to increased risk or to market abnormalities. The studies which have documented abnormal returns have used relative volatility or beta to measure risk. To the extent that one has reason to believe that beta is far from a perfect, or even a useful, risk measure—as I will indicate in Part Three—one should treat the low P/E anomaly with some suspicion.

And don't forget that low P/Es are often justified. Very often companies on the verge of some financial disaster will sell at very low multiples of reported earnings. For example, just prior to declaring bankruptcy in 1983, Continental Illinois Bank sold at an unusually low earnings multiple. The financial community in this case was entirely justified in disbelieving reported earnings. The low multiples reflected not value but a profound concern about the viability of the bank. It turned out that Continental's reported earnings bore little relation to the actual economic earnings of the bank.

Another illustration will show how difficult it is to imple-ment a low P/E strategy. Suppose two identical banks have $10 per share in earnings for the year, half of which represents

Average Quarterly Returns During the 1980s vs P/E Ratio

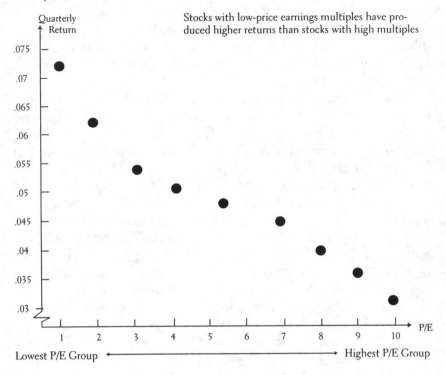

Quarterly Return

Stocks with low-price earnings multiples have produced higher returns than stocks with high multiples

.075
.07
.065
.06
.055
.05
.045
.04
.035
.03

P/E

1   2   3   4   5   6   7   8   9   10

Lowest P/E Group ←————————————————————→ Highest P/E Group

"pay-in-kind" interest from financially weak less-developed countries (LDCs). The LDCs can't pay their interest but instead just write a new IOU for the unpaid interest. Bank One reports the whole $10 in earnings while Bank Two reports only $5 as earnings, preferring to set up the more questionable extra $5 "pay-in-kind" interest as a reserve against future potential defaults. Which bank will show the higher P/E multiple? Most likely it will be the more conservative Bank Two, which reported the *lower* earnings. If both banks sold at $50 per share (and by assumption they are identical except for their accounting policies), then the conservative Bank Two would have a P/E multiple of 10 while Bank One, which set up no reserves and just called everything "earnings," would have a multiple of only 5. It's easy to see how a low P/E criterion could in some instances give a poor measure of true value.

5. Stocks that sell at low multiples of their book values tend to produce higher subsequent returns. Another pattern of return predictably is the relationship between the ratio of a stock's price to its book value (the value of the company's assets as recorded on its books) and its later return. Stocks that represent good value in the sense that they sell at low ratios of price to book value tend to produce higher future returns. This finding is consistent with the views of Benjamin Graham and David Dodd, first expounded in 1934, and later championed by Warren Buffett. The price-book value ratio is used by Standard & Poor's to help construct its "value stock" index. Over the years "value stocks" have tended to outperform more glamorous "growth" stock indexes.

Again, caution is necessary in interpreting these findings. The results are not consistent over time, and stocks selling at very low multiples of book values may be fundamentally riskier. Moreover, some of the studies documenting a price-book value effect may suffer from survivorship bias by not including companies that actually went bankrupt. If the database includes only surviving companies, the measured results from the strategy will exclude the losses from buying "value" stocks that later went bankrupt.

It is also important to realize that book values may often fail to represent the true value of the assets of the company. Some financial institutions may have a portfolio of office buildings on their books whose market values are far below their stated values. Moreover, when companies merge or are recapitalized, their asset values often get restated. Finally, it is important to note that the superior performance of value stocks over the past several decades has been well publicized and during the mid-1990s more glamorous growth stocks sold at historically very modest premiums over so-called "value" issues. It may well be that as "growth" stocks sell at very modest premiums over the market as a whole, that they may produce the superior returns over the next several years.

6. Higher initial dividends have meant higher subsequent returns. Another apparently predictable relationship concerns the returns realized over several quarters or years from stocks and the initial dividend yields at which they were purchased.

For example, 25 percent of the variability of returns for a two-to four-year holding period can, over certain periods, be predicted on the basis of the stocks' initial dividend-price ratios. Such a finding is perfectly consistent, however, with an efficient-market view of security price determination. Stock prices are low relative to dividends (that is, yields are high) when general market interest rates and thus required returns are high. Such a result also is consistent with the findings of mean reversion (return reversals) described above. An economic shock that raises general market interest rates will be associated with a decline in stock prices, which will lower realized returns. But the price decline raises both the dividend yield and the future rate of return. Assuming that the cumulative price effects from fluctuations in market interest rates are roughly zero, the time variation of expected returns can give rise to mean-reverting components of market prices.

The point, then, is that at a time when bond interest rates are high, dividend yields on stocks are also likely to be high and those higher dividend yields will presage higher subsequent stock returns. This is a logical outcome and is entirely consistent with efficient markets. And there is no doubt that, other things being the same, stocks with higher dividend yields represent better value. Unfortunately, a strategy of simply buying those stocks which have the highest dividend yields will not *consistently* beat the market. The strategy often does do well, and a portfolio yielding high dividends may be especially appropriate for certain individuals in low tax brackets or with high income needs for living expenses. But there is no evidence that the market systematically and consistently fails to adjust properly to current and prospective dividend returns.

In sum, while it is true that departures exist from the weak and semi-strong forms of the efficient-market hypothesis, departures from randomness are generally small and are not consistent over time. An investor who pays transactions costs cannot generally formulate an investment strategy that is profitable on the basis of these anomalies. Moreover, the more dependable relationships, such as those associated with general movements in interest rates and with price-to-earnings or price-to-book value ratios, may be perfectly consistent with market efficiency. Although the random-walk hypothesis is not strictly upheld, the documented departures from randomness do not appear to leave significant unexploited investment opportunities that are inconsistent with the efficient-market hypothesis.

Strong Form of the Efficient-Market Hypothesis

We have already suggested that the strongest form of the efficient-market hypothesis is unlikely to hold. We know that stock splits, dividend increases, and merger announcements can have substantial effects on share prices. Consequently, insiders trading on such information can clearly profit before the announcement is made. While such trading is illegal, the fact that the market often at least partially anticipates the announcements suggests that it is possible to profit on the basis of privileged information.

We also know that corporate insiders typically do well when trading stocks of their own companies. Stocks purchased by insiders often outperform the stocks in a randomly selected group. Moreover, distributions by "knowledgeable" sellers have often preceded significant price declines. Thus, the strongest form of the efficient-market hypothesis is clearly refuted.

Of course, it is possible for insiders acting on the basis of information about an important mineral strike to make profits at the expense of public investors not privy to that information. Such things have happened in the past with all too much frequency. But situations like that involving Texas Gulf Sulphur, where insiders allegedly profited from news of mineral discoveries at the expense of the public, are now less likely to occur than in the past. Of course, those who know in advance about a future takeover bid at a large premium over current market prices can profit from that knowledge. But arbitrageurs such as Ivan Boesky who have been convicted of securities violations have, in fact, spent time in jail—albeit a jail that bore some resemblance to a country club. It is also possible for columnists writing in widely read financial publications to profit from advance information of a bullish story concerning a particular security. But when they are caught utilizing this information themselves or selling it to others, they get fired and go to jail, as R. Foster Winans of the *Wall Street Journal* discovered.

In recent years, the Securities and Exchange Commission has taken an increasingly tough stand against anyone profiting from information not generally available to the public. The SEC has put the investment community on notice that corporate officials, arbitrageurs, and anyone else acting on material that is not public information do so at their own peril. More recently, the SEC has extended this warning to *any* investor acting on this information, even if he hears about it thirdhand— such as through his broker. It is small wonder that many a company president who thinks he has told a visiting security analyst some relevant piece of information he has not made available to others will immediately issue a press release to rectify the situation.

Thus, tightened rules on disclosure make time lags in the dissemination of new information much shorter than they may have been in previous years. Of course, the more quickly information is disseminated to the public at large, the more closely the market may be expected to conform to the random-walk model. While the evidence on insider trading indicates that the very strongest form of the theory is not valid, there is considerable evidence that the market comes reasonably close to strong-form efficiency.

The Performance of Professional Investors

As indicated in the preceding chapter, several studies show that randomly selected portfolios or unmanaged indices do as well as, or better than, professionally managed portfolios. This was not good news for highly paid investment pros. And so, the search was on for "better" studies. Sure enough, after wading through mountains of data, some researchers in the late 1980s published findings that challenged the original research. They concluded that, at least before load fees and other expenses, mutual funds actually outperformed the market. Since funds did about the same as the market after expenses, the studies concluded that fund managers have sufficient skill and/or private information to offset their expenses. This finding, even if true, is not inconsistent with a somewhat looser definition of efficiency, however. Presumably, the army of professional security analysts who insure that information does get properly reflected in prices should at least earn their expenses. Otherwise, it wouldn't pay anyone to do the analysis to push market prices back in line if they temporarily stray from their proper values.

Other studies done in the 1990s have gone further by suggesting that mutual-fund returns were predictable. They claim to show that some mutual-fund managers may have a "hot hand" and that past mutual-fund returns dependably predict future returns. Funds that have been superior (inferior) performers in one period predictably perform better (or worse) in a subsequent period, at least over the near term. This result is inconsistent with the findings I have described in Chapter Seven. Some researchers have also suggested that investors could earn significantly better returns by purchasing recently good-performing funds, thus apparently contradicting the efficient-market hypothesis.

Naturally, I have followed this work with great interest. And I am convinced that many studies have been flawed by the phenomenon of "survivorship bias," that is, including in their studies only the successful funds which survived over a long period of time, while excluding from the analysis all the unsuccessful funds that fell by the wayside. Commonly employed data sets of mutual-fund returns, such as those available from the *Morningstar* service, typically show the past records of all funds *currently* in existence. Clearly, today's investors are not interested in the records of funds that no longer exist. This creates the possibility of significant biases in the returns figures calculated from most of the available data sets.

Mutual funds that are unsuccessful with big risky bets usually do not survive. You are not alone in being reluctant to buy a mutual fund with a poor record. Mutual-fund complexes (those with large numbers of funds) typically allow such a fund to suffer a painless death by merging it into a more successful fund in the complex, thereby burying the bad fund's record. Thus, there will be a tendency for only the more successful funds to survive and measures of the returns of such funds will tend to overstate the success of mutual-fund management. Moreover, it may appear that high returns will tend to persist since funds whose bets were unsuccessful will tend to drop out of the sample. The problem for the investor is that at the beginning of any period he or she can't be sure which funds will be successful and survive.

Another little known factor in the behavior of mutual-fund management companies also leads to the conclusion that survivorship bias may be quite severe. A number of mutual-fund management complexes employ the practice of starting "incubator" funds. A complex may start ten small new equity funds with different in-house managers and wait to see which ones are successful. Suppose after a few years only three funds produce total returns better than the broad-market averages. The complex begins to market those successful funds aggressively, dropping the other seven and burying their records. The full records from inception of the successful funds will be the only ones to appear in the usual publications of mutual-fund returns.

In order to get a handle on the possible magnitude of this bias, I obtained from Lipper Analytic Services, a company that publishes information on mutual-fund returns, over 20 years of data on the records of *all* mutual funds that were available to the public each year, whether they survived into the 1990s or not. The following table presents some estimates of survivorship bias over the 1982–1991 period. (Similar findings were confirmed for 15- and 20-year periods.)

The second column presents the average annual net returns of all general equity funds that existed continuously from 1982 through 1991. This is the sample one would obtain from the normal data sources if one asked what was the average annual return for all general equity funds existing on January 1, 1992, which had at least a 10-year record. At the bottom of the table, we find that the (size weighted) average annual total return including dividends and capital changes for the 10-year period was 17.09 percent for all general equity funds versus 17.52 percent return for the Standard & Poor's 500-Stock Index. The rows above show the returns by various categories of funds, where the funds are sorted by the announced objectives of the portfolio managers. These data would suggest that surviving funds came close to matching the broad stock indexes after expenses. But since expenses for equity mutual funds average about one percentage point, the pre-expense returns of surviving funds must have exceeded the Standard & Poor's 500-Stock Index.

The first column of the table shows the average net returns for *all* general equity mutual funds—both survivors and failures—that existed in every year during the 10-year period. The average return for these funds (including those that were liquidated during the period) was only 15.69 percent, 1½ percentage points *less* than the average of surviving funds and almost two percentage points below the returns from the Standard & Poor's 500 Index. The last column of the table adds the total expenses reported by each fund to the net return in order to obtain the fund's gross investment return before expenses. We find that even the gross return before expenses for the universe of funds in existence each year fails to match the broad Standard & Poor's stock-market index. When you read press stories of how

Some Estimates of Survivorship Bias Average Annual Returns 1982–91

	(1) All Mutual Funds in Existence Each Year (Net of Expenses)	(2) Surviving Funds in Existence in 1982 and Still Existing in 1991 (Net of Expenses)	(3) S&P 500 Index	(4) All Mutual Funds in Existence Each Year (Gross of Expenses)
Capital appreciation funds	16.32%	18.08%	17.52%	17.49%
Growth funds	15.81	17.89	17.52	16.81
Small company growth funds	13.46	14.03	17.52	14.53
Growth and income funds	15.97	16.41	17.52	16.89
Equity income funds	15.66	16.90	17.52	16.53
All general equity mutual funds	15.69	17.09	17.52	16.70

well mutual funds do, it is likely you are seeing only the records of surviving funds.

When *all* mutual funds sold to the public are considered, the original thesis propounded by the first edition of *A Random Walk Down Wall Street* in 1973 holds up remarkably well. The results from 1973 through 1994 are presented in the following figure, which shows the performance of all general equity mutual funds sold to the public compared with the broad Wilshire 5,000 Index. In most years, well over half of the equity funds were outperformed by the index. Similar results are found using the Standard and Poor's 500-Stock Index. Over the whole 22-year period since the first edition of this book, about two-thirds of the funds proved inferior to the market as a whole. The same result also holds for professional pension fund managers. Most managers of the equity portfolios of mutual funds and pension funds could have substantially improved their performance by casting their lot with the efficient-market theory and not trying to outguess the market. Indeed, if the Standard & Poor's were an athlete, they would probably be testing it for steroids.

But is it possible that some fund managers are consistently better than the rest? Are fund results predictable from past performance? Is there really a "hot hand" phenomenon that has inspired thousands of advertising campaigns and turned a number of mutual-fund managers into legends during the 1970s and 1980s? The facts are disappointing. The evidence suggests that there was indeed a good deal of consistency in mutual-fund results during the 1970s. Good performing funds tended to continue to perform well, at least over the near term. Unfortunately, these persistent relationships did not continue to hold during the 1980s and early 1990s. Investors would not have been able to earn superior returns by purchasing funds whose recent performance was above average. Indeed, a variety of strategies involving purchase of the top-performing funds, or those funds touted in various financial publications, have sharply underperformed the broad-market indexes during the 1980s and early 1990s.

In conclusion, an analysis of mutual-fund returns does not provide any reason to abandon a belief that securities markets are remarkably efficient. Most investors would be considera-

General Equity Funds Outperformed by the Wilshire 5,000

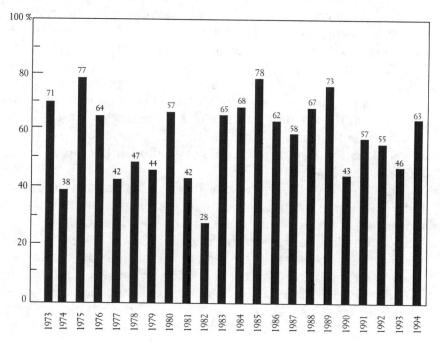

bly better off by purchasing a low-expense index fund that simply bought and held a broad-stock index, than by trying to select an active fund manager who appears to possess a "hot hand." Since active management generally fails to provide excess returns and also tends to generate greater tax burdens for investors because they regularly realize capital gains, the advantage of passive management holds with even greater force.

Some Other Anomalies

While it is clear that evidence in favor of the efficiency of markets remains extremely strong, two other studies published in the late 1980s are disturbing because they cast doubt on some of the key assumptions of the efficient-market hypothesis. The first, authored by Kenneth French and Richard Roll, exam-

ined the key presumption of the efficient-market hypothesis
that market moves are precipitated by the receipt of new information. If the major cause of market movements is the receipt
of news, then market prices should not fluctuate more over
periods when the market is open than when it is closed. French
and Roll demonstrated that this is not the case and that asset
prices are much more volatile during exchange trading hours.
For example, the variability (statistically, the variance) of
prices from the opening to the close of trading on an average
day is over six times as large as the price variances from Friday's close to Monday's opening even though the weekend is
eleven times longer.

One possible explanation for this phenomenon is that new
public information (new economic data, merger announcements, judicial decisions, new contracts, and so forth) is most
likely to arrive during normal business hours. Alternatively,
the greater price volatility during periods when the market is
open could be caused by the provision of private information
(the predictions of market gurus, the recommendations of fundamental security analysts, and so forth) which typically gets
incorporated into market prices when the exchange is open.
Security analysts are more likely to work at this time, and the
benefits of producing such information are larger when the information can be acted upon quickly and conveniently.

In order to distinguish between these two explanations,
French and Roll examined the volatility of prices around regular business days when the exchanges were closed. During the
second half of 1968, the major stock exchanges were closed on
Wednesdays because of a paperwork backlog. This gave these
two men a wonderful research opportunity. Public information
could be expected to be generated without interruption on
those Wednesdays while the flow of private information would
be sharply reduced. Thus, we should expect the volatility of
prices from Tuesday's close to Thursday's opening (when the
market was closed on Wednesday) to be considerably larger
than the variability of prices from Tuesday's close to Wednesday's opening (during Wednesdays when the exchange was
open) if new public information is the major cause of stock
price changes. On the other hand, if the production of *private*
information is an important cause of stock price change, the

Tuesday-Thursday volatility would be far less when the exchange was closed on Wednesday. It turned out that the two-day volatility numbers were, in fact, quite small. They were only a little larger than the one-day numbers, suggesting that the generation of private information is a principal cause of price variances in the market.

The point is that the market makes its own news. Just as the discovery of an important new source of petroleum can affect the price of an oil stock, so can the publication of a bullish report on the stock from a major brokerage firm. Although this is not necessarily inconsistent with markets being efficient, it does open the possibility of there being additional influences in the market besides the receipt of new public information. Surely the sentiment of the professional investment community is not irrelevant.

Roll has also shown in another study that even with hindsight, the ability to explain stock price changes is relatively modest. Less than 40 percent of the volatility in stock prices is explained by news events concerning the economy, industry developments, and specific news about the individual companies. It appears that security valuations and their changes over time are quite complex and that private information and the sentiments of professional and other investors can play an important role in the valuation process.

The Market Crash of October 1987

Can an event such as the October 1987 market crash be explained by rational considerations, or does such a rapid and significant change in market valuations prove the dominance of psychological rather than logical factors in understanding the stock market? Behaviorists would say that a one-third drop in market prices, which occurred early in October 1987, cannot be explained by rational considerations. The basic elements of the valuation equation do not, according to the behavioral view, change rapidly enough to produce such a substantial change in rationally determined market prices. I have already indicated that it is impossible to rule out the existence of behavioral or psychological influences on stock-market pricing.

Nevertheless, it may be useful to review the several logical considerations that could explain a sharp change in market valuations during the first weeks of October 1987.

As a frame of reference, we should recall that common stocks are rationally priced as the present or discounted value of the future stream of dividends expected from them. For a long-term holder of stocks, this rational principle of valuation translates to a simple formula:

Rate of Return to Stockholder = Dividend Yield + Long-run Dividend Growth Rate.

In symbols, we can write the basic valuation equation as

$$r = D/P + g,$$

where r is the rate of return, D/P is the yield (dividend divided by price), and g is the long-term growth rate. Using this equation, it is easy to show how sensitive share prices can be as a result of rational responses to small changes in interest rates and risk perceptions. This equation can also throw the "Monday meltdown" (October 19, 1987) into a more logical setting.

I believe there were very good reasons to think that investors should rationally have changed their views about the proper values of common stocks during October 1987. Specifically, a number of factors tended to increase the "r"—the rate of return required by stock investors—in the equation above. First, there had been a substantial increase in interest rates in the previous two months. Yields on long-term Treasury bonds increased from about 9 percent to almost 10½ percent just before the crash. In addition, a number of events created significantly increased risk perceptions in the market. In early October, Congress threatened to impose a "merger tax" that would have made merger activity prohibitively expensive and could well have ended the merger boom. It is significant to note that the stocks that went down the most in the week preceding October 19 were the stocks of companies that were the subject of takeover attempts. The risk that merger activity might be curtailed increased risks throughout the stock market by weakening the discipline over corporate management that potential takeovers provide. Also, James Baker, then secretary of the Treasury, had threatened in October to encourage a further fall in the price of the dollar, increasing risks for all foreign investors and thereby frightening domestic investors as well.

A numerical illustration will show how sensitive share prices can be as a result of rational responses to small changes in interest rates and risk perceptions. Recalling our previous equation of rational present-value pricing of common stocks, $r = D/P + g$, we will consider r to be the rate of return for the market as a whole and P to be the market price index, such as the price of one of the broad stock-market averages. Suppose initially that the "riskless" rate of interest on government bonds is 9 percent and that the required additional risk premium for equity investors is 2 percent. In this case r, the appropriate rate of return for equity holders (or, equivalently, the proper discount rate for common stocks), will be 11 percent $(0.09 + 0.02 = 0.11)$. If a typical stock's expected growth rate, g, is 6 percent and if the dividend is $5 per share, we can solve for the appropriate price of the stock index (P), obtaining

$$0.11 = \frac{\$5}{P} + 0.06$$
$$P = \$100.$$

Now assume that yields on government bonds rise from 9 to 10½ percent, with no increase in expected inflation (which might increase expected growth rates), and that risk perceptions increase so that stock-market investors now demand a premium of 2½ percentage points instead of the 2 points in the previous example. The appropriate rate of return or discount rate for stocks, r, rises then from 11 percent to 13 percent $(0.105 + 0.025)$, and the price of our stock index falls from $100 to $71.43:

$$0.13 = \frac{\$5}{P} + 0.06$$
$$P = \$71.43.$$

The price must fall to raise the dividend yield from 5 to 7 percent so as to raise the total return by the required 2 percentage points. It is clear that no irrationality is required for share prices to suffer quite dramatic declines with the sorts of changes in interest rates and risk perceptions that occurred in October 1987. Of course, even a very small decline in anticipated growth would have magnified these declines in warranted share valuations.

Critics may still raise the argument that this kind of calculation does not seem to explain why the bulk of the decline in market prices occurred *on a single day*. The Nobel laureate financial economist, Merton Miller, describes how a major revision in valuations can be triggered in a rational market by what might be considered to be only very small changes in immediate objective circumstances. Miller tells the story of the great drought in the midwest United States in the summer of 1988. As the drought persisted, the prices of corn and soybeans rose each day as the anticipated reduction in supply became incorporated into market prices. Suddenly, a very slight sprinkling of rain fell over Chicago—an amount insufficient to make up for even one day's rain shortfall. Nevertheless, the prices of corn and soybeans plummeted.

Miller asks, "Was this rapid readjustment a sign that the prices before the fall had been driven up by irrational buyers in bubble-like fashion to absurd and unsustainable levels? Or that panicky speculators had overreacted to events on both the way up and the way down?" He answers, "No! The response in the market was quite rational." It reflected the recognition that weather patterns tend to be persistent. Once the pattern of persistent drought was broken, even if by a slight amount, market participants made an immediate and substantial change in their climactic forecast and in the likely future supply of corn and soybeans. In suggesting the relevance of this incident for the stock market, Miller suggested that on October 19, after some weeks of external events that may have individually been relatively minor, the cumulative effect of these changes in interest rates and risk perceptions signalled a major change in economic and political climate for equities. He concluded that "many investors simultaneously, and based on the same information, came to believe that they were holding too large a share of their wealth in risky equities and too little in safer (and now more attractive) instruments such as government bonds."

This is not to say that purely psychological factors were irrelevant in explaining the sharp correction of market prices. I am sure that they, too, played a role in the decline. Moreover, the swiftness of the decline was probably accelerated by new trading techniques such as "portfolio insurance," which dictated that some institutional investors should increase their selling as share prices declined. In addition, "program trading," a technique whereby an entire basket of securities can be sold (or purchased) using computerized generation of orders, enables changes in market sentiment (as well as any discrepancies between the value of any stock indices, which trade mainly in Chicago, and the value of the component stocks) to affect the prices of shares with extraordinary speed. But it would be a mistake to dismiss the significant change in the external environment, which can provide a rational explanation of the need for a significant decline in the appropriate values for common stocks.

Concluding Comments

I have emphasized that market valuations rest on both logical and psychological factors. The theory of valuation depends on the projection of a long-term stream of dividends whose growth rate is extraordinarily difficult to estimate. Thus, fundamental value is never a definite number. It is a fuzzy band of possible values and prices can move sharply within this band whenever there is increased uncertainty or confusion. Moreover, the appropriate risk premiums for common equities are changeable and far from obvious either to investors or to economists. Thus, there is room for the hopes, fears, and favorite fashions of market participants to play a role in the valuation process. Indeed, I emphasized in early chapters how history provides extraordinary examples of markets in which psychology seemed to dominate the pricing process, as in the tulip-bulb mania in seventeenth-century Holland and the Japanese stock boom of the late 1980s followed by the crash of the early 1990s. Thus, I harbor some doubts that we should consider that the current array of market prices always represents the best estimates available of appropriate discounted value.

Nevertheless, one has to be impressed with the substantial volume of evidence suggesting that stock prices display a remarkable degree of efficiency. Information contained in past prices or any publicly available fundamental information is rapidly assimilated into market prices. Prices adjust so well to reflect all important information that a randomly selected and passively managed portfolio of stocks performs as well as or better than the portfolios selected by the experts. If some degree of mispricing exists, it does not persist for long. "True value will always out" in the stock market. Moreover, whatever mispricing there is usually is only recognizable after the fact, just as we always know Monday morning the correct play the quarterback should have called.

With respect to the evidence reviewed in this chapter indicating that future returns are, in fact, somewhat predictable, there are several points to make in summary. First, there are considerable questions regarding the long-run dependability of these effects. Many could be the result of "data snooping," letting the computer search through the data sets of past securities prices in the hopes of finding some relationships. With the availability of fast computers and easily accessible stock market data, it is not surprising that some statistically significant correlations have been found, especially since published work is probably biased in favor of reporting anomalous results rather than boring confirmations of randomness. Thus, many of the predictable patterns that have been discovered may simply be the result of data mining—the result of beating the data set in every conceivable way until it finally confesses. There may be little confidence that these relationships will continue in the future. The small firm effect may well be in this category. In the ten years since 1983, after this pattern was discovered, there seems to have been little size effect in the pattern of returns.

Second, even if there is a dependable predictable relationship it may not be exploitable by investors. For example, the transaction costs involved in trying to capitalize on the January effect are sufficiently large that the predictable pattern is not economically meaningful. Third, the predictable pattern that has been found, such as the dividend-yield effect, may simply reflect general economic fluctuations in interest rates or, in the case of the small firm effect, an appropriate premium for risk. Finally, if the pattern is a true anomaly, it is likely to self-destruct as profit maximizing investors seek to exploit it. Indeed, the more profitable any return predictability appears to be, the less likely it is to survive.

An exchange during the 1990s between Robert Shiller, an economist who cannot believe the market is efficient because prices fluctuate far too widely, and Richard Roll, an academic economist who also is a businessman running billions of dollars of investment funds, is quite revealing. After Shiller stressed the importance of fads and inefficiencies in the pricing of stocks, Roll responded as follows:

> I have personally tried to invest money, my client's money and my own, in every single anomaly and predictive device that academics have dreamed up . . . I have attempted to exploit the so-called year-end anomalies and a whole variety of strategies supposedly documented by academic research. *And I have yet to make a nickel on any of these supposed market inefficiencies* . . . I agree with Bob that investor psychology plays an important role. But, I have to keep coming back to my original point that a true market *inefficiency* ought to be an exploitable opportunity. If there's nothing investors can exploit in a systematic way, time in and time out, then it's very hard to say that information is not being properly incorporated into stock prices . . . Real money investment strategies don't produce the results that academic papers say they should.

Pricing irregularities and predictable pattens in stock returns may well exist and even persist for periods of time, and markets can be influenced by fads and fashions. Eventually, however, any excesses in market valuations will be corrected. Undoubtedly, with the passage of time and with the increasing sophistication of our data bases and empirical techniques, we will document further apparent departures from efficiency and further patterns in the development of stock returns. Moreover, we may be able to understand their causes more fully. But I suspect that the end result will not be an abandonment of the belief of many in the profession that the stock market is remarkably efficient in its utilization of information.

PART THREE

The New
Investment
Technology

9

Modern Portfolio and Capital-Asset Pricing Theory

> ... Practical men, who believe themselves to be quite exempt from any intellectual influence, are usually the slaves of some defunct economist. Madmen in authority, who hear voices in the air, are distilling their frenzy from some academic scribbler of a few years back.
> —J. M. Keynes, *General Theory of Employment, Interest and Money*

Throughout this book, I have attempted to explain the theories used by professionals—simplified as the firm-foundation and castle-in-the-air theories—to predict the valuation of stocks. As we have seen, many academics have earned their reputations by attacking these theories. While not denying that these theories tell us a good deal about how stocks are valued, the academics maintain that they cannot be relied upon to yield extraordinary profits.

As graduate schools continued to grind out bright young economists and statisticians, the attacking academics became so numerous that it seemed obvious—even to them—that a new strategy was needed. Ergo, the academic community busily went about erecting its own theories of stock-market valuation. That's what this part of the book is all about: the academic playground called the "new investment technology." Some people prefer to name it "capital-asset pricing theory," or its related cousin "arbitrage pricing theory." None of these titles conveys the heart of the matter, which is that when all is said and done, risk is the only variable worth a damn in the market.

According to the efficient-market theory, the stock market is so good at adjusting to new information that nothing and no one can predict its future course in a superior manner. Because of the actions of the pros, the prices of individual stocks quickly reflect all the news that is available. Thus, the odds of selecting superior stocks or anticipating the general direction of the market are even. Your guess is as good as that of the ape, your stockbroker, or even mine.

Hmmm. "I smell a rat," as Samuel Butler wrote long ago. Money is being made on the market; some stocks do outperform others. Common sense attests that some people can and do beat the market. It's not all chance. Many academics agree; but the method of beating the market, they say, is not to exercise superior clairvoyance but rather to assume greater risk. Risk, and risk alone, determines the degree to which returns will be above or below average, and thus decides the valuation of any stock relative to the market.

Part Three deals with the new investment technology and its (somewhat tarnished) star performer, beta. Being an academic, I hold to the biased viewpoint that this material is important and that every intelligent investor should be acquainted with the theories and models it includes. They explain how to reduce risk through diversification and present some of the ways to measure it. Even the investment professionals have latched on to much of the new investment technology. This section of the book also describes the options and futures markets and the academic theory explaining the determination of option premiums. So, sit down in a straight-backed chair, prop your eyelids open, and read on. There is a lot to do in these chapters, and, as was the case in Chapter Eight, necessarily the discussion must be a bit more formal than in the first seven chapters. (That means it *could* put you to sleep.) The wide-awake reader will be rewarded, however, with an understanding of a good deal of modern financial theory and of what lies behind some of the specific prescriptions for the investment strategy presented in Part Four.

Defining Risk: The Dispersion of Returns

Risk is a most slippery and elusive concept. It's hard for investors—let alone economists—to agree on a precise definition. The *American Heritage Dictionary* defines risk as the possibility of suffering harm or loss. If I buy one-year Treasury bills to yield 7 percent and hold them until they mature, I am virtually certain of earning a 7 percent monetary return, before income taxes. The possibility of loss is so small as to be considered nonexistent. If I hold common stock in my local power and light company for one year on the basis of an anticipated 8 percent dividend return, the possibility of loss is greater. The dividend of the company may be cut, and, more important, the market price at the end of the year may be much lower, causing me to suffer a serious net loss. Risk is the chance that expected security returns will not materialize and, in particular, that the securities you hold will fall in price.

Once academics accepted the idea that risk for investors is related to the chance of disappointment in achieving expected security returns, a natural measure suggested itself—the probable variability or dispersion of future returns. Thus, financial risk has generally been defined as the variance or standard deviation of returns. Being long-winded, we use the accompanying exhibit to illustrate what we mean. A security whose returns are not likely to depart much, if at all, from its average (or expected) return is said to carry little or no risk. A security whose returns from year to year are likely to be quite volatile (and for which sharp losses are typical in some years) is said to be risky.

Exhibit

Expected Return and Variance: Measures of Reward and Risk

This simple example will illustrate the concept of expected return and variance and how they are measured. Suppose you buy a stock from which you expect the following overall returns (including both dividends and price changes) under different economic conditions:

Business Conditions	Probability of Occurrence	Expected Return
Normal economic conditions	1 chance in 3	10 percent
Rapid real growth	1 chance in 3	30 percent
Recession with inflation (stagflation)	1 chance in 3	−10 percent

If, on average, a third of past years have been "normal," another third characterized by rapid growth, and the remaining third characterized by "stagflation," it might be reasonable to take these relative frequencies of past events and treat them as our best guesses (probabilities) of the likelihood of future business conditions. We could then say that an investor's *expected return* is 10 percent. A third of the time the investor gets 30 percent, another third 10 percent, and the rest of the time he suffers a 10 percent loss. This means that, *on average,* his yearly return will turn out to be 10 percent.

$$\text{Expected Return} = \tfrac{1}{3}(0.30) + \tfrac{1}{3}(0.10) + \tfrac{1}{3}(-0.10) = 0.10.$$

The yearly returns will be quite variable, however, ranging from a 30 percent gain to a 10 percent loss. The "variance" is a measure of the dispersion of returns. It is defined as the average squared deviation of each possible return from its average (or expected) value, which we just saw was 10 percent.

$$
\begin{aligned}
\text{Variance} &= \tfrac{1}{3}(0.30-0.10)^2 + \tfrac{1}{3}(0.10-0.10)^2 + \\
&\quad \tfrac{1}{3}(-0.10-0.10)^2 \\
&= \tfrac{1}{3}(0.20)^2 + \tfrac{1}{3}(0.00)^2 + \tfrac{1}{3}(-0.20)^2 = 0.0267.
\end{aligned}
$$

The square root of the variance is called the *standard deviation.* In this example, the standard deviation equals 0.1634.

Dispersion measures of risk such as variance and standard deviation have failed to satisfy everyone. "Surely riskiness is not related to variance itself," the critics say. "If the dispersion results from happy surprises—that is, from outcomes turning out better than expected—no investors in their right minds would call that risk."

It is, of course, quite true that only the possibility of downward disappointments constitutes risk. Nevertheless, as a practical matter, as long as the distribution of returns is symmetric—that is, as long as the chances of extraordinary gain are roughly the same as the probabilities for disappointing returns and losses—a dispersion or variance measure will suffice as a risk measure. The greater the dispersion or variance, the greater the possibilities for disappointment.

While the pattern of historical returns from individual securities has not usually been symmetric, the returns from well-diversified portfolios of stocks do seem to be distributed approximately symmetrically. The following chart shows a twenty-five-year distribution of monthly security returns for a portfolio consisting of equal dollar amounts invested in 100 stocks. It was constructed by dividing the range of returns into equal intervals (of approximately 1¼ percent) and then noting the frequency (the number of months) with which the returns fell within each interval. On average, the portfolio returned about 0.9 percent per month or 10.7 percent per year. In periods when the market declined sharply, however, the portfolio also plunged, losing as much as 13 percent in a single month.

For symmetric distributions such as this one, a helpful rule of thumb is that two-thirds of the monthly returns tend to fall within one standard deviation of the average return and 95 percent of the returns fall within two standard deviations. Recall that the average return for this distribution was just under 1 percent per month. The standard deviation (our measure of portfolio risk) turns out to be about 4½ percent per month. Thus, in two-thirds of the months the returns from this portfolio were between 5½ percent and − 3⅓ percent, and 95 percent of the returns were between 10 percent and −8 percent. Obviously, the higher the standard deviation (the more spread out are the returns), the more probable it is (the greater the risk) that at least in some periods you will take a real bath in the market. That's why a measure of variability such as standard deviation* is so often used and justified as an indication of risk.

---

*Standard deviation and its square, the variance, are used interchangeably as risk measures. They both do the same thing and it's purely a matter of convenience which one we use.

Distribution of Monthly Returns for a 100-Security Portfolio, January 1945–June 1970

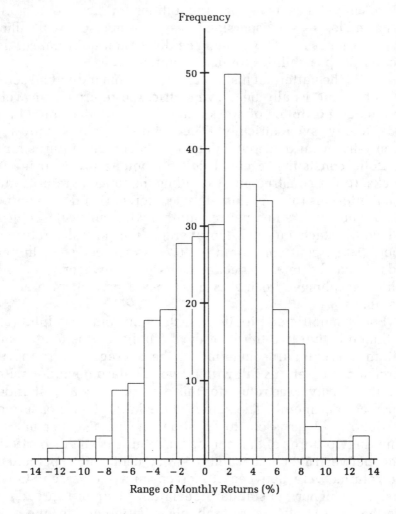

Source: Modigliani and Pogue, "An Introduction to Risk and Return," *Financial Analysts Journal,* March–April 1974.

Documenting Risk: A Long-Run Study

One of the best-documented propositions in the field of finance is that, on average, investors have received higher rates of return for bearing greater risk. The most thorough study has been done by Roger Ibbotson and Rex Sinquefield. Their data cover the period 1926 through 1994. The results are shown in the following table. Appearances notwithstanding, the table was not designed to show one Manhattan skyline and a series of Eiffel Towers. What Ibbotson and Sinquefield did was to take several different investment forms—stocks, bonds, and Treasury bills—as well as the consumer price index, and measure the percentage increase or decrease each year for each item. A rectangle was then erected on the baseline to indicate the number of years the returns fell between 0 and 5 percent; another rectangle indicated the number of years the returns fell between 5 and 10 percent; and so on, for both positive and negative returns. The result is a chart which shows the dispersion of returns and from which the standard deviation can be calculated.

A quick glance shows that over long periods of time, common stocks have, on average, provided relatively generous total rates of return. These returns, including dividends and capital gains, have exceeded by a substantial margin the returns from long-term corporate bonds. The stock returns have also tended to be well in excess of the inflation rate as measured by the annual rate of increase in consumer prices. Thus, stocks have also tended to provide positive "real" rates of return, that is, returns after washing out the effects of inflation.* The data show, however, that common-stock returns are highly variable, as indicated by the standard deviation and the range of annual returns, shown in adjacent columns of the table. Returns from equities have ranged from a gain of over 50 percent (in 1933) to a loss of almost the same magnitude (in 1931). Clearly, the extra returns that have been available to investors from stocks have come at the expense of assuming considerably higher risk. Note that small company stocks have provided an even higher rate of return since 1926 but the dispersion (standard deviation) of those returns has been even larger than

*Similar returns have been earned over even longer periods than those documented by Ibbotson and Sinquefield. For example, from 1871 to 1995 U.S. common stocks have provided an average annual rate of return of 8.8 percent. The average inflation rate was only 2.3 percent over that same 125-year period.

Selected Performance Statistics, 1926–94

Series	Annual (Geometric) Mean Rate of Return	Number of Years Returns Are Positive	Number of Years Returns Are Negative	Highest Annual Return (and Year)	Lowest Annual Return (and Year)	Standard Deviation of Annual Returns	Distribution
Common stocks	10.2%	49	20	54.0% (1933)	−43.3% (1931)	20.3%	
Small company stocks	12.2	48	21	142.9 (1933)	−49.8 (1931)	34.6	
Long-term corporate bonds	5.4	53	16	43.8 (1982)	−8.1 (1969)	8.4	
U.S. Treasury bills	3.7	68	1	14.7 (1981)	−0.0 (1940)	3.3	
Consumer price index	3.1	59	10	18.2 (1946)	−10.3 (1932)	4.6	

Distribution scale: −90%   0%   90%

Source: Ibbotson and Sinquefield, Stocks, Bonds, Bills, and Inflation, 1994 Yearbook.

for equities in general. Again, we see that higher returns have been associated with higher risks.

There have been several periods of five years or longer when common stocks have actually produced negative rates of return. The early 1930s were extremely poor for stock-market investors. The early 1970s also produced negative returns. The one-third decline in the broad stock-market averages during October 1987 is the most dramatic change in stock prices during a brief period since the 1930s. Still, over the long pull, investors have been rewarded with higher returns for taking on more risk. However, given the rate of return they seek, there are ways in which investors can reduce the risks they take. This brings us to the subject of modern portfolio theory, which has revolutionized the investment thinking of professionals.

Reducing Risk: Modern Portfolio Theory (MPT)

Portfolio theory begins with the premise that all investors are like my wife—they are risk-averse. They want high returns and guaranteed outcomes. The theory tells investors how to combine stocks in their portfolios to give them the least risk possible, consistent with the return they seek. It also gives a rigorous mathematical justification for the time-honored investment maxim that diversification is a sensible strategy for individuals who like to reduce their risks.

The theory was invented in the 1950s by Harry Markowitz and, for his contribution, he was awarded the Nobel Prize in Economics in 1990. His book, *Portfolio Selection,* was an outgrowth of his Ph.D. dissertation at the University of Chicago. Markowitz is a scholarly academic "computenick" type with a most varied background. His experience has ranged from teaching at UCLA to designing a computer language at RAND Corporation and helping General Electric solve manufacturing problems by computer simulations. He has even practiced money management, serving as president of Arbitrage Man-

agement Company, which ran a "hedge fund."* What Markowitz discovered was that portfolios of risky (volatile) stocks
might be put together in such a way that the portfolio as a
whole would actually be less risky than any one of the individual stocks in it.

The mathematics of modern portfolio theory (also known as
MPT) is recondite and forbidding; it fills the journals and, incidentally, keeps a lot of academics busy. That in itself is no
small accomplishment. Fortunately, there is no need to lead
you through the labyrinth of quadratic programming for you to
understand the core of the theory. A single illustration will
make the whole game clear.

Let's suppose we have an island economy with only two
businesses. The first is a large resort with beaches, tennis
courts, a golf course, and the like. The second is a manufacturer
of umbrellas. Weather affects the fortunes of both. During
sunny seasons, the resort does a booming business and umbrella sales plummet. During rainy seasons, the resort owner
does very poorly, while the umbrella manufacturer enjoys high
sales and large profits. The following table shows some hypothetical returns for the two businesses during the different seasons:

	Umbrella Manufacturer	Resort Owner
Rainy season	50%	−25%
Sunny season	−25%	50%

Suppose that, on average, one-half the seasons are sunny
and one-half are rainy (i.e., the probability of a sunny or rainy
season is ½). An investor who bought stock in the umbrella
manufacturer would find that half the time he earned a 50 percent return and half the time he lost 25 percent of his invest-

---

*Basically, what Markowitz did was to search with the computer for situations
where a convertible bond sold at a price that was "out of line" with the underlying
common stock. He admitted, however, that it was "no great trick" and that competitors
would be joining him in increasing numbers. "Then when we start tripping over each
other, buying the same bonds almost simultaneously, the game will be over. Two, three
years at most." I spoke to Harry three years later, and he admitted that convertible
hedges were no longer attractive in the market. Consequently, he had moved on to do
hedging operations on the Chicago Board Options Exchange.

ment. On average, he would earn a return of 12½ percent. This is what we have called the investor's *expected return*. Similarly, investment in the resort would produce the same results. Investing in either one of these businesses would be fairly risky, however, because the results are quite variable and there could be several sunny or rainy seasons in a row.

Suppose, however, that instead of buying only one security, an investor with two dollars diversified and put half his money in the umbrella manufacturer's and half in the resort owner's business. In sunny seasons, a one-dollar investment in the resort would produce a 50-cent return, while a one-dollar investment in the umbrella manufacturer would lose 25 cents. The investor's total return would be 25 cents (50 cents minus 25 cents), which is 12½ percent of his total investment of two dollars.

Note that during rainy seasons, exactly the same thing happens—only the names are changed. Investment in the umbrella manufacturer produces a good 50 percent return while the investment in the resort loses 25 percent. Again, however, the diversified investor makes a 12½ percent return on his total investment.

This simple illustration points out the basic advantage of diversification. Whatever happens to the weather, and thus to the island economy, by diversifying investments over both of the firms an investor is sure of making a 12½ percent return each year. The trick that made the game work was that while both companies were risky (returns were variable from year to year), the companies were affected differently by weather conditions. (In statistical terms, the two companies had a negative covariance.*) As long as there is some lack of parallelism in the

*Statisticians use the term *covariance* to measure what I have called the degree of parallelism between the returns of the two securities. If we let R stand for the actual return from the resort and $\overline{R}$ be the expected or average return, while U stands for the actual return from the umbrella manufacturer and $\overline{U}$ is the average return, we define the covariance between U and R (or COV_{UR}) as follows:

$$COV_{UR} = \text{Prob. rain } (U, \text{ if rain} - \overline{U}) (R, \text{ if rain} - \overline{R}) + \text{Prob. sun } (U, \text{ if sun} - \overline{U}) (R, \text{ if sun} - \overline{R}).$$

From the preceding table of returns and assumed probabilities, we can fill in the relevant numbers:

fortunes of the individual companies in the economy, diversification will always reduce risk. In the present case, where
there is a perfect negative relationship between the companies'
fortunes (one always does well when the other does poorly),
diversification can totally eliminate risk.

Of course, there is always a rub, and the rub in this case is
that the fortunes of most companies move pretty much in tandem. When there is a recession and people are unemployed,
they may buy neither summer vacations nor umbrellas. Therefore, one should not expect in practice to get the neat kind of
total risk elimination just shown. Nevertheless, since company
fortunes don't always move completely in parallel, investment
in a diversified portfolio of stocks is likely to be less risky than
investment in one or two single securities.

It is easy to carry the lessons of this illustration to actual
portfolio construction. Suppose you were considering combining General Motors and its major supplier of new tires in a
stock portfolio. Would diversification be likely to give you
much risk reduction? Probably not. It may not be true that "as
General Motors goes, so goes the nation" but it surely does
follow that if General Motors' sales slump, GM will be buying
fewer new tires from the tire manufacturer. In general, diversification will not help much if there is a high covariance between the returns of the two companies.

On the other hand, if General Motors were combined with a
government contractor in a depressed area, diversification
might reduce risk substantially. It usually has been true that as
the nation goes, so goes General Motors. If consumer spending
is down (or if an oil crisis comes close to paralyzing the nation),
General Motors' sales and earnings are likely to be down and
the nation's level of unemployment up. Now, if the government
makes a habit during times of high unemployment of giving out

---

$$COV_{UR} = \frac{1}{2}(0.50-0.125)\,(-0.25-0.125) + \frac{1}{2}(-0.25-0.125)\,(0.50-0.125)$$
$$= -0.141.$$

Whenever the returns from two securities move in tandem (when one goes up the other
always goes up), the covariance number will be a large positive number. If the returns
are completely out of phase, as in the present example, the two securities are said to
have negative covariance.

contracts to the depressed area (to alleviate some of the unemployment miseries there) it could well be that the returns of General Motors and those of the contractor do not move in phase. The two stocks might have very little covariance or, better still, negative covariance.

The example may seem a bit strained, and most investors will realize that when the market gets clobbered just about all stocks go down. Still, at least at certain times, some stocks do move against the market. Gold stocks are often given as an example of securities that do not typically move in the same direction as the general market. The point to realize in setting up a portfolio is that while the variability (variance) of the returns from individual stocks is important, even more important in judging the risk of a portfolio is covariance, the extent to which the securities move in parallel. It is this covariance that plays the critical role in Markowitz's portfolio theory.

True diversification depends on having stocks in your portfolio that are not all dependent on the same economic variables (consumer spending, business investment, housing construction, etc.). Wise investors will diversify their portfolios not by names or industries but by the determinants that influence the fluctuations of various securities.

The following chart illustrates the theory quite nicely. Looking first at the top line of the figure, marked "U.S. Stocks," we see that as the number of securities in the portfolio increases, the total portfolio risk is reduced. By the time the portfolio contains close to 20 equal-sized and well-diversified issues, the total risk (standard deviation of returns) of the portfolio is reduced by about 70 percent. Further increase in the number of holdings does not produce any significant further risk reduction. Of course, we are assuming that the stocks in the portfolio are widely diversified. Clearly, 20 oil stocks or 20 electric utilities would not produce an equivalent amount of risk reduction.

Having learned the twin lessons that diversification reduces risk and that diversification is most helpful if one can find securities that don't move in tandem with the general market, investors in the 1980s and 1990s have sought to apply these principles on the international scene. Since the movement of foreign economies is not always synchronous with that of the

The Benefits of Diversification

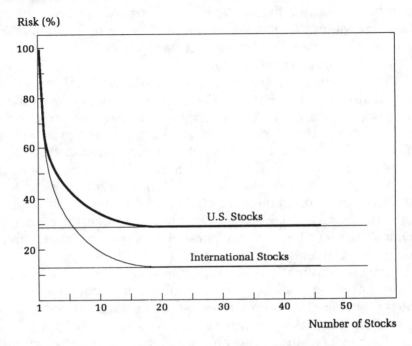

Source: Solnik, "The International Pricing of Risk," *Journal of Finance*, May 1974.

U.S. economy, we should expect some additional benefits from including foreign companies in the portfolio. The potential benefits of international diversification are illustrated in the bottom line of the figure. Here, the stocks are drawn not simply from the U.S. stock market but also from the United Kingdom, France, Germany, Italy, Belgium, the Netherlands, and Switzerland. As expected, the international diversified portfolio tends to be less risky than the one of corresponding size drawn purely from stocks directly traded on the NYSE. Even further benefits would be achieved by including securities from the Pacific Rim countries, such as Japan and Australia, and greater benefits still would be captured by also including investments in various "emerging markets" such as those in the Far East and Latin America.

Modeling Risk: The Capital-Asset Pricing Model (CAPM)

Portfolio theory has important implications for how stocks are actually valued. If investors seek to reduce risk in anything like the manner Harry Markowitz described, the stock market will tend to reflect these risk-reducing activities. This brings us to what is called the "capital-asset pricing model," a creation devised by Stanford professor William Sharpe, the late Harvard professor John Lintner, and Fischer Black. Sharpe received a Nobel Prize for his contribution at the same time Markowitz was honored in 1990.

I've mentioned that the reason diversification cannot usually produce the miracle of risk elimination, as it did in my mythical island economy, is that usually stocks tend to move up and down together. Still, diversification is worthwhile—it can eliminate some risks. What Sharpe and others did was to focus directly on what part of a security's risk can be eliminated by diversification and what part can't.

Can you imagine any stockbroker saying, ' We can reasonably describe the total risk in any security (or portfolio) as the total variability (variance or standard deviation) of the returns from the security"? He'd probably scare away the few individual customers who are left. But we who teach are under no such constraints, and we say such things often. We go on to say that part of total risk or variability may be called the security's *systematic risk* and that this arises from the basic variability of stock prices in general and the tendency for all stocks to go along with the general market, at least to some extent. The remaining variability in a stock's returns is called *unsystematic risk* and results from factors peculiar to that particular company; for example, a strike, the discovery of a new product, and so on.

Systematic risk, also called market risk, captures the reaction of individual stocks (or portfolios) to general market swings. Some stocks and portfolios tend to be very sensitive to market movements. Others are more stable. This relative volatility or sensitivity to market moves can be estimated on the basis of the past record, and is popularly known by the Greek letter beta.

You are now about to learn all you ever wanted to know about beta but were afraid to ask. Basically, beta is the numerical description of systematic risk. Despite the mathematical manipulations involved, the basic idea behind the beta measurement is one of putting some precise numbers on the subjective feelings money managers have had for years. The beta calculation is essentially a comparison between the movements of an individual stock (or portfolio) and the movements of the market as a whole.

The calculation begins by assigning a beta of 1 to a broad market index, such as the NYSE index or the S&P 500. If a stock has a beta of 2, then on average it swings twice as far as the market. If the market goes up 10 percent, the stock tends to rise 20 percent. If a stock has a beta of 0.5, it tends to be more stable than the market (it will go up or down 5 percent when the market rises or declines 10 percent). Professionals often call high-beta stocks aggressive investments and label low-beta stocks as defensive.

Now the important thing to realize is that *systematic risk cannot be eliminated by diversification.* It is precisely because all stocks move more or less in tandem (a large share of their variability is systematic) that even diversified stock portfolios are risky. Indeed, if you diversified perfectly by buying a share in the S&P index (which by definition has a beta of 1) you would still have quite variable (risky) returns because the market as a whole fluctuates widely.

Unsystematic risk is the variability in stock prices (and therefore, in returns from stocks) that results from factors peculiar to an individual company. Receipt of a large new contract, the finding of mineral resources on the company's property, labor difficulties, the discovery that the corporation's treasurer has had his hand in the company till—all can make a stock's price move independently of the market. The risk associated with such variability is precisely the kind that diversification can reduce. The whole point of portfolio theory is that, to the extent that stocks don't move in tandem all the time, variations in the returns from any one security will tend to be washed away or smoothed out by complementary variation in the returns from other securities.

The following chart, similar to the one on page 240, illustrates the important relationship between diversification and total risk. Suppose we randomly select securities for our portfolio that tend on average to be just as volatile as the market (the average betas for the securities in our portfolio will always be equal to 1). The chart shows that as we add more and more securities, the total risk of our portfolio declines, especially at the start.

When 10 securities are selected for our portfolio, a good deal of the unsystematic risk is eliminated, and additional diversification yields little further risk reduction. By the time 20 well-diversified securities are in the portfolio, the unsystematic risk is substantially eliminated and our portfolio (with a beta of

How Diversification Reduces Risk

Risk of Portfolio
(Standard Deviation of Return)

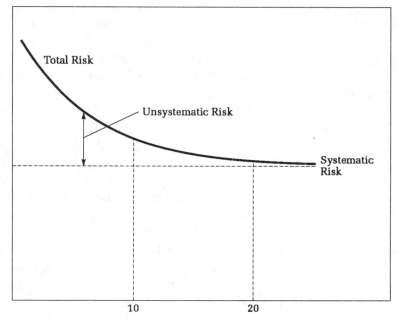

Number of Securities in Portfolio

Source: Modigliani and Pogue, *op. cit.*

1) will tend to move up and down essentially in tandem with the market. Of course, we could perform the same experiment with stocks whose average beta is 1½. Again, we would find that diversification quickly reduced unsystematic risk, but the remaining systematic risk would be larger. A portfolio of 20 or more stocks with an average beta of 1½ would tend to be 50 percent more volatile than the market.

Now comes the key step in the argument. Both financial theorists and practitioners agree that investors should be compensated for taking on more risk by a higher expected return. Stock prices must, therefore, adjust to offer higher returns where more risk is perceived, to ensure that all securities are held by someone. Obviously, risk-averse investors wouldn't buy securities with extra risk without the expectation of extra reward. But not all of the risk of individual securities is relevant in determining the premium for bearing risk. The unsystematic part of the total risk is easily eliminated by adequate diversification. So there is no reason to think that investors will be compensated with a risk premium for bearing unsystematic risk. The only part of total risk that investors will get paid for bearing is systematic risk, the risk that diversification cannot help. Thus, the capital-asset pricing model says that returns (and, therefore, risk premiums) for any stock (or portfolio) will be related to beta, the systematic risk that cannot be diversified away.

The proposition that risk and reward are related is not new. Finance specialists have agreed for years that investors do need to be compensated for taking on more risk. What is different about the new investment technology is the definition and measurement of risk. Before the advent of the capital-asset pricing model, it was believed that the return on each security was related to the total risk inherent in that security. It was believed that the return from a security varied with the instability of that security's particular performance, that is, with the variability or standard deviation of the returns it produced. The new theory says that the *total* risk of each individual security is irrelevant. It is only the systematic component of that total instability that is relevant for valuation.

While the mathematical proof of this proposition is forbidding, the logic behind it is fairly simple. Consider a case where there are two groups of securities—Group I and Group II—with 20 securities in each. Suppose that the systematic risk (beta) for each security is 1; that is, each of the securities in the two groups tends to move up and down in tandem with the general market. Now suppose that, because of factors peculiar to the individual securities in Group I, the total risk for each of them is substantially higher than the total risk for each security in Group II. Imagine, for example, that in addition to general market factors the securities in Group I are also particularly susceptible to climatic variations, to changes in exchange rates, and to natural disasters. The specific risk for each of the securities in Group I will, therefore, be very high. The specific risk for each of the securities in Group II, however, is assumed to be very low, and, hence, the total risk for each of them will be very low. Schematically, this situation appears as follows:

Group I (20 Securities)	Group II (20 Securities)
Systematic risk (beta) = 1 for each security	Systematic risk (beta) = 1 for each security
Specific risk is high for each security	Specific risk is low for each security
Total risk is high for each security	Total risk is low for each security

Now, according to the old theory, commonly accepted before the advent of the capital-asset pricing model, returns should be higher for a portfolio made up of Group I securities than for a portfolio made up of Group II securities, because each security in Group I has a higher total risk, and risk, as we know, has its reward. The advent of the new investment technology changed that sort of thinking. Under the capital-asset pricing model, returns from both portfolios should be equal. Why?

First, remember the preceding chart on page 243. (The forgetful can turn the page back to take another look.) There we saw that as the number of securities in the portfolio approached 20, the total risk of the portfolio was reduced to its systematic level. All of the unsystematic risk had been eliminated. The conscientious readers will now note that in the schematic illustration, the number of securities in each port-folio is 20. That means that the unsystematic risk has essen-tially been washed away: An unexpected weather calamity is balanced by a favorable exchange rate, and so forth. What remains is only the systematic risk of each stock in the port-folio, which is given by its beta. But in these two groups, each of the stocks has a beta of 1. Hence, a portfolio of Group I securities and a portfolio of Group II securities will perform exactly the same with respect to risk (standard deviation) even though the stocks in Group I display higher total risk than the stocks in Group II.

The old and the new views now meet head on. Under the old system of valuation, Group I securities were regarded as offering a higher return because of their greater risk. The capi-tal-asset pricing model says there is no greater risk in holding Group I securities if they are in a diversified portfolio. Indeed, if the securities of Group I did offer higher returns, then all ration-al investors would prefer them over Group II securities and would attempt to rearrange their holdings to capture the higher returns from Group I. But by this very process, they would bid up the prices of Group I securities and push down the prices of Group II securities until, with the attainment of equilibrium (when investors no longer want to switch from security to security), the portfolio for each group had identical returns, related to the systematic component of their risk (beta) rather than to their total risk (including the unsystematic or specific portions). Because stocks can be combined in portfolios to eliminate specific risk, only the undiversifiable or systematic risk will command a risk premium. Investors will not get paid for bearing risks that can be diversified away. This is the basic logic behind the capital-asset pricing model.

In a big fat nutshell, the proof of the capital-asset pricing model (henceforth to be known as CAPM because we econo-mists love to use letter abbreviations) can be stated as follows:

> If investors did get an extra return (a risk premium) for bear-ing unsystematic risk, it would turn out that diversified port-folios made up of stocks with large amounts of unsystematic risk would give larger returns than equally risky portfolios of

stocks with less unsystematic risk. Investors would snap at the chance to have these higher returns, bidding up the prices of stocks with large unsystematic risk and selling stocks with equivalent betas but lower unsystematic risk. This process would continue until the prospective returns of stocks with the same betas were equalized and no risk premium could be obtained for bearing unsystematic risk. Any other result would be inconsistent with the existence of an efficient market.

The key relationship of the theory is shown in the following chart. As the systematic risk (beta) of an individual stock (or portfolio) increases, so does the return an investor can expect. If an investor's portfolio has a beta of zero, as might be the case if all her funds were invested in a government-guaranteed bank savings certificate (beta would be zero since the returns from the certificate would not vary at all with swings in the stock market), the investor would receive some modest rate of return, which is generally called the risk-free rate of interest. As the individual takes on more risk, however, the return should increase. If the investor holds a portfolio with a beta of 1 (as, for example, holding a share in one of the broad stock-market averages) her return will equal the general return from common stocks. This return has over long periods of time exceeded the risk-free rate of interest, but the investment is a risky one. In certain periods, the return is much less than the risk-free rate and involves taking substantial losses. This, as we have said, is precisely what is meant by risk.

The diagram shows that a number of different expected returns are possible simply by adjusting the beta of the portfolio. For example, suppose the investor put half of her money in a savings certificate and half in a share of the market averages. In this case, she would receive a return midway between the risk-free return and the return from the market and his portfolio would have an average beta of 0.5.* The CAPM then asserts very simply that to get a higher average long-run rate of return you should just increase the beta of your portfolio. An investor

*In general, the beta of a portfolio is simply the weighted average of the betas of its component parts.

Risk and Return According to the Capital-Asset Pricing Model*

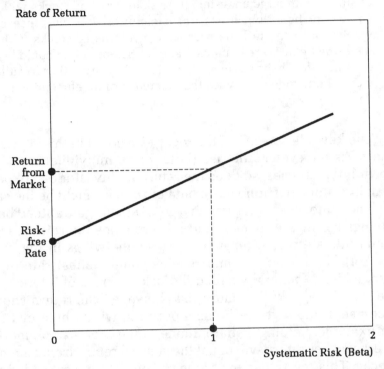

*Those who remember their high school algebra will recall that any straight line can be written as an equation. The equation for the straight line in the diagram is

Rate of Return = Risk-free Rate + Beta (Return from Market − Risk-free Rate).

Alternately, the equation can be written as an expression for the risk premium, that is, the rate of return on the portfolio or stock over and above the risk-free rate of interest:

Rate of Return − Risk-free Rate = Beta (Return from Market − Risk-free Rate).

The equation says that the risk premium you get on any stock or portfolio increases directly with the beta value you assume. Some readers may wonder what relationship beta has to the covariance concept that was so critical in our discussion of portfolio theory. The beta for any security is essentially the same thing as the covariance between that security and the market index as measured on the basis of past experience.

can get a portfolio with a beta larger than 1 either by buying high-beta stocks or by purchasing a portfolio with average volatility on margin. (See the chart and following table.) There was an actual fund proposed by a West Coast bank that would have allowed an investor to buy the S&P average on margin, thus increasing both his risk and potential reward. Of course, in times of rapidly declining stock prices, such a fund would have enabled an investor to lose his shirt in a hurry. This may explain why the fund found few customers in the 1970s.

Illustration of Portfolio Building[a]

Desired Beta	Composition of Portfolio	Expected Return from Portfolio
0	$1 in risk-free asset	10%
½	$.50 in risk-free asset $.50 in market portfolio	½ (0.10) + ½ (0.15) = 0.125, or 12½%[b]
1	$1 in market portfolio	15%
1½	$1.50 in market portfolio borrowing $.50 at an assumed rate of 10 percent	1½ (0.15) − ½ (0.10) = 0.175, or 17½%

[a] Assuming expected market return is 15 percent and risk-free rate is 10 percent.
[b] We can also derive the figure for expected return using directly the formula that accompanies the preceding chart:
$$\text{Rate of Return} = 0.10 + \tfrac{1}{2}(0.15 - 0.10) = 0.125, \text{ or } 12\tfrac{1}{2}\%.$$

Just as stocks had their fads, so beta came into high fashion by the early 1970s. The *Institutional Investor*, the glossy prestige magazine that spent most of its pages chronicling the accomplishments of professional money managers, put its imprimatur on the movement in 1971 by featuring on its cover the letters BETA on top of a temple and including as its lead story "The Beta Cult! The New Way to Measure Risk." The magazine noted that money men whose mathematics hardly went beyond long division were now "tossing betas around with the abandon of Ph.D.s in statistical theory." Even the Securities and Exchange Commission gave beta its approval as a risk measure in its *Institutional Investors Study Report.*

In Wall Street, the early beta fans boasted that they could earn higher long-run rates of return simply by buying a few high-beta stocks. Those who thought they were able to time the market thought they had an even better idea. They would buy high-beta stocks when they thought the market was going up, switching to low-beta ones when they feared the market might decline. To accommodate the enthusiasm for this new investment idea, beta measurement services proliferated among brokers, and it was a symbol of progressiveness for an investment house to provide its own beta estimates. Today, you can obtain beta estimates from brokers such as Merrill Lynch and investment advisory services such as Value Line and Morningstar. The beta boosters on the Street oversold their product with an abandon that would have shocked even the most enthusiastic academic scribblers intent on spreading the beta gospel.

10

The Current State of the Art: Beyond Beta

Everything should be made as simple as possible, but not
more so.   —Albert Einstein

In Shakespeare's *Henry IV,* Glendower boasts
to Hotspur, "I can call spirits from the vasty deep." "Why, so
can I or so can any man," says Hotspur, unimpressed; "but will
they come when you do call for them?" Anyone can theorize
about how security markets work, and the capital-asset pricing
model is just another theory. The really important question is:
Does it work?

Certainly many institutional investors have embraced the
beta concept, if only in an attempt to play down the flamboyant
excesses of the past. Beta is, after all, an academic creation.
What could be more staid? Simply created as a number that
describes a stock's risk, it appears almost sterile in nature.
True, it requires large investments in computer programs, but
the closet chartists love it. Even if you don't believe in beta, you
have to speak its language because back on the nation's cam-
puses, my colleagues and I have been producing a long line of
Ph.D.s and M.B.A.s who spout its terminology.

By the early 1980s, according to a *Wall Street Journal* article, beta had become so popular that it underlay the investment rationale for $65 billion in U.S. pension funds. Beta also
appeared to provide a method of evaluating a portfolio man-

ager's performance. If the realized return is larger than that predicted by the overall portfolio beta, the manager is said to have produced a positive alpha. Lots of money in the market sought out the manager who could deliver the largest alpha.

But is beta a useful measure of risk? Do high-beta portfolios always fall farther in bear markets than low-beta ones? Is it true that high-beta portfolios will provide larger long-term returns than lower-beta ones, as the capital-asset pricing model suggests? Do present methods of calculating beta on the basis of past history give any useful information about future betas? Does beta alone summarize a security's total systematic risk, or do we need to consider other factors as well? In short, does beta really deserve an alpha? These are subjects of intense current debate among practitioners and academics, and not all the evidence is in as yet. This chapter reviews the available evidence and discusses the current state of thinking on the new investment technology.

Batting for Beta: The Supporting Evidence

Tests of the capital-asset pricing model have tried to ascertain if security returns are in fact directly related to beta, as the theory asserts. I have already presented some data on this question in previous chapters. Here I would like to present some additional evidence.

The enthusiasm for beta and for the CAPM in which it is wrapped has been fueled by charts, such as the following, that show the relationship over a particular ten-year period between the performance of a large number of professionally managed funds and the beta measure of relative volatility. The results appear to be quite consistent with the theory. The portfolio returns have varied positively with beta in (almost) a straight-line manner, so that over the long pull, high-beta portfolios have provided larger total returns than low-risk ones.

The next two charts break down the mutual-fund performance over the 1969–1988 period into two subperiods: (1) the fifteen years when the market went up and (2) the five years when it went down. Again, the relationship is exactly as predicted by the theory. In these figures, I have used averages of

many funds with different objectives and different risk structures. In "up" years, the high-beta portfolios well outdistanced
the low-beta ones. In "down" years, however, the high-beta
portfolios did considerably worse than the low-volatility ones.

Evidence in Favor of CAPM
The Decade of the 1970s

Rate of Return (%)

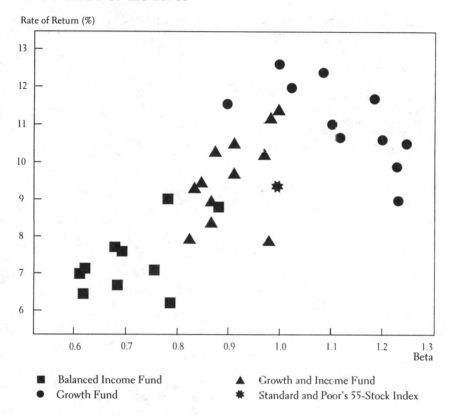

■ Balanced Income Fund   ▲ Growth and Income Fund
● Growth Fund   ✳ Standard and Poor's 55-Stock Index

It was the high-beta portfolios that took the real drubbings in
the bear-market periods of the 1970s. Of course, this is precisely what we mean by the concept of risk, and this is why
betas for diversified portfolios appear to be useful risk measures.

The possibility of obtaining higher returns over the long pull
from higher-beta portfolios is perfectly consistent with the random-walk and efficient-market notions I have discussed earlier. The efficient-market theory asserts that there is no way to

gain superior performance (that is, extra returns) *for a given level of risk.* The beta advocates say that the only way to gain extra returns is to take on more risk. But this is hardly an inefficiency in the market. It is the natural expectation in a market where most participants dislike risk and, therefore, must be compensated (rewarded) to bear it.

Average Annual Return vs. Risk: Selected Mutual Funds
(15 "Up" Years, 1969–88)

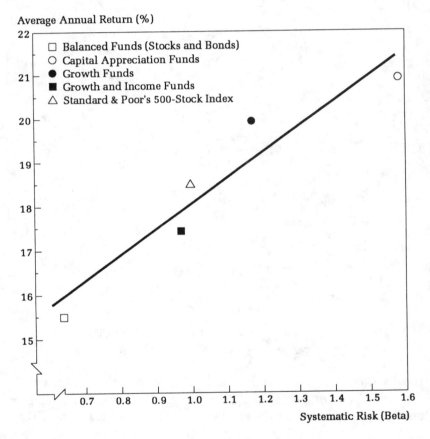

Average Annual Return (%)

Being Bearish on Beta: Some Disquieting Results

Like just about everything in life, beta may work well some of the time, but it certainly doesn't live up to its press billings

Average Annual Return vs. Risk: Selected Mutual Funds
(5 "Down" Years, 1969–88)

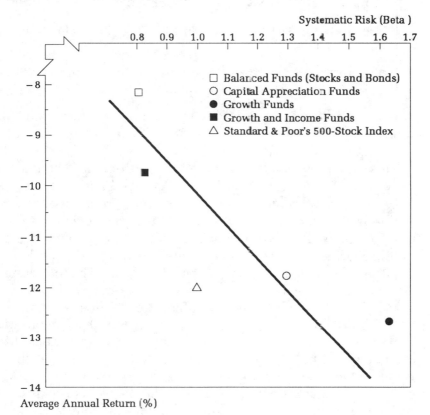

all of the time. Burrowing away at the statistical base of the capital-asset pricing model, the beta bears have uncovered major flaws. The evidence contradicting this fundamental part of the new investment technology has sent some practitioners and academics off in search of ways to improve the CAPM. And even some institutional investors who in the past swore by the model began disavowing it altogether by the late 1980s. In order to understand this reaction, we need to examine the academic studies that led to beta's fall from grace, at least in the minds of some academics and professionals.

Academic Attack 1:
Theory Does Not Measure Up to Practice

Recall that the CAPM could be reduced to a very simple formula:

Rate of Return = Risk-free Rate + Beta (Return from Market
                    —Risk-free Rate).

Thus, a security with a zero beta should give a return exactly equal to the risk-free rate. Unfortunately, the actual results don't come out that way.

This damning accusation is the finding from an exhaustive study of all the stocks on the New York Stock Exchange over a thirty-five-year period. The securities were grouped into ten portfolios of equal size, according to their beta measures for the year. Thus, Portfolio I consisted of the 10 percent of the NYSE securities with the highest betas. Portfolio II contained the 10 percent with the second-highest betas, etc. The following chart shows the relation between the average monthly return and the beta for each of the ten different portfolios (shown by the black dots on the chart) over the entire period. The market portfolio is denoted by O, and the solid line is a line of best fit (a regression line) drawn through the dots. The dashed line connects the average risk-free rate of return with the rate of return on the market portfolio. This is the theoretical relationship of the CAPM that was described in the last chapter.

If the CAPM were absolutely correct, the theoretical and the actual relationship would be one and the same. But practice, as can quickly be seen, is not represented by the same line as theory on the chart. Note particularly the difference between the rate of return on an actual zero-beta common stock or portfolio of stocks and the risk-free rate. From the chart, it is clear that the measured zero-beta rate of return exceeds the risk-free rate. Since the zero-beta portfolio and a portfolio of riskless assets such as Treasury bills have the same systematic risk (beta), this result implies that something besides a beta measure of risk is being valued in the market. It appears that some unsystematic (or at least some non-beta) risk makes the return higher for the zero-beta portfolio.

Systematic Risk (Beta) vs. Average Monthly
Return for Ten Different-Risk Portfolios,
and the Market Portfolio, for 1931–65

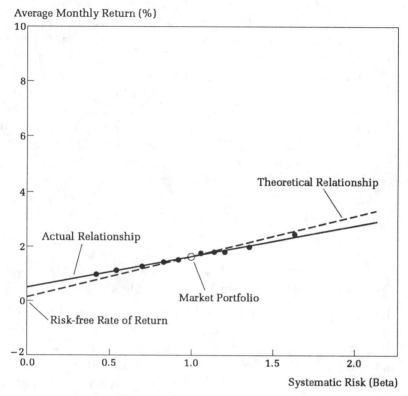

Source: Black, Jensen, and Scholes, "The Capital Asset Pricing Model: Some Empirical Tests," in *Studies in the Theory of Capital Markets,* ed. Jensen, 1972.

Furthermore, the actual risk-return relationship (examined by Black, Jensen, and Scholes) appears to be much flatter than that predicted by the CAPM; low-risk stocks earn higher returns, and high-risk stocks earn lower returns, than the theory predicts. (This is a phenomenon much like that found at the race track, where long shots seem to go off at much lower odds than their true probability of winning would indicate, whereas favorites go off at higher odds than is consistent with their winning percentages.) Shrewd old Adam Smith recognized this way back in 1776 when he wrote, "The ordinary rate of profit always rises more or less with the risk. It does not, however, seem to rise . . . so as to compensate it completely." Recently, Black has confirmed these results for the almost 70-year period from the mid-1920s through the early 1990s.

Black has suggested that practical restrictions on borrowing may explain the flatness of the systematic risk-return relationship. Margin requirements limit the amount that individuals can borrow against their securities' purchases and a variety of legal and other restrictions effectively limit many institutions from borrowing against their equity portfolios. Hence, investors who seek high risk (and, therefore, higher expected return) portfolios do not have the option of buying low-beta stocks and leveraging them by borrowing to increase both risk and return. Instead, those investors who want lots of risk will bid up the prices of high-beta stocks forcing their returns lower than would be anticipated by the capital-asset pricing model.*

Academic Attack 2: Beta Is a Fickle Short-Term Performer (and Sometimes It Fails to Work for Long Periods of Time)

The divergence of theory from evidence is even more striking in the short run: For some short periods, it may happen that risk and return are *negatively* related. In 1972, for example, which was an "up" market year, it turned out that safer (lower-beta) stocks went up *more* than the more volatile securities. *Fortune* magazine commented dryly on this well-publicized failure, "The results defied the textbooks." What happened

---

*Fischer Black has also proposed a more theoretical explanation of these discrepancies between theory and evidence by pointing out that with uncertain inflation, the future real value of any dollar return is also uncertain. Hence, what we have been calling the risk-free rate is actually a risky real rate of return. Indeed, when inflation is taken into account, a truly riskless asset does not exist. It is, therefore, not surprising that the procedure of drawing a line from some supposedly risk-free return through the market portfolio (as in the theoretical relationship depicted in the chart above) does not represent the actual relationship between returns and beta.

Black argues that the true relationship between risk and return can be described by the following equation:

Rate of Return = Zero-beta Return + Beta (Return from Market − Zero-beta Return).

He finds that the data better support this version of the CAPM. It is, however, still subject to many of the other problems that are discussed in the rest of this chapter.

was that in 1972 styles changed in Wall Street as institutional investors eschewed younger, more speculative companies, the "faded ladies" of the late 1960s, and became much more enamored of the highest-quality, most stable leading corporations in the so-called "first tier" of stocks. This was the Nifty Fifty craze chronicled in Chapter Three. It became clear that beta could not be used to guarantee investors a predictable performance over a period of a few months or even a year.

Black, Jensen, and Scholes found a similar type of anomaly for the entire period from April 1957 through December 1965. Their results are shown in the chart below. Not only does the zero-beta return exceed the riskless rate here, but during this period of nearly nine years, securities with higher risk produced *lower* returns than less-risky (lower-beta) securities. Substantial deviations from the relationship predicted by the CAPM were also found for many subperiods.

The experience of the 1980s provided even more dramatic evidence of the folly of relying on beta measures to predict

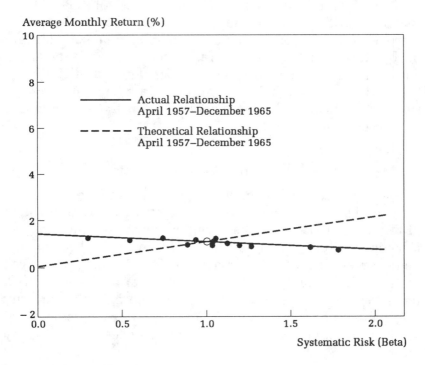

Average Monthly Return (%)

——— Actual Relationship
April 1957–December 1965

– – – – Theoretical Relationship
April 1957–December 1965

Systematic Risk (Beta)

Source: Black, Jensen, and Scholes, *op. cit.*

realized rates of return. It turned out that for the entire decade
of the 1980s realized mutual-fund returns bore no relationship
to their beta measures of risk.

The following chart shows the relationship between mutual-fund returns during the 1981–1991 period and the beta
measures of systematic risk. In this chart, I have categorized
271 funds into ten baskets, the 27 funds with the lowest betas,
the 27 funds with the second lowest betas, and so on, and I
have plotted the average quarterly return for each beta decile.
Note that there is no positive relationship between the beta
risk measures and the mutual-fund returns. (The correlation
coefficient between betas and returns for the 1980s is essentially zero.) There is even a tendency for the highest-beta portfolios to earn a lower rate of return. Thus, investors who
thought they could use the capital-asset pricing model to fashion higher-risk portfolios of mutual funds in order to achieve
higher rates of return during the 1980s were sadly disappointed.

If we maintain that beta summarizes the total systematic
risk of securities, we must accept three uncomfortable conclusions: (1) In some periods, investors may be penalized for taking on more risk; (2) in the long run, investors are not rewarded
enough for high risk and are overcompensated for buying securities with low risk; and (3) in all periods, some unsystematic
risk is being valued by the market. Any of these results is a
serious contradiction of the CAPM.

Academic Attack 3: Estimated Betas Are Unstable

Another problem the theory encounters is the instability of
measured betas. One might well be skeptical about the wisdom
of relying on beta estimates based on historical data. Beta really looks suspiciously like a tool of technical analysis in academic dress—a bastard cousin of the technicians' charts. And
as far as individual securities go, historical betas—used as a
basis for predicting future betas and, hence, expected security
returns—do not seem to be much more reliable as predictors of
security performance than any of the devices cooked up by
technical analysts.

Average Quarterly Returns vs Beta: 271 Mutual Funds 1981–1991

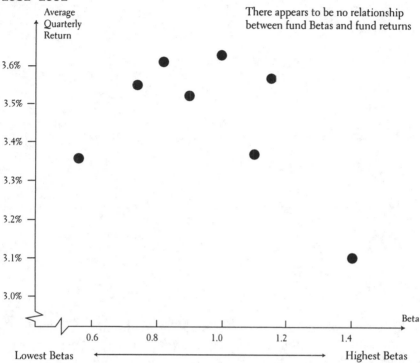

In order to see how beta familiarity breeds contempt, we should know how beta is bred in the first place. The typical procedure in estimating betas for an individual stock is to measure the relationship between the security's past return and the return from the market as a whole. For example, suppose that in the last quarter AT&T's total return (including both dividends and capital gains) was 5 percent and the market return (similarly measured) was 10 percent. We plot this pair of returns on a graph, as is done on the following page.

We can continue the process by measuring the rate of return for AT&T and for the S&P 500 (our proxy for the market) in many other past three-month periods, and we can plot these observations on the same graph. After many pairs of returns for AT&T and for the market have been plotted, a line of best fit (a regression line) is drawn to represent the average relation-

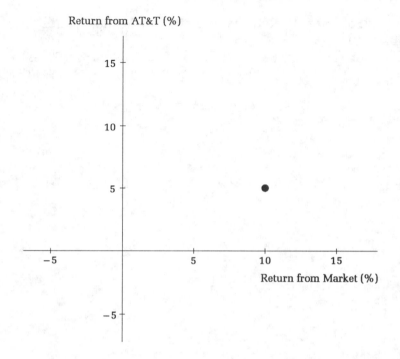

Return from AT&T (%)

ship between the returns from AT&T and those from the S&P 500.* The slope of the regression line (i.e., the ratio between the vertical and horizontal sides of a right triangle having the regression line as its hypotenuse) is our measure of the security's historical beta. This historical beta is then used as an estimate of the security's future beta. In this example, we get a beta estimate for AT&T of ½, or 0.5, as shown in the chart on page 263. This means that AT&T has been about half as volatile as the overall market, and the assumption is that it will continue to be so in the future. It is clear why this last assertion may be wrong. After the divestiture of 1983 and with deregulation of the telecommunications industry, AT&T is not the same company as it previously was. Even without such major changes affecting the characteristics of the company's stock, some unforeseen event(s), not reflected in past returns, may decisively affect the security's future returns.

*The regression line is also called a "least-squares" line, since it is estimated by finding the line that minimizes the sum of the squared vertical distances from each of the black dots to the line.

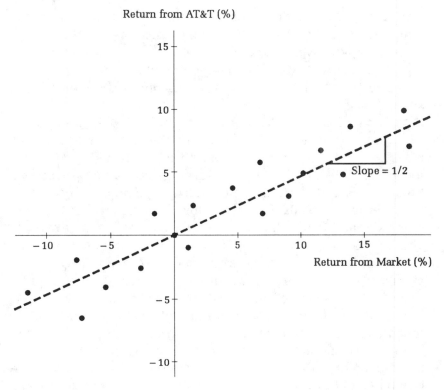

To illustrate this hazard in measuring an individual stock's beta, consider the following example: During some periods in the 1960s, Mead Johnson and Company (now part of Bristol-Myers Company) had a measured beta that was negative; it tended to move against the market and thus appeared to be precisely the kind of stock investors would seek to reduce the risks of their portfolio. But looking behind the reasons for this measured beta's being less than zero did not give one very much comfort that the beta for the future—which is after all what is really relevant—would turn out to be anything like the beta from the past.

What happened in the Mead Johnson case was that in 1962 the company came out with a marvelous new product that became an instant best-seller. The product, called "Metrecal," was a liquid dietary supplement. Consumers were urged to have a can of Metrecal rather than their normal lunch. Metrecal would provide all the vitamins and nutrients needed for health with few of the calories that usually went along with lunch. And so, in 1962, as Americans became more diet-conscious, drinking Metrecal became quite a fad, and the earnings and stock price of Mead Johnson climbed sharply at precisely the time the stock market was taking one of its worst baths since the Great Depression.

Like most fads, the Metrecal boom did not last very long; by 1963 and 1964, just when the general stock market was recovering, Americans got pretty sick and tired of drinking Metrecal for lunch, and the big boost in earnings and stock prices that Mead Johnson had earlier enjoyed began to fade away.

Later in the 1960s, just about the time the market took another slump, Mead Johnson came out with another new product. This one was called "Nutrament." Nutrament was a dietary supplement that was supposed to put on weight, and skinny teenagers bought it by the case to improve their appearance. Yes, you guessed it! Nutrament was the same product as Metrecal except that if you drank Nutrament *in addition* to lunch you could put on weight, rather than lose it. Again, Mead Johnson prospered while the market slumped, and it is this unusual combination of circumstances that produced the negative betas of the period.

The problem is, of course, whether such a fortuitous string of events could reasonably be anticipated to occur in the future. On *a priori* grounds we would expect not. Indeed, what was in fact measured was anything but a systematic relationship with the market. Of course, this is precisely the problem in predicting betas on the basis of past experience. Any changes in the economy, in the characteristics of an individual company, or in the competitive situation facing the company can be expected to change the sensitivity of the company's stock to market fluctuations. It would be surprising to discover that betas of individual stocks did not vary widely over time. In fact, they do vary. The Mead Johnson example is not just an isolated case, the exception that tests the rule.

Marshall Blume, a professor at the Wharton School of Finance, conducted several tests of the stability of historical beta estimates. He found that the smaller the number of securities in the portfolio, the weaker the relationship between portfolio betas for consecutive periods. For a portfolio of one security, the beta calculated from an earlier period is a very poor predictor of the beta in the following period: Past betas are not useful predictors of future betas for individual stocks. Not surprisingly, however, better predictive power is obtained from betas calculated for portfolios containing larger numbers of stocks. Thanks to the law of large numbers, a number of inaccurate beta estimates on individual stocks can be combined to form a much more accurate estimate of the risk of the portfolio as a whole. While the beta estimates for some securities will be much too high, the estimates for many others will be too low.

Mutual-fund betas are not quite as easy to predict from period to period as are betas for unmanaged portfolios because fund managers will often deliberately change the risk composition of the portfolio. Still, the general investment objective of the fund (e.g., growth, stability, etc.) does put a limit on the degree of change possible, and mutual-fund betas also tend to be far more stable from period to period than are the betas for individual stocks. Nevertheless, the general conclusion that should be drawn from this discussion is that historical betas may be quite imperfect indicators of future betas. The people who oversold beta as a useful tool in predicting the behavior of individual stocks did the new investment technology a great disservice. In judging risk, beta cannot substitute for brains.

Many beta boomers, however, have gone to great lengths to legitimize their technical bastard. One of the most celebrated of these is Barr Rosenberg, a former professor at Berkeley, whose new investment technology work and California lifestyle were celebrated in a cover story in *Institutional Investor* during the late 1970s. What Rosenberg did was to come up with a better beta mousetrap. Instead of calculating betas from past history, Rosenberg calculates what he calls "fundamental betas" based on the fundamental characteristics of each company, such as its earnings history, relative size, financial structure, and so forth. (Think of Amdahl, a *relatively* small computer-manufacturing company in an increasingly competitive cyclical industry. No wonder the stock is so volatile.) These risk estimates became known as "Barr's bionic betas."

An academic turned entrepreneur, Rosenberg formed his

own firm, Barr Rosenberg and Associates (or just BARRA, as the name appears on the official company T-shirt). Along with his reputation as the guru of the new investment technology, Barr presented the perfect image. He was into Zen, attended Esalen, and intoned a Sanskrit chant before dinner. He believed in telepathy and clairvoyance. Each year he spent three months on the Hawaiian island of Kauai for work and meditation. Although quiet and unassuming, he projected a kind of authority and omniscience. While the pros have not all jumped to embrace Rosenberg's techniques, he won several converts among the cadre of institutional investors. Unfortunately, however, Rosenberg's betas are still based on historical accounting information and thus are still subject to the same kinds of instability problems as are conventional betas.

Academic Attack 4: Beta Is Easily Rolled Over

Perhaps the most devastating criticism of beta has been delivered by Richard Roll. Like Rosenberg, he is a financial theorist from California. He is also a businessman, managing over a billion dollars of investment funds. The resemblance ends there. The personalities of the two men clash. Barr is a guru, while *Institutional Investor* has characterized Richard Roll as "ebullient and 'laid back'—teaching his UCLA course in jeans and a shirt open to the waist . . .—with a taste for fast motorcycles and (aggressive) skiing." And their theories clash, too. Roll has focused his attack on the CAPM, the model Rosenberg has painstakingly defended.

Roll says that it is impossible to observe the market's return. Because, in principle, the market includes *all* stocks, a variety of other financial instruments, and even nonmarketable assets such as an individual's investment in education, the S&P index (or any other index used to represent the market) is a very imperfect market proxy at best. And when we measure market risk using an imperfect proxy, we may obtain a quite imperfect estimate of market sensitivity. Roll showed that by changing the market index against which betas are measured, one can obtain quite different measures of the risk levels of individual stocks or portfolios. As a consequence, one would make very different predictions about the expected returns from the stocks or portfolios. He further demonstrated that by changing market indexes (from, say, the S&P 500 to the much broader Wilshire 5,000) one could actually reverse the risk-adjusted performance rankings (alphas) of fund managers. But if betas differ according to the market proxy that they are measured against, and if you never can get a measure of the "true" market portfolio, then, in effect, the CAPM has not been (and cannot be) adequately tested.

Academic Attack 5: Has Beta Ever Been a Reliable Predictor of Future Returns?

What has widely been interpreted as the final nail in the beta coffin was delivered in the early 1990s by Eugene Fama and Kenneth French. The two financial economists studied an entire period of almost 40 years from the early 1960s into the 1990s. They looked at all nonfinancial corporation shares traded on the New York, American, and NASDAQ exchanges and grouped stocks into ten portfolios based on their beta levels (as well as groupings based on other characteristics). The returns of the ten portfolios and their associated average beta levels are shown in the figure on the next page.

The figure does show that while the lowest-beta stocks have relatively low rates of return, those with the second lowest-beta level beat out the return for the portfolio made up of the highest-beta stocks. Since their comprehensive study covered a period of almost 40 years, Fama and French concluded that the relationship between beta and return is essentially flat. Beta, the key analytical tool of the capital-asset pricing model, is not a useful measure to capture the relationship between risk and return. Fama and French find instead that the structure of returns is effectively predicted by price-book value (P/BV) ratios (the lower the price relative to the stock's book value, the higher the subsequent return) and size (smaller stocks outperformed larger ones over the period studied). They interpret the P/BV and size variables as proxies for risk. These were two of the "predictable patterns" we discussed earlier in Chapter Eight. And so, by the mid-1990s, not only practitioners but even

Average Monthly Return vs Beta: 1963–1990

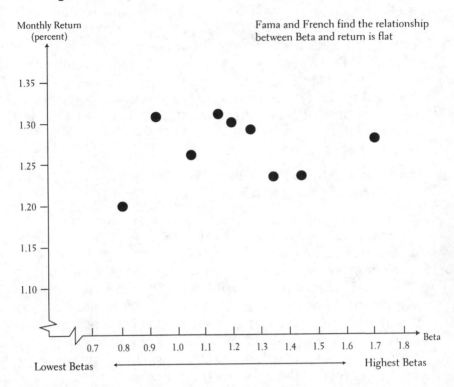

Monthly Return
(percent)

Fama and French find the relationship
between Beta and return is flat

Lowest Betas   Highest Betas

many academics as well, were ready to assign beta to the scrap heap. The financial press, which earlier had chronicled the ascendancy of beta, now ran feature stories with titles such as "The Death of Beta," "Bye, Bye Beta," and "Beta Beaten." The *Institutional Investor* quoted a letter the magazine had just received from a writer known only as "Deep Quant."* The letter began, "There is a very big story breaking in money management. The Capital-Asset Pricing Model is dead." The magazine went on to quote one "turncoat quant" as follows: ". . . advanced mathematics will become to investors what the *Titanic* was to sailing," and so the whole set of tools making up the new investment technology—including even modern portfolio theory (MPT)—came under a cloud of suspicion.

*"Quant" is the Wall Street nickname for the quantitatively inclined financial analyst who devotes attention largely to the new investment technology.

"Does it bother you at all that when you say MPT quickly it comes out 'empty'?"

Source: *Pensions and Investments,* September 15, 1980.

An Appraisal of the Evidence

My own guess is that the "turncoat quant" is wrong. The unearthing of serious cracks in the CAPM will not lead to an abandonment of mathematical tools in financial analysis and a return to traditional security analysis. The evidence that supports the efficiency of capital markets and the existence of long-run relationships between measures of risk and return is far too abundant for anyone to reject the new investment technology out of hand. Moreover, I am not quite ready to write an obituary for beta at this time. There are many reasons, I believe, to avoid a rush to judgment.

First, it is important to remember that stable returns are preferable, that is, less risky, than very volatile returns. Clearly, if one could earn only the same rate of return drilling for oil as could be obtained from a riskless government security, only those who loved gambling for gambling's sake alone would drill for oil. If investors really did not worry at all about volatility, the multi-trillion dollar derivative-securities markets would not be thriving as they are. Thus, the beta measure of

relative volatility does capture at least some aspects of what
we normally think of as risk. And portfolio betas from the past
do a reasonably good job of predicting relative volatility in the
future.

Secondly, we must keep in mind the Roll criticism that it is
very difficult (indeed probably impossible) to measure beta
with any degree of precision. The Standard and Poor's 500-
Stock Index is not "the market." The total stock market contains many thousands of additional stocks in the United States
and thousands more in foreign countries. Moreover, the total
market includes bonds, real estate, precious metals, and other
commodities and assets of all sorts including one of the most
important assets any of us has—the human capital built up by
education, work, and life experiences. Depending on exactly
how you measure the "market," you can obtain very different
beta values. One's conclusions about the capital-asset pricing
model and the usefulness of beta as a measure of risk depend
very much on how you measure beta. Two economists from the
University of Minnesota, Ravi Jagannathan and Zhenyu Wang,
find that when the market index (against which we measure
beta) is redefined to include human capital and when betas are
allowed to vary with cyclical fluctuations in the economy, the
support for the CAPM and beta as a predictor of returns is quite
strong. Their conclusion makes up the title of their mid-1990s
article, "Beta is Alive and Well." One might argue that their
procedures for measuring beta are somewhat *ad hoc,* and we
probably should not be carried away by one study that does
confirm the predicted relationship between risk and return, but
neither should we conclude that beta is necessarily dead.

Finally, investors should be aware that even if the long-run
relationship between beta and return is flat, beta can still be a
useful investment management tool. Were it in fact the case
that low-beta stocks will *dependably* earn rates of return at
least as large as high-beta stocks (a very big "if" indeed), then
beta as an investment tool is even more valuable than it would
be if the capital-asset pricing model held. Investors should
scoop up *low-*beta stocks and earn returns as attractive as for
the market as a whole but with much less risk. And investors
who do wish to seek higher returns by assuming greater risk
should buy and hold low-beta stocks on margin, thereby in-

creasing their risk and returns. Moreover, beta may be a useful risk measure during sharp market swings. High-beta stocks did decline more sharply than low-beta ones during the sharp market sell-off of October 1987. Moreover, high-beta stocks did tend to fall more than low-beta stocks during all of the bear market periods within the 38-year sample period studied by Fama and French. What is clear, however, is that beta, as it is usually measured, cannot be relied upon as a simple predictor of long-run future returns. Nevertheless, reports of beta's total demise are, in my judgment, premature.

The Quant Quest for Better Measures of Risk: Arbitrage Pricing Theory

If beta is badly damaged as an effective quantitative measure of risk, is there anything to take its place? One of the pioneers in the field of risk measurement is the Yale School of Management's, Stephen Ross. Ross has developed a new theory of pricing in the capital markets called "APT," or arbitrage pricing theory. APT has had wide influence both in the academic community and in the practical world cf portfolio management. To understand the logic of the newest APT work on risk measurement, one must remember the correct insight underlying the CAPM: The only risk that investors should be compensated for bearing is the risk that cannot be diversified away. Only systematic risk will command a risk premium in the market. But the systematic elements of risk in particular stocks and portfolios may be too complicated to be capturable by a measure of beta—the tendency of the stocks to move more or less than the market. This is especially so since any particular stock index is a very imperfect representative of the general market. Hence, many quants now feel that beta fails to capture a number of important systematic elements of risk.

Let's take a look at several of these other systematic risk elements. Changes in national income, for one, may affect returns from individual stocks in a systematic way. This was shown in our illustration of a simple island economy, in the preceding chapter. Also, changes in national income mirror changes in the personal income of individuals, and the systematic relationship between security returns and salary income

can be expected to have a significant effect on individual behavior. For example, the laborer in a GM plant will find a holding of GM common stock particularly risky, since job layoffs
and poor returns from GM stock are likely to occur at the same
time. Changes in national income may also reflect changes in
other forms of property income and may, therefore, be relevant
for institutional portfolio managers as well.

Changes in interest rates also systematically affect the returns from individual stocks and are important nondiversifia-
ble risk elements. To the extent that stocks tend to suffer as
interest rates go up, equities are a risky investment, and those
stocks that are particularly vulnerable to increases in the general level of interest rates are especially risky. Thus, many
stocks and fixed-income investments will tend to move in parallel, and these stocks will not be helpful in reducing the risk of
a bond portfolio. Since fixed-income securities are a major part
of the portfolios of many institutional investors, this systematic
risk factor is particularly important for some of the largest
investors in the market. Clearly, then, investors who think of
risk in its broadest and most meaningful sense will be sensitive
to the tendency of certain stocks to be particularly affected by
changes in interest rates.

Changes in the rate of inflation will similarly tend to have a
systematic influence on the returns from common stocks. This
is so for at least two reasons. First, an increase in the rate of
inflation tends to increase interest rates and thus tends to
lower the prices of equities, as just discussed. Second, the increase in inflation may squeeze profit margins for certain
groups of companies—public utilities, for example, which often
find that rate increases lag behind increases in costs. On the
other hand, inflation may benefit the prices of common stocks
in the natural-resource industries. Thus, again there are important systematic relationships between stock returns and economic variables that may not be captured adequately by a simple beta measure of risk.

Statistical tests of the influence on security returns of several systematic risk variables have shown somewhat promising results. Better explanations than those given by the CAPM
can be obtained for the variation in returns among different

securities by using, in addition to the traditional beta measure of risk, a number of systematic risk variables, such as sensitivity to changes in national income, in interest rates, and in the rate of inflation. Of course, the evidence supporting many-risk-factor models of security pricing has only begun to accumulate and the APT measures of risk are beset by some of the same problems faced by the CAPM beta measure. It is not yet certain how these new theories will stand up to more extensive examination.

If, however, one wanted for simplicity to select the one risk measure most closely related to expected returns, the traditional beta measure would not be most analysts' first choice. In my own work with John Cragg, the best single risk proxy turned out to be the extent of disagreement among security analysts' forecasts for each individual company. Companies for which there is a broad consensus with respect to the growth of future earnings in dividends seem to be considered less risky (and, hence, have lower expected returns) than companies for which there is little agreement among security analysts. It is possible to interpret this result as contradicting modern asset pricing theory, which suggests that individual security variability *per se* will not be relevant for valuation. The dispersion of analysts' forecasts, however, may actually serve as a particularly useful proxy for a variety of systematic risks.

Consider, for example, two companies. One, a machinery manufacturer, is heavily in debt and extremely sensitive to systematic influences. The other, an all-equity pharmaceutical firm, is quite insensitive to economic conditions. It could be that Wall Street analysts agree completely on how economic conditions will affect the companies but differ greatly on their economic forecasts. If so, there could be a big dispersion in earnings forecasts for the machinery manufacturer (because of the difference in economic forecasts and the extreme sensitivity of the company to economic conditions) and very small differences in the forecasts for the drug company (because economic conditions have little effect on that company). Thus, if two different analysts have very different forecasts for GNP, inflation, and interest rates, a highly debt-leveraged company in a heavy industry would be greatly affected by differences in underlying economic forecasts, while an unleveraged drug company might show no effect whatsoever. Hence, differences in analysts' forecasts could be a most useful proxy for systematic risk in the broadest sense of the term.

While we still have much to learn about the market's evaluation of risk, I believe it is fair to conclude that risk is unlikely to be captured adequately by a single beta statistic, the risk measure of the CAPM. It appears that several other systematic risk measures affect the valuation of securities. In addition, as was indicated in the preceding chapter, there is some evidence that security returns are related to size (smaller firms tend to have higher rates of return) and also to price-earnings multiples (firms with low P/Es tend to produce higher returns) and price-book value ratios (stocks that are cheap relative to their book values tend to earn higher total returns). All three of these measures may be effective proxies for systematic risk. Whether individual risk plays any role at all in the valuation process is still, however, an open question.

My results with Cragg can be interpreted as showing that individual security variability does play a role in the valuation process. This would not be hard to explain. Because of transactions and information costs, a large number of individual portfolios may not be diversified. Individuals own between one-half and two-thirds of all NYSE stocks and an even larger fraction of stocks traded on other exchanges. Thus, these security holders might well be concerned with the variability of individual stocks. Even well-diversified institutional investors may worry about the behavior of individual stocks when they must report to finance committees the breakdown of their performance results over the preceding period. Still, there is a powerful argument on the other side. Any role in the valuation process that may consistently be provided by individual security variability will create an arbitrage opportunity for investors able to diversify widely. It is difficult to believe that these arbitrage opportunities will not eventually be exploited. Returning to the theme we played earlier, eventually "true value will out."

A Summing Up

Chapters Nine and Ten have been an academic exercise in the modern theory of capital markets. The stock market appears to be an efficient mechanism that adjusts quite quickly to new information. Neither technical analysis, which analyzes the past price movements of stocks, nor fundamental analysis, which analyzes more basic information about the prospects for individual companies and the economy, seems to yield consistent benefits. It appears that the only way to obtain higher long-run investment returns is to accept greater risks—and those risks can be horrendous, as any investor who has lived through the great bear market of October 1987 can tell you.

Unfortunately, a perfect risk measure does not exist. Beta, the risk measure from the capital-asset pricing model, looks nice on the surface. It is a simple, easy-to-understand measure of market sensitivity. Unfortunately, beta also has its warts. The actual relationship between beta and rate of return does not correspond to the relationship predicted in theory. Moreover, the relationship is undependable in the short run and has even failed to work for very long periods. Some analysts doubt if betas have ever been useful predictors of future returns. Finally, betas are not stable from period to period, and they are very sensitive to the particular market proxy against which they are measured.

I have argued here that no single measure is likely to capture adequately the variety of systematic risk influences on individual stocks and portfolios. Returns are probably sensitive to general market swings, to changes in interest and inflation rates, to changes in national income, and, undoubtedly, to other economic factors such as exchange rates. And if the best single risk estimate were to be chosen, the traditional beta measure is unlikely to be everyone's first choice. The mystical perfect risk measure is still beyond our grasp.

To the great relief of assistant professors who must publish or perish, there is still much debate within the academic community on risk measurement, and much more empirical testing needs to be done. Undoubtedly, there will yet be many improvements in the techniques of risk analysis, and the quantitative analysis of risk measurement is far from dead. My own guess is that future risk measures will be even more sophisticated—not less so. Nevertheless, we must be careful not to accept beta or any other measure as an easy way to assess risk and to predict future returns with any certainty. You should know about the best of the modern techniques of the new investment technology—they can be useful aids. But there is never going to be a handsome genie who will appear and solve all our investment problems. And even if he did, we would probably foul it up—as did the little lady in the following favorite story of Robert Kirby of Capital Guardian Trust:

> She was sitting in her rocking chair on the porch of the retirement home when a little genie appeared and said, "I've decided to grant you three wishes."
>
> The little old lady answered, "Buzz off, you little twerp, I've seen all the wise guys I need to in my life."
>
> The genie answered, "Look, I'm not kidding. This is for real. Just try me."
>
> She shrugged and said, "Okay, turn my rocking chair into solid gold."
>
> When, in a puff of smoke, he did it, her interest picked up noticeably. She said, "Turn me into a beautiful young maiden."
>
> Again, in a puff of smoke, he did it. Finally, she said, "Okay, for my third wish turn my cat into a handsome young prince."
>
> In an instant, there stood the young prince, who then turned to her and asked, "Now aren't you sorry you had me fixed?"

11

How Pork Bellies Acquired
an Ivy League Suit:
A Primer on Derivatives

The gambling known as business looks with austere disfavor upon the business known as gambling.
— Ambrose Bierce, *The Devil's Dictionary*

Once upon a time, long, long ago—at least 150 years—American farmers and other commodity producers worked out a market system to provide some financial sanity in their lives. In essence, it was a kind of insurance and, as with all insurance, it involved paying a relatively small price as a guarantee against future loss. The system, explained more fully below, became known as the futures market and was centered in Chicago. Because of that city's historic association with the processing and sale of sides of beef and pork, the catchy commodity component "pork belly" was used as a bellwether for all commodity futures trading. If the price of pork bellies went up, traders on LaSalle Street smiled; if it sank, there were grimaces.

All that emotion—and the brokerage commissions that went with it—attracted the interest of those whose sole role in life was to buy and sell financial instruments. Why not, they successfully reasoned, create a system similar to commodity futures but restricted to stocks and other financial instruments? The result was an activity that became known as stock options and financial-futures trading (also more fully explained below). Though option trading has been practiced in one form or another for centuries, it was considered such a minute, specialized aspect of investing that I devoted little attention to it in the first edition of this book in 1973.

How times do change! Those fat little pork bellies and those arcane options and financial futures now comprise a multi-trillion dollar financial scramble. And they've also acquired a new name. After all, what self-respecting MBA in a pinstripe suit and white shirt or blouse—a person who sacrificed any personal life to work at least 12 hours every day—would publicly admit that all such effort was on behalf of pork bellies? Nary a one! This was big-time, sophisticated activity and it deserved a big-time, sophisticated name: derivatives.

Dealing in derivatives was the most dynamic and rapidly growing part of the securities business in the mid-1990s. It was the sure way to impress even the marginally financially literate at cocktail parties. Despite the complicated-sounding name, the term derivative is really self-explanatory. Derivatives are simply financial instruments whose value is determined by (or "derived" from) the price of some underlying asset, such as stocks, bonds, currencies, or commodities. As we shall see below, what they do is to permit the transfer of risks and broaden the investment and hedging opportunities available to individuals and institutions. They also provide the means to undertake highly leveraged speculative positions.

This chapter seeks to present a proper perspective on derivatives by (1) explaining their function and history, (2) giving examples not only of how they work but also of how they can cause both tremendous gains and losses, and (3) presenting guidelines for their use.

The Basic Types of Derivatives

The two most popular forms of financial derivative securities are futures and options contracts. They are derivatives because they take their value from their connected underlying securities. While we will concentrate on simple options and futures, it should be noted that there are many other derivative-type instruments that build upon these two basic forms. These complex derivatives have fancy and often forbidding names, such as swaps, inverse floaters, leaps, lookbacks, swaptions, quantos, rainbows, floors, caps, and collars. Then there are instruments that look as though they belong on an eye chart, such as REMICS, M-CATS, and TIGRS.

A futures, or forward, contract involves the obligation to purchase (or deliver) a specified commodity (or financial instrument) at a specified price at some specific future period. For example, suppose it is now June, and I want to get a delivery of 42,000 gallons of heating oil (the typical contract size) in December. I might buy a December heating oil future at a price of 60 cents. This commits me to take delivery of 42,000 gallons of heating oil in mid-December at a price of 60 cents per gallon. The seller of the futures contract commits to make delivery of the oil at that time.*

Futures are traded on single commodities such as gasoline, wheat, sugar, coffee, orange juice, corn, soybeans, cattle, and so on. In addition, active markets exist in precious metals, such as gold, silver, and platinum. A burgeoning market exists in financial futures, where one can buy for future delivery a variety of bonds, currencies, and stock-market indexes such as the S&P 500. These financial futures are typically settled in cash based on the difference between the initial contract price and the final cash market price of the financial instrument. No physical delivery is made. Not to be outdone in innovation on new contract designs and specifications, the options markets have developed options on futures contracts. If we can create derivatives, it is only natural to trade derivatives on derivatives.

A stock option, just as the name implies, gives the buyer the right (but not the obligation) to buy or sell a common stock (or group of stocks) at a specific price on or before a set date. For example, a call option on IBM might cost the buyer $10 a share (the option premium) expiring the third Friday in July (the expiration date) with an exercise price of $100 a share (the striking

---

*Futures contracts have standardized terms and are traded on organized futures exchanges. Forward contracts are individualized arrangements between two parties. Buyers (and sellers) of futures and forward contracts often close out their obligations by selling (or buying back) their contracts prior to the expiration date.

price). Thus, for a premium of $10, the buyer of this call option has the right to purchase a share of IBM at $100 at any time up through the third Friday in July. The seller (or writer) of the option receives the premium and takes on the corresponding potential obligation to sell the share at the contract price. A put option reverses the situation. A put on IBM gives the holder the right to sell IBM shares at a specific price. The seller of the put (called the writer) takes on the potential obligation to buy the shares.

Options exist on the major traded individual stocks as well as on a variety of stock indexes, bonds, and foreign currencies. Options on the S&P 500 Index are traded in Chicago, while options on (a very close substitute for) the Dow Jones industrial average are traded in New York. In addition, options are traded on a variety of smaller capitalization indexes as well as specific industry indexes. The volume of trading in basic options and futures has at times actually exceeded the volume of trading in the underlying assets. What makes the market important, however, is not simply its size but also the significant role it plays in providing new tools to manage risk.

The Futures Markets: Functions and History

Despite their association in the financial press with speculation and gambling, futures markets have a valuable economic role. They permit both producers and consumers to transfer risks in such a way that all market participants can be better off. Contracts in the wheat futures markets, for example, typically stipulate the purchase and sale of specific quantities of wheat at fixed prices on a designated future date. At planting time, Farmer Jones might enter into a contract to *sell* his output of wheat at the end of the growing season at a fixed price. Knowing what he will receive for his wheat, Jones can then budget the purchase of supplies, such as fertilizer and irrigation equipment, offer labor contracts to his workers, and guarantee himself a profit—no matter what happens to the price of wheat over the season. Farmer Jones sleeps well at night with a wheat futures contract.

Baker Smith has a different problem. She has agreed to sell her output of bread to several elegant restaurants at a fixed price. Smith, knowing the revenues she will get for her bread, can guarantee herself a profit by entering into a futures contract to *buy* wheat at a fixed price. So both Smith and Jones are made better off by transacting in the futures market.

The concept of a futures market seems to have had its roots in the Book of Genesis. The Egyptian pharaoh had summoned Joseph to interpret a dream in which seven fat cows and seven plump ears of corn were succeeded by seven gaunt cows and seven thin, blighted ears of corn. Joseph said the dream meant that seven years of famine would follow seven years of great plenty. He also proposed a solution: Essentially, Egypt should initiate future-buy contracts during the seven-year period of oversupply to avoid famine during the period of undersupply that would follow. While the Egyptians did not open the first Nile Board of Trade, clearly the idea of futures contracting was born.

The origins of actual markets in futures are somewhat obscure, but it appears that such contracts have had a very long history. Some authors have suggested that futures trading began in India as early as 2000 B.C. Others have traced the origins of the practice to Roman and even to Classical Greek times. There appears to be strong evidence that Roman emperors entered into futures contracts to assure their subjects an adequate supply of Egyptian grain. Whatever the actual origin, it seems clear that the immediate predecessor to modern futures trading was the "to arrive" contract used in Europe during the eighteenth century. These were contracts for the purchase of goods when they would be available in the future, as, for example, when a ship's cargo would arrive in port. Such contracts played an important role in the development of the United States' grain trade.

During the early stages of the development of American agriculture, grain prices were subject to seemingly perpetual cycles of boom and bust as prices fell when farmers flooded the market with grain at harvest time and then rose later as shortages developed. Buyers and sellers began to contract for future delivery of specific quantities of grain at agreed upon prices and delivery dates. These "to arrive," or forward, contracts were themselves bought and sold in anticipation of changes in market prices and became the basis for the standardized futures contracts traded on the Chicago Board of Trade, the first organized commodities futures market in the United States.

The Chicago Board of Trade was founded in 1848. It initially served as the exchange for all types of commodities trading, including grain, beef, pork bellies, and so on. A rival exchange, the Chicago Mercantile Exchange, was established in 1874 as a successor organization to an organization trading butter and eggs. While several other futures exchanges have been formed in the United States, the two Chicago exchanges remain the major locus of trading.

Though they serve a beneficial economic function, futures exchanges have always looked somewhat like gambling casinos, and some of the traders have tried to manipulate the market. Perhaps the boldest futures manipulation of the twentieth century was Bunker and Herbert Hunt's attempt to corner the silver market. Together with their co-conspirators, the brothers at one time controlled over $17 billion worth of silver, in the process engineering a price rise from about $6 an ounce at the start of 1979 to a high of over $50 an ounce on one trading day in January 1980.

What the Hunts did was quite simple—and quite daring. They cornered the silver market by accumulating gigantic positions in the futures market to buy silver and then demanding delivery when the contracts came due. Simultaneously, they accumulated enormous stocks of silver in the spot market (the market in which physical quantities of the metal were bought for immediate delivery) and held this silver off the market, making it difficult for those who had sold silver futures to fulfill their obligations. Thus, they increased demand in the futures market while restricting supply in the spot market. The price of silver skyrocketed.

One amusing story reported by author Stephen Fay recounts an incident about the Hunts' activities in hoarding and storing silver abroad that involved flying 6 million ounces of silver bullion across the Atlantic. The silver was carefully arranged around the hold of the aircraft to balance its weight. The large gap in the middle was filled by an enormous cage containing a circus elephant. Over the middle of the ocean, the plane began to yaw uncontrollably. One of the Hunts and a brother-in-law rushed back to discover that the elephant had pushed his trunk through the side of the cage and was playing with the wires controlling the aircraft's wing flaps. As Stephen Fay tells the tale, "Acting with the inspiration that is prompted only by impending death, our heroes opened the cage and threw a rubber tire at the elephant—which transferred its attention to its new toy—and thus saved their own lives and the family silver."

Corners have been a fact of life in the commodities markets since their inception and so has the attempt at regulation. In the United States, the Commodities Futures Trading Commission (CFTC) attempts to avoid corners by insuring that there are limits on the amount of futures contracts any individual or group can hold. The Hunts were able to avoid these constraints for a while. They did so by arguing that the two brothers were operating independently, so that any constraints were interpreted as applying to their individual rather than to their joint holdings. They also pointed out that they owned a significant interest in a silver mine, which was considered a member of the commercial silver market—not a speculator. And they denied categorically that their ownership of significant quantities of silver through various corporate entities, trusts, and partnerships (including one with a wealthy group of Saudi Arabians) was part of a global coalition engaged in a blatant attempt to corner the market.

The regulators and the courts finally saw it differently. Early in 1980, the CFTC ruled that no *new* purchases of silver contracts could be made in the futures markets. At the same time, the Chicago Board of Trade raised margin requirements on silver and lowered the amount of silver future contracts any single speculator could hold. Traders were given until mid-February 1980 to liquidate their extra holdings. This prospective increase in supply came at the same time that high prices were bringing silver out of the woodwork as people began melting everything from coins to the family tea set to cash in. There was a dramatic loss of luster in the silver market and prices plunged.

By early March 1980, the price of silver had declined to

about $20 an ounce. Of course, as the price sank, those who had long positions in silver futures contracts (those who had bought silver for future delivery) suffered a financial loss and had to find additional cash to maintain their margin positions. Otherwise, they would have to sell some of their positions. The Hunts desperately struggled to come up with the required margin—even mortgaging hundreds of their prized racehorses. But as silver continued to plummet, their efforts failed. On March 19, the Hunts defaulted on their margin obligation. Their brokers, Bache and Merrill Lynch, began selling off the collateral behind the loans, but this collateral was, of course, silver. In one final ploy to prop up the market, the Hunts announced a plan on March 26 to issue bonds backed by their holdings of silver. The market correctly interpreted this announcement as a desperation move. On March 27, a day which came to be known as Silver Thursday, silver opened at about $16 an ounce and plunged to about $10 by the end of the day. Rumors circulated that Bache and other Hunt creditors would fail.

Later a jury found that the Hunts had indeed manipulated the silver market. Monetary judgments and punitive damages were imposed against the Hunts, their co-conspirators, and their brokers. However, the full settlement was never collected against the Hunts. The two brothers—the world's richest men at the outset of the 1980s—sought protection in bankruptcy in 1990. So ended one of history's greatest corners of a commodities market. The meltdown continued, however, and by the early 1990s, silver was selling at four dollars an ounce.

Though the shine was off silver, a new category of futures was making a sterling debut. A bevy of new products, called financial futures, propelled a spectacular growth of futures trading over the 1980s and 1990s. These came into being as a result of the increased price variability of many financial assets. And they were polished by the innovativeness and entrepreneurial abilities of the futures markets in designing products to cope with this variability.

The demise of the Bretton Woods system of fixed international exchange rates and the change to a floating or flexible exchange rate regime dramatically increased the variability in foreign currency values. Leo Melamed, of the Chicago Mercantile Exchange, recognized that this new system, where markets rather than governments determined the prices of currencies, created the opportunity for the inception of futures trading. He introduced highly successful currency futures contracts in a variety of foreign currencies. At the same time, it became apparent that the forces of inflation would greatly increase the price volatility of fixed-income securities. Thus, in 1975 the Chicago Board of Trade initiated trading in bonds issued by the Government National Mortgage Association (GNMAs). This was the beginning of futures trading on a variety of fixed-income instruments. In January 1976, futures on 90-day Treasury bills began trading, and in August of 1977, the first U.S. Treasury bond contract was introduced.

The next major landmark for financial futures occurred in spring of 1982 when the Kansas City Board of Trade introduced a stock index futures contract based on the price of the Value Line Stock Index. Exchanges now trade contracts on the Standard & Poor's 500-Stock Index, the Major Market Index designed to track the Dow Jones industrial average, and the New York Stock Exchange Index. More recently, trading has commenced on a variety of foreign-stock indexes. These newer contracts also incorporated the feature of cash settlement. Thus, if one bought a futures contract on the S&P 500-Stock Index at a price of $500, the seller would not deliver a package of the 500 stocks on the expiration date. Rather, the contract would be settled in cash based on the difference between $500 and the value of the index on the settlement date. Today, trading in financial futures represents well over half of the total futures trading. Most industry observers expect the continued growth of the futures market to center around such financial instruments.

The Options Markets: Functions and History

Most people know of options as a device to speculate on an expected rise, or fall, in the price of a stock while putting up little money. For example, suppose IBM was selling at $75 a share, and you thought it would rise to $90 a share within a short period of time. If you purchased 100 shares of IBM it would cost you $7,500 (plus commissions), and, if your forecast of the price increase was correct, you would be able to sell the shares later for $9,000 (less commissions). Your profit would be $1,500, or 20 percent of your initial investment, ignoring brokerage commissions. Suppose now, instead, you bought a call option on 100 shares of IBM at $75 per share at a premium of $5 per share. You would put up only $500 (plus commissions). If the price of IBM did rise to $90, you could simultaneously exercise your option, buying the 100 shares for $7,500 and selling them in the market for $9,000. Your profit, again ignoring brokerage commissions, would be $1,500 minus the $500 you paid for the option, or $1,000. Note that in percentage terms, however, your return would be 200 percent ($1,000 profit for a $500 investment) rather than the 20 percent return that would have been earned from an outright purchase. Thus, options allow an investor who makes correct forecasts about stock-price movements to increase substantially her percentage return. We shall see below, however, that options and futures can also play an extremely important role as a tool for risk reduction as well as risk enhancement.

Stock options can be used in another way, however: They can transfer risks as well as broaden the investment opportunities available to individuals and institutions. Let us illustrate this by looking at the case of Widower White and Gambler Green. Widower White cannot afford to suffer a large drop in the value of his stock. He no longer works and depends on his investments as his major source of support. Gambler Green thinks White is a Nervous Nelson and is willing to bet money that she is right. White reduces some of his risk by selling a call option to Green. By purchasing the call, Green receives the right to buy White's shares at an agreed-upon price up to a fixed date. For this privilege, Green pays White a sum of money called the option premium.

By selling the call, White has transferred to Green the opportunity to profit if, by a specific time, the price of his stock has risen above the contract price, called the striking price. In turn, he has received an option premium which gives him some revenue and partially protects him if the stock declines in value. Thus, the option does not create any new risks for White. Rather, it redistributes both some risk and all potential profit to Green. And Green may actually be a shrewd, rather than reckless, gambler because the call option can be used as a substitute for buying the stock outright and, thus, as an efficient diversification strategy.

Options have a long and checkered history. Once again the Bible (Genesis 29) contains the earliest reference to a business option. The incident occurred when Jacob wished to marry Rachel, youngest daughter of Laban. Laban agreed provided that Jacob would first pay him with seven years of labor. After that period, Jacob would have an option on Rachel's hand. One can see that options were already off to a bad start since Laban reneged on the contract and delivered to Jacob his elder daughter, Leah, instead.

Options were prominently mentioned in Book I of Aristotle's *Politics*. Aristotle told the story of the philosopher Thales who had been ridiculed by the populace for his poverty, which they took as proof that philosophy was of no practical use. But Thales, who possessed exceptional skill in reading the stars, had the last laugh. One winter, Thales foresaw that the next autumn's olive harvest would be a bumper crop, far above normal. He took the little money he had and quietly visited all the owners of olive presses in the area, placing small deposits with each for an option on the use of their presses at normal rents when fall arrived. Aristotle concludes the story as follows, "When the harvest-time came, and many [presses] were wanted all at once and of a sudden, he let them out at any rate he pleased, and made a quantity of money. Thus he showed the world that philosophers can easily be rich if they like."

Options made their first major mark on financial history during the tulip-bulb craze in seventeenth-century Holland, chronicled in Chapter Two. Options were initially used in this time period for hedging. By purchasing a call option on tulip bulbs, a dealer who was committed to a sales contract could be assured of obtaining a fixed number of bulbs for a set price. Similarly, tulip-bulb growers could assure themselves of selling their bulbs at a set price by purchasing put options. Later, however, options were increasingly used by speculators who found that call options were an effective vehicle for obtaining maximum possible gains per guilder of investment. As long as tulip prices continued to skyrocket, a call buyer would realize returns far in excess of those that could be obtained by purchasing tulip bulbs themselves. The writers (that is, sellers) of put options also prospered as bulb prices spiralled since writers were able to keep the premiums and the options were never exercised. Of course, when the tulip-bulb market collapsed in 1636, speculators lost everything. Hardest hit were the put writers who were unable to meet their commitments to purchase bulbs. As a result of the involvement of put and call options in this classic speculative mania, options acquired a bad name which they have retained, more or less, to the present time.

Because of their association with excessive speculation, options were declared illegal in England by Barnard's Act of 1733 and continued to be illegal at various times until 1860. Opposition to options was particularly strong on the part of members of the Labor Party, who regarded their use as *prima facie* evidence that the stock exchange was merely a den of gamblers. But Barnard's Act was even less effective than alcohol prohibition in the United States in restraining the options trade. Trading in options flourished on the London Stock Exchange despite their illegality, and London became the most important options market in the world.

As was the case in Britain, options have had a controversial history in the United States. The first mention of options in American history dates back to 1790. By the time of the Civil War, options and futures trading was a flourishing activity. As the progressive movement swept the country, however, all kinds of speculative activity fell into disfavor, and around the turn of the century, options on commodities came to be regarded as gambling contracts and, hence, illegal and unenforceable. Stock options were never banned, however, despite several attempts to abolish them as part of a general program to restrain speculation.

Interest in options increased dramatically in the United States during the bull market of the 1920s. The most flagrant abuses of these instruments also occurred during this period. As described in Chapter Three, options played an important role in several pools designed to manipulate stock prices. Trading in this period was largely in two- and three-day call options. There was even a one-day call option known as a "seven-cigar call" because it sold for one day's worth of stogies. In 1932 and 1933, a congressional investigation found that many of the financial abuses of the 1920s were related to the use of options. In 1934, a bill called for an outright ban on stock options, but the Securities Act of 1934 stopped short of forbidding options trading and only empowered the SEC to regulate it. In fact, the industry itself developed a highly organized, self-policing organization so that direct government regulation was averted.

Stock options began to be traded on organized options exchanges in 1973 following the formation of the Chicago Board Options Exchange (CBOE). In 1975, the American Stock Exchange began option trading, and later many of the regional exchanges followed suit. With the advent of exchange-traded options, many of the risks that formerly existed in options trading were eliminated. A centralized clearing entity, the Options Clearing Corporation (OCC), was organized as the issuer and *guarantor* of each option traded on a U.S. exchange. This essentially eliminated the credit risk that existed when traders had to rely on the counterparties to the transaction to live up to their obligations. In addition, the exchanges significantly reduced the transactions costs of dealing in options and the existence of continuous options markets allowed investors both to initiate and offset options transactions at competitively determined prices. These developments paved the way for a rapid expansion of the market that has continued to the present time.

The Exciting Dangers of Derivatives

Probably the most important factor to keep in mind about derivatives is that their use can often involve considerable risk. If anyone tries to sell you a derivative strategy that involves a sure profit and no risk, watch out. She's selling snake oil. If something sounds too good to be true, it undoubtedly is too good to be true.

From one standpoint, buying a $500 call option on a specific stock involves limited risk because all you can lose is $500. Looking at it another way, however, the strategy is extremely risky since that $500 can be 100 percent of your capital. A futures transaction can be even more disastrous. When you buy a $100,000 position in the Treasury bonds for future delivery, you may have to put up an initial margin as little as $1,000. But if the Treasury securities suddenly drop in price by just two percent, a movement that could happen in a single day, you will be liable for a loss of $2,000, double the amount of your initial capital. This explains how some traders can suffer extraordinary losses even if they put up relatively small amounts of money.

Even the pros can get badly burned. During the mid-1990s, Procter and Gamble entered into a customized derivative transaction they thought would achieve their borrowing objectives. It turned out that they lost over $100 million when German and U.S. interest rates both rose sharply. The company officially responsible for the trade was placed on "special assignment" and P&G sued Banker's Trust (which it doesn't *trust* anymore) for recommending the transaction. Not even staid public finance officials were immune from taking flyers in the derivatives market. Orange County, California announced that its Christmas greeting in 1994 was to file for bankruptcy protection after taking a two billion dollar loss in risky investments. While derivatives played only a part in the Orange County debacle, they came in for the most criticism in the media. At the end of February 1995, one of Britain's most venerable banks, Barings PLC—the oldest investment firm in the U.K., collapsed after suffering more than a one billion dollar loss from trading Japanese stock-index futures contracts.

The possibility that an ordinary investor could take a sum as small as $1,000 and, by shrewd trading, turn it into $100,000 in a few months (as Hillary Rodham Clinton claims to have done) is about as likely as going to Las Vegas, putting a dollar in a slot machine, winning the $50 million grand prize, and then walking away never to enter a casino again.

The risk involved can be enormous even if the market participant is hedged as some fund managers learned during the

"Hey, there's always tomorrow. Well, unless you're in derivatives."

mid-1990s. In a hedge fund, the manager might sell short a derivative instrument on one stock or bond index and buy another instrument. Suppose, for example, you believed that the prices of stocks of smaller companies would rise *relative* to stocks of larger companies. You might buy a three-month future on the Russell 2,000 index (an index of smaller firms) and sell an equivalent futures contract on the S&P 500 (an index of the biggest companies). Note that you would be hedged in the sense that if all stocks went down, you would lose on your Russell 2,000 contract but gain on the S&P contract. As long as small stocks did better than large stocks on a relative basis, you could gain whatever the direction of the general market. However, if the relative performance figures went the other way—that is, big-company stocks did better than small-company stocks—you could lose substantial sums of money. This is so because futures markets allow you to control *billions* of dollars worth of securities while putting up a security deposit of only *millions*. Derivatives truly provide investors with staggering amounts of leverage.

George Soros, a famous hedge-fund manager, supposedly endowed with a "Midas touch," made hundreds of millions when he correctly "bet" that some currencies would be stronger than others and translated his bet into hedged-futures contracts. The Midas touch turned to a minus touch, however, when he lost more than half a billion dollars during 1994 on a single currency deal. Leverage is a double-edged sword.

Another factor to keep in mind is that derivative transactions can involve substantial trading costs. If an option is quoted as 5 bid–5¼ asked, it means you buy the option at 5¼, while if you sell it, you only get 5. That ¼ point spread is a 5 percent transactions charge on the purchase or sale of that particular instrument (a so-called round-trip transaction) and does not include brokerage commissions. Even discount brokers exact their tolls: most often a minimum brokerage charge of $35 on each purchase and sale—or $70 for 100 shares of a $5 option for each round-trip transaction. This translates to an additional 14 percent charge.

The experiences of the Princeton Students Investment Club in the early 1990s illustrate the potential pitfalls in dealing in derivatives. Four Princeton students, interested in learning about stock markets firsthand, put up $500 each and formed an investment club. Since it would be impossible to purchase a portfolio of individual stocks with only $2,000, they decided to pursue an options-buying strategy. At any one time, they would buy four or five call options on individual stocks they thought attractive and occasionally one or more put options on stocks considered overpriced and due for a fall. The students made some excellent choices during the club's two years of operation.

During a period when high-technology stocks were hot, they made lots of money in call options on Intel and Micron Technology. Similarly, they timed their put option purchases well, making a good profit betting that Snapple Beverages would retreat after a speculative frenzy drove its price to unsustainable levels. When Boston Chicken laid an egg and became Boston Turkey for a time, the club also benefited handsomely.

Of course, not all of their trades proved to be profitable. The club bought options on Paramount Communications and Grumman Aircraft, mistakenly predicting that a bidding war would erupt after initial tender offers were made for Paramount and Grumman shares. In both cases, their call options expired worthless. After two years of operation, the participants in the club graduated and divided their spoils. The final accounting showed that the original $2,000 had grown to $2,125 for an annual rate of return of approximately 3 percent. This was far below the 10 percent rate of return for the stock market as a whole over the same period. How could such brilliant pickers underperform the market? The answer: brokerage commissions, pure and simple. These totaled $980, almost 50 percent of their original stake. These budding entrepreneurs had done more to fatten the coffers of their stock broker than to contribute toward their tuition bills.

Some Illustrations of the Potential Profits and Pitfalls from Options and Futures

It is much easier to understand the potential profits and losses from derivative transactions with some simple numerical examples and charts. In this section, we will illustrate some basic strategies using Micron Technology, one of the hottest technology stocks of the mid-1990s.

Bullish on Micron Technology Stock—Alternative Profit and Risk Positions

Suppose you believed Micron would continue to advance and wanted to analyze the pros and cons of taking a position by buying the stock directly or by purchasing a three-month call "at-the-money" for $4 per share. (In the Appendix to this chapter, I explain what determines the size of the option premium for different contracts.) "At-the-money" means that if the stock is currently selling at $40, the contract, or striking price, is also $40, right at the current market price. In options terminology, if the investor bought an option with a striking price of $45, that option would be "out-of-the-money" since the contract price was higher than the current market price. Alternatively, a call option with a $35 striking price and a market price of the stock at $40 would be $5 "in-the-money." For our purposes, and to keep the examples simple, all charts illustrate "at-the-money" calls.

Buying the stock outright results in gains or losses exactly equivalent to Micron Technology stock's price movements. If Micron increases by 50 percent to 60, a 100-share investment—initially worth $4,000—will increase to $6,000, a 50 percent gain. (In this and future illustrations, we will also ignore brokerage costs to keep the number simple.) On the other hand, a 100-share investment in three-month options at $4 per share with a striking price of $40 increases in value by 400 percent, or $1,600. You can exercise your option at $40 and simultaneously sell the shares on the open market at $60. Your profit is the $2,000 of appreciation on the underlying stock minus the $400 you paid for the option. It is clear that if you are correct in your stock picks, the percentage gains are eye catching, and you're even protected on the downside. If Micron declines, you let your option expire and the most you can lose is the $400 you spent to buy the contract.

The scenario is even more dramatic if you put all your money into options. Had you invested the whole $4,000 into Micron call options, profits from a 50 percent stock increase would be $16,000 ($1,600 times 10) as opposed to a $2,000 profit from direct ownership. As shown in Chart 1, the leverage of options in enhancing profits is beautiful to behold when everything goes well.

Leverage, as we all know, works two ways. Let's continue the example where the investor puts all $4,000 into call options, and let's suppose that Micron doesn't move within the three-month option period. The stock buyer still has his original stake intact and has lost nothing. Indeed, he has collected any dividends paid out during the three-month period. The option buyer, however, receives no dividends and has lost $4,000, 100 percent of his investment. Thus, anyone who tells you that buying options isn't risky is not telling the truth. Option buyers have to be right not only on the direction of the movement in the stock but also on the *exact timing* of when the move will take place. If Micron makes its move in four months, an option

Chart 1
The Allure of Fattening Your Purse With Call Options Rather Than Stocks

Micron Technology Stock—Current Price $40
Call Option $4.00 Per Share: Striking Price $40

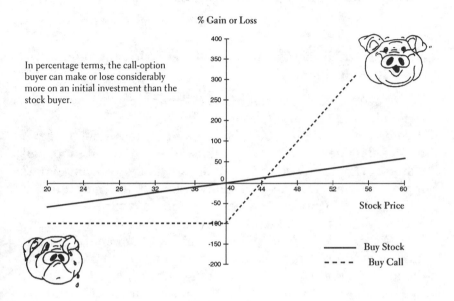

% Gain or Loss

In percentage terms, the call-option buyer can make or lose considerably more on an initial investment than the stock buyer.

Stock Price

——— Buy Stock
- - - - Buy Call

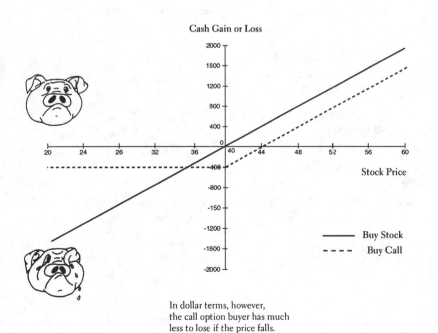

Cash Gain or Loss

Stock Price

——— Buy Stock
- - - - Buy Call

In dollar terms, however, the call option buyer has much less to lose if the price falls.

buyer can still lose everything, whereas the stock buyer would be fully rewarded. Before you engage in an options-buying strategy, consider how difficult it is not only to pick the right stock but also to time its upward move perfectly.

Bearish on Micron Technology Stock—Alternative Profit and Risk Positions

Suppose you believe that Micron Technology is now posed to decline. You can profit from this by buying a put option. A put gives you the right to sell the stock at a guaranteed price. If the price declined to $30, you could exercise your option to sell the stock at $40. How can you sell the stock if you don't own it? Simple. You buy it in the open market for $30 and sell it to the put writer for $10 more.* Thus, a put-option buyer profits only if the stock declines—and declines by more than the option premium. For example, if the put option costs $4 per share, the put option buyer would not make any money until the price of Micron stock fell below $36 a share. If the stock declines sharply, however, the put buyer can reap exciting gains. If the stock price stays even or advances, the put buyer will lose her entire stake.

Put buying can also be combined with stock ownership. Suppose you own Micron Technology but are having trouble sleeping at night because you are worried the price could decline sharply. In this case, you might buy a put option on Micron Technology at $40. This is called a protective put. If the stock goes down, you exercise your option to sell the shares at $40. If the stock goes up, you allow the option to expire unexercised and profit from any rise in the price of the stock. Foolproof? Not quite. The put costs $4 per share. If the stock goes down, you would have been $4 per share better off to have sold in the first place. If the stock goes up, your profits are reduced by the $4 per share put premium. Think of the $4 as a three-month insurance premium. You pay for the peace of mind that

---

*In practice, you would simply sell the put option rather than exercising it. The put would have risen in price to reflect the greater worth of an instrument that allows you to sell the stock at $10 more than its market value.

Chart 2
How to Put Your Best Foot Forward

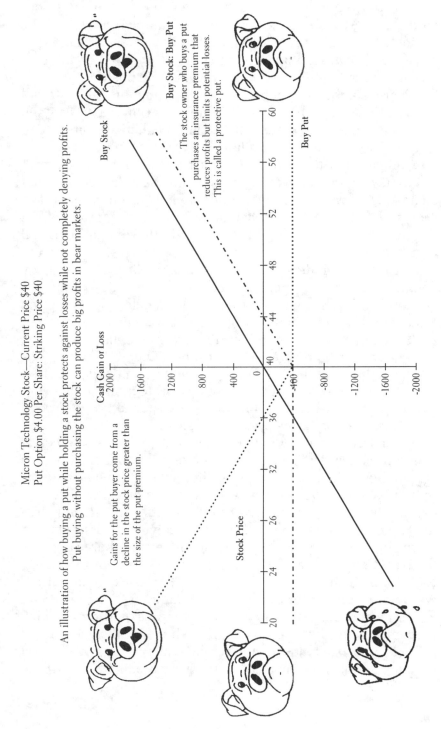

Micron Technology Stock—Current Price $40
Put Option $4.00 Per Share: Striking Price $40

An illustration of how buying a put while holding a stock protects against losses while not completely denying profits. Put buying without purchasing the stock can produce big profits in bear markets.

Buy Stock

Gains for the put buyer come from a decline in the stock price greater than the size of the put premium.

Buy Stock: Buy Put

The stock owner who buys a put purchases an insurance premium that reduces profits but limits potential losses. This is called a protective put.

Cash Gain or Loss

2000
1600
1200
800
400
0
-400
-800
-1200
-1600
-2000

Stock Price

20 24 26 32 36 40 44 48 52 56 60

Buy Put

comes from knowing you need not worry about losing your gains from Micron stock. Like auto insurance, however, the protection is not cheap. Chart 2 shows the results for a put buyer who owns the underlying stock as well as for the purchaser of a put option who has no ownership position.

There is another way to gain some protection against a fall in the price of Micron stock. The owner of the stock can sell (write) a call against his position. This is called "covered" call writing and is explained in Chart 3.

Compared with buying a put for protection, there are both advantages and disadvantages as can be seen from the visual summary shown in the bottom of the chart. If the price of Micron stock stays within 20 percent of the starting price within the three-month period, you are much better off selling a call option on the stock and *collecting* the premium as opposed to paying for a put. Indeed, even if the price of Micron Technology declines to $32, a 20 percent decline, you are in exactly the same position using either strategy. Thus, as long as you think Micron will sell within a range of plus or minus 20 percent within a three-month period, writing covered calls offers some protection and is never a poorer strategy. Only if Micron stock rises or falls more than 20 percent would put buying be better. The put-buying strategy produces more protection against very severe price declines and allows the investor to profit more in the event of a very large price increase.

Of course, for every buyer of a call or put there is a corresponding seller. And just as many option buyers do not own the stock in question, so there are sellers who write call and put options without ever owning a single share of stock. Selling a call option without owning the stock is called naked call writing. Remember that the call writer receives a lump sum for taking on the potential obligation to deliver 100 shares of stock to the option buyer at a set striking price (in all our examples, $40). Thus, if the stock price goes to $60, $1,600 goes out the window for the writer of a 100-share contract. The naked call writer must spend $6,000 to obtain 100 shares of Micron, which then must be turned over to the option buyer at the guaranteed price of $4,000. That $2,000 difference, minus the $400 option premium, makes up the $1,600 loss. Naked call writers freeze

Chart 3
How to Keep Your Shirt—and Only Your Shirt—In a Rising Market While Muting Your Agonized Squeals in a Plunging One

Micron Technology Stock—Current Price $40
Call Option $4.00 Per Share: Striking Price $40

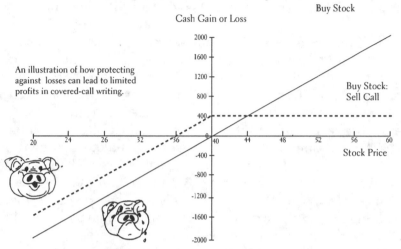

An illustration of how protecting against losses can lead to limited profits in covered-call writing.

This shows what happens when an individual who buys (or already owns) 100 shares of Micron Technology at $40 per share writes (sells) a call option at $4 per share. This is called "covered" call writing. If the stock stays at $40 at the end of three months, the option will expire unexercised. The investor will own 100 shares worth $4,000 while keeping the $400 option premium in cash: a 10 percent return over a three-month period. Not bad for a stock that has gone nowhere. Now suppose the stock price goes up to $60. The covered writer does not benefit from the rise because the option buyer will call the stock away at $40, the strike price. The writer ends up with $4,000 from the sale of the stock plus, of course, the $400 option premium. Thus, the covered writer makes a 10 percent return at any price for Micron of $40 or above. Should Micron fall in price, the owner of the stock would lose, but that loss would be reduced by the $400 premium on the option, which would expire unexercised.

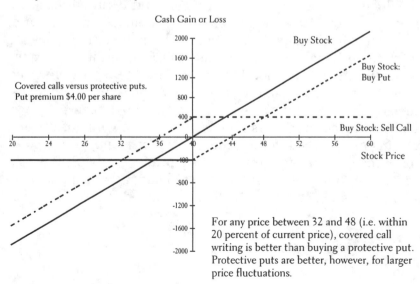

Covered calls versus protective puts.
Put premium $4.00 per share

For any price between 32 and 48 (i.e. within 20 percent of current price), covered call writing is better than buying a protective put. Protective puts are better, however, for larger price fluctuations.

when stocks go up. On the other hand, if Micron Technology declines to $36 per share, the buyer would not want to pay $4,000 for a stock valued at $3,600 and thus does not exercise the option—permitting the seller of the naked call to pocket a $400 profit. Obviously, the risk associated with such profit is enormous.

The situation is similar for put writers. Put writers pocket the premium when stocks go up and lose heavily when stocks go down. It is actually difficult to figure out the percentage gains and losses from naked option writing because brokers will demand that the writer put up sufficient margin so as to give the broker comfort that the writer will be able to fulfill his contract obligation. It is clear, however, that naked writing is a very risky strategy. If the options remain unexercised, the gains to the writer are extremely large. But the potential losses can be staggering. Writers of naked puts were the ones who lost everything during the crash of 1987 (and the sharp decline in 1989), while writers of naked calls lost heavily earlier in the 1980s when takeovers sent stock prices spiraling.

Strategies Involving Financial Futures

If you want a really flashily attired portfolio, dress it up in financial futures. The most popular of these instruments are futures on the Standard & Poor's 500-Stock Index and on a long-term Treasury bond. Recall that a futures contract represents an obligation to deliver or receive a commodity (in this case an underlying bond or basket of stocks) at a specified price at a designated future date. The price to be paid is the price at which the original contract is bought or sold in the open market. Unlike actual commodity transactions, there is no physical delivery of goods in financial futures. The settlement takes place by the payment of the cash difference between the price at which the contract was purchased and the value of the underlying asset on the final trading day. For example, suppose you purchase three-month futures contracts on the S&P Stock Index at $500 per contract and on settlement day suppose the index stands at $480. You would be obligated to pay the seller of the contracts the $20 per contract that was lost on the transaction.

Both purchasers and sellers of futures contracts are subject to margin requirements, which determine both the initial deposit and the maintenance level. Not only that, financial futures have a special pay-as-you-lose system. At the end of each trading day, the value of a futures contract is determined and the party suffering the loss pays that loss to the gainer. (This is called marking to market.) Thus, whether a buyer or a seller of a financial futures contract, you must pay all losses as they accrue. Unless a trader closes out his futures position, he would be required, in the event of an uninterrupted market slide, to continue to pay unrealized losses as they occurred.

Obviously, as shown in Chart 4, the ability to call turns in the stock market correctly can yield extraordinarily large profits. Economists disbelieve, and you should too, that such ability really exists. The results of managers seeking solely to profit from such transactions are as random as any other walk down Wall Street. It must be emphasized, however, that not all futures traders are speculators. S&P futures are widely used by index mutual funds as a method of investing a temporary influx of funds; in this way, the fund is always fully invested and can closely track the index. S&P futures are also widely used for hedging purposes. An investor who was very confident about the prospects for her stock holdings, but very nervous about the overall level of stock prices, might sell S&P futures in the hope that even if the stock market declined sharply, the profit from the sale of the futures would exceed the losses from any individual stock holdings.

The Controversy Over Derivatives

Controversy always accompanies great financial gains or losses. Derivatives have received more than their fair share of such attention. Two lines of criticism have been prominent. First, the squealing by players losing heavily in the derivatives markets led some regulators and politicians to worry aloud about the potential fragility of the whole financial system.

Chart 4
How to Look into the Future and Wind Up a Sartorial Genius or an Out-of-Pocket Bum
Three-Month Future Bought at $500; 2 Percent Margin Required

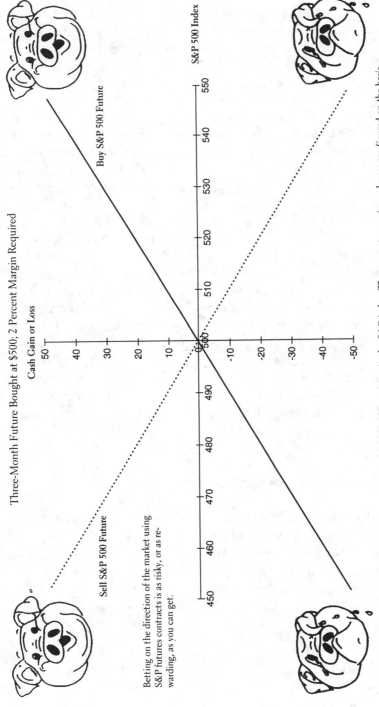

Three-Month Future Bought at $500; 2 Percent Margin Required

Cash Gain or Loss

50 40 30 20 10 0 -10 -20 -30 -40 -50

S&P 500 Index

450 460 470 480 490 500 510 520 530 540 550

Buy S&P 500 Future

Sell S&P 500 Future

Betting on the direction of the market using S&P futures contracts is as risky, or as rewarding, as you can get.

In this example, an investor with $2,000 would control a $100,000 position in the S&P index. The percentage gains or losses are figured on the basis of the original investment. The buyer of an S&P future profits dollar for dollar from any rise in the price of the index while sustaining an equivalent loss if the future market p rice of the index declines below the price at which her contract was originally executed. Just the opposite is true for the futures seller.

While trading in standardized options and futures is centrally cleared and guaranteed by well-capitalized clearing corporations, individually designed derivatives are simply bilateral transactions between buyer and seller. These customized derivatives are the ones responsible for the large losses suffered by many corporations during the mid-1990s. And since the counterparties to some derivative transactions were institutions in many different countries, some people who like to wallow in doom even imagined the possibility of a collapse of the international financial system if derivatives trading was not somehow regulated and contained.

A second line of attack on derivatives proclaims that they make stock and bond markets more volatile. Critics viewed the leverage available to options and futures traders as destabilizing because large positions can be taken and abandoned very quickly. The search to find villains is particularly intense after stock prices plunge dramatically, as they did during the crash of October 1987. Today's wicked financial pigs are said to be the proliferation of index futures (where one can buy or sell a basket of stocks) and computer program trading strategies (where one automatically enters orders for the simultaneous purchase or sale of a group of stocks, such as the S&P 500). I disagree.

Options and futures have flourished as an inexpensive mechanism for tracking and adjusting positions in underlying securities. Institutions wishing to change a portfolio's equity mix or hedge against market declines can do so more quickly and at lower brokerage costs in the futures market than in the underlying securities markets. This is why futures markets often react to new information first and give the impression that they cause price movements in the stock market.

I am particularly sorry to see the slop thrown at program trading. The technique follows the precept—advocated in every edition of this book—of using "passive portfolio management." Profits are eaten away by commissions and taxes when investors switch from security to security to catch good buying and selling opportunities. Indeed, two-thirds of active portfolio managers have consistently been outperformed by the unmanaged Standard & Poor's 500-Stock Index—a figure that amply demonstrates the wisdom of simply buying and holding the index (as is done by many "index funds"). Program trading is the technique whereby index funds can add or subtract from their investment portfolios. It is a healthy development that has improved the effectiveness of portfolio management.

"Index arbitrage" is another form of program trading. The goal is to create a perfectly hedged position and an abnormally large return by combining a portfolio of stocks with an index futures contract. Arbitrage opportunities arise whenever the value of an index future and the value of the underlying securities diverge. For example, suppose the value of the 500 stocks in the S&P index is $500 while the value of the S&P 500 future is $510. An index arbitrageur simultaneously sells the index at $510 and buys the underlying stocks through a program trade at $500 guaranteeing her a $10 profit, less commissions and carrying costs. The benefits of index arbitrage are twofold. First, by increasing trading, liquidity in both the securities and futures markets is enhanced. Second, arbitrage trades link markets together and insure that both the underlying securities and futures are appropriately priced. When new information arises about the stock market, the futures market is the natural entry point for this information because of the low cost of futures trading. And such news (or change in sentiment) may well be carried into the stock market through computer-driven index arbitrage. But arbitrage is merely the medium—not the message. Technology does not move markets, people do.

Futures markets arose to cope with underlying volatility. Blaming futures and related program trading for the volatility in the stock market is as illogical as blaming the thermometer for measuring uncomfortable temperatures. By making the market more quickly responsive to changes in underlying conditions or the sentiment of large institutions, program trading increases the efficiency of the stock market. To eliminate new instruments and techniques would be to make our markets less efficient. And because of the increasing integration of world financial markets, traders abroad would be sure to utilize any opportunities we discard.

After the 1929 crash, legislation was introduced to prohibit the use of telephones to transmit margin orders. Now derivatives and program trading are the target. But technology does not move markets, it merely facilitates the flow of orders. Program trading is not the mindless computer-driven technique that keeps the market from reflecting fundamental values. It reflects human decisions about the value of stocks, made easier to execute because of computers. If institutions decide to sell, they will do so whether by computers, telephones, or even hand signals from open windows to brokers outside, as was the case in earlier times.

Yes, sudden large movements in stock prices are upsetting to individual investors who feel at the mercy of large institutional traders. But to paraphrase a common expression, "If you can keep your head when those around you are losing theirs, you *do* understand the problem." The long-term investor can and should ignore short-term market volatility and not leave the stock market. The losers from volatility will be institutions which trade frequently in a futile attempt to time the market, not the steady investor who buys and holds for the long term.

Hysteria seems especially out of place when people proclaim that the large losses triggered by derivatives could threaten the stability of the world financial system. While enormous leverage and extraordinary potential losses from derivatives will continue to receive banner headlines, a number of international study groups have concluded that a spreading worldwide financial crisis caused by derivatives is highly unlikely. Speculators who take large risks will continue to risk ruin, and some financial institutions—even large ones—will continue to fail. But a systematic undermining of world financial stability caused by derivatives trading does not deserve to be on the top of anyone's worry list.

Some Rules for Individual Investors

How can you as an individual investor take advantage of derivatives? It is not easy because the risks are large and the transactions-cost savings available to institutions are usually not available for smaller players. Not surprisingly, many investment counselors suggest that individuals "just say no" to the futures market and "not exercise their options." I believe, however, that the following three situations provide acceptable opportunities for an individual's use of derivatives.

1. *Options buying as an adjunct to investing in index mutual funds*

As I have mentioned repeatedly, most investors would be far better off owning low-cost index mutual funds (diversified to include bonds, smaller companies, and international stocks as well as the major U.S. stocks included in indexes such as the S&P 500). I recognize, however, that many investors, particularly those with a gambling temperament, will not be satisfied unless they do some picking of individual stocks. If you are one of these people, you might want to commit 95 percent of your funds to index mutual funds and speculate with the remaining 5 percent. The option market allows you to buy a few positions for a moderate amount of money and the odds are certainly better than either the horse races or your state lottery. Be prepared to lose your entire 5 percent stake because that is a real possibility, and take to heart the lessons of the Princeton Students Investment Club. You may well enrich only your broker by undertaking an option-buying strategy. Moreover, your gains, if any, will be taxed at ordinary income-tax rates. And never forget, you are gambling and not investing.

2. *Option writing as an adjunct to portfolio management*

A strategy that is more likely to be profitable and may even save on taxes is an option-writing strategy undertaken in connection with the management of a diversified stock portfolio. As someone who believes largely in the efficient market theory, I advocate a buy-and-hold strategy. Doing very little trading minimizes both transactions charges and taxes. The only time it makes sense to sell a stock is when it no longer fulfills your expectations and it has *declined* in price. Selling a stock that has gone down will usually reduce your taxes.

Consider, however, the situation facing Dr. Brown. Dr. Brown was proud of her portfolio, which included a substantial number of pharmaceutical stocks that she knew from her work. Merck & Co., Inc. was her most successful holding at the start of 1993. It was trading at about $50 per share while her cost was below $5 per share. Though proud of her overall portfolio, Dr. Brown became worried about Merck because appreciation in the stock had made it very much overweighted in her holdings. She also felt that a combination of competitive market pressures and governmental jawboning would restrain future increases in drug prices. Finally, she felt that Merck's vaunted research department had produced a less than blockbuster product pipeline of future drugs, and this too suggested a slowing of future earnings growth. Dr. Brown preferred not to have almost half of her portfolio in just one stock.

The dilemma facing Dr. Brown seemed insoluble. She was overinvested in a stock that she confidently believed would have a far less rosy future than its past. Moreover, industry changes and political pressures could make Merck's stock vulnerable to a substantial price decline. But selling all or part of her shares would generate a large capital gains liability. Figuring both the federal and state capital gains tax, she would lose more than 30 percent of her investment to taxes.

Option writing gave Dr. Brown a way out of her dilemma. Dr. Brown began a program of writing call options of approximately three months in length "at-the-money," that is, with a striking price at or about the then current market price of $50. For this, she received an option premium of about $4 per share, or 8 percent of the market price. Because Merck is a relatively stable stock, its option premiums tend to be a smaller percentage of the price of the stock than options on a volatile stock such as Micron Technology. The main determinants of option premiums "at-the-money" are (1) the stock's characteristic volatility and (2) the length of time the option runs. The Appendix to this chapter presents a fuller discussion of what determines futures prices and option premiums.

At the end of the three-month period, the price of Merck stock remained at about $50. The option expired unexercised and she then wrote (sold) another three-month call option for $400. At the end of the next period, her fears began to be realized. The price of Merck fell to $45 and again the option re-

mained unexercised. Dr. Brown in effect lost $5 per share in the
market value of the stock but pocketed the $400 option pre-
mium as well as the generous quarterly dividend paid by
Merck. Hence, she largely avoided the loss she would have
suffered if she had taken no offsetting action in the options
market.

Dr. Brown continued to write call options on Merck stock
each three months. At times the price of Merck actually rose
during these periods. She had to cover her call (buy it back in
the open market). She would lose money on the option transaction only if Merck rose by more than the amount of the option
premium. And, of course, since she still owned the stock, any
losses would be offset by her gain on the shares.

Two years passed and Dr. Brown then calculated the results from her strategy. It turned out she was correct in her
worries about Merck's prospects during this period. Over the
two-year period during 1993 and 1994, Merck's stock declined
from $50 to $35 a share, a $1,500 loss for each 100 shares she
owned. Had Dr. Brown taken no action, she would have seen
the value of her portfolio investment in Merck shrink by 30
percent. By continuously writing options, however, Dr. Brown
actually came out ahead:

Value of premiums collected	$26.00
(8 call options written—average price	
$3.25/share net of transactions costs)	
Less cost to buy back options which	(−4.00)
did not expire	
Dividends for two years	2.24
Total gain per share	$24.24

She collected $24.24 per share from the holding and option-
writing strategy, which, even after paying income taxes on the
value of the expired option premiums, more than offset the capital loss from the shares. And eventually, when she felt that
Merck had declined sufficiently to make it an attractive holding
again (and a much smaller percentage of her total portfolio),
she discontinued option writing and simply held her long position in the stock.

3. *The use of index options and futures as hedging instruments*

Marcus Pincus, Esq., was named executor of a multimillion dollar estate, invested in a diversified portfolio of stocks—including the stocks of a number of very small companies. His assignment was a profitable but messy one. There were many beneficiaries, some who wanted to receive pro rata share in the stock, others who wished to receive cash. Moreover, there were a number of complicated legal challenges that had to be dealt with and which made it prudent to make no changes in the estate's assets. The problem was that Pincus was quite nervous about the high level of stock prices that prevailed in the mid-1990s. He worried that since it would be a long time before the estate would be settled, he would be criticized if stock prices declined sharply. What he needed was a hedge that would protect the corpus of the estate if the market took a nose dive.

Derivative markets provided just such a hedge. Some alternatives were ruled out immediately. For example, it was not possible to sell call options against the entire portfolio since many of the smaller stocks did not have active option markets. Pincus could have sold futures contracts against the portfolio but he knew that would be likely to eliminate any chance for big gains if the market rose. While the portfolio was likely to increase in value, losses would be suffered on the futures contracts. What Pincus simply wanted was an insurance policy that would insulate the portfolio from catastrophic losses during the time period that the estate was being settled. The vehicle that enabled Pincus to accomplish his objective was a "deep out-of-the-money" put option.

At the time of his decision, the S&P stock index was selling near the $500 level. While Pincus could have bought three-month S&P puts with a striking price of $500 (at or slightly in-the-money), they would have been very expensive. With each put option purchased costing about 10 percent, a year's worth of protection for the entire portfolio would have cost about 40 percent of its total value. Pincus, however, only wanted protection against a major drop in the market. He found that deep out-of-the-money puts (puts with a striking price of $440, almost 15 percent below current market levels) could be bought for a cost of about ¾ of 1 percent, or for about 3 percent per year. Pincus knew that this bought him protection only from a disaster, that is, a 15 percent drop in the market. But the cost was low. And even though he never exercised the options prior to the settlement of the estate, he was very happy for the protection. Just as he was happy to continue to pay premiums on his homeowners insurance policy, even though his house never burned down, so he was delighted to have been able to use the options market to buy catastrophe insurance for the estate.

Appendix to Chapter 11:
What Determines Prices
in the Futures and
Options Markets?

One probably does need to be a rocket scientist to figure out the latest wrinkles in the pricing formulas used by professionals to determine the appropriate price to pay for any specific futures or options contract. It is possible, however, for any individual to understand the basic determinants of these prices and, therefore, to have at least a general idea why some options may sell at 15 percent and others at only 5 percent of the market value of the underlying stock.

Let's deal with the futures market first and see what is involved in the pricing of a silver future. Let's suppose that the spot price of silver for immediate delivery is $6.00 an ounce. Suppose further that the price of a silver future for delivery in three months time is $6.10. Is the futures market some kind of con game whereby buyers are, in effect, cheated out of an extra ten cents? Not at all. Consider the situation faced by an individual who needs a certain quantity of silver in three months time. He could buy the silver now at $6.00 per ounce and hold onto it until it was needed. This would involve two kinds of costs, however. First, he would have to store the silver for 90 days and this would involve storage costs of perhaps $0.01 per ounce. Second, buying silver in the spot market would involve an immediate payment of the $6.00 price and, thus, what economists call an opportunity cost. By paying for the silver now, one foregoes the opportunity to invest the money for 90 days in a perfectly safe investment such as a Treasury bill. If Treasury bill yields were 6 percent per year (or 1.5 percent per quarter), the spot buyer would have foregone the opportunity to earn $0.09 (the $6.00 times 1.5 percent). Hence, the buyer in need of silver would be indifferent between buying silver in the spot market at $6.00 or buying it in the futures market at $6.10. Similarly, the seller would be equally happy to receive $6.00 now, which would enable her to save on storage costs and earn interest on the receipts, or receive $6.10 at the end of the quarter.

From this simple illustration, the basic determinants of the spread between spot and futures prices can be made clear. Futures prices depend on the interest rate and storage costs. Moreover, one additional factor is likely to enter the equation—the so-called "convenience yield" of having the inventory directly on hand. In general, the futures price will be above the spot price because of the interest and storage factors, but it could in some circumstances be lower when the convenience yield is very high, as might happen if the commodity was in very short supply.

Similarly, we can list the factors determining option prices. The factors have to do with the characteristics of the options contract and those of the underlying stock and the market. Five factors are important:

1) *The Exercise Price*

   Suppose Micron Technology is selling at $40 per share. A call option exercisable at $40 is clearly more valuable than one exercisable at $50 per share, well "out-of-the-money." The higher the exercise price, the lower the value of the option. Of course, the value of the option can never go below zero. As long as there is some probability that the market price of the stock could exceed the exercise price in the future, the option will have some value.

2) *The Stock Price*

   All other things being the same, the higher the stock price, the higher will be the price of the call option. Obviously, if a stock is selling at $1 per share, the option could not possibly be worth more than $1, since purchasing the stock directly would allow the investor to realize whatever appreciation develops while the investor's risk would be limited to the purchase price. An option premium on such a stock might run 5 or 10 cents per share. On the other hand, the value of an at-the-money call on a $100 stock could be $5 or $10 per share.

3) *Expiration Date*

The longer the option has to run, the greater its value. Consider two options on Micron Technology with an exercise price of $40 per share. Obviously, a six-month option is worth more than a three-month option, since it has an additional three months within which the call on the stock can be exercised. Thus, if something good happens to the company, the buyer of the longer option will have a longer period over which she can take advantage of any favorable outcome.

4) *The Volatility of the Stock*

This is the key factor determining the value of a stock option. The greater the volatility of the underlying stock in question, the higher the cost of a call option. An at-the-money call on Micron Technology, which is an extremely volatile stock, is likely to sell for very much more than an at-the-money call of similar length on a more stable stock such as AT&T. For the stable stock, it is unlikely that the call buyer will make a killing since the stock characteristically doesn't fluctuate much. Similarly, on the down side, buying the stock directly does not involve great risk. On the other hand, buying Micron Technology, which is very volatile, does involve considerable risk which is limited when the investor buys the call option. At the same time, very favorable outcomes could lead to a big rise in Micron Technology stock, making the potential worth of the option far greater than in the AT&T case.

5) *Interest Rates*

Call prices are also a function of the level of interest rates. The buyer of a call option does not pay the exercise price until and unless he exercises the option. The ability to delay payment is more valuable when interest rates are high and, therefore, earnings opportunities on cash are very attractive.

A model has been developed by Fischer Black and Myron Scholes to make quantitative estimates of options values based upon the factors just outlined. While the mathematics of these formulas are quite forbidding, they are easily programmed on a personal computer and they are used extensively by option buyers and traders to determine the appropriate value of option premiums. It turns out that option premiums fluctuate reasonably closely around the values suggested by the Black-Scholes model.

A Practical Guide for Random Walkers and Other Investors

12

A Fitness Manual for Random Walkers

In investing money, the amount of interest you want should depend on whether you want to eat well or sleep well.
—J. Kenfield Morley, *Some Things I Believe*

Part Four is a how-to-do-it guide for your random walk down Wall Street. In this chapter, I shall offer general investment advice that should be useful to all investors, even if they don't believe that security markets are highly efficient. In Chapter Thirteen, I try to explain the recent fluctuations that have occurred in stock and bond returns and survey the stock and bond markets of the mid-1990s. In that chapter, I will indicate how investors can at least roughly gauge the long-run returns they are likely to achieve from different investment programs. In Chapter Fourteen, I present a life-cycle investment guide indicating how the stage of your life plays an important role in determining the mix of investments that is most likely to enable you to meet your financial goals.

In the final chapter, I outline three specific strategies for equity investors who believe at least partially in the random-walk theory or who are convinced that even if real expertise does exist, they are unlikely to find it. I have yet to see any compelling evidence that past stock prices can be used to predict future stock prices, and I am convinced that new information quickly gets reflected in market prices. I can't, however, keep in step with a "strong" random walker. While markets are reasonably efficient, I doubt that there will ever be a time when no one possesses any useful nonpublic information. Moreover, I have seen enough castles in the air to leave me skeptical about the market's vaunted ability to price all assets perfectly at all times. In economic jargon, I am a weak or semi-strong random walker and, as such, I believe useful techniques and unique investment opportunities often exist.

Remember, you'll need the highest possible returns on your investment funds to keep up with inflation. If inflation proceeds at, say, a 4 percent rate, the price level will double and your dollars will lose half their value in just over seventeen years. Hence, if you are sensible, you will take your random walk only after you have made detailed and careful plans with regard to all your investments, including your cash reserves. Even if stock prices move randomly, you shouldn't. Think of the advice that follows as a set of warm-up exercises that will enable you to reduce your income taxes and risk and at the same time increase your returns.

Exercise 1: Cover Thyself with Protection

Disraeli once wrote that "patience is a necessary ingredient of genius." It's also a key element in investing; you can't afford to pull your money out at the wrong time. You need staying power to increase your odds of earning attractive long-run returns. That's why it is so important for you to have noninvestment resources, such as medical and life insurance, to draw on should any emergency strike you or your family.

It used to be that there were only two broad categories of life insurance products available: high-premium whole-life and low-cost term insurance. The standard whole-life insurance policy combines an insurance scheme with a type of savings plan; the latter was supposed to be attractive because the savings accumulate tax free. But when double-digit inflation battered the U.S. economy, insurance buyers had second thoughts about the savings aspect of whole-life policies. Many of the assets of these policies had been invested in pre-inflation bonds and the yields on the savings part of the policies were as low as 3 or 4 percent per year. Since older whole-life policies generally allowed you to borrow the amount saved at attractive interest rates as low as 4 or 5 percent, consumers in the early 1980s borrowed over $45 billion against the cash value of their policies and many invested these dollars in money-market funds paying double-digit yields. Other consumers just gave up totally on whole-life policies and switched to term insurance, which I recommended in earlier editions. Term insurance provides death benefits only and provides no buildup of cash value. By 1981, this form of insurance accounted for more than half the volume of individual life sales.

Into this changing insurance market stepped two new products: universal life and variable life. Some companies appear to be trying to cover all bases by offering "universal-variable" policies. With a universal life insurance policy, you can raise or lower the premium or death benefit according to your changing needs. You do this by, in effect, buying more or less term insurance, which is what provides for death benefits. In addition, interest rates on the cash value are allowed to change with market interest rates, rather than being tied to an insurance company's portfolio yield at the time you buy your policy. With variable life, the premium does not vary but the rate on which your cash value builds up does. This is possible because you choose the investment medium in which your cash values are invested. In effect, it is like having money with a mutual-fund family. If you choose the right investment plan (say a growth-stock fund during a period when they are booming), you come out ahead. The "universal-variable" policies give the policyholder universal's flexibility in premiums and death benefits and variable's menu of investment choices.

Increasingly, however, there is less difference between these "new wave" policies and ordinary whole life. Many traditional whole-life policies are now becoming somewhat more "interest sensitive." But, as with any cash value policy, your early premiums go mainly for sales commissions and other overhead rather than for buildup of cash value. Thus, not all your money goes to work. Hence, for most people, I continue to favor the do-it-yourself approach. Buy term insurance for protection—invest the difference yourself (preferably in tax-deferred plans such as IRAs).

Many people, however, will not regularly and consistently

invest what they have saved by paying lower insurance premiums. If you are not confident of your ability to set up and maintain an investment program but nevertheless want to be sure there will be a certain amount of money available to your family when you die, you do need to buy permanent whole-life insurance, and you may find one of the flexible new wave policies useful.

But if you have the discipline to save, my advice is to buy renewable term insurance; you can keep renewing your policy without the need for a physical examination. So-called decreasing term insurance, renewable for progressively lower amounts, should suit many families best, since as time passes (and the children and family resources grow), the need for protection usually diminishes. Unless you will incur heavy penalties for discontinuing your present coverage, have a special tax reason for buying permanent insurance (and there are significant tax advantages for some people in buying an interest-sensitive insurance policy), or are able to save money only when a bill from your insurance company forces you to do so, look for a term-insurance plan. You should understand, however, that term-insurance premiums escalate sharply when you reach the age of sixty or seventy or higher. If you still need insurance at that point, you will find that term insurance has become prohibitively expensive. But the major risk at that point is not premature death; it is that you will live too long and outlive your assets. You can increase those assets more effectively by buying term insurance and using the money you save for the investments I'll discuss below.

Take the time to shop around for the best deal. There is considerable variation in insurance-company rates, and you can often get a better deal by looking around.

In addition, you should keep some reserves in safe and liquid investments. That, surely, is to many the antithesis of investing. Why put money in a safe place when you could be picking the next winner on the stock market? To cover unforeseen emergencies, that's why! It's the height of folly to gamble that nothing will happen to you. Every family should have a reserve of funds to pay an unexpected medical bill or to provide a cushion during a time of unemployment.

The old rule of thumb was that a year's living expenses should be kept in assets that could be converted to cash quickly and without loss. If you are protected by medical and disability insurance, this emergency reserve can be reduced safely. Indeed, even some bank trust departments—the acme of conservative money management—now estimate that a reserve that will cover living expenses for three months is satisfactory. In no case, however, should you be without at least some assets near the safe and liquid end of the spectrum. Moreover, any large future expenditures (such as junior's college tuition bill) should be funded with short-term investments whose maturity matches the date on which the funds will be needed.

Exercise 2: Know Your Investment Objectives

This is a part of the investment process that too many people skip, with disastrous results. You must decide at the outset what degree of risk you are willing to assume and what kinds of investments are most suitable to your tax bracket. The securities markets are like a large restaurant with a variety of products, suitable for different tastes and needs. Just as there is no one food that is best for everyone, so there is no one investment that is best for all investors.

We would all like to double our capital overnight, but how many of us can afford to see half our capital disintegrate just as quickly? J. P. Morgan once had a friend who was so worried about his stock holdings that he could not sleep at night. The friend asked, "What should I do about my stocks?" Morgan replied, "Sell down to the sleeping point." He wasn't kidding. Every investor must decide the trade-off he or she is willing to make between eating well and sleeping well. The decision is up to you. High investment rewards can be achieved only at the cost of substantial risk-taking. This has been one of the fundamental lessons of this book. So what's your sleeping point? Finding the answer to this question is one of the most important investment steps you must take.

To help raise your investment consciousness, I've prepared

a sleeping scale on investment risk and expected rate of return, as of the mid-1990s. At the stultifying end of the spectrum are a variety of short-term investments. A bank account appears to be the safest investment of all. You are *certain* to be able to withdraw every dollar you put in. The dollar value of your investment will never fluctuate. But even this investment does have a risk, because with continued inflation, you are, unfortunately, just about certain to lose out in real purchasing power even with the interest added, especially if you pay taxes on the interest. Next come special six-month certificates, money-market deposit accounts, and money-market funds—somewhat less flexible, but far more likely to offer inflation protection. If this is your sleeping point, you'll be interested in the information on these kinds of investments in Exercise 4.

Corporate bonds are somewhat riskier, and some dreams will start intruding in your sleep pattern if you choose this form of investment. In the mid-1990s, the yield on good-quality, long-term public-utility bonds was around 8 percent when held to maturity. Should you sell before then, your return will depend on the level of interest rates at the time of sale. If they rise in yield, your bonds will fall to a price that makes their yield competitive with new bonds offering a higher stated interest rate. Thus, there is a chance of loss. Your capital loss could be enough to eat up a whole year's interest—or even more. On the other hand, if interest rates fall, the price of your bonds will rise and you will get not only the promised percent interest but also a capital gain. Thus, if you sell prior to maturity, your actual yearly return could vary considerably, and that is why bonds are riskier than short-term instruments, which carry almost no risk of principal fluctuation. Generally, the longer a bond's term to maturity, the greater the risk and the greater the resulting yield.* You will find some useful information on how to buy both short- and long-term bonds in Exercises 4 and 5.

*This isn't always the case. During some periods of unusually high interest rates in the 1980s, for example, short-term securities actually yielded more than long-term bonds. The catch was that investors could not count on continually reinvesting their short-term funds at such high rates, and by later in the decade, short-term rates had declined sharply. Thus, investors can reasonably expect that continual investment in short-term securities will not produce as high a return as investment in long-term bonds. In other words, there is a reward for taking on the risk of owning long-term bonds even if short-term rates are temporarily above long-term rates.

No one can say for sure what the returns on common stocks will be. But the stock market, as Oskar Morgenstern once observed, is like a gambling casino where the odds are rigged in favor of the players. Although stock prices do plummet, as they did so disastrously during October 1987, the overall return over the whole twentieth century has been about 9 to 10 percent per year, including both dividends and capital gains. I believe that a portfolio of common stocks such as those that make up a typical mutual fund will have similar average annual rates of return during the twenty-first century. The actual yearly return in the future can and probably will deviate substantially from this target—in down years you may lose as much as 25 percent or more. Can you stand the sleepless nights in the bad years?

How about dreams in full color with quadraphonic sound? You may want to choose a portfolio of somewhat riskier (more volatile) stocks, like those in aggressive growth-oriented mutual funds. These are the stocks in younger companies in newer technologies, where the promise of greater growth exists. Such companies are likely to be more volatile performers, and portfolios of these issues can easily lose half of their value in a bad market year. But your average future rate of return for the twenty-first century could be in the neighborhood of 10–11 percent per year. Portfolios of smaller stocks have tended to outperform the market averages by small amounts. If you have no trouble sleeping during bear markets, and if you have the staying power to stick with your investments, an aggressive common-stock portfolio—made up of smaller companies—may be just right for you.

Real estate is a very tricky and often sleepless investment for most individuals. Nevertheless, the returns from real estate have been quite generous, similar to those from common stocks. I'll argue in Exercise 6 that individuals who can afford to buy their own homes are well advised to do so. In Exercise 7, I will discuss how individuals can invest in commercial real estate.

I realize that my table slights gold and omits art objects, commodities, and other more exotic investment possibilities. Many of these have done very well, especially when inflation was accelerating, and can serve a useful role in balancing a

The Sleeping Scale of Major Investment Choices

Sleeping Point	Type of Asset	Expected Rate of Return, 1995 (before Income Taxes)	Length of Time Investment Must Be Held to Get Expected Rate of Return	Risk Level
Semicomatose state	Bank accounts	2½–3%	No specific investment period required. Many thrift institutions calculate interest from day of deposit to day of withdrawal.	No risk of losing what you put in. Deposits up to $100,000 guaranteed by an agency of the federal government. An almost sure loser with high inflation, however.
Long afternoon naps and sound night's sleep	Money-market deposit accounts	3½–4%	No specific investment period required but check withdrawals limited to 3 per month.	No risk of losing what you put in. Deposits guaranteed as above. Rates geared to expected inflation. Will vary over time.
Sound night's sleep	Money-market funds	4½–5%	No specific investment period required. Most funds provide check-writing privileges.	Very little since most funds are invested in bank certificates. Not usually guaranteed, however, and some funds have taken risky positions in derivatives. Some funds buy only government securities. Rates vary with expected inflation.
	Special six-month certificates	5%	Money must be left on deposit for the entire six months to take advantage of higher rate.	Early withdrawals subject to penalty. Rates geared to expected inflation. Will vary.
An occasional dream or two—some possibly unpleasant	High-quality corporate bonds (prime-quality public utilities)	8–8¼%	Investments must be made for the period until the maturity of the bond (20–30 years) to be assured of the stated rate. (The bonds also need to be protected against redemption.) The bonds may be sold at any time, however, in which case the net return will depend on fluctuations in the market price of the bonds.	Very little if held to maturity. Moderate to substantial fluctuations can be expected in realized return if bonds are sold prior to maturity. Rate geared to expected long-run inflation rate. This may differ from *actual* rate over the term to maturity of the bond. "Junk bonds" promise much higher returns but with much higher risk.

The Sleeping Scale of Major Investment Choices (Continued)

Sleeping Point	Type of Asset	Expected Rate of Return, 1995 (before Income Taxes)	Length of Time Investment Must Be Held to Get Expected Rate of Return	Risk Level
Some tossing and turning before you doze and vivid dreams before awakening	Diversified portfolios of blue-chip common stocks (such as an index fund)	9%	No specific investment period required, and stocks may be sold at any time. The average expected return assumes a fairly long investment period and can only be treated as a rough guide based on current conditions.	Moderate to substantial. In any one year, the actual return could in fact be negative. Diversified portfolios have at times lost 25% or more of their actual value. Contrary to some opinion—a good inflation hedge.
Nightmares not uncommon, but over the long run well rested	Diversified portfolios of relatively risky stocks (such as aggressive growth-oriented mutual funds)	9–10%	Same as above. The average expected return assumes a fairly long investment period and can only be treated as a rough guide based on current conditions.	Substantial. In any one year the actual return could be negative. Diversified portfolios of very risky stocks have at times lost 50% or more of their value. Good inflation hedge.
Vivid dreams and occasional nightmares	Real estate	Similar to common stocks	Only makes sense as a very long-term investment. Heavy transactions costs in trading.	Can't sell in a hurry without substantial penalties. Hard to diversify. Very good inflation hedge if bought at reasonable price levels.
Bouts of insomnia	Gold	Impossible to predict	High returns could be earned in any new speculative craze as long as there are greater fools to be found.	Substantial. Believed to be a hedge against doomsday and hyperinflation. Can, however, play a useful role in balancing a diversified portfolio.

well-diversified portfolio of paper assets. Because of their substantial risk, and thus extreme volatility, it's impossible to describe them in the kind of terms applied to other investments; Exercise 8 reviews them in greater detail.

In all likelihood, your sleeping point will be greatly influenced by the way in which a loss would affect your financial survival. That is why the typical "widow" is often viewed in investment texts as unable to take on much risk. The widow has neither the life expectancy nor the ability to earn, outside her portfolio, the income she would need to recoup losses. Any loss of capital and income will immediately affect her standard of living. At the other end of the spectrum is the "aggressive young businesswoman." She has both the life expectancy and the earning power to maintain her standard of living in the face of any financial loss. At what stage you are in the "life cycle" is so important that I have devoted a special chapter (Chapter Fourteen) to this determinant of how much risk is appropriate for you.

In addition, your psychological makeup will influence the degree of risk you are willing to assume. One investment adviser suggests that you consider what kind of Monopoly player you once were (or still are). Were you a plunger? Did you construct hotels on Boardwalk and Park Place? True, the other players seldom landed on your property, but when they did, you could win the whole game in one fell swoop. Or did you prefer the steadier but moderate income from the orange monopoly of St. James Place, Tennessee Avenue, and New York Avenue? The answers to these questions may give you some insight into your psychological makeup with respect to investing, and may help you to choose the right categories of securities for you. Or perhaps the analogy breaks down when it comes to the money game, which is played for keeps. In any event, it is critical that you understand yourself before choosing specific securities for investment. Chapter Fourteen presents a special test you can take to help determine your ability to bear risk.

A second key step is to review how much of your investment return goes to Uncle Sam and how much current income you need. Check your last year's income-tax form (1040) and the taxable income you reported for the year. The table on the following page shows the 1994 marginal tax brackets (rates paid on the last dollar of income) as well as the tax advantage of municipal (tax-exempt) bonds. If you are in a high tax bracket, with little need for current income, you will prefer bonds that are tax exempt and stocks that have low dividend yields but promise favorably taxed long-term capital gains (where taxes do not have to be paid until gains are realized—perhaps never, if the stocks are part of a bequest). On the other hand, if you are in a low tax bracket and need a high current income, you will be better off with taxable bonds and high-dividend-paying common stocks, so that you don't have to incur the heavy transactions charges involved in selling off shares periodically to meet current-income needs.

The two steps in this exercise—finding your risk level, and identifying your tax bracket and income needs—seem obvious. But it is incredible how many people go astray by mismatching the types of securities they buy with their risk tolerance and their income and tax needs. The confusion of priorities so often displayed by investors is not unlike that exhibited by a young woman whose saga was recently written up in a London newspaper:

RED FACES IN PARK

London, Oct. 30.

Secret lovers were locked in a midnight embrace when it all happened.

Wedged into a tiny two-seater sports car, the near-naked man was suddenly immobilised by a slipped disc, according to a doctor writing in a medical journal here.

Trapped beneath him his desperate girlfriend tried to summon help by sounding the hooter button with her foot. A doctor, ambulancemen, firemen and a group of interested passers-by quickly surrounded the couple's car in Regents Park.

Dr. Brian Richards of Kent said: "The lady found herself trapped beneath 200 pounds of a pain-racked, immobile man.

"To free the couple, firemen had to cut away the car frame," he added.

The distraught girl, helped out of the car and into a coat,

1994 Taxable Equivalent Yield Table[a]

| If Taxable Income is: (Thousands) | | Your Federal Tax Bracket Is | With a Tax-Free Yield of: | | | | | | | | | |
Single Return	Joint Return		3.50%	4.00%	4.50%	5.00%	5.50%	6.00%	6.50%	7.00%	7.50%	8.00%
			You Need to Find a Taxable Investment Yielding (%)									
$22.8–55.1	$38–91.9	28.0%	4.86	5.56	6.25	6.94	7.64	8.33	9.02	9.72	10.42	11.11
55.1–115	91.9–140	31.0	5.07	5.80	6.52	7.25	7.97	8.70	9.42	10.14	10.87	11.59
115–250	140–250	36.0	5.47	6.25	7.03	7.81	8.59	9.37	10.16	10.94	11.72	12.50
Over $250	Over $250	39.6	5.79	6.62	7.45	8.28	9.11	9.93	10.76	11.59	12.42	13.25

[a]To see what a taxable security would have to yield to equal the yield of a tax-free security, find your taxable income and read across. The table is based on federal income-tax rates established by the Revenue Reconciliation Act of 1993 and assumes that all income would otherwise be taxable at the investor's highest tax rate. Federal income tax brackets will be adjusted annually to reflect changes in the Consumer Price Index; therefore, an individual's tax bracket may differ from the tax bracket shown in the table. Certain taxpayers may find their effective marginal federal tax rates to be greater than the federal tax rates shown in this table. Those investors would need a higher taxable return than those shown here to equal the corresponding tax-free yield. Income may be subject to state and local taxes.

sobbed: "How am I going to explain to my husband what has happened to his car?"

—Reuters.

Investors are often torn by a similar confusion of priorities. You can't seek safety of principal and then take a plunge with investment into the riskiest of common stocks. You can't shelter your income from high marginal tax rates and then lock in returns of 8 percent from taxable corporate bonds, no matter how attractive these may be. Yet, the annals of investment counselors are replete with stories of investors whose security holdings are inconsistent with their investment goals.

Exercise 3: Dodge Uncle Sam Whenever You Can

One of the best ways to obtain extra investment funds is to avoid taxes legally. We've already discussed tax-exempt bonds and the tax advantages of unrealized capital gains. But did you know that you pay no income taxes on money invested in a retirement plan (or on the earnings from this investment) until you actually retire and use the money? At that time, you may be in a lower tax bracket. Even if you are not then in a lower bracket, you will have paid no taxes on your retirement savings over the years. This exercise makes you fit enough to reap these benefits.

First, check to see if your employer has a pension or profit-sharing plan, such as a 401(k) and 403(b)7 savings plan. If so, you are home free. But what if your employer doesn't have such a plan? If you're single, as of 1994 you can contribute up to $2,000 of your annual income a year to an Individual Retirement Account (IRA). If you're married and both you and your spouse work, you can contribute $4,000. If your spouse is not working, you can contribute $2,250. While the contribution to your IRA is no longer tax deductible, if your income exceeds $25,000 (and you are single), IRAs are still a good deal, because

the interest earnings on your contributions compound free of
tax.* The chart below compares a $2,000 annual contribution to
an IRA, where the interest earnings are not taxed, with the
equivalent contribution to a taxable (a 28 percent rate is assumed) investment. The chart assumes funds are invested at a
10 percent interest rate and that contributions are made for a
25-year period. While it is true that the earnings withdrawn
from a tax-deferred account will ultimately be taxed, a 25-year
deferral of taxes paid implies almost a $77,000 advantage for
the IRA account, as the chart shows. If your income is low
enough to qualify for a deduction on the IRA contributions as
well, you will be even further ahead.

For self-employed people, Congress has created the Keogh

The Advantage of Tax-deferred Compounded Earnings*

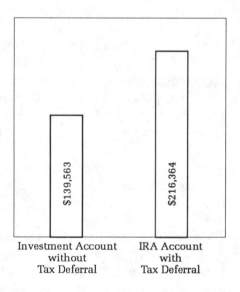

Investment Account   IRA Account
       without   with
    Tax Deferral   Tax Deferral

Source: Vanguard Group of Investment Companies.
*Value of $2,000 yearly investment at 10 percent rate for 25 years with and without tax
deferral of interest earnings.

*The contributions to IRAs are fully deductible if your income is under $25,000 and
you are single or if you and your spouse have joint income under $40,000. IRAs are
partially deductible for single incomes between $25,000 and $34,999 and for joint incomes between $40,000 and $49,999.

plan. Since 1984, all self-employed individuals—from accountants to Avon ladies, barbers to real estate brokers, doctors to decorators—are permitted to establish such a plan, to which they can contribute as much as 20 percent of their income, up to $30,000 annually. If you moonlight from your regular job, you can establish a Keogh for the income you earn on the side. The money paid into a Keogh is deductible from taxable income, and the earnings are not taxed until they are withdrawn. If you qualify for this plan, you'll be making a big mistake not to take advantage of this perfectly legal way to checkmate the Internal Revenue Service and maximize your retirement savings to help you cope with the effects of inflation.

Millions of taxpayers are currently missing what is one of the truly good deals around. Unless we look at a few numbers, it's impossible to realize what a difference these plans can make. Let's say you're thirty-five years old and contribute $1,000 to a Keogh plan this year, placing this sum in fixed-income investments yielding 10 percent. In thirty years (when you are sixty-five), your $1,000 investment will have compounded tax free to $17,449.* Now suppose you withdraw the whole amount at age sixty-five, when you retire. If you are then in the 28 percent tax bracket, you will retain $12,563 *after all taxes.* If you are in a lower bracket when you retire, you will obviously be even better off.

Consider now the alternative of not establishing a Keogh plan. Your $1,000 will then be taxed at the regular rate. That means that if you are presently in the 28 percent bracket, you will retain only $720 for investment in 10 percent securities. What's more, each year's interest will be taxed, so that your net earnings rate, after a tax of 28 percent, will be only 7.2 percent. At age sixty-five, you will end up with only $5,834 *after taxes,* assuming you haven't blown the money on a good toot sometime along the way. In this conservative example, a Keogh plan (or deductible IRA) allows you to end up with over two times as much income, after taxes, at retirement. And we've just looked at a single $1,000 contribution; suppose you contrib-

*The calculation assumes you can continue to reinvest the interest earnings at the same 10 percent rate.

ute $1,000 every year or, better still, the maximum amount you can contribute to a Keogh or other deductible retirement plan. My advice is to save as much as you can through these tax-sheltered means. Use up any other savings you may have for current living expenses, if you must, so you can contribute the maximum allowed.

Is there a fly in the ointment? Yes, as the favorite expression of economists goes, "There ain't no such thing as a completely free lunch." You can't touch IRA or Keogh funds before turning fifty-nine and a half or becoming disabled. If you do, the amount withdrawn is taxed, and in addition you must pay a 10 percent penalty on it.

But even with this catch, I believe IRAs and Keoghs are a good deal. While 10 percent of what you withdraw is indeed a stiff penalty, it's really not too much to pay for having been able to compound your savings tax free and to defer taxes on the income you put into the plan. Certainly, the advantages of staying in the plan for a few years far outweigh the penalty, even if you do withdraw some funds.

The important point is that if you plan to have any money saved up by the time you are fifty-nine and a half, you may as well do your saving by means of a tax-free retirement fund. Whatever your savings and investment decisions, it's always better to keep the sums involved tax free.

What can Keogh and IRA funds be invested in? You name it—stocks, bonds, mutual funds, savings certificates, annuity contracts, and other investments. Your choice should depend on your risk preferences as well as the composition of your other investment holdings. You can choose from a wide variety of plans offered by savings institutions, securities dealers, insurance companies, and mutual funds. My own preference would be stock and bond funds, and I'll give you specific advice later on choosing the best vehicle for you. You certainly don't want to invest in lower-yield tax-exempt securities, however, since your retirement fund will accumulate tax free anyway.

Any further questions regarding the plans? You can call your local office of the Internal Revenue Service for answers to specific questions. Also, IRS publications 560 (Keoghs) and 590 (IRAs) cover all the detailed regulations.

Another strategy to foil the tax collector is the use of tax-deferred annuities. This instrument is useful if you have exceeded the limitations involved in other tax-advantaged savings programs. A tax-deferred annuity is a contract between you and an insurance company, purchased with one or more payments; the funds deposited accumulate tax-deferred interest, and the money is used to provide regular income payments at some later time. Usually, this type of contract involves no risk to your principal; the insurance company guarantees return of your original deposit at any time. Alternatively, variable annuities are usually invested in equity funds and their returns will depend on how well the particular investment you choose performs in the years ahead.

As with the IRA and the Keogh plan, you pay no income tax on the interest, dividends, or gains accrued during the accumulation period. Thus, all of your interest—as well as the principal—keeps working for you. When you start receiving payments from your annuity, a portion of each payment is considered to be a return of principal and is, therefore, tax free. Furthermore, if—like most people—you use the annuity to provide a regular income during retirement, you will possibly be in a lower tax bracket when you finally do pay the taxes. A deferred annuity can also avoid the cost and delay of probate in the event of death, since your funds pass automatically to your beneficiaries. But make sure you check the fee tables published at the front of each annuity prospectus. With some very expensive deferred annuities, what you gain in tax deferral you can lose in extra fees. In general, annuities are more expensive than IRAs and Keoghs invested in mutual funds. Therefore, you should invest in an annuity only after you have placed the maximum amount in a regular retirement plan, such as a 401(k), 403(b)7, Keogh, or IRA. Finally, remember the age-old maxim that has served investors well over the past years, "Never buy anything from someone who is out of breath."

Exercise 4: Be Competitive; Let the Yield on Your Cash Reserve Keep Pace with Inflation

As I've already pointed out, some ready assets are necessary for pending expenses, such as college tuition, possible emergencies, or even psychological support. Thus, you have a real dilemma. You know that if you keep your money in a savings bank and get, say, 3 percent interest in a year in which the inflation rate exceeds 3 percent, you will lose real purchasing power. In fact, the situation's even worse because the interest you get is subject to regular income taxes. So what's a small saver to do?

The investor of substantial means has no problems. He or she can buy Treasury bills (short-term IOUs issued by the U.S. government) or large certificates of deposit (short-term IOUs issued by banks, called bank CDs). But many of these instruments are issued only in large denominations, such as $10,000. If you have only a small amount of liquid assets, you can't get into this market directly. So how does the small saver avoid getting shafted? How do you get a rate of return that protects you against inflation? That is what this exercise is all about.

There are four short-term investment instruments that can at least help you stand up to inflation. These are (1) money-market mutual funds; (2) money-market deposit accounts; (3) bank certificates; and (4) tax-exempt money-market funds.

Money-Market Mutual Funds

In my judgment, the money-market mutual funds (or money funds) provide the best instrument for many investors' needs. They combine safety, high yields, and the right to withdraw money with no penalty attached. Most funds allow you to write large checks against your fund balance, generally in amounts of at least $250. Interest earnings continue until the checks clear. These money funds are the best alternative to bank accounts, and they have been extraordinarily popular. A list of names of some of the largest money funds is presented below. At the end of Chapter Fifteen, I have included "A Random

Walker's Address Book and Reference Guide to Mutual Funds." The first two pages of that guide list the addresses, telephone numbers, and detailed pertinent financial information concerning a selected number of funds.

Selected Money-Market Funds

Dreyfus Basic MMF	Prudential Money Market Assets
Fidelity Spartan MMF	Smith Barney Cash Portfolio
Merrill Lynch CMA MF	T. Rowe Price Prime Reserve
USAA MMF	Vanguard Money Market (Prime)

These money funds invest in large bank CDs, commercial paper (short-term corporate IOUs), government securities, and other instruments. Their yield, therefore, fluctuates fairly closely with the available yield on these short-term securities. To date, this yield has always outpaced—by a significant margin—the interest offered on cash savings accounts. Since they pool the funds of many small investors, the money funds can buy larger issues, beyond the individual's financial reach. The funds sell for a dollar a share and aim to keep that principal constant. While there's no guarantee against a loss of principal, you shouldn't have trouble sleeping nights if you invest in any of the funds in my table. Even during volatile market periods, these funds were able to keep the principal value constant at a dollar, although in some cases this was accomplished only through not paying out all of the interest earnings of the fund for periods of several days. In judging the funds that are best for your sleeping scale, you should know that those with longer average maturities and with riskier investments (such as Eurodollar CDs, described below) tend to offer somewhat higher returns as well as occasional dreams.

A Eurodollar is a dollar on deposit outside the United States, and these certificates, even when issued by foreign branches of U.S. banks, are not subject to the same regulations as dollars on deposit within the United States. A foreign government can impose restrictions on foreign branches of U.S. banks. For example, it can impose exchange controls that block payment of the interest and principal on these certificates. However unlikely such an event may be, these investments do entail some additional risk. Is the extra interest worth it? That depends on your psychological makeup.

For those who deep in their hearts prefer the semicomatose state of safety that banks provide, a new class of money-market funds has been formed. These are funds that invest only in Treasury bills or in federally guaranteed securities. As you might expect, they tend to yield less than comparable funds investing in bank obligations. During the mid-1990s, the differential in yields was between ¼ and ½ of 1 percent. Is the yield sacrifice worth the extra safety? Again, the answer depends on your psychological makeup.

My personal answer is to go with the higher-yielding regular funds. While I would be the first to agree that money saved for a rainy day should not be allowed to go down the drain, I think that the risk of the prime-quality funds is, as my lawyer friends like to put it, *de minimus.* Even funds that held obligations of the incontinent Continental Illinois Bank in 1984 got paid off in full. I should also tell you, however, that I am not a worrier.

Beware of management-fee waivers and "teaser" rates. In general, money-market funds will all be invested in very similar securities. The difference in yields they produce is largely determined by the funds' expense ratios (the costs of running and managing the funds, which are charged to the funds' shareholders). Other things being the same, lower expenses mean higher net returns for the shareowners. This is why expense ratios are particularly important in comparing money-market funds. Some mutual-fund companies promote low-expense (or no-expense) funds for a limited and often unspecified length of time. They do so by temporarily waiving their investment management fees and/or absorbing other fund operating expenses. These exceptionally high "loss-leader" yields are then promoted heavily in the print media with full-page ads to attract a large asset base on which full fees and expenses could eventually be charged. *Temporarily,* such promotional funds can be a good deal for investors. But watch out when the full expenses get socked to the investor and the certain reduction in net yields results. If you do try to take advantage of a teaser yield, check the fund's yield weekly in the newspaper so you can move back to a higher-yielding fund when it is appropriate to do so. You should never own a money fund whose yields are not published.

One final warning needs to be issued for those who are fitful sleepers and are very averse to risk. Some money funds have enhanced their yields by investing in derivatives. With the development of complex and exotic derivative instruments, even obligations originally issued by the U.S. Treasury or by Federal agencies can in quite subtle ways become very risky. My advice is to read your money fund's prospectus carefully, especially the discussion of risk factors. The two most important determinants of whether a particular money fund is right for you is the degree of risk assumed and the fund's expense ratio. Most investors will be most comfortable with funds that have low expenses and which accept only moderate risks.

Money-Market Deposit Accounts

The money funds became so popular that hundreds of billions of dollars were drained out of bank deposits into these higher-yielding mutual funds. Needless to say, the banks sought ways to compete. And so, in another example of how deregulation benefits the consumer, the banks were allowed to offer money-market deposit accounts to individuals. At the outset, banks offered promotional rates that were well above the yields offered by the money funds. Indeed, initially some money-market deposit accounts had a yield advantage of 2 percentage points. Savvy consumers, chasing the prettiest rate in the market, deserted the money funds in droves.

In the mid-1980s, however, the money funds enjoyed a renaissance. The banks, having reestablished themselves, quietly reduced the rates they were offering so that the money funds then had a ½ to 1 percentage point advantage over the deposit accounts. Money began to return to the funds and now both types of investments have hundreds of billions of consumers' dollars. Through the first half of the 1990s, the money-market funds have usually enjoyed a somewhat higher net yield.

How should you decide between the two? Each has its own advantages. The banks enjoy important attractions. First, like other bank deposits, money-market deposit accounts are insured by an agency of the federal government. Thus, they score at the top of the scale for worried insomniacs. In addition, it's convenient to invest in money-market deposit accounts, since banks have branches, while money funds only have post office boxes and toll-free telephone numbers. But the money funds have their own advantages. Their yields tend to be higher than the bank accounts, as noted above. Indeed, during periods when interest rates have been rising, the differential in favor of the money funds has tended to widen as the banks have been slow in raising posted rates. In addition, the money funds allow an unlimited number of checks to be written against balances (although each check must be written for at least $250 or $500 depending on the fund). The deposit accounts allow only three checks per month (for any amount).* Money funds also offer wire transfer facilities that permit money to be moved around overnight. Moreover, since money funds are typically part of a large mutual fund or brokerage complex, they are an ideal place to "park" cash at high earning rates awaiting movement into more permanent investments. Finally, it is possible to find money funds that invest only in tax-exempt securities so that high-bracket investors can earn considerably higher after-tax yields. I'll discuss these tax-exempt money funds below.

Bank Certificates

Banks also offer certificates of deposit with a variety of periods to maturity. Yields on these instruments are typically higher than those on either money-market deposit accounts or money funds. These certificates are government insured up to $100,000 per buyer ($200,000 with your spouse). Thus, the certificates are even safer than the money funds and are an excellent medium for investors who can tie up their liquid funds for at least six months.

The certificates do have a number of disadvantages, how-

*Banks do offer so-called Super NOW deposit accounts that allow unlimited checking and these accounts can be very useful for investors who can meet the minimum deposit requirements. The interest rates on Super NOWs are, however, substantially below the returns on money-market deposit accounts.

ever. First, you need to have a substantial nest egg—usually
$10,000—before you can buy. Second, you can't write checks
against the certificates as you can with shares in the money
funds. Most important, as in other aspects of life, there is a
substantial penalty for premature withdrawal. If you redeem
your certificate prior to maturity, federal regulations stipulate a
minimum penalty of the loss of one month's interest. Some
banks impose even greater penalties. Fourth, the yield on bank
certificates is subject to state and local taxes (Treasury bills,
also obtainable for $10,000, are exempt from these).

Tax-Exempt Money-Market Funds

This instrument may be useful for some investors, particularly those who pay taxes at the top marginal rate and who live
in states with high income-tax rates. A disadvantage of all the
vehicles previously described is that the interest is fully taxable. Investors in very high brackets will find that, after taxes,
even the highest of the yields offered will not compensate for
inflation. This situation led to the establishment of tax-exempt
money-market funds.

These funds invest in portfolios of short-term, high-quality,
tax-exempt issues. They produce daily tax-exempt income.
Like the regular money-market funds, they provide instant li-

Drawing by Lorenz, © 1984 The New Yorker Magazine, Inc.

quidity and free checking for large bills ($250 or more). Some sample funds are listed on pages 465–466 of the Reference Guide. The yields on tax-exempt funds are considerably lower than those on taxable funds. Nevertheless, individuals in the highest tax brackets will find the earnings from this investment more attractive than the after-tax yield of the regular money funds.

If you live in a state which has high income-tax rates, you may want to consider a fund that only holds securities issued by entities within your home state. Tax-exempt bonds issued, for example, by New York municipalities are *taxable* in other states. Thus, the only way for, say, a Californian to avoid both federal and state taxes is to buy a fund that holds only California securities. Fortunately, there are now tax-exempt money funds (as well as bond funds) available that invest in the securities of a single state. These are not available for all states. You should call one of the mutual-fund complexes such as Fidelity or Vanguard to check on the availability of a fund that invests in securities of the state in which you pay taxes.

Exercise 5: Investigate a Promenade through Bond Country

Let's face it, bonds were a lousy place to put your money during the 1960s and 1970s. Inflation had eaten away at the real value of the bonds with a vengeance. For example, savers who bought U.S. savings bonds for $18.75 in the early 1970s and redeemed them five years later for $25 found, much to their dismay, that they had actually lost real purchasing power. The trouble was that, while the $18.75 invested in such a bond five years before might have filled one's gas tank twice, the $25 obtained at maturity did little more than fill it once. In fact, an investor's real return was negative, as inflation had eroded purchasing power faster than interest earnings were compounding. Small wonder many investors view the "bond" as an unmentionable four-letter word.

In fact, the U.S. savings bond program, with its touching appeals to patriotism and good citizenship, has been a monumental rip-off. Interest rates on Series EE savings bonds were far below the inflation rates of the late 1960s and 1970s and were not much more than half what the government was paying on regular bonds sold on the open market. Fortunately, the government improved the terms of U.S. savings bonds so that they can pay 85 percent of the rate the Treasury pays for funds in the open market. The bonds also have some tax advantages. Still, as I'll show you below, far more attractive investment opportunities are available.

Of course, other bonds have also been poor investments during the 1960s and 1970s, since the interest rates they carried often proved insufficient to offer adequate inflation protection. Investors thirty years ago simply did not realize how high inflation could go. But remember Part Two. Markets are reasonably efficient, and investors now refuse to buy bonds unless their yields offer a reasonable degree of compensation for the expected loss in the dollar's purchasing power. In the mid-1990s, good-quality long-term bonds were yielding close to 8 percent in the open market. This yield translates freely into protection against a long-term inflation of 3 percent and pro-

vides a real rate of return above that inflation of about 5 percent. Of course, it is always possible that the actual long-run
rate of inflation may be considerably greater than the 3 percent
inflation premium that was implicit in this bond yield. But the 5
percent real return they promise gives a reasonably generous
margin of safety, as I will argue in the next chapter.

In my view, there are three kinds of bond purchases you
may especially want to consider: (1) zero-coupon bonds (which
allow you to lock in high yields for a predetermined length of
time); (2) bond mutual funds (which permit you to buy shares in
bond portfolios); and (3) tax-exempt bonds and bond funds (for
those who are fortunate enough to be in high tax brackets).

Zero-Coupon Bonds Can Generate Large Future Returns

Suppose you were told you could invest $10,000 now and be
guaranteed by the government that you would get more than 5
times that amount back in 20 years. The ability to accumulate
such a $50,000+ nest egg is possible through the use of zero-
coupon securities.

These securities are called zero coupons or simply zeros
because owners receive no periodic interest payments as they
do in a regular interest-coupon-paying bond. Instead, these securities are purchased at deep discounts from their face value
(for example, 20 cents on the dollar) and gradually rise to their
face or par values over the years. If held to maturity, the holder
is paid the full stated amount of the bond. These securities are
available on maturities ranging from a few months to almost 30
years. As of the mid-1990s, long-term zero-coupon Treasury
securities sold to yield about 7½ percent per year.

The first zero-coupon obligations were created by major
brokerage houses. They were introduced in 1982 by Merrill
Lynch under the proprietary acronym TIGRs (Tigers), Treasury
Investment Growth Receipts. Other brokerage houses followed
suit and marketed similar products bearing such names as
CATS, LIONS, COUGARS, and TEDDY BEARS. Small-denom-
ination zeros marketed by Merrill Lynch are known as "tiger
cubs." In 1985, the Treasury itself began to provide zero-
coupon bonds directly. Zero-coupon securities have also been

offered by corporations, insurance companies, and banks. They are available at somewhat higher yields than Treasury zeros, but with not quite the same degree of safety.

The principal attraction of zeros is that the purchaser is faced with no reinvestment risk. It would, of course, be possible to duplicate a zero with a regular bond by taking the interest coupons and reinvesting them over the life of the issue. Indeed, the typical yield to maturity calculation assumes that interest payments are reinvested at a constant rate. In fact, however, the interest rate at which you could reinvest the coupons could fall, so that the realized yield to maturity could be a good bit lower. A zero-coupon Treasury bond guarantees an investor that his or her funds will be continuously reinvested at the yield to maturity rate. Thus, the zeros offer a convenient way to lock in high yields for many years to come.

The main disadvantage of zeros is that the Internal Revenue Service requires that taxable investors declare annually as income a pro rata share of the dollar difference between the purchase price and the par value of the bond. This is not required, however, for investors who hold zeros in IRAs or Keogh plans. Here the investor can defer all taxes until retirement. Thus, zero-coupon securities are a superb vehicle for retirement plans.

Two warnings are in order. Often brokers will charge small investors fairly large commissions for the purchase of zero-coupon bonds in small denominations. It would, therefore, be worthwhile to check the net yields available on, say, twenty-year zeros with two or three brokers to ascertain the best quotes. As I will discuss in Exercise 9 below, commission rates are not random and some comparison shopping could pay big yields. In addition, you should know that redemption at face value is guaranteed *only* if you hold the bonds to maturity. In the meantime, prices can be highly variable as interest rates change.

No-Load Bond Funds Are Appropriate
Vehicles for Individual Investors

Open-end bond (mutual) funds give some of the long-term advantages of the zeros but are much easier and less costly to buy or sell. Those that I have listed on pages 467–470 of the Reference Guide all invest in long-term securities. While there is no guarantee that you can reinvest your interest at constant rates, these funds do offer long-run stability of income and are particularly suitable for investors who plan to live off their interest income.

Bond mutual funds typically hold a diversified portfolio of high-quality bonds. Purchasers of shares in such a fund in essence buy a pro rata share in all of the assets of the fund and are entitled to a pro rata share of the income. Thus, a small investor would be able to obtain the same kind of broad-scale diversification available to a large institutional investor.

These open-end funds issue shares in unlimited quantities and stand ready to redeem their shares at net asset value calculated each day on the basis of the market prices of the bonds they hold. Many funds charge a loading fee or commission fee that can be as high as 8½ percent to invest in the fund. The funds that I especially recommend are all no-load; that is, there is neither a fee to buy into the fund nor a fee to redeem shares. The investment performance of bond mutual funds is totally unrelated to the fees they charge (including the expenses they incur in managing the investments). Thus, I recommend no-load funds. There's no point in paying for something if you can get it free. Moreover, I prefer funds with low expense ratios.

The Reference Guide shows a sample of bond funds available from some of the largest mutual-fund complexes. I list in the tables several types of funds: those specializing in prime-quality corporate bonds and those that buy a portfolio of GNMA mortgage-backed bonds. In separate tables, I list those funds investing in tax-exempt bonds (which I will discuss in the next section), as well as high-yield and index bond funds.

All of the funds listed in my Reference Guide (except high-yield funds) are invested in prime-quality issues with minimal risk of default. I personally favor the GNMA funds. These funds invest exclusively in GNMA (Ginnie Mae) mortgage pass-through securities. These are bonds backed by a pool of government-insured mortgages (either VA or FHA) and are, therefore, a general obligation of the U.S. government. Interest and principal payments on the bonds come from the interest and principal repayments of the underlying mortgages. Not only is the security on these bonds of the highest quality, but also the yields are comparable to those on corporate bonds. Mortgage bonds have one disadvantage in that when interest rates fall, many homeowners refinance their high-rate mortgages and some high-yielding mortgage bonds get repaid early. It is that potential disadvantage that makes the yield on government-guaranteed mortgage bonds so high. Mutual funds that diversify among mortgage bonds backed by mortgages issued at many different initial rates offer some protection, however, against premature redemption. Hence, I think that a Ginnie Mae fund is a particularly attractive investment in today's bond market.

Tax-Exempt Bonds Are Useful for High-Bracket Investors

If you are in a very high tax bracket, taxable money funds, zeros, and taxable bond funds may not be right for you. You need the tax-exempt bonds issued by state and local governments and by various governmental authorities, such as port authorities or toll roads. The interest from these bonds doesn't count as taxable income on your federal tax form, and bonds from the state in which you live are typically exempt from any state income taxes.

This tax exemption gives a subsidy to state and local governments, since they can issue bonds at lower interest rates than if the bonds were fully taxable. Economists have argued that it's an inefficient subsidy (it would be cheaper, so this argument goes, for the U.S. Treasury just to pay the state and local governments to issue taxable bonds). But since that's the present law, there is no reason why you shouldn't take advantage of it.

By now, if you've carefully followed Exercise 2, you know

whether municipal bonds are compatible with your tax bracket and your income needs. In the mid-1990s, good-quality long-term corporate bonds were yielding about 8 percent, and tax-exempt issues of comparable quality yielded about 6 percent. Suppose your tax bracket (the rate at which your last dollar of income is taxed—not your average rate) is about 36 percent, including both federal and state taxes. The table below shows that the after-tax income is $88 higher on the tax-exempt security, which is clearly the better investment for a person in your tax bracket. Even if you are in a lower tax bracket, tax-exempts may still pay, depending on the exact yields available in the market when you make your purchase.

Look carefully at new long-term revenue bond issues of various public authorities, such as port authorities, established turnpikes, power authorities, etc. These bonds (called term bonds) often serve as very attractive tax-exempt investment vehicles. I suggest that you buy new issues rather than already outstanding securities, because new-issue yields are usually a bit sweeter than the yields of seasoned outstanding bonds and you avoid paying transactions charges on new issues. I also suggest that to keep your risk within reasonable bounds, you stick with issues rated at least A by Moody's and Standard & Poor's rating services. These term bonds usually mature in twenty years or more, but they often enjoy a good trading market after they have been issued. Thus, if you want to sell the bonds later you can do so with reasonable ease, particularly if you own at least $10,000 worth of a single issue.

For those who sleep poorly at night, consider guaranteed tax-exempt bonds that are insured against default by a consortium of banks, insurance companies, and securities firms. Their yields are a bit lower, but they generally carry a AAA rating. Also consider so-called AMT bonds. These bonds are subject to the alternative minimum (income) tax and, therefore, are not

Tax-Exempt vs. Taxable Bonds ($10,000 face value)

Type of Bond	Interest Paid	Applicable Taxes (36% Rate)	After-Tax Income
6% tax-exempt	$600	$0	$600
8% taxable	800	288	512

attractive to individuals who have sheltered a significant part of their income from tax. But if you are not subject to the alternative minimum tax (and the overwhelming majority of people are not), you can get some extra yield from AMT bonds.

It is usually wise to avoid serial bonds. These are tax-exempt bonds that mature serially over perhaps thirty different years or more. These are usually tougher to sell than term bonds if you have to raise funds prior to their maturity. Also, yields on serial issues (especially the shorter-term ones) usually tend to be lower than on term bonds, in part because they are particularly attractive to institutions, like banks, that pay taxes at high corporate rates. Unless you have funds to invest for some specific period of time and want to match the maturity of the bond you buy with the timing of your fund requirements, these bonds are best left to institutional buyers. So ask your broker how the "new-issue calendar" looks. By waiting a week or so until a new high-yielding revenue term bond comes out, you may be able to improve your interest return substantially.

There is one nasty "heads I win, tails you lose" feature of bonds that you should know about. If interest rates go up, the price of your bonds will go down, as I noted earlier. But if interest rates go down, the issuer can often "call" the bonds away from you (repay the debt early) and then issue new bonds at lower rates.

To protect yourself, make sure your bonds have a call-protection provision that prevents the issuer from calling your bonds in order to issue new ones at lower rates. Many tax-exempt revenue issues offer ten years of call protection. After that the bonds are callable, but typically at a premium over what you paid for them. Make sure to ask about call protection, especially during periods when interest rates are higher than usual.

There are good tax-exempt bond funds available as well. I have listed these in the table on pages 471–472 of the Reference Guide. If you have substantial funds to invest in tax-exempts ($25,000 or more), however, I see little reason for you to make your tax-exempt purchases through a fund and pay the management fees involved. If you follow the rules already presented and confine your purchases to a few high-quality bonds, particularly those that are insured, there is little need for you to diversify by purchasing a large number of different securities. And you'll get more interest return if you invest directly. On the other hand, if you have just a few thousand to invest, you will find it costly to buy and sell small lots of bonds, and a fund will provide convenient liquidity and diversification for you. In addition to the bond funds listed in the table, there are funds available that confine their purchases to the bonds of a single state so that you can avoid both state and federal income taxes.

Should You Be a Bond-Market Junkie?

Is the bond market immune to the maxim that investment risk and reward are related? Not at all! During most periods, so-called junk bonds (lower credit quality, higher-yielding bonds) have given investors a *net* rate of return about 2 percentage points higher than the rate that could be earned on "investment-grade" bonds with high-quality credit ratings. In the mid-1990s, investment-grade bonds yielded about 8 percent while "junk" bonds often yielded 10 percent or more. Thus, even if 2 percent of the lower-grade bonds defaulted on their interest and principal payments and produced a total loss, a diversified portfolio of low-quality bonds would still produce a larger net return than would be available from a high-quality bond portfolio. For this reason, many investment advisers have recommended *well-diversified* portfolios of high-yield bonds as sensible investments. They find the higher yields quite tempting and offering more than adequate compensation for the moderately larger investment risk involved.

There is, however, another school of thought which advises investors to "just say no to junk bonds." These people view the risks involved as far too large. Most junk bonds have been issued since the mid-1980s as a result of a massive wave of corporate mergers, acquisitions, and leveraged (mainly debt-financed) buyouts. The junk-bond naysayers point out that lower credit bonds are most likely to be serviced in full only during good times in the economy. But watch out, they say, if the economy falters and we go into a broad-based recession. In such an environment, many analysts worry that defaults on lower-grade bonds could be substantially larger than has been the case historically—far exceeding the 2 percent in the previous example. In such an environment, the net returns on lower-grade bond portfolios could even be lower than the returns on high-grade portfolios.

So what's a thoughtful investor to do? There's no easy solution. Again, the answer depends in part on how well you sleep at night when you assume substantial investment risk. Clearly, high-yield or junk-bond portfolios are not for insomniacs. Even with diversification, there is substantial risk in these investments. Moreover, they are not for investors who depend solely on high-yield bond payments as their major source of income. And they are certainly not for any investors who do not adequately diversify their holdings either through direct investment or through the medium of mutual funds. However, the gross yield premium from junk bonds is substantial, and, at least historically, it has more than compensated for actual default experience. If the U.S. economy remains on a relatively even keel and avoids a doomsday scenario, investors with high risk tolerances and the access to adequate diversification will probably continue to earn attractive returns. Page 473 of the address book lists a selected number of high-yield bond funds.

Exercise 6: Begin Your Walk at Your Own Home; Renting Leads to Flabby Investment Muscles

Remember Scarlett O'Hara? She was broke at the end of the Civil War, but she still had her beloved plantation, Tara. A good house, on good land, keeps its value no matter what happens to money. As long as the world's population continues to grow, the demand for real estate will be among the most dependable inflation hedges available.

One hundred years ago, Henry George sounded the call for real estate investment:

> Go, get yourself a piece of ground, and hold possession. . . .
> You need do nothing more. You may sit down and smoke your

pipe; you may lie around like the lazzaroni of Naples or the leperos of Mexico; you may go up in a balloon, or down a hole in the ground and without doing one stroke of work, without adding one iota to the wealth of the community, in ten years you will be rich.

By and large, George's advice turned out to be pretty good.

Although the calculation is tricky, it appears that the returns on residential real estate have been quite generous. While returns in the late 1980s and early 1990s were poor, the longer-run record has been excellent. But the real estate market is less efficient than the stock market. There may be hundreds of knowledgeable investors who study the worth of every common stock. Perhaps only a handful of prospective buyers assess the worth of a particular real estate property. Hence, individual pieces of property are not always appropriately priced. Finally, real estate returns seem to be higher than stock returns during periods when inflation is accelerating, but to do less well during periods of disinflation. In sum, real estate has proved to be a good investment providing generous returns and excellent inflation-hedging characteristics.

The natural real estate investment for most people is the single-family home or the condominium. You have to live somewhere, and buying has several tax advantages over renting. Because Congress wanted to encourage home ownership and the values associated with this, it gave the homeowner a number of tax breaks: (1) While rent is not deductible from income taxes, the two major expenses associated with home ownership—interest payments on your mortgage and property taxes—are fully deductible; (2) any realized gains in the value of your house can be postponed if you reinvest the proceeds in a more expensive house; and (3) if you sell your house after age fifty-five, a portion of the gains are tax exempt. In addition, ownership of a house is a good way to force yourself to save, and a house provides enormous emotional satisfaction. My advice is: Own your own home if you can possibly afford it.

How do you know if you can afford a home? The general rule of thumb is that a family should not spend more than 30 percent of its income on mortgage payments. With long-term fixed-rate mortgages, that used to be easy to calculate. You told the lending institution how much you needed for how long and they would tell you what your monthly payments would be at the prevailing interest rate. When that rate hit 14 percent or more in the first half of the 1980s, however, the monthly payments effectively priced many families out of their pursuit of the American dream—an affordable home. Enter the red-hot adjustable-rate mortgage, known as the ARM. By the mid-1980s, two out of every three homes were financed with ARMs.

There are literally thousands of different variations of the adjustable-rate mortgage. Their basic feature is that the contract interest rate is subject to periodic adjustment based on the movements of a selected interest-rate index, such as the rate on short-term Treasury securities. In general, the initial rates on ARMs are considerably lower than on fixed-rate mortgages. However, the home buyer takes the risk of future increases in interest rates. Many mortgage experts have warned that if rates rise in the future, this could lead to "payment shock"—payments rising so sharply that they wreck the household budget or, at worst, that high rates could strong-ARM some families out of their homes.

Fortunately, ARMs are now usually available with a cap on interest payments. The cap typically limits yearly rate adjustments to, say, 1 to 2 percent and sets a lifetime or maximum cap on total increases at, say, 5 percent. While these caps are very useful for consumers, they can at times lead to a false sense of security. If, for example, the capped interest payments are not enough to cover interest-rate increases called for by the rise in the index interest rate on which the ARM is based, the home-buyer could be faced with something called "negative amortization." That awful-sounding term means that, if your payments don't cover all the interest due, the unpaid interest is added to your mortgage loan. Thus, you've got more debt to pay off instead of less. The result is that you may be paying over a longer term or get a reduced net proceeds from the sale of your home.

As you can see, getting a home mortgage these days is not nearly as simple as it used to be. Personally, I favor ARMs, but as I've suggested in other places in the book, shopping around is absolutely essential. There are many variations and many different arrangements offered and it would be well worth your while to look for the best deal. My advice is to look for the lowest-priced ARM you can find provided you can get a good cap along the lines described above. Make sure that if interest rates rose to the cap limit, you could still afford your mortgage interest payments without wrecking your budget. In addition, look for a deal with no negative amortization and no pre-payment penalty. Despite a lot of the negative publicity about ARMs, they can be a very good deal for the home-buyer.

Once you find a successful investment, why not repeat it? For example, the rent from another well-located well-maintained single-family house or condominium can provide generous returns—especially if you know the property well. If you have the temperament to accept a 2 A.M. call from your neighbor complaining that the furnace doesn't work, you may even adore the house next door and purchase it as a rental property. You're likely to have the best knowledge of the market and the specific characteristics of the property in your own neighborhood. The rent should provide you a reasonable yield above covering your interest and taxes. The depreciation of the house provides good tax write-offs and any capital gain from a rise in value of the property can be deferred until the gain is realized.

Despite the recent rash of fabulous get-rich-quick stories about real estate investing, there are risks aplenty. A few deserve special mention. There is a maxim in the real estate field that there are three principles of real estate investment: location, location, and location. And location is a fickle thing. A country home without access to public transportation is no longer as desirable as it used to be. Now that family size is shrinking, six- and seven-bedroom homes are no longer *de riguer.* There is also another real estate maxim: "The buyer needs 100 eyes; the seller not one." As mentioned above, the market can be inefficient and a particular property not appropriately priced. Keep in mind, too, that demographic trends that have helped inflate house prices from the 1950s to the 1980s have diminished as the growth in household formation has slowed considerably. The baby-bust generation cannot provide the demand for single-family houses that the baby boomers did in the

1970s and early 1980s. There are also particular risks in specific real estate investments. For example, local restrictions can prevent you from building on land in which you have invested. Rent controls can turn a profitable apartment-house investment into a sour lemon, especially since property taxes go on whether you can rent on favorable terms or not. It's also important to remember that real estate cannot be sold quickly or inexpensively. And it's very difficult for an investor to obtain adequate diversification by purchasing one or two houses. Finally, the greatest risk facing real estate investment is the risk of disinflation. If inflation disappears in the late 1990s, the returns from real estate are likely to be inferior to those from stocks and bonds.

Despite the risks, well-located single-family homes that are not excessively priced remain a useful investment medium—capable of producing generous returns and providing an excellent inflation hedge. And single-family real estate in most areas of the country was quite reasonably priced as of early 1995. Every investing household should plan to own its own home.

Exercise 7: After the Real Estate Depression of the Early 1990s, Some Attractive Opportunities Exist in Commercial Real Estate

If you want to insure that your portfolio is on *terra firma,* consider owning some commercial real estate. This is a prudent investment move for many reasons. First, ownership of real estate (as is possible through the purchase of equity Real Estate Investment Trusts, which I will describe below) has produced comparable rates of return to common stocks over the 25-year period from the 1970s through the mid-1990s. Equally important, real estate is an excellent vehicle to provide the benefits of diversification described in Chapter Nine. Because real estate returns have relatively little correlation with other assets, putting some share of your portfolio into real estate can reduce the overall risk of your investment program. Moreover, real estate is probably a more dependable hedge against inflation than common stocks in general. During the inflationary binge of the 1970s, real estate returns were considerably higher than those of the broad stock market indices. Finally, during the mid-1990s, real estate appeared to be priced more moderately than blue-chip common equities. The broad market averages were selling at relatively high multiples of earnings and book values and extraordinarily low dividend yields. Real estate prices, on the other hand, had just gone through a severe sinking spell during the late 1980s and early 1990s and appeared poised for recovery.

It is impractical for most individual investors to own commercial property directly as they lack both the expertise to appraise property investments and the large sums required to purchase them. Moreover, most investors require liquidity— the ability to turn their investment into cash if an emergency funding requirement arises. Thus, REITs (Real Estate Investment Trusts) offer the only practical vehicle for small individual investors to add some real estate to their portfolios. Equity REITs are basically packages of actively managed commercial real estate. Mortgage REITs are different animals; their portfolios consist largely of mortgages on property, as opposed to ownership interests. The total supply of REITs available in the market mushroomed in the 1990s from about $5 billion at the start of the decade to about $50 billion by the middle of the 1990s.

Unfortunately, the job of sifting through the hundreds of outstanding REITs, as well as the flood of new REIT offerings that hit the market during the mid-1990s, is a daunting one for the individual investor. Moreover, a single equity REIT is unlikely to provide the necessary diversification across property types and regions of the country. Many REITs specialize in a particular property type, such as apartment houses, shopping malls, industrial warehouses, commercial office buildings, etc., and often they concentrate their purchases in one area of the country. And, certainly, individuals could stumble badly by purchasing the wrong REIT. Now, however, investors have a rapidly expanding group of real estate mutual funds that are more than willing to do the job for them. The funds cull through the available offerings and put together a diversified portfolio of REITs, insuring that a wide variety of property types and regions are represented. Moreover, investors have the ability to liquidate their fund holdings whenever they wish. A representative sample of real estate mutual funds is presented in the table on page 356. These funds offer a quite serviceable vehicle for individual investors to place a portion of their investable fund in real estate equity. For a prospectus and application, call one of the 800 numbers listed under each fund.

While real estate offers attractive diversification benefits for individual investors, there are very important caveats to keep in mind. As is the case with common stocks, there are large fluctuations in real estate prices and in the prices of REITs. Had you purchased REITs at the peak of the real estate boom of the 1980s you would have been quite disappointed. The investment situation in the mid-1990s is somewhat mixed. On the one hand, the prices of commercial real estate had fallen well below the peak levels of the 1980s and in some cases property was available at well below the cost to replace the structure. Moreover, it appeared that the bottom had been reached and already some property types, such as apartment houses in the Southwest, had begun to rise in price. Certainly in an historical context, and in relation to common stock valuations, real estate appeared to be quite attractive.

The potential pitfall for investors is that REITs, like other common stocks, can become inflated relative to the value of the underlying real estate in its portfolio. And REITs were the hottest part of the stock market in the mid-1990s. Yields on money-market funds were relatively low and investors were attracted by the 6 and 7 percent yields on the REITs. Prices of REITs were bid up and a literal flood of new issues hit the market. The situation was a godsend for developers and financial institutions who wanted to lighten up on their real estate holdings. They just packaged their real estate properties (often including the bad with the good) into REITs and sold them to the public. The managers of the REITs received generous annual fees and the valuation of the REIT typically was well above the value at which the actual properties could be sold.

The investment firm of Salomon Brothers monitors these premiums by comparing the multiples of cash flow at which properties sell in the private market (the actual market for property) and in the public market (the REIT market on the stock exchanges). The figure on page 357 shows that by the

Some Information on Real Estate Mutual Funds (Telephone numbers in parenthesis)

Fund	Sales Charge	Year Organized	Expense Ratio (%)	Assets 1994 ($Millions)	1-Year Total Return to 12/31/94	3-Year Total Return to 12/31/94	Risk Measure (Beta)
Fidelity Real Estate (800-544-8888)	no	1986	1.18	539	2.04	11.12	0.54
Cohen & Steers Realty (800-437-9912)	no	1991	1.18	440	8.31	15.60	0.41
PRA Real Estate Securities (800-497-2494)	no	1989	1.22	103.5	3.00	13.32	0.44

mid-1990s, the public market multiples had soared almost 30 percent above the private market multiples before a bear market in REITs late in 1994 brought prices somewhat back in line. Investors in real estate should watch these relationships because, in the long run, REITs can only be as prosperous as the properties they own. Investors can get burned buying at the peak of euphoria regarding these instruments and, therefore, need to approach REITs cautiously. REITs are a wonderful vehicle for investors but, unlike Mae West's view of the world, too much of a good thing is not always wonderful. As a popular bumper sticker in Houston in the mid-1980s put it, "Please, God, give us another oil boom and we promise not to screw it up." Real estate is a trusted asset and deserves a role in individual portfolios, but the industry has made egregious errors in the past and, undoubtedly, will do so again in the future.

Private and Public Multiples for Real Estate*

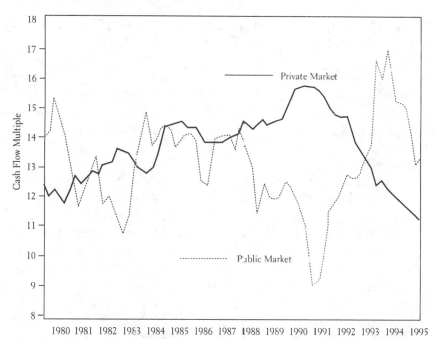

Source: Salomon Brothers and author's estimates.
*When investors are very enthusiastic about REITs, the ratio of REIT prices to their cash flows (lighter line) soars above the multiples in the property markets themselves (dark line).

While on the subject of errors you can make, a special note of caution should be raised about those late-night cable TV real estate gurus who promise unlimited wealth by buying real estate with "nothing down." Don't buy their books and manuals and by all means avoid their get-rich-quick schemes that could lead you to personal bankruptcy and even jail. The gifted financial columnist, Jane Bryant Quinn, studied a group of these programs and the materials they sold and came to the following conclusion:

> I found them misleading, fantastical, false, and in some cases, flatly illegal. The dream they sell—that you can buy profitable property with no credit, no job, no experience, even with a bankruptcy behind you—shouldn't pass anyone's first-round BS test. Gurus earn their Rolls-Royces and their diamond pinky rings not by extracting value from real estate but by extracting cash from *you*.

Exercise 8: Tiptoe through the Investment Fields of Gold and Collectibles

In the early editions of this book, I took a very negative view of gold and other "things" as investment vehicles. At the start of the 1980s, gold had risen past $800 an ounce. Diamonds glittered, metals such as copper and silver shone, and collectibles such as art, rugs, and porcelains all became popular investment vehicles.

Publishers jumped on this golden bandwagon and a number of "how-to-beat-inflation" books came out, touting investments in "things" rather than paper securities. The premise was that since you and everybody else consume "things," if you want to preserve real purchasing power, you can do so by owning specific commodities. For example, if you eat TV dinners and drive Honda Accords, the way to preserve real purchasing power is to store away TV dinners and Hondas. There's something to this advice. Indeed, in countries which have suffered from hyperinflation, one can often see cars up on blocks in the backyards of middle-class neighborhoods, for it is by accumulating objects of this sort that people hedge their savings against inflation.

The problem is that "things" often don't yield a stream of benefits, such as dividend returns. Moreover, they can be costly to store and protect. They can even spoil. The Honda Accord in your backyard can rust, and the three-year-old TV dinner in your freezer may not taste very good. I tend to prefer the kinds of assets that produce a return while they are giving inflation protection. That's why I like real estate and common stocks.

Still, there's no denying that for those who feed on economic paranoia, 1979, with its gold rush, was a banner year. People who early in the year pooh-poohed gold at a price of less than $300 an ounce swallowed awfully hard when they saw it rise to more than $600. In early 1980, gold continued to soar—approaching the $900-an-ounce mark. The doomsday groupies, on the other hand, were ecstatic, having long recommended a portfolio consisting entirely of gold. The price of gold feeds on anxiety, and we certainly have had much cause for worry.

The problem, as I pointed out, was that gold is a sterile

"I'm putting all my money into 'things.' "

Drawing by Geo. Price. © 1979 The New Yorker Magazine, Inc.

investment in a rational world. It does not yield dividends and can be costly to store and protect. Moreover, the sharp run-up in prices in 1979–80 was uncomfortably close in my mind to the price increases during the tulip-bulb craze described in Chapter Two. I said in 1980 that I am not panning gold for all time. "Investment in gold can help to reduce risks because gold prices generally move counter to trends in the U.S. market. Moreover, anything can happen when it's tulip time in the market. If gold can sell at $900 an ounce, it can just as easily sell for $1,800 an ounce (or $450 an ounce)." But I did conclude that at 1980s prices, gold was "an extraordinarily risky investment." I rested my case with the following calculation. "Suppose gold continues to rise and sells at the astronomical price of $3,000 an ounce in December 1990. If you made your purchase at the January 1980 price, your total money return when you sell in 1990 will actually be less than that provided by an 11½ percent bond." In fact, gold traded in the $300 to $400 level during the first half of the 1990s.

In mid-1990s, gold was selling at just over $350 an ounce, and I am more positive about gold as an investment but far from enthusiastic. While I would recommend against putting a major proportion of your assets into gold, there is a modest role for gold in a well-diversified portfolio. Returns from gold tend to be very little correlated with the returns from paper assets. Hence, even modest holdings (say, 5 percent of the portfolio) can be of considerable help to an investor in reducing the variability of the total portfolio, as was clearly shown in Chapter Nine. Small gold holdings can easily be obtained now by purchasing shares in one of the specialized mutual funds concentrating on gold.

The volatile movements in gold prices remind me of the story of the wily Chinese merchant who made an excellent living trading in sardines. His business was so successful that he hired a bright young college graduate to assist him in his endeavors. One day when the young man was entertaining his in-laws for dinner, he decided to bring home a couple of cans of sardines to have as an appetizer. Upon opening the first can, he found, to his great chagrin, that the can was filled with sand. He then opened the second can and found that it, too, was filled with sand. Upon informing the Chinese merchant of his experience the next day, the wily trader simply smiled and said, "Oh, those cans are for trading, not for eating."

In a sense, this story is very similar to the situation that occurs in gold trading. Practically all gold trading is for the purpose of hoarding or speculating so that the bullion can be sold later at a higher price. Almost none of the gold is actually used. While there is some small demand for such uses as dental work, jewelry, and a few other specialized industrial needs, the current inventory of gold is some fifty times its annual industrial requirement—not to mention the large amounts of yet-to-be-mined metal stored below ground. In this kind of market, no one can tell where prices will go. Prudence suggests—at best—a limited role for gold as a vehicle for obtaining broader diversification.

What about other collectibles? They have not had the kind of price correction that has occurred in the gold market and are generally not suitable as investment mediums for the layperson. Diamonds, for example, are often described as everybody's best friend. But there are enormous risks and disadvantages for individual investors. One must remember that buying diamonds involves large commission costs. Furthermore, there are fads in the way diamonds are cut. Despite assurances to the contrary, you will seldom be able to buy at true wholesale prices. It's also extraordinarily hard for an individual to judge quality, and I can assure you that the number of telephone calls you get from folks wishing to sell diamonds will greatly exceed the calls from those who want to buy them.

Another popular current strategy is investment in collectibles. Thousands of salesmen are touting everything from Renoir to rugs, Tiffany lamps to rare stamps, art deco to airsick bags. I think there's nothing wrong in buying "things" you can love—and God knows people do have strange tastes—but my advice is buy those things because you love them, not because you expect them to appreciate in value. Contrary to popular belief, the inflation-adjusted value of art objects and collectibles does not generally increase. In addition, enormous commissions are paid when you buy and sell. Suppose you buy some collectibles from a dealer for $1,000; the dealer keeps 50 percent, which, after sales tax and various charges, leaves $400 for the original seller. Suppose in five years, the market value increases to four times what the seller got, from $400 to $1,600. Now suppose you sell your collectibles at auction. The auction house may take its commission of $350 and send you a check for $1,250. In this scenario, then, you've made a profit of 25 percent in five years, less than the rate on bank CDs—and these calculations are based on the assumption that your collectibles appreciated to an astronomical 400 percent of their original value, certainly an unlikely event.

Ask yourself why everyone is so willing to part with things whose value is supposedly increasing. And don't forget that fakes and forgeries are common. A portfolio of collectibles also often requires hefty insurance premiums and endless maintenance charges—so you are making payments instead of receiving dividends or interest. To earn money collecting, you need great originality and taste. You must buy first-class objects when no one else wants them, not inferior schlock when a vast uninformed public enthusiastically bids it up. In my view, most people who think they are collecting profit are really collecting trouble.

Another popular instrument these days is the commodities futures contract. As mentioned in Chapter Eleven, you can buy not only gold but also contracts for the delivery of a variety of commodities from grains to metals. It's a fast market where professionals can benefit greatly but individuals who don't know what they are doing can easily get clobbered. My advice to the nonprofessional investor: Don't go against the grain.

Exercise 9: Remember that Commission Costs Are Not Random; Some Are Cheaper than Others

With the advent of competitive commission rates, it has now become possible to buy your brokerage services at wholesale prices. A number of brokers around today will execute your stock orders at discounts of as much as 75 percent off the standard commission rates charged by the leading brokerage houses. The discount broker provides a plain-pipe-rack service. If you want your hand held, if you want opinions and investment suggestions, if you want a broker you can call for quotations and other information, the discount broker is *not* for you. If, however, you know exactly what you want to buy, the discount broker can get it for you at much lower commission rates than the standard full-service house. Make sure, however, that your discount broker is actually transacting your orders for stocks like IBM or Exxon on the New York Stock Exchange. Some discounters actually do the transactions off the exchange and the net price you end up paying is actually higher than that charged by a full-service broker.

It's not too hard to find discount brokers. Just read the financial pages of your daily or Sunday paper and you'll find their ads with such catchy headlines as "Full commissions are for the herds" and "There's nothing discount about [our service] except [our] commission rates." Purely for the execution of stock-market orders, you can use an honest discounter. The discounters all belong to the Security Investors Protection Corporation, which insures all accounts up to $100,000.

While on the subject of commission costs, you should be aware of a 1990s Wall Street innovation called the "wrap account." For a single fee, your broker obtains the services of a professional money manager, who then selects for you a portfolio of stocks, bonds, and perhaps real estate. Brokerage commissions and advisory fees are "wrapped" into the overall fee. One problem is that it is difficult, or impossible, for you to assess the manager selected by your broker. More importantly, the costs involved in wrap accounts are extremely high. Annual fees are usually about 3 percent per year, and there may be additional execution fees and fund expenses (if the manager uses mutual funds or REITs). With those kinds of expenses, it will be virtually impossible for you to beat the market. My advice here is: Avoid taking the wrap.

Exercise 10: Diversify Your Investment Steps

In these warm-up exercises, we have discussed a number of investment instruments. The most important part of our walk down Wall Street will take us to the corner of Broad Street—to a consideration of sensible investment strategies with respect to common stocks. A guide to this part of our walk is contained in the final three chapters, since I believe common stocks should form the cornerstone of most portfolios. Nevertheless, in our final warm-up exercise we recall the important lesson of modern portfolio theory—the advantages of diversification.

A biblical proverb states that "in the multitude of counselors there is safety." The same can be said of investments. Diversification reduces risk and makes it far more likely that you will achieve the kind of good average long-run return that meets your investment objective. Therefore, within each investment category you should hold a variety of individual issues, and while common stocks should be a major part of your portfolio, they should not be the sole investment instrument. Whatever the investment objectives, the investor who's wise diversifies.

A Final Checkup

Now that you have completed your warm-up exercises, let's take a moment for a final checkup. The theories of valuation worked out by economists and the performance recorded by the professionals lead to a single conclusion: There is no sure and easy road to riches. High returns can be achieved only through higher risk-taking (and perhaps through acceptance of lesser degrees of liquidity).

The amount of risk you can tolerate is partly determined by your sleeping point. The next chapter discusses the risks and rewards of stock and bond investing and will help you determine the kinds of returns you should expect from different financial instruments. But the risk you can assume is also significantly influenced by your age and by the sources and dependability of your non-investment income. Chapter Fourteen—"A Life-Cycle Guide to Investing"—will help give you a clearer notion of how to decide what portion of your capital should be placed in common stocks, bonds, and short-term investments. The final chapter presents specific stock-market strategies that will enable amateur investors to achieve results as good as or better than the most sophisticated professionals.

13

The Determinants of Stock and Bond Returns and How You Can Roughly Project the Future Returns from Financial Assets

No man who is correctly informed as to the past will be disposed to take a morose or desponding view of the present.   —Thomas B. Macaulay, *History of England*

This chapter presents a method by which you can assess, in a rough way, the attractiveness of current valuation levels. At the very least, it should help you judge the return levels it is reasonable to expect from different financial investments. The plan for the chapter is as follows. First, I will outline the major determinants of stock and bond returns. Next, I will review their 30-year history paying special attention to the role of inflation in influencing the returns that investors receive. Finally, and this is where you might make some money, I will survey the bond and stock markets as of the mid-1990s, as well as the long-term inflation outlook, and offer recommendations that can take you into the twenty-first century. While price levels will undoubtedly fluctuate, the general methodology to assess yield expectations from financial instruments should serve you well in realistically adapting your investment program to your financial needs.

Long-run returns from common stocks are driven by two critical factors: the initial dividend yield at the time the stocks were purchased and the future growth rate of the dividends. In principle, a share of common stock is worth the "present" or "discounted" value of its stream of future dividends. Recall that this "discounting" reflects the fact that a dollar received tomorrow is worth less than a dollar in hand today. A stock buyer is purchasing an ownership interest in a business and hopes to receive a growing stream of dividends. Even if a company pays very small dividends today and retains most (or even all) of its earnings to reinvest in the business, the investor implicitly assumes that such reinvestment will lead to a more rapidly growing stream of dividends in the future.

The discounted value of this stream of dividends can be shown to produce a very simple formula for the long-run total return for the stock market:*

> Long-Run Equity Return = Initial Dividend Yield + Growth Rate of Dividends.

We can use this formula to estimate the long-run return likely for the stock market in the future. Long-term data testify to its validity. From 1926 through 1994, for example, common stocks have provided an average annual rate of return of about 10 percent. The dividend yield for the market as a whole on January 1, 1926, was about 5 percent. The long-run rate of growth of dividends was also approximately 5 percent.

Over shorter periods, such as a year or even several years, a third factor is critical in determining returns. This factor is the change in valuation relationships—specifically, the change in the price-dividend multiple.† (Increases or decreases in the price-dividend multiple tend to move in the same direction as the more popularly used price-earnings multiple.)

---

*This formula, long-run return = initial dividend yield + long-run growth rate, can be derived from the mathematical statement that a share is worth the present or discounted value of the stream of dividends it produces.

†The price-dividend multiple is simply the reciprocal of the dividend yield. A stock that sells at a dividend yield of 5 percent has a price-dividend multiple of 20.

Price-dividend and price-earnings multiples vary widely from year to year. For example, in times of great optimism, such as early October 1929 and early October 1987, stocks sold at 35 times dividends (and at very high price-earnings multiples as well). At times of great pessimism, such as the early 1950s, stocks sold at less than 15 times dividends. The price-dividend multiple is also influenced by interest rates. When interest rates are low, stocks, which compete with bonds for an investor's savings, tend to sell at low dividend yields or high price-dividend multiples. When interest rates are high, the yield on stocks rises to be more competitive. And, of course, the higher the yield, the lower the price-dividend multiple. As we will see below, one of the worst recent decades for common stocks was the decade from 1968 to 1978 when returns were only 2½ percent per year. Stocks sold at a dividend yield of 3 percent at the start of the decade and dividend growth was 5.1 percent per year, a bit above the long-run average. Had price-dividend multiples (and dividend yields) remained constant, stocks would have produced an 8.1 percent annual return. But a large increase in dividend yields (a large fall in the price-dividend multiple) reduced the average annual return by over 5½ percentage points per year. The following figure, adapted from John Bogle's excellent book on mutual funds, shows the price-dividend multiple for stocks from 1926 through 1994.

Future long-run returns from bonds are even easier to calculate. Over the long-run, the yield that a bond investor receives is approximated by the yield to maturity of the bond at the time it is purchased. For a zero-coupon bond (a bond that makes no periodic interest payments, but simply returns a fixed amount at maturity), the yield at which it is purchased is precisely the yield that investor will receive, assuming no default. For a coupon-paying bond (a bond that does make periodic interest payments), there could be a slight variation in the yield that is earned over the term of the bond depending upon whether and at what interest rates the coupon interest is reinvested. Nevertheless, the initial yield on the bond provides a quite serviceable estimate of the yield that will be obtained by an investor who holds the bond until maturity.

Estimating bond returns becomes murky when bonds are

The Price of $1.00 of Dividends
(The Price-Dividend Multiple)

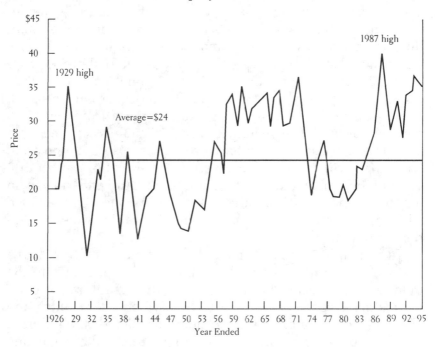

not held until maturity. Changes in interest rates (bond yields) then become a major factor in determining the net return received over the period during which the bond is held. For example, suppose an investor bought a ten-year zero-coupon bond to yield 8 percent and then sold it next year when interest rates had risen to 8½ percent. Instead of earning 8 percent for the year, the investor would have received a return of only about 3½ percent. The reason is that when interest rates rise, bond prices fall so as to make existing bonds competitive with bonds that are currently being issued at the higher interest rates. A one-half of one percent increase in interest rates would make the price of the bond drop by about 4½ percent, creating a capital loss that reduces the net rate of return. The principle to keep in mind is that bond investors who don't hold to maturity will have their return increased or decreased depending upon what happens to interest rates in the interim.

Bond investors suffer to the extent that interest rates rise—they gain to the extent that rates fall.

We are now ready to talk about the final major factor influencing bond and stock returns—changes in the rate of inflation. In the bond market, an increase in the inflation rate is unambiguously bad. To see this, suppose that there was no inflation and bonds sold on a 5 percent yield basis, providing investors with a real (that is, after inflation) return of 5 percent. Now assume that the inflation rate increases from zero to 5 percent per year. If investors still require a 5 percent real rate of return, then the bond interest rate must rise to 10 percent. Only then will investors receive an after-inflation return of 5 percent. But, this will mean that bond prices fall and those who previously purchased 5 percent long-term bonds will suffer a substantial capital loss. Inflation then is the deadly enemy of the bond investor.

In principle, common stocks should be an inflation hedge and stocks are not supposed to suffer with an increase in the inflation rate. Recall that the long-run rate of return for common stocks consists of the initial dividend yield plus the growth rate of the dividend. In theory at least, if the inflation rate rises by one percentage point, all prices should rise by one percentage point including the values of factories, equipment, and inventories. Consequently, the growth rate of earnings and dividends should rise with the rate of inflation. Thus, even though bond yields will rise with inflation and so will the required return on common stocks, to make them competitive with bonds, no change in dividend yields (or the price-dividend ratio) will be required. This is so because expected growth rates should rise along with increases in the expected inflation rate. Whether this happens in practice we will examine below.

The Acceleration of Inflation in the Late 1960s and 1970s

From the late 1960s through the early 1980s, the major influence on the securities markets was the sharp and unanticipated upward ratcheting of the underlying or core rate of inflation in the U.S. economy. By the core rate of inflation (prop your eyes open now) I mean the rate of increase of unit labor costs, measured by the increase in compensation per hour adjusted for any offsetting increase in productivity. Since labor costs are the major expense in the production of most goods and in the provision of most services, this measure of the increase in unit labor costs provides a better estimate of the underlying inflationary pressure in the economy than does the more popular (but more variable) consumer price index (CPI).

In the mid-1960s, inflation was essentially unnoticeable—running at a rate of just over 1 percent. When our involvement in Vietnam increased in the late 1960s, however, we had classical, old-fashioned "demand-pull" inflation—too much money chasing too few goods. This raised the core rate of inflation to something like 4 or 4½ percent. Once inflation ratcheted up, it appeared to be impervious to slack in the economy. We saw this happen often in the 1970s.

Then the economy was beset by the oil and food shocks of 1973–74. It was a classic case of Murphy's Law at work—whatever could go wrong did. OPEC contrived to produce an artificial shortage of oil and Mother Nature produced a real shortage of foodstuffs through poor grain harvests in North America and disastrous ones in the Soviet Union and sub-Saharan Africa. When even the Peruvian anchovy crop mysteriously disappeared (anchovies are a major source of protein), it appears that O'Toole's commentary had come into play. (It was O'-Toole who suggested that "Murphy was an optimist.") Again, the inflation rate ratcheted up. The core rate hit the 6 to 6½ percent level—measured rates of inflation, such as the CPI, were even higher.

During the 1974–75 recession, the core rate of inflation stubbornly remained at about 6 percent. Then in 1978 and 1979, a combination of policy mistakes—leading to considerable excess demand in certain sectors—and another 125 percent increase in the price of oil kicked the inflation rate up again, taking with it wage costs and thus unit labor costs. Once again, the 1980 recession failed to dampen the core rate of inflation, which rose to around 8 to 9 percent. The problem then was that from the mid-1960s to the early 1980s, the core rate of inflation steadily ratcheted upward. Each economic shock was built into the wage-cost structure and once a higher level of inflation became embedded in the system, there seemed to be no way of getting rid of it, at least with the unsustained doses of deflationary policies we were willing to accept in the 1970s.

The Agony of the Bond Investor

Because the inflation was unanticipated and allowance for it was not incorporated into the prices of most paper assets, investors in bonds had disastrous results. For example, in 1966, 30-year long-term bonds offered a yield to maturity of about 6 percent. This provided protection against the going inflation rate of about 3 percent and an anticipated after-inflation real rate of return of 3 percent. Unfortunately, the actual rate of inflation over the 15-year period 1966–81 was well in excess of 6 percent, wiping out any positive real rate of return. That's the good news part of this dreary story. The bad news was that there were capital losses. Who wanted to buy a bond yielding 6 percent in the late 1970s, when the rate of inflation was in double digits? No one! If you had to sell your bonds you sold at a loss so the new buyer could get a yield consonant with the higher rate of inflation. Yields rose even further as the risk premium on bonds rose to take into account their increased volatility. To make matters worse, the tax system delivered the unkindest blow of all to bond investors. Even though bond investors often actually earned negative pre-tax rates of return, their bond coupons were taxed at regular income-tax rates.

The Sorrow of the Stock Investor

Common stocks also failed to provide adequate inflation protection during the late 1960s and 1970s. It used to be widely believed that sensible investors should buy common stocks, representing ownership claims on real property, for generous long-run returns and for protection against inflation. But let's face it—during the 1970s, stock-market investing created a nouveau poor in the United States. The Dow Jones industrial average, which supposedly crossed the 1,000 barrier "for good" in 1973, ended the 1970s languishing near the 800 level. Because this disastrous performance occurred at the same time that the general price level increased about 70 percent, it became fashionable to believe that stocks were no longer an effective hedge against inflation. In 1979, *Business Week* published a cover story on the death of equities. Institutional investors who did not believe in capital punishment rushed to the sidelines, and individuals were consistent net sellers of their equity mutual funds.

Investors in the 1970s found little comfort in the satisfactory long-run performance record of common stocks. As was shown in Chapter Nine, over the long pull common stocks have produced an annual rate of return of 10 percent—considerably above the long-run rate of inflation. But investors were well aware of Lord Keynes' admonition, "In the long run we are all dead"; and over the shorter run investors expect to enjoy themselves and earn satisfactory returns. Between 1968 and 1979, the annual rate of return on U.S. common stocks was a paltry 3.1 percent. The annual rate of return on gold and various objets d'art was more than six times as large. Robert S. Salomon, Jr., of the renowned investment firm of Salomon Brothers, plotted the 1968–79 investment records of several major assets. The results, shown in the following table, leave little doubt as to why money left the stock market in the 1970s.

In the eleven years 1968–79, common stocks actually underperformed long-term bonds, while gold, Chinese ceramics, stamps, and other nontraditional investments produced extraordinary returns.

Why Did Common Stocks Fail in the 1970s?—
Some False Clues

The failure of bonds to protect investors against an *unanticipated* inflationary episode is hardly surprising. The common-stock flop was something else. Since stocks represent claims on real assets that presumably rise in value with the price level, stock prices—according to this line of logic—should have risen also. It's like the story of the small boy on his

Traditional vs. Nontraditional Investments, 1968–79

Investment	Compound Annual Growth in Value, 1968–79
Gold	19.4%
Chinese ceramics	19.1
Stamps	18.9
Rare books	15.7
Silver	13.7
Coins (U.S. nongold)	12.7
Old masters' paintings	12.5
Diamonds	11.8
Farmland	11.3
Single-family house	9.6
U.S. consumer price index	6.5
Foreign currencies[a]	6.4
High-grade corporate bonds	5.8
Common stocks	3.1

Source: Salomon Brothers.
[a]West German mark, Japanese yen, Swiss franc, and Dutch guilder.

first trip to an art museum. When told that a famous abstract painting was supposed to be a horse, the boy asked wisely, "Well, if it is supposed to be a horse, why isn't it a horse?" If common stocks were supposed to be an inflation hedge, then why weren't they?

Many different explanations involving faltering dividends and earnings growth have been offered that simply don't hold up under careful analysis. One common explanation was that inflation had caused corporate profits to shrink drastically, especially when reported figures were adjusted for inflation. Inflation was portrayed as a kind of financial neutron bomb, leaving the structure of corporate enterprise intact, but destroying the lifeblood of profits. Many saw the engine of capitalism as running out of control, so that a walk down Wall Street—random or otherwise—could prove extremely hazardous.

It used to be easy to measure profits. They were the excess of income over expenses. Not so in an era of inflation, when figuring out true profitability can be quite complex. The problem is that inflation tends to make reported profits appear misleadingly large. Inflation swells reported profits (as well as actual tax liabilities) through two fictitious elements—the overstatement of income (because of the inclusion of inventory profits) and the understatement of expenses (because depreciation charges are calculated on original rather than replacement costs).

Inventory profits provide the same kind of illusory benefits for a business firm that real estate gains provide for homeowners. Homeowners have paper capital gains from the rising values of their homes, but unless they obtain additional mortgages at high interest rates, they cannot use this wealth until they sell their homes. Even worse, as soon as their property is reassessed, property taxes go up. Similarly, inventory profits are not the benefit to a firm that they seem. As the firm disposes of its appreciated inventory, the goods must be replaced at higher prices. Thus, inventory profits provide no cash flow for the firm. Indeed, just the opposite is true, for these paper profits are taxed at regular income-tax rates.

Depreciation charges are another factor in the inflation-swollen profit picture. These are the expenses, charged against taxable income, for the wearing out of the firm's plant and equipment during the production process. The lower the charge, the more income (and profit) will be reported. Because depreciation charges are based on low original cost rather than higher current replacement cost, they are usually not as high as they should be. This makes the remaining income appear as healthy profit when it should be set aside to provide for the necessary replacement of the depreciating assets. Thus, we must be careful, in looking at profits, to judge them as nearly as possible on a true economic basis.

The facts are, however, that after making all the necessary adjustments to reported profits, there was no evidence that true profits had been "sliding down a pole greased by cruel and inexorable inflation," as some in the financial community believed in the early 1980s. Over the long pull, corporate profits, both in the aggregate and as a percentage of invested capital (figured at inflated replacement cost), have held up extremely well. Indeed, through the 1980s and into the 1990s, thanks to lower inflation rates and higher depreciation allowances al-

lowed by the tax law, any inflation illusion on reported corporate profits has been more than wiped out. For the entire
decade of the 1980s, reported profits were actually lower than
true economic profits.

Perhaps, however, we are looking in the wrong place for a
clue to the seventies slump. Remember the well-known story of
the government bureaucrat searching on his hands and knees
on Pennsylvania Avenue for some object during the midday
rush?

"What are you looking for?" asked a passerby.

"My watch."

"Do you remember where you lost it?"

"Over on Connecticut Avenue."

"Then why are you looking here?"

"The light is better here."

There is much light placed on corporate earnings in the financial press; but perhaps the experts would be wiser to focus
on dividends rather than earnings. Maybe the relevant question is not the amount of earnings—however adjusted—but
rather what dividends U.S. corporations are able to pay. The
acid test of whether true earning power is increasing is the
ability of corporations to provide a stream of dividends whose
growth will keep up with inflation. Let us, then, move our light
over from earnings to dividends.

The following chart shows the progression of both dividends and the consumer price index from 1926 through 1994.
Dividends have more than held their own. Even during the
stagflation period of the 1970s and the recession of the early
1980s, dividends rose by nearly the same rate as the CPI.
Clearly, then, common stocks have proved to be a dependable
inflation hedge with respect to their ability to produce dividends that have grown at rates equal to or exceeding the rate of
growth of the price level.

Movie buffs may recall the marvelous final scene from
Casablanca. Humphrey Bogart stands over the body of a Luft-
waffe major, a smoking gun in his hand. Claude Rains, a cap-
tain in the French colonial police, turns his glance from Bogart
to the smoking gun to the dead major and finally to his assistant, and says, "Major Strasser has been shot. Round up the
usual suspects." We, too, have rounded up the usual suspects,

Inflation vs. Dividends

Index (1926=100)

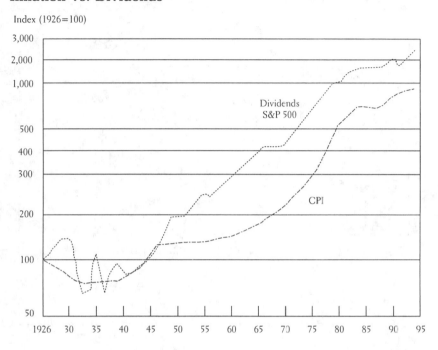

but we have yet to find out who shot the stock market. Nor have we discovered a rational motive for the crime. Now let's look at the smoking gun.

The Smoking Gun: The Price-Dividends, Price-Earnings Crash of the 1970s

The major reason for the decline in equity prices during the 1970s was that investors' evaluations of dividends and earnings—the number of dollars they were willing to pay for a dollar of dividends and earnings—fell by roughly half. Stocks failed to provide investors with protection against inflation not because earnings and dividends failed to grow with inflation, but rather because price-earnings multiples quite literally collapsed over the period.

The graph on page 369 shows the collapse in price-dividend multiples. The following figure shows that the price-earnings multiple for the S&P index was cut by more than 50 percent

S&P 500 P/E Multiples

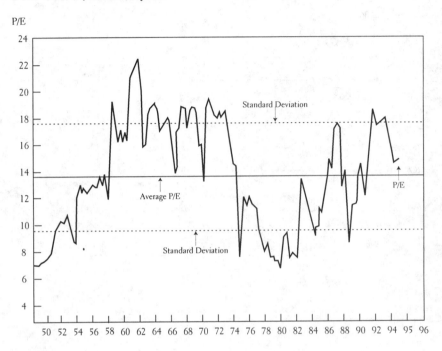

during the decade of the 1970.* The multiples of growth stocks dropped even more drastically, falling by two-thirds. It was this decline in multiples that produced such extraordinarily poor returns for investors in the seventies and that prevented stock prices from reflecting the real underlying progress most companies made in earnings and dividend growth. Thus, the internationally respected financial economist Franco Modigliani (writing with Richard Cohn in the *Financial Analysts Journal*) concluded that the market was simply irrational during the 1970s and early 1980s—it simply didn't know how to capitalize earnings during an inflationary period.

It is, of course, quite possible that stock investors may have become irrationally pessimistic in the early 1980s, just as they were probably irrationally optimistic in the mid-1960s. But

*The graph also shows the standard deviation, a measure of the variability of P/E multiples. Note that multiples went from well above average in 1970 to well below average in 1980.

while I do not believe the market is always perfectly rational, if forced to choose between the stock market and the economics profession, I'd put my money on the stock market every time. I suspect that stock investors weren't irrational when they caused a sharp drop in price-dividend and earnings multiples—they were just scared. In the mid-1960s, inflation was so modest as to be almost unnoticeable and investors were convinced that economists had found the cure for serious recessions—even mild downturns could be "fine-tuned" away. No one would have imagined in the 1960s that the economy could experience either double-digit unemployment or double-digit inflation, let alone that both could appear simultaneously. Clearly, we learned that economic conditions were far less stable than had previously been imagined.

We also realized more fully that inflation is not a benign phenomenon, as it used to be described in some textbooks. When prices rise by 10 percent, all prices do not rise by the same amount. Rather, relative prices (and the relationship between input and output prices) are far more variable at higher levels of inflation. Furthermore, the higher the rate of inflation, the more variable and unpredictable inflation becomes. Thus, more volatile levels of real output and higher inflation rates, as well as the accompanying greater volatility of interest rates, increased uncertainty throughout the economy. Equity securities (dare I say equity insecurities) were, therefore, considered riskier and deserving of higher risk compensation.*

The market provides higher risk premiums through a drop in prices relative to earnings and dividends; this produces larger returns in the future consistent with the new riskier environment. Paradoxically, however, the same adjustments that produced very poor returns in the late 1960s and throughout the 1970s created some very attractive price levels in the early 1980s. The experience makes clear, however, that if one wants to explain the generation of returns over a decade or shorter

---

*Economists often put the proposition in terms of the risk premium—that is, the extra return you can expect from an investment over and above the return from perfectly predictable short-term investments. According to this view, the risk premiums in the 1960s were very small—perhaps 1 or 2 percentage points. During the early 1980s, risk premiums demanded by investors to hold both stocks and bonds expanded to a range of probably 4 to 6 percentage points, as I shall show below.

time period, a change in valuation relationships plays a critical role. The growth rate of dividends did compensate for inflation during the 1970s, but the drop in price-dividend multiples, which I believe reflected increased perceived risk, is what killed the stock market.

The 1980 Paper-Asset Thesis

Let me turn now to the thesis I presented in late 1980 that the decade of the 1980s would be the age of paper assets. I argued that both bonds and stocks had fully adjusted—and perhaps even overadjusted—to the changed economic environment. I suggested that stocks and bonds were priced not only to provide adequate protection against the likely rate of inflation, but also to give unusually generous real rates of return.

Let us consider the argument for the bond market first. In the early 1980s, this market was in disgrace. *The Bawl Street Journal,* in its 1981 annual comedy issue, wrote, "A bond is a fixed-rate instrument designed to fall in price." At the time, the yield on high-quality corporate bonds was close to 15 percent. The underlying rate of inflation (as measured by the growth of unit labor costs) was then about 8 percent. Thus, corporate bonds provided a prospective real rate of return of about 7 percent, a rate unusually generous by past historical standards. (According to Ibbotson and Sinquefield, the long-term real rate of return on corporate bonds was only 2 percent.) To be sure, bond prices had become volatile and, thus, it was reasonable to suppose that bonds ought to offer a somewhat larger risk premium than before. But I suggested then that panic-depressive institutional investors probably overdiscounted the risks of bond investments. Like generals fighting the last war, investors had been loathe to touch bonds because experience over the past fifteen years had been so disastrous. But at some price, bonds are appropriately valued in the market, and it was my thesis in 1980 that, because so many investors "would never buy a bond again," the market may even have overreacted. Even if inflation remained at its 1980–81 levels, bonds were a smart investment, particularly for tax-exempt investors (including Keogh and IRA participants).

What about stocks? As I mentioned above, it is possible to calculate the anticipated long-run rate of return on stocks of the Dow Jones industrial average by adding the dividend yield of the average to the anticipated growth of dividends per share. The calculations I performed during 1980 suggested a total expected rate of return from common stocks of 16 to 17 percent. The 16 percent rate was 8 percentage points more than the core rate of inflation and was again very generous by historical standards.

Common stocks were also selling at unusually low multiples of cyclically depressed earnings, at below average price-dividend multiples, and at prices that were only a fraction of the replacement value of the assets they represented. Small wonder we saw so many corporate takeovers during the 1980s. Whenever assets can be bought in the stock market at less than the cost of acquiring them directly, there will be a tendency for firms to purchase the equities of other firms, as well as to buy back their own stocks. Thus, I argued that in the early 1980s, we were presented with a market situation where paper assets had adjusted and perhaps overadjusted to inflation and the greater uncertainty associated with it. On the other hand, hard assets, despite their extraordinary performance during the 1970s, seemed fully priced. I concluded that the question was not how badly equity investors had done in the past—it was what investors would be kicking themselves about five years from now for not having bought today.

The 1980s—A Decade for Paper Assets

The stock and bond markets in the last half of 1982 finally reacted to what were apparently severely undervalued price levels of the earlier 1980s. Until October 1987, the stock market rallied almost continuously. Bonds also did well.

Then, in a single week during October 1987, market prices dropped by one-third. In one day, October 19, 1987, the popular Dow Jones industrial average dropped over 500 points, the largest single-day decline in history. Still, for the decade as a whole, stocks and bonds provided investors with extraordinarily generous returns. Indeed, the return from stocks ex-

"Let me put it this way. It's five years from now. What am I kicking myself
for not having bought?"

Drawing by Whitney Darrow, Jr. © 1956 The New Yorker Magazine, Inc.

ceeded the 16 percent calculated by adding the initial dividend
yield to the growth rate at the start of the decade. This was so
because the the price-dividend multiple (and price-earnings
multiple) rose over the decade. On the other hand, hard assets
such as gold experienced a decade of relatively poor performance.

The following chart, again using data prepared by Robert
Salomon of the firm of Salomon Brothers Incorporated, presents returns from 1980 through 1989 for selected investment
assets. Paper assets, especially common stocks, were the clear
winners during the 1980s. On the other hand, while some collectibles, such as coins and old masters' paintings, did reason-

The 1980s—A Decade for Financial Assets
(Compound Annual Rates of Return)

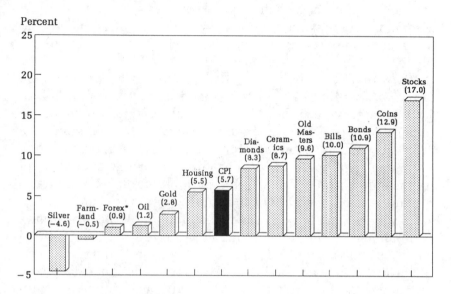

Source: Salomon Brothers.
*West German mark, Japanese yen, Swiss franc, and Dutch guilder.

ably well, the worst returns were provided by hard assets, such as silver, gold, and oil.

Returns During the First Half of the 1990s

In the fifth edition of this book, published in 1990, I used the same techniques to assess the likely long-run returns from stocks and bonds. By adding the dividend yield to the anticipated long-run growth rate for the Dow Jones industrial average, I calculated that the stock market as a whole was priced to provide a long-run return of about 9½ percent, far less generous than the extraordinary over 17 percent returns during the 1980s, but not too much different from the long-run rates of return earned by stock investors during the twentieth century. Stocks then were considered, at best, only of average attractiveness. I pointed out, however, that good-quality long-term corporate bonds offered a rate of return (when held to maturity) of 9 to 9½ percent—almost as high as the rate of return from stocks and much higher than their historical returns. I argued that bonds, which carried less risks, in general, than common stocks, seemed *relatively* attractive offering close to the same rate of return as common stocks, but with considerably less volatility and sleepless nights.

Now that about half of the 1990s have passed, we can look at the returns that have been realized through the first half of 1994. Again, we use the Salomon Brothers return numbers to illustrate the returns. The data are shown in the table on page 385. We see that common stocks did provide approximately their long-run 10 percent rate of return. While one cannot count on the sum of the dividend yield and long-term growth rate to provide a good estimate of the short-run return from common stocks, the estimate will prove reasonably reliable when there is no change in the price-dividend ratio. And as the graph on page 369 shows, yields of common stocks (and, therefore, their reciprocals, the price-dividend ratios) remained relatively constant over the first half of the 1990s, although dividend multiples did rise a bit. Bond returns were also very close to the number forecast at the start of the decade, although the last months of 1994 reduced the return somewhat below the yield shown in the table. Recall that even in the short-term, bond investors will earn the promised yield to maturity if there is no change in interest rates. And despite some gyrations in yields during the first half of the 1990s, yields in mid-1994 were approximately the same as they were in January 1990. Thus, bonds and stocks did give investors roughly equivalent returns during the first half of the 1990s.

Judging Returns for Financial Investments during the Late 1990s and into the Twenty-First Century

While I remain convinced that no one can predict short-term movements in securities markets, I do believe it is possible to judge the long-run appropriateness of levels of stock prices and interest rates. While investment opportunities dur-

Returns from Various Investments, 1990–94

Investment	Compound Annual Growth in Value 1990 to mid-1994
Foreign exchange[a]	10.6%
Common stocks	10.4
Bonds	9.9
Treasury bills	5.6
Consumer price index	3.5
Housing	2.7
Farmland	2.4
Silver	1.9
Diamonds	1.4
Gold	1.3
Stamps	1.1
Oil	−1.9

Source: Salomon Brothers.
[a]Combines money-market returns with changes in exchange rates.

ing the mid-1990s are not nearly so compelling as those existing at the start of the 1980s, many factors suggest that paper assets still offer reasonable rates of return for investors. This section will summarize the rough guidelines investors can use to estimate the long-run returns one can expect from financial assets.

Looking at the stock market, it is well to remember that the market has, like Alice in *Through the Looking Glass,* been on a treadmill—essentially selling at very near the same levels as in the mid-1960s. The following chart indicates that in "real" or inflation-adjusted terms, stocks in the mid-1990s were selling somewhat below the peak levels of the 1960s and early 1970s, despite their substantial increase.*

Price-earnings multiples, however, indicate that the stock market of the mid-1990s was priced well above the bargain-basement levels reached in the early 1980s. As indicated in the figure on page 378, multiples were somewhat above average in the mid-1990s, but were at least within the general historical range of the past thirty-five years. Comparing price-earnings multiples with historical precedent is far from an infallible way to judge the reasonableness of security valuations but it is at least a guide.

*The inflation-adjusted level of the S&P index is calculated by dividing the index number by the general price level.

S&P 500-Stock Index—Inflation-adjusted Level 1947–94

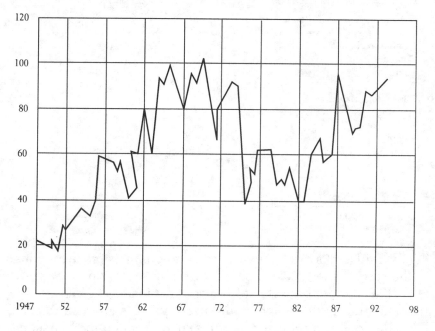

Another guide is to compare the dividend yield of the stock market or the price-dividend multiple with yields and multiples available in the past. The price-dividend comparison is shown on page 369 and indicates that valuations were on the rich side. The chart on page 387 presents data on dividend yields for the S&P 500 index going back into the 1920s. Again, the comparison is not as favorable for common stocks. Dividend yields at 2.8 percent were clearly very low relative to historical precedent during the mid-1990s. Investors should certainly be aware of the relationship of the dividend yield for the market as a whole relative to the historical norm.

I emphasize dividends for two reasons. First, the initial dividend yield is one component of the long-run rate of return from common stocks. It is obviously better to purchase stocks at a six percent dividend yield rather than a three percent yield, other things being the same. Second, to the extent that one can predict shorter-run returns from common stocks, the initial dividend yield has historically been a useful indicator. Histori-

Dividend Yield, S&P 500-Stock Index

Yeild %

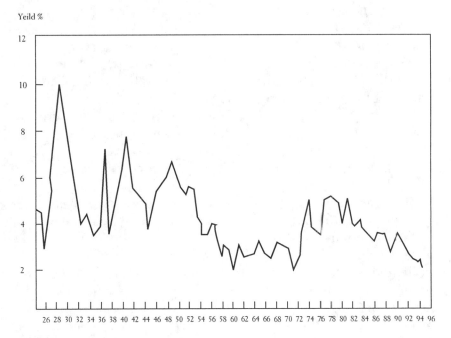

cally, investors have *never* received *above-average* rates of
return when dividend yields for the market have been under
three percent. The problem is that if dividend yields rise (or
equivalently price-dividend ratios fall), investors will suffer
from such valuation changes as they did in the 1970s. Unless
growth rates are far more rapid in the decade ahead than has
been the case historically, investors should not anticipate unusually generous returns from common stocks.

The charts on page 389 summarizes the effect of the initial
dividend yield (D/P) and the P/E multiple at which stocks were
purchased and the 10-year future returns realized from those
valuation levels. The charts demonstrate that there is a fair
amount of predictability in the future 10-year rate of return
earned by stock investors and the initial P/E and D/P at which
the stocks were bought. The dividend chart was constructed by
measuring, at the start of each quarter from 1926 to 1985, the
yield (D/P) for the market as a whole. All the observations
were then divided into 10 groupings (deciles) according to the
levels of yields. Ten percent of the time, dividend yields were

very low (below 3.0 percent). At these times the market was very expensive. The next grouping had the second-lowest dividend yields (about 3.1 percent). The bottom of the chart shows the average D/P for each decile. Similarly, the P/E chart divides the quarters from 1926 through 1985 into deciles depending on the P/E for the market at the start of the period. The ten percent of the time when stocks were the most conservatively valued (very cheap), they had P/E levels below 9.8. The grouping to the far right shows the periods when stocks were extremely expensive (had the highest multiples of 20.1 and above). Again, the bottom of the chart shows the average P/E multiple for each decile.

The candles in the graphs show the following 10-year rate of return from the different initial valuation levels. The candles in the dividend figure show the average returns following the various initial dividend yields. The candles in the P/E figure indicate the average returns following different initial P/E multiples. The pattern is very clear. While on average, investors have earned about 10 percent from the stock market, rates of return from equities have been above average when it was possible to buy them at low P/Es and high yields. Returns from equities have been well below average when P/Es were high and yields were low. While no one can forecast short-run returns from the market, the charts can be very helpful to investors in estimating the longer-run returns that are most likely. My advice to investors is to look up the yield and multiple for one of the broad-market indexes, such as the S&P 500, and compare the P/E and D/P valuation levels with those in the charts. The method is far from foolproof, but it will be a useful indication of the relative attractiveness of equities.

Another indicator, and one that puts stocks in a more favorable light, is to compare the total market value of the equities in the S&P 400 Industrial Stock Index with the replacement value of the assets represented. The chart on page 390 presents thirty years of data for this indicator. Price to replacement cost ratios are somewhere in the middle of their historical range. By this measure, stocks are more attractively valued than they were in the 1960s though not nearly as inexpensive as they were during the early 1980s.

Finally, let me update the yield plus growth calculations, in-

The Future 10-Year Rates of Return When Stocks Are Purchased at Alternative Initial
Dividend Yields (D/P)
Future returns are higher when stocks are purchased at high dividend yields.

Return (%)

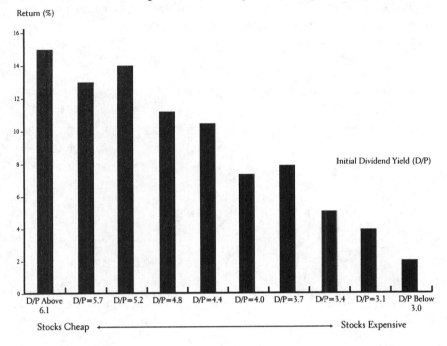

Initial Dividend Yield (D/P)

Stocks Cheap ←————————————————————————→ Stocks Expensive

The Future 10-Year Rates of Return When Stocks Are Purchased at Alternative Initial
Price-to-Earnings (P/E) Multiples
Future returns are higher when stocks are purchased at low price-earnings multiples.

Return (%)

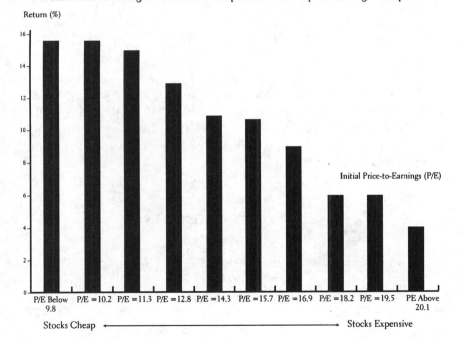

Initial Price-to-Earnings (P/E)

Stocks Cheap ←————————————————————————→ Stocks Expensive

Source: The Leuthold Group.

cluded in earlier editions, to show that stocks still appear to provide acceptable prospective returns. I believe that you can obtain
a 9½ percent return even on a stodgy stock like good old Exxon.

S&P's 400-Stock Index (Ratio of Price to
Replacement Value of Assets, 1960–94)

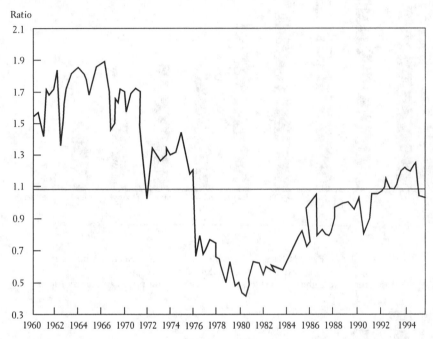

Source: Goldman, Sachs and Co.

Exxon is not a spectacular investment and its image was
badly sullied by the Valdez oil spill of 1989. But it is a high-
quality bellwether stock and very widely held by the public.
Early in 1995, the basic investing measurements for an Exxon
share were as shown below:

Price: $60.00

1995 Earnings (est.): $4.00

P/E Multiple: 15

1995 Dividend (est.): $3.00

Yield: 5%

Exxon's Early 1995 Investment Profile

We see that, for openers, an investor could expect a 5 percent rate of return in 1995 just from a continuation of the $3.00 dividend. Exxon doesn't leap and bound, but it has been able to produce growing dividends. Even during the 1970s (a decade most equity investors would rather forget), the dividend grew at a rate of better than 10 percent. Let's be really cautious and suppose that during the remainder of the 1990s the dividend grows at only a 4½ percent rate (certainly a conservative assumption and actually somewhat below some estimates currently being made in Wall Street). Now we all know that when earnings and dividends grow at an average rate of, say, 4½ percent, we don't expect the growth to come in at exactly that rate every year. Prosperous years for the economy may bring much larger increases; recession years may even bring declines, especially in earnings. But let's suppose that 1996, for example, is an average year. We now have the picture shown below:

1996 Earnings (est.): $4.18
($4.00 + 4½%)

1996 Dividend (est.): S3.14
($3.00 + 4½%)

Exxon's 1996 Estimated Growth

Before we can project an Exxon investor's overall rate of return during 1995—including both dividends and changes in the worth of a share—we need to project what the stock price will be at the start of 1996. Suppose we project that the market will be just as pessimistic about Exxon and its tarnished image at the start of 1996 as it was at the start of 1995. It's easier to get into a state of depression than to get out of it (like the old saw about making love to a gorilla: You don't quit when *you* get tired; you quit when the *gorilla* gets tired). With the same degree of pessimism prevailing at the start of 1996, the market will continue to assign a price-earnings multiple of 15 and a dividend yield of 5 percent to Exxon stock. Thus, it will sell at about $62.75 per share—15 times its estimated earnings of $4.18—while still producing a 5 percent yield with its then projected $3.14 dividend. We have now completed our investment profile.

Price: $62.75 (15 × $4.18 earnings)

1996 Earnings (est.): $4.18

P/E Multiple: 15

1996 Dividend (est.): $3.14

Yield: 5%
    ($3.14 dividend ÷ $62.75 price)

Exxon's Early 1996 Estimated Investment Profile

Under these circumstances, the holder of Exxon stock can expect a yearly return of 9½ percent—5 percent from the dividend yield and 4½ percent from the growth of the company. The investor gets $3.00 in dividends and $2.75 in capital gains, for a total return of $5.75, which is approximately 9½ percent of the original $60 investment.

Purchase Price Early 1995: $60.00

Market Price Early 1996: $62.75

Capital Gain: $2.75

Dividend during Period Held: $3.00

$$\frac{\text{Total Return}}{\text{Purchase Price}} = \frac{\$5.75}{\$60.00} \approx 9\frac{1}{2}\%$$

Returns to Holder of Exxon Stock
(12 Months, Early 1995 to Early 1996)

Our Exxon example provides another illustration of finding the prospective rate of return on any stock by adding the expected growth rate of the company to its dividend yield. The rule works whenever there is no change in the general level of P/E or price-dividend multiples. Obviously, such neat calculations are not likely to work out year after year. Nevertheless, over longer periods of time results do average out so that total returns can well be approximated by adding the growth rate to the dividend yield. The moral is clear. Exxon was priced in early 1995 to provide a return of about 9½ percent.

What about the rest of the market? I've done similar calculations for the thirty stocks of the Dow Jones industrial average as of mid-1995. When you add the dividend yields for each stock to the long-run growth rates, the prospective return is around 9 percent. (Growth rate estimates are obtained from Wall Street security analysts. Individuals can find growth prospects for a wide variety of companies from the *Value Line Investment Survey*. While these estimates are subject to considerable error, the *Value Line* estimates have as good a record as any others.) This average prospective return of 9 percent is roughly equal to (though slightly below) the long-run historical return earned by equity investors since 1926.

Let's now turn to an assessment of the bond market. High-quality corporate bond yields, while well below the early 1980s peak, were in mid-1995 around 8 percent and still reasonably generous. Remember that inflation rates have also come down sharply. While it is true that the measured rate of inflation in the United States rose to about 5 percent at the end of the 1980s, recent wage behavior and productivity trends suggest a core inflation rate at the start of 1995 of no more than 3 to 4 percent. This gives a projected very generous real rate of return of something in the vicinity of 4 to 5 percent, not too much lower in real terms than earlier in the eighties. Thus, bonds in mid-1995 were priced to be a very serviceable investment that should provide unusually generous real rates of return. Over the long pull in the United States, corporate bonds have historically produced a real rate of return of only 2 percent, as measured by Ibbotson and Sinquefield.

Comparisons of prospective stock and bond yields can potentially be very helpful to investors. The following figure plots bond yields and prospective rates of return on common stocks (the Dow Jones industrial average), calculated using the growth-rate estimates of Wall Street analysts. The figure shows that bond yields rose above the prospective returns from stocks only once. That was during the early autumn of 1987. When even U.S. government bonds rose above 10 percent, this proved far too competitive for common stocks and the market collapsed. While I would never claim that any statistic can reliably predict turns in the market, such comparisons can at least be helpful in providing warning signals and revealing periods of attractive relative values in the bond market. As of mid-1995, bonds appeared to offer return possibilities almost as attractive as stocks but with less risk.

Expected Total Return: Stocks and Bonds

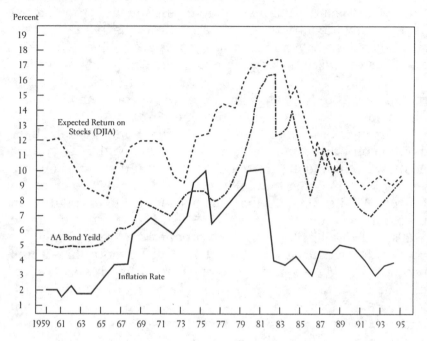

Percent

19
18
17
16
15
14
13   Expected Return on
12   Stocks (DJIA)
11
10
9
8
7
6   AA Bond Yeild
5
4
3   Inflation Rate
2
1

1959 61   63   65   67   69   71   73   75   77   79   81   83   85   87   89   91   93   95

Bonds are the Rodney Dangerfield of financial investments. They don't get much respect. The arguments against bonds are easy to make. Over the long pull, their total return (interest payments plus capital gains and losses) has been far inferior to that of common stocks. Over the past sixty years, stocks have returned a compound annual rate of 10 percent, about 7 percentage points better than the average rate of inflation over the period. On the other hand, high-grade corporate bonds have eked out a rate of return of only about 5 percent. In inflation-adjusted terms, bonds yielded 2 percent versus 7 percent for stocks; thus, stocks did 3½ times as well as bonds.

With the benefit of hindsight, we now know that bonds were inappropriately priced thirty years ago (as they also were in the forties and early fifties when their yields were pegged at artificially low levels). If investors had known thirty years ago that inflation would become a major problem—if they had correctly forecast that the general economy, inflation rates, exchange rates, and, therefore, interest rates would become increasingly volatile—bonds would not have been priced to give such inadequate total returns. But remember that our smartest economists were claiming in the early 1960s that inflation (then at 1 percent) was dead and that even minor fluctuations in economic activity could easily be offset. Economists and investors were egregiously wrong. But they are not likely to be wrong forever.

The point is that you shouldn't invest with a rearview mirror. What was a poor investment over the past sixty years will not necessarily be one over the next sixty. Investors learn, and new information about inflation and volatility does get incorporated into market prices. Bonds today reflect the poorer inflation outlook and the greater instability of bond prices. The issue is not how poorly bond investors fared in the 1950s, 1960s, and 1970s. The issue is: Will bonds produce a generous return in the future? I believe that when purchased at the 8 percent yield levels existing as of mid-1995, the answer is yes.

While I believe that bonds were priced more attractively relative to stocks in the mid-1990s, I do want to point out the one area of the U.S. stock market that at least on a relative basis seems most attractive. The relative P/E multiple for small company growth stocks was very near a historical low, during the mid-1990s, as is shown in the next figure. Over long periods of time, rates of return on small stocks have been higher than for the market as a whole and that should be especially true when they can be bought at the valuation levels existing during 1995. So to the extent that one is in stocks (and I believe all investors should have some part of their assets in the stock market), there appears to be greater relative value in smaller growth stocks and recognized growth stocks selling at small premiums to the general market.

Small Company Growth Stocks Relative P/E Multiple
(Price-Earnings Multiple of Index of Small
Growth Companies Relative to S&P 500-Stock Index)

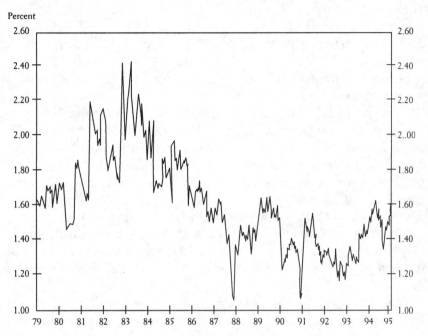

Source: Smith, Barney & Co.

Could I Be Wrong?

The thesis presented is that at the price levels existing in mid-1995, attractive prospective returns are likely to come in the future from investment in bonds. Stocks appear to be, at best, of average attractiveness. A popular maxim warns, however, "If you can remain calm when everyone around you is panicked, perhaps you don't understand the problem." Could the problem be worse than I have described? Could the market actually be underestimating the long-run inflation dangers to economic instability? What if the core rate of inflation is about to ratchet back up to the double-digit level, as some investors fear? This is precisely the situation that would make my investment thesis wrong as it concerns long-term bonds. (And it would undoubtedly make investment in tangible assets far more attractive than was the case in the 1980s.) So the critical final question I must address is the likelihood that the current core inflation rate will remain at a restrained level.

While many forecasters anticipate a sharp acceleration of inflation in the late 1990s, I would suggest to you that there are at least some reasons for optimism as well as some for concern. The most favorable part of the picture concerns the behavior of wage settlements. Average hourly earnings are still rising at less than a 4 percent rate. I realize that many analysts believe that the recent period of wage restraint is an aberration and that a significant acceleration of wage settlements is likely. But even if this were true, the tightening of controls throughout American industry and the increasing experience mix of our labor force augur well for a better productivity performance in the late 1990s. Thus, the rise in unit labor costs (which I have suggested is a good proxy for the core rate of inflation) should not increase by more than 4 percent and may do even better.

Over the longer term, however, there are also reasons to be sanguine. I think we have learned throughout the Western world that our economies do not work well with high and variable rates of inflation, and there is now a willingness to accept far harsher demand management policies than was previously thought politically feasible. The level of unemployment throughout the Western world was higher in the mid-1990s, and was expected to stay higher than at similar points of postwar economic cycles. Moreover, even socialist European Economic Community countries were experiencing unprecedented high rates of unemployment. While there should be considerable growth in the less-developed world and in formerly communist countries, it seems quite likely that the world economy will not be characterized by excess demand and increases in the prices of basic commodities. Our past problem with inflation was associated with worldwide excess demand or at least tight supply conditions.

Moreover, U.S. labor clearly recognizes that our economy is now sufficiently open to world trade that continued reasonable moderation in industrial wage demands and acceptance of changes in work rules are essential if we are to keep from becoming a service economy. An industry-by-industry analysis suggests that heightened competitive pressures in both domestic and foreign markets (and including substantially increased competition from developing countries) have significantly changed the wage-setting process. Moreover, the deregulation of such industries as airlines, trucking, and telephone service has triggered increased wage competition in many industries. While no one can tell if we will succeed, there are certainly reasons for optimism that the upward ratcheting of the core inflation rate has ended.

There is, however, one disturbing part of the picture that has not yet fallen into place in the United States and is, I believe, the reason interest rates are still as high as they are and threaten to return to even higher levels. The projected federal budget deficit in the mid-1990s is still far too large. More disturbing is the fact that most projections show the deficit rising in the late 1990s with the aging of the U.S. population. It is clear that political action with respect to the budget will be necessary to remove the legitimate fear that interest rates will increase as private and federal demands overwhelm the supply of savings or that continued deficit spending will eventually lead to inflation. Progress on the deficit would remove an important question mark on the thesis presented, at least as it concerns investment in bonds. Even if less progress is made than desirable, I believe that bonds will provide reasonable real rates of return over the remainder of the 1990s. At the very least, investors should assign some substantial probability to this continued moderate inflation scenario (or at least no return to the 1970s inflation scenario) and balance their equity positions with some portion of their investment funds in bonds.

It is also well to remember the lessons of the theories we examined in Part Two, which suggested that capital markets are at least reasonably efficient over the long pull. Fears about renewed inflation and economic instability are not reflected in stock and bond prices at some time in the future; they are reflected in the market now. If investors perceive that investment risk has increased, the financial pages reflect such thinking very quickly. In well-functioning financial markets, such as ours, investors are willing to buy only those assets that will provide the higher future rates of return sufficient to compensate them for added risk.

Does my expectation for reasonably attractive rates of return from bonds and stocks mean that I am predicting a bull market rally during some specific period of the late 1990s? Not at all! As a random walker through Wall Street, I am skeptical that anyone can predict the course of short-term stock price movements, and perhaps we are better off for it. I am reminded of one of my favorite episodes from the marvelous old radio serial "I Love a Mystery." This mystery was about a greedy stock-market investor who wished that just once he would be allowed to see the paper, with its stock price changes, twenty-four hours in advance. By some occult twist his wish was granted, and early in the evening he received the late edition of the next day's paper. He worked feverishly through the night planning early-morning purchases and late-afternoon sales which would guarantee him a killing in the market. Then, before his elation had diminished, he read through the remainder of the paper—and came upon his own obituary. His servant found him dead the next morning.

Since I, fortunately, do not have access to future newspapers, I cannot tell how stock and bond prices will behave in any particular period ahead. Nevertheless, I am convinced that the long-run estimates of bond and stock returns presented here are the most reasonable ones that can be made for investment planning during the remainder of the 1990s and into the twenty-first century. Investors will, I believe, be well served by putting their money where my mouth is and investing a substantial part of their wealth in paper assets, including bonds.

14

A Life-Cycle Guide to Investing

There are two times in a man's life when he should not speculate: when he can't afford it, and when he can.
—Mark Twain, *Following the Equator*

Investment strategy must be keyed to a life cycle. It is simple common sense to say that a thirty-four-year-old and a sixty-four-year-old saving for retirement may prudently use different financial instruments to accomplish their goals. A thirty-four-year-old—just beginning to enter the peak years of income earnings—can use wages to cover any losses from increased risk. A sixty-four-year-old, on the other hand, does not have the long-term luxury of relying on salary income. This person cannot afford to lose money that will be needed in the near future.

In essence, these strategic considerations have to do with a person's *capacity* for risk. Heretofore, most of the discussion about risk in this book has dealt with one's *attitude* toward risk. While the thirty-four-year-old and the sixty-four-year-old may both invest in a certificate of deposit, the younger will do so because of an *attitudinal* aversion to risk and the older because of a reduced *capacity* to accept risk. In the first case, one has more choice in how much risk to assume; in the second, one does not.

The most important investment decision you will probably ever make concerns the balancing of asset categories (stocks, bonds, real estate, money-market securities, etc.) at different stages of your life. According to Roger Ibbotson, who has spent a lifetime measuring returns from alternative portfolios, over 90 percent of an investor's total return is determined by the markets in which the investor chooses to invest and in what proportions. Less than 10 percent of investment success is determined by the specific stocks or mutual funds that an individual may choose. In this chapter, I will show you that whatever your aversion to risk—whatever your position on the eat-well, sleep-well scale—your age, income from employment, and specific responsibilities in life go a long way to helping you determine the mix of assets in your portfolio.

Before we can determine a rational basis for making asset-allocation decisions, certain principles must be kept firmly in mind. We've covered some of them implicitly in earlier chapters but treating them explicitly here should prove very helpful. The key principles are:

1. History shows us that risk and return are related.
2. The risk of investing in common stocks and bonds depends upon the length of time the investments are held. The longer an investor's holding period, the lower the risk.
3. Dollar-cost averaging is a useful technique that can further reduce the risk of stock and bond investment.
4. You must distinguish between your attitude toward and your capacity for risk.

The risks you can afford to take depend on your total financial situation, including the types and sources of your income exclusive of investment income.

1. Risk and Reward Are Related

By now you are tired of hearing that investment rewards can be increased only by the assumption of greater risk. But there is no lesson more important in investment management. This fundamental law of finance is supported by literally centuries of historical data. The following table, summarizing data presented earlier, is as good as any to illustrate the point.

Total Annual Returns for Basic Asset Classes, 1926–94

	Average Annual Return	Risk Index[a] (Year-to-Year Volatility of Returns)
Small company common stocks	12.2%	34.6%
Common stocks in general	10.2	20.3
Long-term bonds	5.4	8.4
U.S. Treasury bills	3.7	3.3
Inflation rate	3.1	

Source: Ibbotson Associates, *Stocks, Bonds, Bills, and Inflation: 1994 Yearbook.*
[a]The risk or volatility index is a statistical measure of the "standard deviation" of the return series showing the extent to which the yearly returns differ from the average observation of the series. Approximately 66.7 percent (95 percent) of the yearly return observations lie within one (two) standard deviation(s) of the average yearly return.

Common stocks have clearly provided very generous long-run rates of return. It has been estimated that if George Washington had put just one dollar aside from his first presidential salary and invested it at the rate of return earned by common stocks, his heirs would have been millionaires about seven times over by 1995. Roger Ibbotson estimates that stocks have provided a compounded rate of return of 8.2 percent per year since 1790. (As the table shows, returns have been even more generous since 1926, when common stocks in general earned 10.2 percent.) But this return came only at substantial risk to investors. Total returns were negative in about three years out of ten. So as you reach for higher returns, never forget that "There ain't no such thing as a free lunch." Higher risk is the price one pays for more generous returns.

2. Your Actual Risk in Stock and Bond Investing Depends on the Length of Time You Hold Your Investment

The length of time you hold on to your investment, and thus your "staying power," plays a critical role in the actual risk you assume from any investment decision. It is this important factor that makes your stage in the life cycle such a critical element in determining the allocation of your assets. Let's see why the length of your holding period is so important in determining your capacity for risk.

We saw in the table above that long-term bonds over a period of almost seventy years have provided an average annual rate of return of almost 5½ percent. The risk index, however, showed that in any single year this rate of return could stray far from the yearly average. Indeed, in many individual years, the rate of return from holding long-term bonds was actually negative. What if I told you that today you could invest in a 7½ percent, twenty-year bond and that if you promise to hold it for exactly twenty years you will earn exactly 7½ percent. Impossible, you say! Not at all. If you buy a twenty-year zero-coupon U.S. government bond today and *if you hold it until maturity* you will earn exactly 7½ percent—no more, no less—all guaranteed by the U.S. Treasury. Of course, the rub is that if you find you have to sell it next year, your rate of return could be 20 percent, 0 percent, or even a substantial loss if interest rates rise sharply with existing bond prices falling to adjust to the new higher interest rates. I think you can see why your age and the likelihood that you can stay with your investment program not only affect the risks you can assume but even determine the amount of risk involved in any specific investment program.

What about investing in common stocks? Could it be that the risk of investing in stocks also decreases with the length of time over which you hold your investments? The answer is yes. A substantial amount (but not all) of the risk of common-stock investment can be eliminated by adopting a program of *long-term* ownership of common stocks and sticking to it through thick and thin (the buy-and-hold strategy discussed in earlier chapters).

The picture on the following page is worth a thousand words so I can be brief in my explanation. Note that if you held a diversified stock portfolio (such as the Standard & Poor's 500-Stock Index) during the period from 1950 through the mid-1990s, you would earn, on average, a quite generous return of about 10 percent. But the range of outcomes is certainly far too wide for an investor who has trouble sleeping at night. In one year, the rate of return from a typical stock portfolio was over 52 percent, while in another year it was negative by more than 26 percent. Clearly, there is no dependability of earning an adequate rate of return in any single year. If you have money to

Range of Annual Returns on Common Stocks
for Various Time Periods, 1950–94

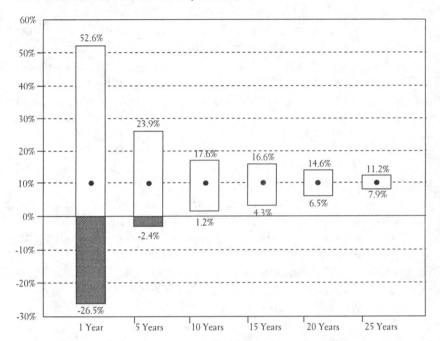

The ● represents the average of the annual returns for various periods.

invest for only a single year and you want to be certain that you will earn a positive rate of return, a one-year U.S. Treasury security or a one-year government-guaranteed certificate of deposit is the investment for you.

But note how the picture changes if you can hold on to your common-stock investments for twenty-five years. While there is some variability in the return achieved depending upon the exact twenty-five-year period in question, that variability is minuscule. On average, investment over the twenty-five-year periods covered by this figure has produced a rate of return of close to ten percent. This long-run expected rate of return was reduced by less than two percentage points if you happened to invest during the worst twenty-five-year period ending in the mid-1990s. It is this fundamental truth that makes a life-cycle view of investing so important. *The longer the time period over* *which you can hold on to your investments, the greater should be the share of common stocks in your portfolio.* In general, you are reasonably sure of earning the generous rates of return available from common stocks only if you can hold them for relatively long periods of time, such as twenty years or more. Moreover, these returns are gained by the steady strategy of *buying* and *holding* your diversified portfolio. Switching your investments around in a futile attempt to time the market will only involve extra commissions for your broker, extra taxes for the government, and poorer net performance.*

3. Dollar-Cost Averaging Can Reduce the Risks of Investing in Stocks and Bonds

If, like most people, you will be building up your investment portfolio slowly over time with the accretion of yearly savings, you will be taking advantage of "dollar-cost averaging." This technique helps you avoid the risk of putting all your money in the stock or bond market at the wrong time.

Don't be alarmed by the fancy-sounding name. Dollar-cost averaging simply means investing the same fixed amount of money in, for example, the shares of some mutual fund at regular intervals—say, every month or quarter—over a long period of time. Periodic investments of equal dollar amounts in common stocks can substantially reduce (but not avoid) the risks of equity investment by ensuring that the entire portfolio of stocks will not be purchased at temporarily inflated prices. The investor who makes equal dollar investments will buy fewer shares when prices are high and more shares when prices are low. As illustrated in the following table, the average cost per share is actually lower than the average of the share prices during the period when the investments are made.

In this example, I assume you put $150 per period into a mutual fund whose share price fluctuates between $25 and $75. By the process of dollar-cost averaging, you have purchased 11 shares, now worth $50 apiece, for a total market value of $550.

---

*Technically, the finding that risk is reduced by longer holding periods depends on the mean-reversion phenomenon described in Chapter Eight. The interested reader is referred to Paul Samuelson's Fall 1989 article in the *Journal of Portfolio Management*, "The Judgement of Economic Science on Rational Portfolio Management."

Period	Investment	Price of Fund Shares	Shares Purchased
1	$150	$75	2
2	150	25	6
3	150	50	3
Total cost	$450		
Average price		$50	
Total shares owned			11
Average cost: approximately $41			

You have invested only $450 over the period. In other words, your average share cost ($450/11 = $40.91) is lower than the average ($50) of the market price of the fund's shares during the periods in which they are accumulated. So you've actually made money despite the fact that the average price at which you bought is the same as the current price. It works because you bought more shares when they were cheap and fewer when they were dear.

Don't think that dollar-cost averaging will solve all of your investment problems. No plan can protect you against a loss in market value during declining stock markets. And a critical feature of the plan is that you have both the cash and the courage to continue to invest during bear markets as regularly as you do in better periods. No matter how pessimistic you are (and everybody else is), and no matter how bad the financial and world news is, you must not interrupt the plan or you will lose the important benefit of ensuring that you buy at least some of your shares after a sharp market decline. Indeed, if you can buy a few extra shares whenever the market declines by 20 to 25 percent, your dollar-cost averaging will work even better.

There is one drawback to dollar-cost averaging. Remember, brokerage commissions are relatively high on small purchases, even when you use a discount broker. For that reason, it is usually advisable to buy larger blocks of securities over longer time intervals. For example, it is cheaper to buy $150 worth of stock each quarter, or $300 semiannually, than to invest $50 each month. Of course, if you pick a no-load mutual fund (such as I used in my example) for your dollar-cost averaging, this problem disappears. You can invest as little as $50 per month in most no-load funds, with no brokerage charges at all. Another way to get some of the advantages of dollar-cost averaging is to join the dividend-reinvestment programs of those companies that have them. You can buy your shares at zero or only nominal brokerage costs, and some companies even price their shares at a discount for stockholders who reinvest their dividends.

To further illustrate the benefits of dollar-cost averaging, let's move from a hypothetical to a real example. The following table shows the results (ignoring taxes) of a $500 initial investment made on January 1, 1974, and thereafter $100 per month, in the shares of the T. Rowe Price Growth Stock Fund, a no-load mutual fund.

Of course, no one can be sure that the next twenty years

Illustration of Dollar-Cost Averaging with T. Rowe Price Growth Stock Fund[a]

Year Ended December 31	Total Cost of Cumulative Investments	Total Value of Shares Acquired
1974	$1,600	$1.242
1975	2,800	2.942
1976	4,000	4.560
1977	5,200	5.459
1978	6,400	7,359
1979	7,600	9,470
1980	8,800	13,769
1981	10,000	13,177
1982	11,200	16,817
1983	12,400	20,053
1984	13,600	21,040
1985	14,800	29,896
1986	16,000	37,687
1987	17,200	40,162
1988	18,400	43,842
1989	19,600	56,320
1990	20,800	55,091
1991	22,000	74,875
1992	23,200	80,761
1993	24,400	94,601
1994	25,600	96,597

Source: T. Rowe Price.
[a]$500 initial investment on January 1, 1974, and $100 monthly investment thereafter. All dividends and capital gains distribution were reinvested.

A Practical Guide for Random Walkers

will provide the same returns as the past twenty. But even though growth stocks were out of favor through most of the period and T. Rowe Price's record was only average, the results are quite spectacular. Thus, the table does illustrate the tremendous *potential* gains possible from consistently following a dollar-cost averaging program even through a period where there was a negative environment for growth-stock investing. Because there is a long-term uptrend in common stock prices, however, this technique is not necessarily appropriate if you need to invest a lump sum such as a bequest.

If possible, keep a small reserve (in a money fund) to take advantage of market declines and buy a few extra shares if the market is down sharply. I'm not suggesting for a minute that you try to forecast the market. However, it's usually a good time to buy after the market has fallen out of bed and no one can think of any reason why it should rise. Just as hope and greed can sometimes feed on themselves to produce speculative bubbles, so do pessimism and despair react to produce market panics. The greatest market panics are just as unfounded as the most pathological speculative explosions. No matter how bleak the outlook has been in the past, things usually got better. For the stock market as a whole, Newton's law has always worked in reverse: What goes down must come back up. But this does not necessarily hold for individual stocks, just for the market in general.

4. The Risks You Can Afford to Take Depend on Your Total Financial Situation

As I mentioned at the beginning of this chapter, the kinds of investments that are appropriate for you depend importantly on your sources of income other than income derived from your investment portfolio. Your earning ability outside your investments, and thus your capacity for risk, is usually related to your age. Three illustrations will help you understand this concept.

Mildred G. is a recently widowed sixty-four-year-old. She has been forced to give up her job as a registered nurse because of her increasingly severe arthritis. Her modest house in Home-wood, Illinois, is still mortgaged. While this fixed-rate home mortgage was taken out some time ago at a relatively low rate, it does involve a substantial monthly payment. Apart from monthly Social Security payments, all Mildred has to live on are the earnings on a $250,000 group insurance policy on which she is the beneficiary and a $50,000 portfolio of small growth stocks that had been accumulated over a long number of years by her late husband.

It is clear that Mildred's capacity to bear risk is severely constrained by her financial situation. She has neither the life expectancy nor the physical ability to earn income outside her portfolio. Moreover, she has substantial fixed expenditures on her mortgage. She would have no ability to recoup a loss on her portfolio. A portfolio of safe investments that can generate substantial income is what is appropriate for Mildred. Bonds and high-dividend-paying stocks from relatively safe companies are the kinds of investments that are suitable. Risky (often non-dividend-paying) stocks of small growth companies—no matter how attractive their prices may be—do not belong in Mildred's portfolio.

Tiffany B. is an ambitious, single twenty-six-year-old who was recently graduated from the Graduate School of Business at Stanford and has just entered a training program that will lead to a position as a loan officer at San Francisco's Wells Fargo Bank. She has just inherited a $50,000 legacy from her grandmother's estate. Her goal is to build a sizable portfolio which in later years could finance the purchase of a home and be available as a retirement nest egg.

For Tiffany, one can safely recommend an "aggressive young businesswoman's" portfolio. She has both the life expectancy and the earning power to maintain her standard of living in the face of any financial loss. While her personality will determine the precise amount of risk exposure she is willing to undertake, it is clear that Tiffany's portfolio belongs toward the far end of the risk-reward spectrum. Mildred's portfolio of small growth stocks would be far more appropriate for Tiffany than for a sixty-four-year-old widow who is unable to work.

Carl P., a forty-three-year-old foreman at a General Motors production plant in Pontiac, Michigan, makes close to $40,000 per year. His wife, Joan, has a $12,500 annual income from selling Avon products. The Ps have four children ranging in age from six to fifteen. Carl and Joan would like to see all the children attend college. They realize that private colleges are probably beyond their means but do hope that an education within the excellent Michigan state university system will be feasible. Fortunately, Carl has for some time been saving money regularly through the GM payroll savings plan and has chosen the option of purchasing GM stock under the plan. He has accumulated GM stock worth $89,000. He has no other assets but does have substantial equity in a modest house with only a small mortgage remaining to be paid off.

Carl and Joan have the resources to meet their financial needs. They have a most inappropriate portfolio, however, especially in view of their major source of income. First, the portfolio is completely undiversified. A negative development that caused a sharp loss in GM's common stock would directly affect the value of the portfolio. There would be no offsetting effects from other common stocks or other types of securities. Moreover, a serious negative development at GM could affect Carl's livelihood as well. It might not be true that "as General Motors goes so goes the nation," as a self-aggrandizing former chief executive officer of GM once suggested. But it certainly is true that as GM goes so go the fortunes of Carl and Joan. A serious depression in the auto industry could subject Carl to a double whammy—it could cost Carl his job as well as his investment portfolio. Carl and Joan's investment portfolio should be diversified, and it should not take on the same risks that attach to Carl's major source of income.

The Life-Cycle Investment Guide, with Some Individual Adjustments to the Game Plan

Now that I have set the stage, this section presents a life-cycle guide to investing. We will look at some general rules that will be serviceable for most individuals at different stages of their lives, and at the end of the section I will summarize them in an investment guide. Of course, no guide will fit every individual case just as no general game plan will prove appropriate for the same sports team during every game of the season. Any game plan will require some alteration to fit the individual circumstances. Its usefulness, however, is that it provides an excellent starting point for building a sensible investment strategy for individual investors.

One change to the general guidelines must always be kept in mind—*a specific need must be funded with specific assets dedicated to that need.* Suppose, for example, we are planning the investment strategy for a young couple in their twenties attempting to build a retirement nest egg. The advice in the life-cycle investment guide table, which follows, is certainly appropriate to meet those long-term objectives. But suppose also that the couple expects to need a $30,000 down payment to purchase a house in one year's time. That $30,000 to meet a specific need should be invested in a safe security, maturing when the money is required, such as a one-year certificate of deposit. Similarly, if college tuitions will be needed in three, four, five and six years, funds might be invested in CDs or zero-coupon securities of the appropriate maturity.

Another adjustment you may want to make concerns the mixing of assets in your long-run plan. The guide advises more common stocks for individuals earlier in the life cycle and more bonds for those nearer to retirement. But as this guide was put together during the mid-1990s, bonds provided unusually generous rates of return compared with common stocks. As Chapter Thirteen indicated, the spread between bond yields and the inflation rate was relatively wide and the extra benefits from common-stock investments appeared to be considerably lower than the historical average. Hence, the guide has a slightly higher percentage of bonds recommended than many invest-ment counselors often suggest. Even younger investors are ad-vised to hold substantial amounts of bonds given the invest-ment environment of the mid-1990s. Should bond rates fall relative to inflation as we move through the later nineties, the proportion of bonds should be slightly reduced.

By far the biggest individual adjustment to the general guidelines suggested concerns your own attitude toward risk. It is for this reason that successful financial planning is more of an art than a science. General guidelines can be extremely helpful in determining what proportion of a person's funds should be deployed among different asset categories. But the key to whether any recommended asset allocation works for you is whether you are able to sleep at night. Risk tolerance is an essential aspect of any financial plan and only you can eval-uate your attitude toward risk. You can take some comfort in the fact that the risk involved in investing in common stocks and long-term bonds is reduced the longer the time period over which you accumulate and hold your investments. But you must have the temperament to accept considerable year-to-year fluctuations in your portfolio's value. Even though the market collapse that occurred on October 19, 1987, may be a very rare event—quite possibly one that will never be re-peated—fluctuations in stock values of 20 to 30 percent over very short periods of time are likely to happen again, as the crashette of October 13, 1989, demonstrated. If such an occur-rence is likely to make you physically ill when a large propor-tion of your assets is invested in common stocks, then clearly you should pare down the stock portion of your investment program. Thus, subjective considerations also play a major role in the asset allocations you can accept and you may legiti-mately stray from those recommended here depending on your aversion to risk.

A simple questionnaire is unlikely to provide you with a completely reliable index of your tolerance for risk. Neverthe-less, the following quiz is designed to help you discover your investment risk tolerance level. It was designed by the per-sonal finance expert William E. Donoghue and the editors of

Donoghue's Money Letter to help you determine how much risk you are likely to feel comfortable accepting.

One final preliminary before presenting the asset-allocation guide. What do you do if right now you have no assets to allocate? So many people of limited means believe it is impossible to build up a sizable nest egg. Accumulating meaningful amounts of retirement savings such as $50,000 or $100,000 often seems completely out of reach. Don't despair. The fact is that a program of regular savings each week—persistently followed, as through a payroll savings plan—can in time produce substantial sums of money. Can you afford to put aside $23 per week? Or $11.50 per week? If you can, the possibility of eventually accumulating a large retirement fund is easily attainable, if you have many working years ahead of you.

The table on page 416 shows the results from a regular savings program of $100 per month. A conservative interest rate of 8 percent is assumed as an investment rate. The last column of the table shows the total values that will be accumulated over various time periods.* If we assume a 10 percent interest rate instead of 8 percent, total accumulations in Year 30 would exceed $228,000, as the next table shows. It is clear that *regular* savings of even moderate amounts of money make the attainment of meaningful sums of money entirely possible, even for those who start off with no nest egg at all. If you can put a few thousand dollars into the savings fund to begin with, the final sum will be increased significantly.

If you are able to save only $50 per month—just over $11.50 per week—cut the numbers in the table in half; if you are able to save $200 per month, double them. You will need to pick one or more no-load mutual funds to accumulate your nest egg since direct investments of small sums of money would be prohibitively expensive. Also, mutual funds permit automatic reinvestment of interest, or dividends and capital gains, as is assumed in the table. Finally, make sure you check if your employer has a matched savings plan. Obviously, if by saving

---

*I assume that the savings can be made in an IRA or other tax-favored savings vehicle, so income taxes on interest earnings are ignored.

How much risk is right? A quick quiz

Smart—and happy—investors know their risk comfort zones and make money in ways they feel at ease with. Here's a quiz to help you determine how much risk you can handle.

1. Your investment loses 15 percent of its value in a market correction a month after you buy it. Assuming that none of the fundamentals have changed, do you:
    - ☐ (a) Sit tight and wait for it to journey back up.
    - ☐ (b) Sell it and rid yourself of further sleepless nights if it continues to decline.
    - ☐ (c) Buy more—if it looked good at the original price it looks even better now.

2. A month after you purchase it, the value of your investment suddenly skyrockets by 40 percent. Assuming you can't find any further information, what do you do?
    - ☐ (a) Sell it.
    - ☐ (b) Hold it on the expectation of further gain.
    - ☐ (c) Buy more—it will probably go higher.

3. Which would you have rather done:
    - ☐ (a) Invested in an aggressive growth fund which appreciated very little in six months.
    - ☐ (b) Invested in a money-market fund only to see the aggressive growth fund you were thinking about double in value in six months.

4. Would you feel better if:
    - ☐ (a) You doubled your money in an equity investment.
    - ☐ (b) Your money-market fund investment saved you from losing half your money in a market slide.

5. Which situation would make you feel happiest?
    - ☐ (a) You win $100,000 in a publisher's contest.
    - ☐ (b) You inherit $100,000 from a rich relative.
    - ☐ (c) You earn $100,000 by risking $2,000 in the options market.
    - ☐ (d) Any of the above—you're happy with the $100,000, no matter how it ended up in your wallet.

6. The apartment building where you live is being converted to condominiums. You can either buy your unit for $80,000 or sell the option for $20,000. The market value of the condo is $120,000. You know that if you buy the condo, it might take six months to sell, the monthly carrying cost is $1,200, and you'd have to borrow the down payment for a mortgage. You don't want to live in the building—what do you do?
    - ☐ (a) Take the $20,000.
    - ☐ (b) Buy the unit and then sell it on the open market.

7. You inherit your uncle's $100,000 house, free of any mortgage. Although the house is in a fashionable neighborhood and can be expected to appreciate at a rate faster than inflation, it has deteriorated badly. It would net $1,000 monthly if rented as is; it would net $1,500 per month if renovated. The renovations could be financed by a mortgage on the property. You would:
    - ☐ (a) Sell the house.
    - ☐ (b) Rent it as is.
    - ☐ (c) Make the necessary renovations, and then rent it.

8. You work for a small, but thriving, privately held electronics company. The company is raising money by selling stock to its employees. Management plans to take the company public, but not for four or more years. If you buy the stock, you will not be allowed to sell until shares are traded publicly. In

the meantime, the stock will pay no dividends. But when the company goes public, the shares could trade for 10 to 20 times what you paid for them. How much of an investment would you make?

☐ (a) None at all.
☐ (b) One month's salary.
☐ (c) Three months' salary.
☐ (d) Six months' salary.

9. Your longtime friend and neighbor, an experienced petroleum geologist, is assembling a group of investors (of which he is one) to fund an exploratory oil well which could pay back 50 to 100 times its investment if successful. If the well is dry, the entire investment is worthless. Your friend estimates the chance of success is only 20 percent. What would you invest?

☐ (a) Nothing at all.
☐ (b) One month's salary.
☐ (c) Three months' salary.
☐ (d) Six months' salary.

10. You learn that several commercial building developers are seriously looking at undeveloped land in a certain location. You are offered an option to buy a choice parcel of that land. The cost is about two months' salary and you calculate the gain to be ten months' salary. Do you:

☐ (a) Purchase the option.
☐ (b) Let it slide; it's not for you.

11. You are on a TV game show and can choose one of the following. Which would you take?

☐ (a) $1,000 in cash.
☐ (b) A 50 percent chance at winning $4,000.
☐ (c) A 20 percent chance at winning $10,000.
☐ (d) A 5 percent chance at winning $100,000.

12. It's 1992, and inflation is returning. Hard assets such as precious metals, collectibles, and real estate are expected to keep pace with inflation. Your assets are now all in long-term bonds. What would you do?

☐ (a) Hold the bonds.
☐ (b) Sell the bonds, and put half the proceeds into money funds and the other half into hard assets.
☐ (c) Sell the bonds and put the total proceeds into hard assets.
☐ (d) Sell the bonds, put all the money into hard assets, and borrow additional money to buy more.

13. You've lost $500 at the blackjack table in Atlantic City. How much more are you prepared to lose to win the $500 back?

☐ (a) Nothing—you quit now.
☐ (b) $100.
☐ (c) $250.
☐ (d) $500.
☐ (e) More than $500.

Your score

Now it's time to see what kind of investor you are. Total your score, using the point system listed below for each answer you gave.

1. a–3, b–1, c–4	6. a–1, b–2	10. a–3, b–1
2. a–1, b–3, c–4	7. a–1, b–2, c–3	11. a–1, b–3, c–5, d–9
3. a–1, b–3	8. a–1, b–2, c–4, d–6	12. a–1, b–2, c–3, d–4
4. a–2, b–1	9. a–1, b–3, c–6, d–9	13. a–1, b–2, c–4,
5. a–2, b–1, c–4, d–1		d–6, e–8

If you scored...

Below 21: You are a conservative investor, allergic to risk. Stay with sober, conservative investments.

21 to 35: You are an active investor, willing to take calculated, prudent risks to gain financially.

36 or more: You are a venturesome, aggressive investor.

Source: **Donoghue's Money Letter.** Reprinted by permission.

How Retirement Funds Can Build:
What Happens to an Investment of $100 a Month,
Earning an 8 Percent Return Compounded Monthly

Year	Cumulative Investment	Annual Income	Cumulative Income	Total Value
1	$1,200	$53	$53	$1,253
2	2,400	157	210	2,610
3	3,600	270	480	4,080
4	4,800	392	872	5,672
5	6,000	524	1,396	7,396
6	7,200	667	2,063	9,263
7	8,400	822	2,885	11,285
8	9,600	990	3,875	13,475
9	10,800	1,175	5,046	15,846
10	12,000	1,368	6,414	18,414
11	13,200	1,581	7,995	21,195
12	14,400	1,812	9,807	24,207
13	15,600	2,062	11,869	27,469
14	16,800	2,333	14,202	31,002
15	18,000	2,626	16,828	34,828
16	19,200	2,944	19,772	38,972
17	20,400	3,288	23,060	43,460
18	21,600	3,600	26,720	48,320
19	22,800	4,063	30,783	53,583
20	24,000	4,501	35,284	59,284
21	25,200	4,973	40,257	65,457
22	26,400	5,486	45,743	72,143
23	27,600	6,041	51,784	79,384
24	28,800	6,642	58,426	87,226
25	30,000	7,293	65,719	95,719
26	31,200	7,998	73,717	104,917
27	32,400	8,761	82,478	114,878
28	33,600	9,588	92,066	125,666
29	34,800	10,106	102,172	136,972
30	36,000	11,422	113,594	149,594

Retirement Funds Build Even Faster at 10 Percent

Year	Cumulative Investment	Annual Income	Cumulative Income	Total Value
1	$1,200	$67	$67	$1,267
2	2,400	200	269	2,667
3	3,600	353	622	4,222
4	4,800	509	1,131	5,931
5	6,000	688	1,819	7,819
6	7,200	886	2,705	9,905
7	8,400	1,105	3,809	12,209
8	9,600	1,345	5,154	14,754
9	10,800	1,612	6,766	17,566
10	12,000	1,906	8,672	20,672
11	13,200	2,231	10,903	24,103
12	14,400	2,591	13,494	27,894
13	15,600	2,987	16,481	32,081
14	16,800	3,426	19,907	36,707
15	18,000	3,910	23,817	41,817
16	19,200	4,446	28,263	47,463
17	20,400	5,036	33,299	53,699
18	21,600	5,689	38,988	60,588
19	22,800	6,411	45,379	68,199
20	24,000	7,207	52,606	76,606
21	25,200	8,088	60,694	85,894
22	26,400	9,060	69,754	96,154
23	27,600	10,134	79,888	107,488
24	28,800	11,313	91,201	120,001
25	30,000	12,640	103,841	133,841
26	31,200	14,081	117,922	149,122
27	32,400	15,680	133,602	166,002
28	33,600	17,447	151,049	184,649
29	34,800	19,400	170,449	205,249
30	36,000	21,556	192,005	228,005

through a company-sponsored payroll savings plan you are able to match your savings with company contributions and gain tax deductions as well, your nest egg will grow that much faster. Moreover, a company savings/retirement program, such as a 403(b) or 401(k) plan, shelters your earnings from tax.

The chart on page 420 presents a summary of the life-cycle investment guide. The general ideas behind the recommendations have been spelled out in detail above. For those in their twenties, a very aggressive investment portfolio is recommended. At this age, there is lots of time to ride out the peaks and valleys of investment cycles and you have a lifetime of earnings from employment ahead of you. The portfolio is not only heavy in common stocks but also contains a substantial proportion of higher-risk stocks such as smaller companies and growth stocks. In addition, the portfolio contains a significant share of international stocks. As mentioned in Chapter Nine, one important advantage of international diversification is risk reduction. Since cycles in economic activity are not perfectly correlated across countries, a portfolio that is diversified internationally will tend to produce more stable returns from year to year than one invested only in domestic issues. Plus, international diversification enables an investor to gain exposure to other growth areas in the world. The U.S. stock market now accounts for only about one-third of the total value of the stocks traded in the world financial markets. Growth opportunities are probably greater in many parts of the world than they are now in the United States.

As investors age, they should start cutting back on the riskier investments and start increasing the proportion of the portfolio committed to bonds. By the age of fifty-five, investors should start thinking about the transition to retirement and moving the portfolio toward income production. The proportion of bonds increases and the stock portfolio becomes more conservative and income producing and less growth oriented. In retirement, a portfolio mainly in a variety of intermediate-term bonds (five to ten years to maturity) and long-term bonds (over ten years to maturity) is recommended. A general rule of thumb that will make sense for many investors is to make the proportion of bonds in one's portfolio almost equal to your age. The small proportion of stocks is included to give some income growth to cope with inflation. While I have not specifically recommended "index" funds in my guide, the discussion of Chapter Fifteen makes clear that such funds would certainly be appropriate for a major portion of your common-stock investments.

Note that I have recommended only mutual funds to form your portfolios. I do so for two reasons. First, most people do not have sufficient capital to diversify properly. Obviously, if you have enough money to buy *portfolios* of stocks yourself of the types recommended, you may do so. Second, I recognize that most younger people will not have substantial assets and will be *accumulating* portfolios by monthly investments. This makes mutual funds almost a necessity. You don't have to use the exact types of funds I suggest, but do make sure they are truly "no load" and pick safer, income-producing funds later in life. Chapter Fifteen will give you advice on the selection of specific common-stock mutual funds.

You will also see that I have not included real estate explicitly in my recommendations. I have said earlier that everyone should attempt to own his or her own home. I believe everyone should have substantial real estate holdings and, therefore, some part of one's equity holdings should be in real estate investment trusts (REITs) or real estate mutual funds described in Chapter Twelve. With respect to your bond holdings, the guide recommends taxable bonds. If, however, you are in the highest tax bracket and live in a high-tax state such as New York, I recommend that you use tax-exempt money funds and bond funds tailored to your state so that they are exempt from both federal and state taxes.

Life-Cycle Investment Guide Recommended
Asset or Savings Allocations

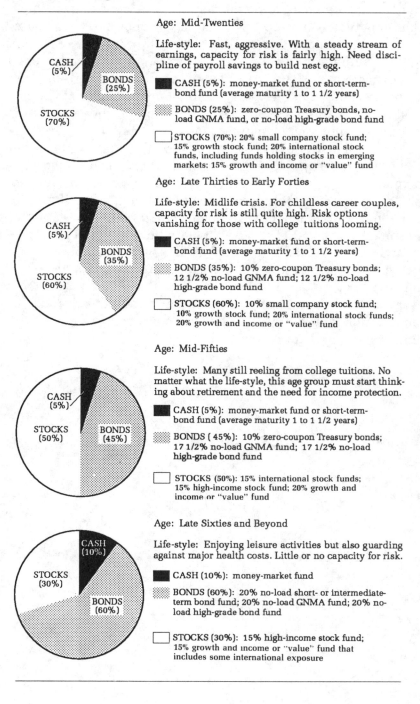

Age: Mid-Twenties

Life-style: Fast, aggressive. With a steady stream of earnings, capacity for risk is fairly high. Need discipline of payroll savings to build nest egg.

■ CASH (5%): money-market fund or short-term-bond fund (average maturity 1 to 1 1/2 years)

▒ BONDS (25%): zero-coupon Treasury bonds, no-load GNMA fund, or no-load high-grade bond fund

☐ STOCKS (70%): 20% small company stock fund; 15% growth stock fund; 20% international stock funds, including funds holding stocks in emerging markets: 15% growth and income or "value" fund

Age: Late Thirties to Early Forties

Life-style: Midlife crisis. For childless career couples, capacity for risk is still quite high. Risk options vanishing for those with college tuitions looming.

■ CASH (5%): money-market fund or short-term-bond fund (average maturity 1 to 1 1/2 years)

▒ BONDS (35%): 10% zero-coupon Treasury bonds; 12 1/2% no-load GNMA fund; 12 1/2% no-load high-grade bond fund

☐ STOCKS (60%): 10% small company stock fund; 10% growth stock fund; 20% international stock funds; 20% growth and income or "value" fund

Age: Mid-Fifties

Life-style: Many still reeling from college tuitions. No matter what the life-style, this age group must start thinking about retirement and the need for income protection.

■ CASH (5%): money-market fund or short-term-bond fund (average maturity 1 to 1 1/2 years)

▒ BONDS (45%): 10% zero-coupon Treasury bonds; 17 1/2% no-load GNMA fund; 17 1/2% no-load high-grade bond fund

☐ STOCKS (50%): 15% international stock funds; 15% high-income stock fund; 20% growth and income or "value" fund

Age: Late Sixties and Beyond

Life-style: Enjoying leisure activities but also guarding against major health costs. Little or no capacity for risk.

■ CASH (10%): money-market fund

▒ BONDS (60%): 20% no-load short- or intermediate-term bond fund; 20% no-load GNMA fund; 20% no-load high-grade bond fund

☐ STOCKS (30%): 15% high-income stock fund; 15% growth and income or "value" fund that includes some international exposure

15

Three Giant
Steps Down
Wall Street

Annual income twenty pounds, annual expenditure nineteen nineteen six, result happiness. Annual income twenty
pounds, annual expenditure twenty pounds ought and six,
result misery.   —Charles Dickens, *David Copperfield*

By now you have made sensible decisions on
taxes, housing, insurance, and how to get the most out of your
cash reserves. You have reviewed your objectives, your stage
in the life cycle, and your attitude toward risk, and decided
how much of your assets to put into the stock market. Now it is
time for quick prayer at Trinity Church and then some bold
steps forward, taking great care to avoid the graveyard on either side of you. In this chapter, I'll present some sensible rules
for buying stocks. These rules can help you to avoid costly
mistakes and unnecessary sales charges and to increase your
yield a mite without undo risk. I can't offer anything spectacular, but I do know that often a percent or two increase in the
yield on your assets can mean the difference between misery
and happiness.

How do you go about buying stocks? Basically, there are
three ways: I call them the No-Brainer Step, the Deep-Thinker
Step, and the Substitute-Player Step.

In the first case, you simply buy a share of the market index
through a so-called index fund. You're assured of the market's
rate of return—a return that I believe for the long-term holder
will continue to average near 10 percent per year, its long-run

421

historical norm. This method also has the virtue of being absolutely simple. Even if you have trouble chewing gum while walking randomly, you can master it. You simply send one check, need make no further decisions, and are guaranteed the same yearly rate of return as the market as a whole. The market, in effect, pulls you along with it.

Under the second system, you jog down Wall Street, picking your own stocks and getting—in comparison with the yield obtained with the index fund—much higher or much lower rates of return. This involves work, but also, in the opinion of those who wouldn't play the game any other way, a lot of fun. To help tilt the odds of success a bit more in your favor, I've provided a series of rules to guide you in picking stocks.

Third, you can sit on a curb and choose a professional investment manager to do the walking down Wall Street for you. The only way investors of modest means can accomplish this is to purchase mutual funds. For this reason, my life-cycle investment guide was presented in terms of the appropriate types of mutual funds. Later in the chapter (and in the Random Walker's Address Book which follows), I will present some helpful suggestions on how to go about picking the right funds for you.

Earlier editions of my book described a strategy called the Malkiel Step: buying closed-end investment company shares at a discount. Alas, that strategy was so successful that it is generally no longer available. The story of its virtual disappearance is useful, however, in resolving the paradox careful readers will have noted throughout this book—namely, how markets can be both reasonably efficient and yet sometimes inefficient at the same time. The Malkiel Step is described near the end of the chapter.

The No-Brainer Step: Buying the Market

The Standard & Poor's 500-Stock Index, a composite that represents 70 percent of the value of all U.S.-traded common stocks, beats most of the experts over the long pull. Buying a portfolio of all companies in this index would be an easy way to own stocks. I argued back in 1973 (in the first edition of this book) that the means to adopt this approach was sorely needed for the small investor:

> What we need is a no-load, minimum-management-fee mutual fund that simply buys the hundreds of stocks making up the broad stock-market averages and does no trading from security to security in an attempt to catch the winners. Whenever below-average performance on the part of any mutual fund is noticed, fund spokesmen are quick to point out, "You can't buy the averages." It's time the public could.

Shortly after my book was published, the "index-fund" idea caught on. At first, only large pension clients were offered this investment opportunity. But one of the great virtues of capitalism is that when there is a need for a product, someone usually finds the will to produce it. In 1976, a fund was created that allowed the public to get into the act as well. The Vanguard Index Trust (also known as the "500 portfolio") is a mutual fund that is internally managed and, therefore, pays no investment advisory fee. The investments of the trust are the 500 stocks of the S&P 500, purchased in the same proportions as their weight in the index. Each investor shares proportionately in the net income and in the capital gains and losses of the fund's portfolio.

Since its inception, the Vanguard Index Trust has closely "tracked" the S&P 500. There are no so-called loading fees for buying the trust's shares. Management expenses (custodian fees, the costs of collecting and distributing dividends, and preparing summary reports for investors, etc.) run at less than one quarter of one percent of assets, far less than the expenses incurred by most mutual funds or bank trust departments. You can now buy the market conveniently and inexpensively.*

The logic behind this strategy is the logic of the efficient-market theory. The above-average long-run performance of the

---

*A Vanguard Index Trust prospectus and application form can be obtained by writing to Vanguard Financial Center, Valley Forge, PA 19482. or by calling 1-800-662-7447. I must remind the reader that I am a director of this fund.

S&P 500 compared with that of major institutional investors has been confirmed by numerous studies described in previous chapters of this book. Between 1974 and 1994, for example, the S&P 500 outperformed three-quarters of the public equity mutual funds—the average annual total return for the S&P 500 was approximately 1 percentage point better than that of the median fund.

Similar studies done of pension funds and of bank and insurance company pooled equity funds confirm the same results. The S&P beat approximately two-thirds of professionally managed portfolios in the decade of the 1980s. The same results were recorded during the twenty-year period since 1974, as was reported in Chapter Eight.

Despite all the evidence to the contrary, suppose an investor still believed that superior investment management really does exist. Two issues remain: First, it is clear that such skill is very rare and, second, there appears to be no effective way to find such skill *before* it has been demonstrated over time. Paul Samuelson sums up the difficulty in the following parable. Suppose it was demonstrated that one out of twenty alcoholics could learn to become a moderate social drinker. The experienced clinician would answer, "Even if true, act as if it were false, for you will never identify that one in twenty, and in the attempt five in twenty will be ruined." Samuelson concludes that investors should forsake the search for such tiny needles in huge haystacks.

Stock trading among institutional investors is like an isometric exercise: Lots of energy is expended, but between one investment manager and another it all balances out, and the commissions the managers pay detract from performance. Like greyhounds at the dog track, professional money managers seem destined to lose their race with the mechanical rabbit. Small wonder that many institutional investors, including Exxon, Ford, American Telephone and Telegraph, Harvard University, the College Retirement Equity Fund, and the New York State Teachers Association, have put substantial portions of their assets into index funds. In 1977, $1 billion in assets were invested in index funds. By 1995, literally hundreds of billions of dollars of institutional funds were "indexed," representing about one-quarter of all institutionally managed equities.

How about you? When you buy an index fund, you give up the chance of boasting at the golf club about the fantastic gains you've made by picking stock-market winners. Broad diversification rules out extraordinary losses relative to the whole market; it also, by definition, rules out extraordinary gains. Thus, many Wall Street critics refer to index-fund investing as "guaranteed mediocrity." But experience conclusively shows that index-fund buyers are likely to obtain results exceeding those of the typical fund manager, whose large advisory fees and substantial portfolio turnover tend to reduce investment yields. And index investors will *predictably* receive the market return. Many people will find the guarantee of playing the stock-market game at par every round a very attractive one. Of course, this strategy does not rule out risk: If the market goes down, your portfolio is guaranteed to follow suit.

The index method of investment has other attractions for the small investor. It enables you to obtain very broad diversification with only a small investment. It also allows you to reduce brokerage charges. When an individual investor buys stocks, he or she pays a brokerage fee of almost a dollar a share on small trades (even if a discount broker is used). The index fund, by pooling the moneys of many investors, trades in larger blocks and can negotiate a brokerage fee of pennies per share on its transactions. The index fund does all the work of collecting the dividends from all of the stocks it owns and sending you each quarter one check for all of your earnings (earnings which, incidentally, can be reinvested in the fund if you desire). In short, the index fund is a sensible, serviceable method for obtaining the market's rate of return with absolutely no effort and minimal expense.

The indexing strategy is one that I have recommended since the first edition in 1973—even before index funds existed. It was clearly an idea whose time had come. By far the most popular index used is the Standard & Poor's 500-Stock Index, an index that well represents the major corporations in the U.S. market. But now, as one of the earliest supporters of the 500-Stock Index, I want to alter my advice. While I still recommend indexing or so-called passive investing, I now believe the best general U.S. index to emulate is the broader Wilshire 5,000-Stock Index—not the S&P 500.*

There are two reasons for my change of heart. First, the S&P indexing strategy has become so popular that it has actually affected the pricing of the component stocks in the index. This can clearly be seen when changes are made in the composition of the index as unavoidably happens from time to time. During the merger and buyout boom of the late 1980s, many S&P 500 companies disappeared and had to be removed from the index. These companies were then replaced by others, which previously had not been included in the index. It turned out that newly included companies tended to appreciate in price by about 5 percent—simply because they were now a part of the S&P. Portfolio managers who ran index funds were required to purchase the stocks of the new companies (in proportion to their relative size and, therefore, their weight in the index) so that their portfolio's performance would continue to conform to that of the index. Thus, the very popularity of S&P 500 indexing may well have tended to make the stocks included in the index a bit pricier than comparable non-S&P-index stocks. Any investment idea that becomes extremely popular can become overvalued.

There is a second reason to favor a broader, more inclusive index. Almost seventy years of market history confirm that, in the aggregate, smaller stocks have tended to outperform larger ones. For example, from 1926 to 1994 a portfolio of smaller stocks produced a rate of return of approximately 12 percent annually while the returns from larger stocks (such as those in the S&P 500) were about 10 percent. While the smaller stocks were riskier than the major blue-chips, the point is that a well-diversified portfolio of small companies is likely to produce significantly enhanced returns. For both reasons, I now favor investing in an index that contains a much broader representation of U.S. companies, including large numbers of the small dynamic companies that are likely to be in early stages of their growth cycles.

*While more publicity is given to the Dow Jones and Standard & Poor's indices, the *Wall Street Journal* does publish the value of the Wilshire index daily.

I did suggest in *Random Walk*'s fourth edition that the S&P index was far from a perfect proxy for the market. I stated then: "It would be nice to have a fund available that bought an index of smaller companies—such as perhaps the American Stock Exchange or NASDAQ with their heavy weighting of younger growth companies and natural resource stocks." Fortunately for investors, one of the mutual-fund complexes—the Vanguard Group—was listening.

Annualized Returns—Indexes vs. Average Equity Mutual Funds Manager (20 years to December 31, 1994)

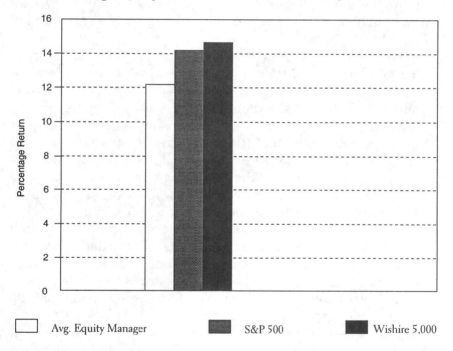

Recall that the S&P 500 represents approximately 70 percent of the market value of all outstanding U.S. common stocks. Literally thousands of companies represent the remaining 30 percent of the total U.S. market value. These are in many cases the emerging growth companies that offer higher investment rewards (as well as higher risks). The Wilshire 5,000 index contains all publicly traded U.S. common stocks on the New York and American stock exchanges and in the NASDAQ over-the-counter market. The Wilshire 5,000 Index is actually composed of more than 6,000 securities and is the best representation available of the entire U.S. market.

While there are several mutual funds based on the S&P 500 index, it was only recently that an instrument became available to enable the investor to match the performance of the total Wilshire index. The vehicle is called the Vanguard Index Trust: Total Stock Market Portfolio. It does have a nominal (one quarter of one percent) transactions charge but this should not be considered a loading fee. The commission is charged for new investments into the fund so that the higher-than-normal cost of buying small stocks can be fairly distributed among all shareholders. As in the Vanguard Group's regular 500-Index Fund, the expense ratio is extremely low.

The chart on the previous page illustrates how the annualized returns of the S&P 500 and the Wilshire 5,000 compare with the returns of the average equity-fund manager. The following chart shows the distribution of returns for all equity mutual funds pursuing "growth" and "value" investment strategies compared with the actual 10-year results after expenses of the Vanguard Index Trust (S&P 500 portfolio). Note how few individual mutual funds beat the index and how much more likely it has been that your actively managed fund has substantially underperformed the index. While past performance can never assure future results, the evidence clearly indicates that both the S&P 500 and the Wilshire 5,000 have provided higher returns than the average equity mutual-fund manager.

As I have indicated earlier, the investor who is wise, diversifies. That means purchasing not only index funds holding U.S. equities, but also those consisting of foreign equities. The most popular international index is calculated by the investment firm of Morgan Stanley and is called the EAFE Index, standing for the European, Australian, and Far East Index. One mutual fund is available that holds the European stocks in the index; another holds the Pacific portfolio. Investors can further diversify by holding countries whose markets are rapidly developing. The Random Walker's Address Book gives you information on both EAFE funds and on emerging-markets index funds that are available for individual investors.

**Growth and Value Funds versus Index Trust 500
Ten Years Ended December 31, 1994**

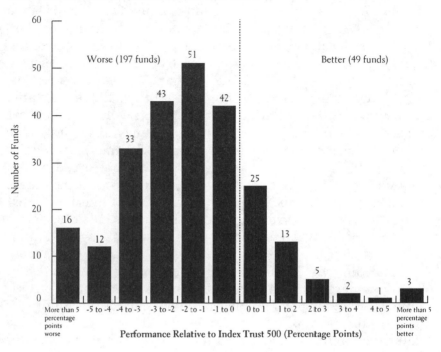

The Tax-Managed Index Fund

One of the advantages, noted earlier, of passive portfolio management (that is, simply buying and holding a diversified index fund) is that such a strategy minimizes transactions costs as well as taxes. To the extent that the long-run uptrend in stock prices continues in the future, switching from security to security involves realizing capital gains that are subject to income tax. Taxes are a crucially important financial consideration, as shown by two Stanford University economists, Joel Dickson and John Shoven. Utilizing a sample of 62 mutual funds with long-term records, they found that, pre-tax, one dollar invested in 1962 would have grown to $21.89 in 1992. After paying taxes on income dividends and capital gains distributions, however, that same dollar invested in mutual funds by a high-income investor would have grown to only $9.87.

To a considerable extent, an index mutual fund helps solve the tax problem. Index funds simply buy and hold a diversified group of securities that make up one of the broad indexes of common stocks. They do not trade from security to security and, thus, they tend to avoid capital gains taxes. Nevertheless, even index funds do realize some capital gains that are taxable to the holders. These gains generally arise involuntarily: either because of a buyout of one of the companies in the index, as when American Home Products bought out American Cyanamid during the mid-1990s; or because sales are forced on the mutual fund. The latter occurs when mutual fund shareholders decide on balance to redeem their shares and the fund must sell securities to raise cash. Thus, even regular index funds are not a perfect solution for the problem of minimizing tax liabilities.

Enter the new mutual fund for the tax conscious investor, The Vanguard Tax-Managed Fund: Growth and Income Portfolio. Despite the portfolio designation, which is not totally revealing, this is an S&P 500 index fund that minimizes taxes by deferring capital gains realizations. Here's an illustration of how it works. Suppose the fund earns a pre-tax 10 percent return over 20 years (the average return for the stock market over long periods of time); 3 percent comes from dividends and 7 percent from growth, i.e., capital gains. The table on the following page shows the results for a hypothetical initial investment of $10,000 in each of three portfolios. Portfolio A distributes taxable dividend income and capital gains each year. Portfolios B and C distribute only taxable dividend income; they realize no capital gains. In Portfolio B the fund is sold after 20 years and gains are realized and taxed at that time. For Portfolio C, the fund is inherited and the gains are never taxed. Capital gains taxes are avoided because when a fund (or any individual stock) is inherited, the cost basis of the security is "stepped up" to current market value. It turns out that Portfolio B accumulates almost $6,700 more than Portfolio A, while Portfolio C accumulates excess cash of $16,500.

The fund is able to defer capital gains by the following techniques. First, the portfolio is indexed to the S&P 500 so there is

The Impact of Taxing Capital Gains
After-Tax Value of $10,000
Invested for 20 Years*

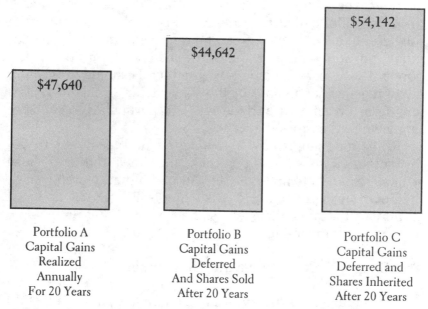

$47,640	$44,642	$54,142
Portfolio A Capital Gains Realized Annually For 20 Years	Portfolio B Capital Gains Deferred And Shares Sold After 20 Years	Portfolio C Capital Gains Deferred and Shares Inherited After 20 Years

Source: Vanguard Group of Investment Companies.
*This hypothetical example assumes a 3% return from dividend income (taxed at a marginal income tax rate of 39.6%) and a 7% return from capital gains (taxed at 28%). In Portfolio A, capital gains are realized, distributed, and taxed annually. In Portfolio B, capital gains accumulate unrealized until they are taxed in the 20th year. Portfolio C is identical to Portfolio B except that the shares are bequeathed, and no capital gain taxes are paid.

no active management that tends to realize gains. Second, when securities do have to be sold (to meet redemptions, for example), the fund sells the highest-cost securities first. Such forced sales from liquidations should be minimized, however, by the assessment of a two percent redemption if fund shares are held less than one year and a one percent redemption fee for fund shares held between one and five years. Third, the fund offsets unavoidable gains by judiciously selling other securities on which there is a loss. As a result, the fund may not perfectly track the benchmark index, but it should come very close.

Vanguard has two additional tax-managed funds. One, called the Capital Appreciation Portfolio, is identical to the income and growth (S&P 500) portfolio except that the index used is the Russell 1,000 index which includes many smaller companies with lower dividend yields. While undoubtedly more aggressive, this portolio is even more effective in minimizing taxes because it distributes less dividend income. A third portfolio, called the Balanced Portfolio, is composed of roughly equal parts of the capital-appreciation (Russell 1,000 index) portfolio and a group of intermediate-term tax-exempt bonds. These low-cost index-oriented funds should prove very advantageous for people in the highest tax brackets with a long-term investment horizon and are particularly useful for funds earmarked for inheritance.

While indexing is now a serviceable and feasible strategy for individual investors, I do realize that it's a dull one. Those with speculative temperaments will undoubtedly prefer using their own steps (and wits) to pick winners. For those who insist on playing the game themselves, the Deep-Thinker Step below may be more appealing.

The Deep-Thinker Step: Doing It Yourself

Having been smitten with the gambling urge since birth, I can well understand why many investors have not only a compulsion to pick the big winners on their own but also a total lack of interest in a system that promises results merely equivalent to those in the market as a whole. The problem is that it takes a lot of work to do it yourself, and as I've repeatedly shown, consistent winners are very rare. For those who regard investing as play, however, this section demonstrates how a sensible strategy can produce substantial rewards and, at the very least, minimize the risks in playing the stock-picking game.

Before putting my strategy to work, however, you need to know the sources of investment information and how to choose an appropriate broker. Most information sources can be obtained at public libraries. You should be an avid reader of the financial pages of daily newspapers, particularly the *New York Times* and the *Wall Street Journal*. Weeklies such as *Barron's* should also be on your "must-read" list. Business magazines such as *BusinessWeek, Fortune,* and *Forbes* are also valuable for gaining exposure to investment ideas. The major investment advisory services are also good. You should, for example, try to have access to Standard & Poor's *Outlock* and the *Value Line Investment Survey.* The first is a weekly publication which contains lists of recommendations; the second presents historical records, current reviews, and risk (beta) ratings of all the major securities, as well as weekly recommendations.

When choosing a broker, you may find that it does not pay to utilize the kind of discount firm recommended in Chapter Twelve if you really do want help. The most important criterion for an investor who wants to be exposed to investment ideas is whether a brokerage firm can furnish investment information. The major question to ask is: Does your broker's firm have a large and well-respected research department? Does it produce comprehensive research reports—as opposed to one-page fly sheets—on the major investment alternatives? Also, the firm should be one that does a substantial amount of institutional business, ensuring your contact with the ideas that are making the rounds of the investment community. While, on average, the value of these reports and ideas may be negligible, you've got to be exposed to them if you truly believe you are one of the rare individuals who can consistently win the game of guessing which idea is likely to catch on. Armed with solid information sources and a good broker, you can then begin the process of selecting individual stocks.

In the first edition of *A Random Walk Down Wall Street,* written in the early 1970s, I proposed four rules for successful stock selection. I find them just as serviceable today. Indeed, as I'll argue below, the stock-market environment of the mid-1990s may be especially conducive to their success. In abridged form, the rules, some of which have been mentioned in earlier chapters, are as follows:

Rule 1: Confine stock purchases to companies that appear able to sustain above-average earnings growth for at least five years. As difficult as the job may be, picking stocks whose earnings grow is the name of the game. Consistent growth not only increases the earnings and dividends of the company but may also increase the multiple that the market is willing to pay for those earnings. This would further boost your gains. Thus, the purchaser of a stock whose earnings begin to grow rapidly has a potential double benefit—both the earnings and the multiple may increase.

Rule 2: Never pay more for a stock than can reasonably be justified by a firm foundation of value.   While I am convinced that you can never judge the exact intrinsic value of a stock, I do feel that you can roughly gauge when a stock seems to be reasonably priced. The market price-earnings multiple is a good place to start: You should buy stocks selling at multiples in line with, or not very much above, this ratio. My strategy, then, is to look for growth situations that the market has not already recognized by bidding the stock's multiple to a large premium. As has been pointed out, if the growth actually takes place you will often get a double bonus—both the earnings and the price-earnings multiple can rise, producing large gains. By the same token, beware of the stock with a very high multiple and many years of growth already discounted in the price. If earnings decline rather than grow, you will usually get double trouble—the multiple will drop along with the earnings, and heavy losses will result.*

Note that, while similar, this is not simply another endorsement of the currently popular "buy low P/E stocks" strategy. Under my rule it is perfectly all right to buy a stock with a P/E multiple slightly above the market average—as long as the company's growth prospects are substantially above average. You might call this an adjusted low P/E strategy. Buy stocks whose P/E's are low relative to their growth prospects. If you can be even reasonably accurate in picking companies that do indeed enjoy above-average growth, you will be rewarded with above-average returns.

---

*In 1973, I cautioned readers not to buy those premier growth stocks (the one-decision Nifty Fifty stocks) whose multiples had soared in some cases to as much as 60, 70, and 80 times earnings, and I mentioned several of those stocks by name. Following Rule 2, therefore, could have enabled you to avoid one of the most notorious investment follies of the 1970s. It would also have kept you safe from the biotechnology craze of the late 1980s.

***Rule 3: It helps to buy stocks with the kinds of stories of antic-
ipated growth on which investors can build castles in the air.***
I stressed in Chapter Two the importance of psychological elements in stock price determination. Individual and institutional
investors are not computers that calculate warranted price-
earnings multiples and then print out buy and sell decisions.
They are emotional human beings—driven by greed, gambling
instinct, hope, and fear in their stock-market decisions. This is
why successful investing demands both intellectual and psychological acuteness. Of course, the market is not totally subjective either; if a positive growth rate appears to be established, the stock is almost certain to develop some type of
following. But stocks are like people—some have more attractive personalities than others, and the improvement in a stock's
multiple may be smaller and slower to be realized if its story
never catches on. The key to success is being where other
investors will be, several months before they get there. So my
advice is to ask yourself whether the story about your stock is
one that is likely to catch the fancy of the crowd. Is it a story
from which contagious dreams can be generated? Is it a story
on which investors can build castles in the air—but castles in
the air that really rest on a firm foundation?

Rule 4: Trade as little as possible. I agree with the Wall
Street maxim "Ride the winners and sell the losers," but not
because I believe in technical analysis. Frequent switching accomplishes nothing but subsidizing your broker and increasing
your tax burden when you do realize gains. I do not say, "Never
sell a stock on which you have a gain." The circumstances that
led you to buy the stock may change, and, especially when it
gets to be tulip time in the market, many of your successful
growth stocks may become way overpriced and overweighted
in your portfolio, as they did during the Nifty Fifty craze of the
1970s or the small company speculative bubble of 1983. But it is
very difficult to recognize the proper time to sell, and heavy tax
costs may be involved. My own philosophy leads me to minimize trading as much as possible. I am merciless with the losers, however. With few exceptions, I sell before the end of each
calendar year any stocks on which I have a loss. The reason for

this timing is that losses are deductible (up to certain amounts) for tax purposes, or can offset gains you may already have taken. Thus, taking losses can actually reduce the amount of loss by lowering your tax bill. I don't always take all losses. If the growth I expect begins to materialize and I am convinced that my stock will work out a bit later, I may hold on for a while. But I do not recommend too much patience in losing situations, especially when prompt action can produce immediate tax benefits.

Do these rules work? They have for me, and they have for some of the few truly successful fund managers on the Street, as I will describe below. But perhaps first it might be instructive to once again visit the Smiths, a pseudonym for the couple whose investments have been described in previous editions of *A Random Walk Down Wall Street.*

Readers who have followed the fortunes of the Smiths may recall that in the last edition they had become parents and their time for perusing investment possibilities had been drastically curtailed. They had naïvely thought that when their daughters were older there would be more opportunity for such a pursuit. This was not the case. Mrs. Smith found herself driving the girls to choir lessons, Girl Scout meetings, and other accoutrements of suburban life. Mr. Smith joined the parade of fathers walking their children's dogs in the mornings and coaching soccer teams on Saturdays.

Mutual funds had become the primary stock investment vehicle for the Smiths' retirement funds. Still, every once in a while they would almost inadvertently come across an individual stock that they could not resist. Once again, my book provided a clue. In the 1981 edition, I used the American Telephone & Telegraph Company as an example of how one could obtain a 15 percent annual rate of return on even a stodgy stock with only moderate growth prospects. The Smiths liked the logic behind my argument and the return it promised. In January 1982, they bought AT&T at $59 a share.

As I repeatedly argued, no one can perfectly predict the future—certainly not me. AT&T's status as a stodgy company was soon obliterated when Judge Harold Green declared that AT&T could no longer exist in its then current form and had to be disconnected.

The Smiths soon found themselves holding shares not only in the new, slimmed-down AT&T but also in the seven regional Bell operating companies, having received one share of each for every ten shares of AT&T that they owned. Because their holding was not that large, the Smiths decided to consolidate their regional shares into that of the company that served them—Bell Atlantic.

Though the picture had changed completely, the Smiths held on. A free-lance writer, Mrs. Smith had done work for AT&T prior to divestiture and had had a chance to work with several managers in the telephone system who cared for the company as much as if not more than for their own individual advancement. Such concern, she reasoned, could only be beneficial in the long run. The Smiths simply do not have the time to dabble in market timing; they invest for the long term. Under these conditions, they felt that the depth of talent in the AT&T organization would eventually bode well.

In addition, the Smiths reasoned correctly that the change from monopoly status to a more competitive environment created many more opportunities for growth both for AT&T and for the regional Bell operating companies, such as Bell Atlantic. Convinced that communications, and especially the cellular telephone segment, was a growth industry, they believed that Rule 1 was satisfied. Moreover, the Smiths loved the below-market P/E ratios for AT&T and the baby Bells and their well-above-average dividend yields. The Smiths had no trouble convincing themselves that Rule 2 was also met. Finally, a spate of newspaper and magazine articles began to talk glowingly about the bright future prospects for the communications industry. While that was not the sort of story on which to build large castles in the air, the Smiths were convinced that investors, who were initially skeptical about AT&T and its spin-offs, would eventually recognize the growth opportunities.

As is well known today, the regional Bells have provided an extremely generous return since they were originally created. Whether investors accepted shares in all the baby Bells or consolidated their holdings, as did the Smiths, the combined investment of AT&T and one or more regionals was one of the smarter investment moves of the decade.

Rather than read investment journals and financial magazines for picking stocks, the Smiths have capitalized on situations they came across in their everyday lives. In May 1985, for example, Mr. Smith was asked to set up a new commercial lending office by the bank he worked for. Original plans called for one secretary for the first year and two by the second. Mrs. Smith asked him what he would do when the secretary was sick or on vacation. Mr. Smith replied that he would hire a "Kelly Girl."

Now, as a freelance writer, Mrs. Smith had been without stretches of income when she was younger and had worked as a "Kelly Girl." That experience had given her a favorable impression of the company. In addition, she knew that the central New Jersey economy was expanding at a tremendous rate and had only to drive down the Route 1 corridor to realize that all the new office buildings going up would eventually require clerical assistance. She took her daughters to the library one afternoon, and while they checked out the children's section, she went to the business area and copied the S&P and Value Line reports on Kelly Services.

What the Smiths had noticed in the New Jersey economy was being felt across the country. The health of the national economy was glowing. Reports of major increases in employment around the country would almost certainly lead to a strong growth in the demand for Kelly Services. And while the P/E for Kelly was somewhat above the general market multiple, it was nevertheless not far from the market norm. In May 1985, the Smiths bought Kelly Services at $43 a share. Despite the 1987 crash, by early 1989 the value of those shares had doubled.

Do the Smiths have a golden touch? Should they be publishing an investment letter? As I've stressed repeatedly, luck often plays an important role in any investor's success. But by following my rules, the Smiths have often managed to buy the right stock at the right time. Often, but not always—as the case of Sears, Roebuck & Company illustrates.

Mrs. Smith had talked to the Sears public relations department in connection with an article on new trends in banking. A former PR person herself, she was impressed with the openness of the company and its willingness to talk with the press.

She had also been a longtime customer of Sears' major appliances and knew that they were always ranked highly by *Consumer Reports*. And in contrast to the prevailing publicity about most major companies, she was impressed with the fact that Sears was willing to invest for the long term in its introduction of the Discover card.

At the same time, Sears was selling at a below-market earnings multiple. Articles were touting that its breakup value was more than the listed stock price. Mrs. Smith viewed this company as a sleeping giant and bought it at $37.25 a share in July 1985.

Had Mrs. Smith talked to me, she would have been told that Sears was often a rather clumsy giant and that its low P/E ratio may have been more than justified by the low growth prospects for the company's core business. But the Smiths were optimistic and at least the stock was moderately priced in relation to its earnings.

Sears roller-coastered around for the next two years—dropping down to the low 30s with the release of lackluster earnings reports and climbing up to the high 40s on rumors of takeovers or breakups. By September 1987, however, Sears was over 50 and Mrs. Smith felt that her intuition was finally justified. Of course, she was wrong. Sears had been pulled along in the wave of euphoria pushing the market to its 1987 high. Three months later, Sears was down to 33—having lost one-third of its value along with the rest of the market.

Mrs. Smith stubbornly refused to sell the stock—partly from a financially debilitating reluctance to acknowledge that she was wrong and partly from lack of time to focus on an alternative investment strategy. She justified her action by thinking that the outlook had not changed dramatically since buying the stock and thus she was not violating my rule to sell losers. Too many investors convince themselves that their actions are correct, even when they know they are not.

Mrs. Smith did follow one practice that I do thoroughly approve of: She participated in a dollar-cost averaging scheme by having all her Sears dividends reinvested. Thus, by July 1989, four years after she had bought the stock, she had accumulated 20 percent more shares. With Sears management announcing a restructuring and with some price appreciation to reflect earnings growth, Mrs. Smith has had a positive rate of return. She could, however, have done a great deal better buying a no-load index fund.

The experience of the Smiths illustrates the potential profits, pitfalls, and fun obtainable from employing my strategy. These are all at least partial success stories (losers, after all, rarely brag), but they did entail some nocturnal anxiety. The Smiths did not sleep well when the price of their Sears stock fell below their initial purchase price. It also takes a lot of time and effort to invest wisely. The Smiths recognize this and they now invest all of their funds in a selection of the mutual funds I name in the Random Walker's Address Book at the end of this chapter. They realize the risk involved in not having a diversified portfolio and how one really disastrous investment could have wiped out a substantial part of their capital.

These small investors also felt a keen sense of ignorance in that they were not always sure they could trust earnings reports and they did not have the contacts and the up-to-the-minute information available to the "experts." They realized that once a story is out in the regular press, it's likely that the market has already taken account of the information, as the efficient-market theory supposes. Even today, they feel that they are neophytes in a very tricky business and agree with me that picking individual stocks is like breeding thoroughbred porcupines. You study and study and make up your mind, and then proceed very carefully. In the final analysis, as much as I hope their successful record resulted from following my good advice, their success may have been mainly a matter of luck.

For all its hazards, picking individual stocks is a fascinating game. My rules do, I believe, tilt the odds in your favor while protecting you from the excessive risk involved in high-multiple stocks. The market environment during the mid-1990s remained particularly favorable for the successful application of my rules. Like the ends of a closing accordion, the price-earnings multiples of stocks with superior growth prospects and those of the more prosaic stocks had come together and stayed relatively close. Because recent speculative investment crazes involved the overpricing of the premier growth stocks, an over-

reaction may even have set in, causing these stocks to be un-
derpriced relative to the market. Recall the chart in Chapter
Thirteen which shows the contraction of the multiple of the
Smith, Barney Emerging Growth Stock Index relative to that of
the S&P 500. While growth stocks tended to sell at more than
double the multiple of the S&P at the height of the growth-stock
craze, they sold at only a 20 percent premium over more run-of-
the-mill stocks during the mid-1990s. Precisely the most interesting stocks in the market—those whose earnings and dividends had been far outdistancing inflation—were selling at
their most reasonable market valuations in years. Therefore,
the late 1990s could prove to be the ideal time to pick individual
stocks on the basis of my rules. Unlike the early 1970s, it should
not be hard to find an abundant selection of strong companies
to fill the bill.

But if you choose this course, remember that a large number
of other investors—including the pros—are trying to play the
same game. And the efficient-market theory suggests that the
odds of anyone's consistently beating the market are pretty
slim. Nevertheless, for many of us, trying to outguess the market is a game that is much too much fun to give up. Even if you
were convinced you would not do any better than average, I'm
sure that most of you with speculative temperaments would
still want to keep on playing the game of selecting individual
stocks. My rules, at least, permit you to do so in a way that
significantly limits your exposure to risk.

The Substitute-Player Step: Hire a
Professional Wall-Street Walker

There's an easier way to gamble in your investment walk:
Instead of trying to pick the individual winners (stocks), pick
the best coaches (investment managers). These "coaches"
come in the form of mutual-fund managers, and there are over
1,000 for you to pick from.

In addition to offering risk reduction through diversification, the mutual funds provide freedom from having to select
stocks, and relief from paperwork and record-keeping for tax

purposes. Most funds also offer a variety of special services, such as automatic reinvestment of dividends and regular cash-withdrawal plans. A mutual fund is particularly attractive as the investment vehicle for an Individual Retirement Account or Keogh plan, as described in Chapter Twelve.

In previous editions of this book, I provided the names of several investment managers who had enjoyed long-term records of successful portfolio management as well as brief biographies explaining their investment styles. These managers were among the very few who had shown an ability to beat the market over long periods of time. I have abandoned that practice in the current edition for two reasons.

First, most of those managers have now retired from active portfolio management or are about to do so. The legendary Peter Lynch, who performed brilliantly as manager of the Magellan Fund, the equity mutual fund with far and away the best record over the decades of the 1970s and 1980s, retired at the start of the 1990s at the ripe old age of 47. John Marks Templeton, who initiated the idea of global investing to the mutual fund world, has sold his group of mutual funds and spends his time relaxing in the quiet seclusion of Lyford Cay, in the Bahamas. John Neff, the brilliant practitioner of value investing, is scheduled to retire soon after the publication date of this sixth edition. Warren Buffett, the sage of Omaha, whose successful application of the firm foundation theory has produced spectacular returns for the holders of his Berkshire Hathaway investment company shares is not yet retired from the management of his company. But as of the mid-1990s, Berkshire Hathaway shares were selling at a hefty premium over the value of the portfolio of assets it owned, and Buffett's reputation for infallibility has been somewhat tarnished by his less than brilliant investments in Champion International, U.S. Air, and Salomon Brothers.

My second reason for refraining from suggesting individual fund managers is that I have become increasingly convinced that the past records of mutual fund managers are essentially worthless in predicting future success. The few examples of consistently superior performance occur no more frequently than can be expected by chance.

Assuming that you prefer to invest in an actively managed equity mutual fund, is it really possible to select a fund that will be a top performer? One plausible method, favored by many financial planners and editors, is to choose funds with the best recent performance records. The financial pages of newspapers and magazines are filled with fund advertisements claiming that a particular fund is number one in terms of its performance record. There are at least two problems with this approach. First, investors should be aware that many fund advertisements are quite misleading. The number one ranking is typically for a self-selected specific time period and compared with a particular (usually small) group of common stock funds. For example, one fund advertised itself as follows: "Now Ranked #1 for Performance.* The Fund That's Performed Through Booms, Busts and 11 Presidential Elections." It is implied that this fund was a top performer over a period of 44 years. The truth of the matter, revealed in a small footnote referenced by the asterisk, was that the fund was number one only during one specific three-month period and only compared with a specific category of funds with an asset value between $250 and $500 million.

The more important reason to be skeptical of past performance records is that, as I have mentioned earlier, there is no consistent long-run relationship between performance in one period and investment results in the next. I have studied the persistence of mutual-fund performance over a quarter of a century and conclude that it is simply impossible for investors to guarantee themselves above-average returns by purchasing those funds with the best recent records. While there have been particular periods (such as the 1970s) where considerable year-to-year persistence in fund performance existed, and while one can find a few examples (such as Lynch's Magellan Fund and Buffett's Berkshire Hathaway) of fairly consistent long-run superb performance, the general result is that there is no dependable long-term persistence. You can't assure yourself of superior performance by buying mutual funds which may have beaten the market in some past period. Once again, the past does not predict the future.

I have tested a strategy where at the start of each year

investors would rank all general equity funds based on the funds' records over the past 12 months. In alternative strategies, I have assumed that the investor buys the top 10 funds, the top 20 funds, and so on. Each year the investor would switch to the top funds the preceding year. I ignored all load and redemption fees, which were considerable for some funds. The results did show above-average performance during the 1970s. During the 1980s, however, and in the early 1990s, the strategy produced returns not only below the mutual-fund average but also below the Standard & Poor's 500-Stock Index. Similar analyses showed the same results when funds were ranked by their past two-year, five-year, and 10-year records. Even ignoring sales charges, you can't consistently beat the market by purchasing the mutual funds that have performed best in the past.

I also tested a strategy of purchasing the "best" funds as ranked by one of the leading financial magazines. *Forbes* magazine, the most widely read investment magazine, has published an "honor roll" of mutual funds annually since 1975. To earn a place on the honor roll, a fund not only had to have an extraordinary long-run performance record (usually based on total returns measured over a ten-year period) but also had to meet certain consistency goals. Performance is measured in both up and down markets, and funds must be at least top-half performers in down markets to qualify for honor status.

Again, I ignored any load charges that might be imposed on the purchase of these mutual fund shares. I found that during the eight years from 1975 through 1983, the honor roll funds did do substantially better than the Standard & Poor's Index. During the next eight years to 1991, however, the *Forbes* honor-roll funds did substantially worse than the index. Over the entire 16-year period, the *Forbes* honor-roll funds underperformed the S&P 500-Stock Index, and an investor paying sales fees would have been further penalized.

The clear implication of these tests in the laboratory of fund performance, as well as the academic work reported in Part Two of this book, is that you cannot depend on an excellent record of any particular manager continuing persistently in the future. Nevertheless, in the Random Walker's Address Book, I have presented the names of a number of funds with moderate risks and expense ratios that do have excellent long-run performance records.

If recent performance is not a reliable indicator in choosing a mutual fund, what is? Three factors that considerably influence the kind of performance you will receive are the risk level of the fund, the amount of the fund's unrealized gains, and the fund's expense ratio.

Risk Level

For equity funds, the beta level is a start. It will indicate the fund's sensitivity to swings in the general market. If you don't sleep well at night, avoid funds with betas much greater than one (the beta for a general index fund). Remember though that beta is not a reliable guide to the return you can expect from a fund. In addition to beta, you should consider other risk characteristics of the fund you buy. Funds owning relatively small companies, funds that are undiversified, such as sector funds investing in just one industry, and funds that employ lots of derivative instruments all tend to be riskier than broad-index funds. For bond funds, the biggest risk-takers hold bonds of longer maturities and of lower quality. Risky bond funds also tend to use a significant amount of leverage (borrowing) and/or derivative instruments.

Unrealized Gains

Avoid purchasing funds with large amounts of unrealized capital gains. This factor is almost invariably overlooked by investors. A large amount of unrealized capital gains in a fund's portfolio is a distinct disadvantage because, when those gains are realized, an investor will be subject to capital gains taxes. Suppose, for example, you buy a fund with a net asset value of $10.00 per share but with a per-share cost basis of only $5.00. If the fund turns over its whole portfolio to buy other stocks, you are liable for a capital gains tax on the $5.00 gain even though you purchased the stock at $10.00. Also, never purchase a fund just before it distributes its realized capital gains. You will have to pay a capital-gains tax on that distribution. Buy the shares just after the gain is distributed and the shares decline in price by the amount of the distribution.

Expense Ratios

There is one element of predictability in mutual-fund performance, however, that may at least help you avoid the poorest performing funds. Mutual funds with abnormally high expense ratios tend to be below-average performers. Moreover, those funds that persist in charging high fees tend to persist in generating poor performance. My advice is pay particular attention to the annual fees charged by your mutual fund. Avoid high-expense funds just as you should avoid funds with high sales charges. Particularly in an era when returns are likely to be far more modest than they were in the 1980s, expenses will become increasingly important. Investors need to realize that, for example, a bond fund charging two percent per year in expenses will be syphoning off 25 percent of the income from eight percent bonds, and that's not chopped liver. A primer on how to analyze mutual-fund costs is presented later in this chapter.

The Morningstar Mutual-Fund Information Service

I have often said that the two best things that have happened to the mutual-fund industry are the arrival of Jack Bogle (who started the low-cost consumer-friendly Vanguard Group of mutual funds during the mid-1970s) and Don Phillips (who in the early 1990s initiated the extremely useful Morningstar Service, which publishes information on mutual funds). For each mutual fund, Morningstar publishes a single page of information crammed full of relevant data. A sample report is presented on the following page for the Vanguard Index Trust: S&P 500 Portfolio.

Basically, Morningstar is one of the most comprehensive sources of mutual-fund information an investor can find. Its reports show past returns, risk ratings, portfolio composition, and the fund's investment style (for example, seek established

Volume 24, Issue Number 4, February 3, 1995. Reprinted with permission.

Vanguard Index 500

		Ticker	Load	NAV	Yield	SEC Yield	Assets	Objective
		VFINX	None	$42.97	2.7%	2.88%	$9356.4 mil	Growth/Inc.

Vanguard Index Trust 500 Portfolio seeks investment results that correspond to the price and yield performance of the S&P 500 Index.

The fund allocates the percentage of net assets each company receives on the basis of the stock's relative total-market value: its market price per share multiplied by the number of shares outstanding.

Shareholders are charged an annual account-maintenance fee of $10.

Prior to Dec. 21, 1987, the fund was named Vanguard Index Trust. Prior to 1980, it was named First Index Investment Trust.

Portfolio Manager(s)

George U. Sauter. Since 10-87. BA'76 Dartmouth College. MBA'80 U. of Chicago. Sauter joined Vanguard Group in 1987. As vice president of core management, he is responsible for the management of Vanguard's index funds. He previously spent two years as a trust investment officer with FNB Ohio. He manages several offerings, including Vanguard Index Total Stock Market and Vanguard Index Value.

Historical Profile

- Return: Above Avg
- Risk: Average
- Rating: ★★★★ Above Avg

Investment Style History
Equity
Average Stock %

	99%	97%	97%	97%	100%	99%	100%	98%

Growth of $10,000

- Investment Value ($000)
- Strength Relative to S&P 500
- ▼ Manager Change
- ▽ Partial Manager Change
- ► Mgr Unknown After
- ◄ Mgr Unknown Before

Performance Quartile (Within Objective)

History

	1983	1984	1985	1986	1987	1988	1989	1990	1991	1992	1993	12-94	
	19.70	19.52	22.99	24.27	24.65	27.18	33.64	31.24	39.32	40.97	43.83	42.97	NAV
	21.29	6.21	31.23	18.06	4.71	16.22	31.37	-3.33	30.22	7.42	9.89	1.18	Total Return %
	-1.17	-0.05	-0.51	-0.62	-0.55	-0.39	-0.32	-0.21	-0.26	-0.20	-0.16	-0.14	+/- S&P 500
	-2.17	3.16	-1.34	1.96	2.34	-1.72	2.19	2.86	-3.98	-1.55	-1.39	1.25	+/- Wilshire 5000
	4.78	4.67	4.54	3.69	2.42	4.56	4.33	3.54	3.87	2.96	2.83	2.69	Income Return %
	16.51	1.55	26.69	14.37	2.28	11.66	27.04	-5.86	26.35	4.46	7.06	-1.52	Capital Return %
	35	46	21	32	24	24	11	66	26	53	67	12	Total Rtn %Rank All
	49	38	26	35	26	45	14	46	37	49	54	20	Total Rtn %Rank Obj
	0.87	0.88	0.91	0.89	0.69	1.10	1.20	1.17	1.15	1.12	1.13	1.17	Income $
	0.71	0.48	1.61	2.02	0.17	0.32	0.75	0.10	0.12	0.10	0.03	0.20	Capital Gains $
	0.28	0.27	0.28	0.28	0.26	0.22	0.21	0.22	0.20	0.19	0.19	0.19	Expense Ratio %
	4.22	4.53	4.09	3.40	3.15	4.08	3.62	3.60	3.07	2.81	2.65	2.68	Income Ratio %
	35	14	36	29	15	10	8	23	5	4	6	7	Turnover Rate %
	233.7	289.7	394.3	485.1	826.3	1055.1	1803.8	2173.0	4345.3	6517.7	8272.7	9356.4	Net Assets ($mil)

Performance 12-31-94

	1st Qtr	2nd Qtr	3rd Qtr	4th Qtr	Total
90	-3.07	6.24	-13.78	8.88	-3.33
91	14.47	-0.29	5.28	8.36	30.22
92	-2.57	1.87	3.08	5.00	7.42
93	4.33	0.43	2.52	2.30	9.89
94	-3.84	0.40	4.86	-0.05	1.18

Trailing	Total Return %	+/- S&P 500	+/- Wil 5000	% Rank All Obj	Growth of $10,000
3 Mo	-0.05	-0.03	0.72	23 18	9,995
6 Mo	4.80	-0.06	0.18	12 12	10,480
1 Yr	1.18	-0.14	1.25	12 20	10,118
3 Yr Avg	6.10	-0.17	-0.51	33 46	11,944
5 Yr Avg	8.50	-0.19	-0.32	28 35	15,036
10 Yr Avg	14.05	-0.33	0.19	17 14	37,239
15 Yr Avg	14.13	-0.36	0.15	22 25	72,573

Best Similar Funds in MMF

Index S&P 500 Index	Strong Fit
Fidelity Market Index	Strong Fit
Schwab 1000	Strong Fit

Analysis

	Tax-Adj Return %	% Pretax Return
3 Yr Avg	5.00	82.0
5 Yr Avg	7.33	86.3
10 Yr Avg	12.17	86.6
Potential Capital Gain Exposure	11% of assets	

Risk Analysis

Time Period	Load-Adj Return %	Risk %Rank All Obj	Morningstar Return	Morningstar Risk	Morningstar Risk-Adj Rating
1 Yr	1.18				
3 Yr	6.10	66 49	0.75[3] 0.74	★★★	
5 Yr	9.50	67 56	0.94[3] 0.80	★★★	
10 Yr	14.05	63 67	1.28 0.86	★★★★	
Average Historical Rating (109 months)			4.0 ★s		

[1]=low, 100=high [3] 1.00 = Equity Avg [3] 1.00 = 90-day T-bill return

Other Measures

	Standard Index S&P 500	Best Fit Index S&P 500
Standard Deviation	7.94	Alpha -0.2 -0.2
Mean	6.25	Beta 1.00 1.00
Sharpe Ratio	0.34	R-Squared 100 100

Portfolio Analysis 12-31-94

Share Chg (11-94) 000	Amount 000	Total Stocks: 502 / Total Fixed-Income: 0	Value $000	% Net Assets
239	4776	General Electric	243597	2.60
208	4367	AT & T	219435	2.35
178	3468	Exxon	210706	2.25
174	3592	Coca-Cola	184991	1.98
77	1498	Royal Dutch Petroleum	161000	1.72
92	2401	Philip Morris	138058	1.48
329	6421	Wal-Mart Stores	136442	1.46
176	3516	Merck	134031	1.43
95	1640	IBM	120571	1.29
103	1915	Procter & Gamble	118718	1.27
99	1902	El duPont de Nemours	107002	1.14
101	1627	Microsoft	99454	1.06
91	1795	Johnson & Johnson	98294	1.05
139	1638	Motorola	94797	1.01
55	1110	Mobil	93548	1.00
118	2105	General Motors	88948	0.95
44	883	American International Group	86535	0.92
77	1427	Bristol-Myers Squibb	82570	0.88
72	1388	Amoco	82079	0.88
153	2688	GTE	81638	0.87
94	1821	Chevron	81246	0.87
113	2213	PepsiCo	80212	0.86
178	2852	Ford Motor	79844	0.85
71	1386	BellSouth	75037	0.80
46	1158	Intel	73659	0.79

Investment Style

Style Value Blend Growth		Stock Portfolio Avg	Rel S&P 500	Rel Objective
Price/Earnings Ratio		18.5	1.00	1.05
Price/Book Ratio		3.4	1.00	1.15
5 Yr Earnings Gr %		5.6	1.00	0.90
Return on Assets %		7.5	1.00	1.10
Debt % Total Cap		28.3	1.00	0.98
Med Mkt Cap ($mil)		12983	1.00	1.69

Special Securities % of assets 06-30-94

○ Private/Illiquid Securities	0.0
○ Exotic Mortgage-Backed	0.0
○ Structured Notes	0.0
● Options/Futures	Yes

Composition
% of assets 01-19-95

Cash	0.0
Stocks	100.0
Bonds	0.0
Other	0.0

Index Allocation
% of stocks

S&P 500	99.7
S&P Mid	0.0
US Sm Cap	0.3
Foreign	3.7

Sector Weightings

	% of Stocks	Rel S&P
Utilities	12.4	1.00
Energy	10.1	1.00
Financials	10.6	1.00
Industrial Cyclicals	16.4	1.00
Consumer Durables	6.2	1.00
Consumer Staples	12.5	1.00
Services	8.1	1.00
Retail	5.8	1.00
Health	8.7	1.00
Technology	9.2	1.00

Analysis by Alice Lowenstein 01-20-95

Vanguard Index Trust 500 Portfolio's 1994 showing provides additional ammunition for index-fund proponents.

More than three fourths of all U.S. diversified equity funds failed to show a year-to-date gain in 1994. The S&P 500, however, managed a positive performance last year, as did this index fund, with its 1.18% return—an impressive act for a fully invested fund.

A key reason for the fund's outperformance was its charter-mandated diversification. By tracking the S&P's broad sector exposure, the fund was in place to avoid the losses shown by more-concentrated portfolios. The fund's greater-than-objective weighting in hard-hit financials was a boon, for example. Also, as the past year offered few long-lasting sector winners, this fund was blessed. Its exposure to sectors ensured that it was in the right place when a particular sector—such as industrial cyclicals early in the year and health care in the third quarter—pulled ahead.

These 1994 results highlight the essential nature of this fund. Its super-diversified portfolio of more than 500 individual equities can miss out on exaggerated losses, as happened last year. Conversely, it will not generate the booming returns of aptly timed sector plays. Thus the fund's volatility is also moderate, as illustrated by its below-objective-average standard deviation (the measure of how far returns have historically deviated from the fund's mean) and its average Morningstar risk score.

This type of fund also offers certain tax advantages. By keeping turnover to a minute level, the fund postpones realizing capital gains, helping to minimize the capital gains for long-term shareholders. (The fund's above-average income level, however, could be a disadvantage for those in high tax brackets.)

Tracking accuracy, combined with its hallmark low expenses, make this fund the standard bearer for S&P 500 index vehicles.

Address	Vanguard Financial Ctr. P.O. Box 2600	Minimum Purchase	$3000	Add: $100	IRA: $500
	Valley Forge, PA 19482	Min Auto Inv Plan	$3000	Systematic Inv: $50
Phone	800-662-7447 / 610-669-1000	Date of Inception	08-31-76
	Vanguard's Core Management Group	Expenses & Fees	
Advisor	None	Sales Fees	No-load
Subadvisor	Vanguard Group	Management Fee	Provided at cost.
States Available	All plus PR,VI,GU	Actual Fees	Mgt: N/A Dist: N/A
Morningstar Grade	B+	Expense Projections	3Yr: $36 5Yr: $60 10Yr: $123
Income Distrib	Quarterly	Annual Brokerage Cost	0.02%

Morningstar Mutual Funds User's Guide

Below is an explanation of key terms found on each Morningstar Mutual Funds report dated after 1/4/1994. If you have questions about your page, please call Product Support at 800-876-5005.

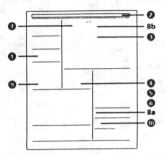

❶ Total Return
Total return is calculated by dividing the change in a fund's net asset value, assuming reinvestment of income and capital-gains distributions, by the initial net asset value. Total returns are adjusted for management, administrative, and 12b-1 fees, and other costs automatically deducted from fund assets. Total returns indicated here are not adjusted for sales load. (Load-adjusted total returns are located in the Risk Analysis section.) Total returns for periods longer than one year are compounded average annual returns.

❷ Yield
Yield represents a fund's income return on capital investment. There are two yield measures on the page, distributed yield and SEC yield. Morningstar computes distributed yield by summing all income distributions for the past 12 months and dividing by the previous month's NAV (adjusted for capital gains distributions). SEC yield is a standardized figure that the Securities and Exchange Commission requires funds to use when mentioning yield in advertisements. An annualized calculation based on a trailing 30-day period, SEC yield can differ significantly from distributed yield.

❸ Performance Graph
The top line of this graph expresses the growth of a $10,00 investment as of the more recent date: the fund's inception or the earliest date indicated on the graph. The horizontal dotted line shows the fund's performance relative to a benchmark (the S&P Index for equity funds and the Lehman Brothers Aggregate Bond Index for fixed-income funds). When the dotted line slopes upward, the fund has outperformed its index; when it slopes downward, it has underperformed its index.

❸ Morningstar Return
Morningstar Return rates a fund's performance relative to other funds within the same class. Morningstar calculates a fund's total return as the excess of the 90-day Treasury bill return, adjusted for fees, and compares this figure to the average excess return of the fund's class or the 90-day T-bill, whichever is higher. The average figure for any investment class is set at 1.00.

❺ Morningstar Risk
Morningstar Risk evaluates a fund's downside volatility relative to that of other funds in its class. To calculate risk, we add up the amounts by which the fund's returns trail those of the three-month Treasury bill, and divide that sum by the number of months in the rating period. The average Morningstar Risk rating for any class is set equal to 1.00.

❻ Morningstar Risk-Adjusted Ratings
These star ratings represent a fund's historical risk-adjusted performance compared with the other funds in its class. To determine a fund's rating for a given period, Morningstar subtracts the fund's Risk score from its Return score, then plots the result along a bell curve to determine the fund's rating: If the fund scores in the top 10% of its class it receives 5 stars; the next 22.5%, 4 stars; the middle 35%, 3 stars; the next 22.5%, 2 stars; and the bottom 10%, 1 star. Ratings are recalculated monthly.

❼ Historical Profile
This provides an overall assessment of a fund's historical returns and risk, and its overall risk-adjusted star rating. The three time periods (three-, five-, and 10-year) are combined as a weighted average, with more weight given to the longer periods. The same bell curve used in the calculation of the risk-adjusted rating is used for a fund's historical risk and return profiles.

❽ Style Box
This proprietary tool reveals a fund's true investment strategy, which may or may not match its stated objective. For equity funds, the vertical axis categorizes funds by size: Funds with median market capitalizations of less than $1 billion are small cap; $1 billion to $5 billion, medium cap; and more than $5 billion, large cap. The horizontal axis denotes investment styles: value-oriented, growth-oriented, or a blend of the two. A stock-fund portfolio's average price/earnings and price/book ratios are computed relative to the combined averages of the S&P 500 Index (set at 2.00). Funds with a combined relative P/E and P/B figure of less than 1.75 are considered value funds; 1.75 to 2.25, blend funds; and more than 2.25, growth funds. Along the vertical axis of fixed-income style boxes lies the average quality

rating of a bond portfolio. Funds with an average credit rating of AA or higher are categorized as high quality; between BBB and AA-, medium quality; and BBB- or below, low quality. The horizontal axis focuses on interest-rate sensitivity; it shows the bond portfolio's average effective maturity (average weighted maturity for municipal-bond funds). Funds with an average effective maturity of less than four years qualify as short-term; four to 10 years, intermediate; and more than 10 years, long-term.

The style box located in the lower right (8a) of the page represents the fund's investment style as of the most recent month-end. The style boxes located above the performance graph (8b) represent the fund's investment style at the beginning of each calendar year.

❾ Tax Analysis
Tax-adjusted historical returns show the fund's average annualized after-tax total return for three-, five-, and 10-year periods. It is computed by diminishing each income and capital-gain distribution by the maximum tax rate in effect at the time of the distribution. Percentage pre-tax return is derived by dividing after-tax returns by pre-tax returns. The highest possible score is 100% for funds with no taxable distributions. Potential capital-gain exposure gives an idea of an investment's potential tax bite. This figure shows what percentage of a fund's total assets represent capital appreciation, either unrealized or realized. If unrealized, the fund's holdings have increased in value, but the fund has not sold these holdings; taxes are not due until the fund does so. Realized gains represent actual gains achieved by the sale of holdings, on which taxes must be paid. Unrealized appreciation may turn into realized gains at any time if the fund's management decides to sell profitable holdings.

❿ Special Securities %
Here we show whether a fund can and does hold a variety of complex or illiquid securities, including derivatives. ● indicates that a fund holds the securities; ○ indicates that the fund may but doesn't currently hold them; — means that the fund cannot own the securities. Percentages held in each category also appear.

large companies or smaller growth companies; favor "value" stocks with low P/E ratios; buy foreign or domestic stocks or both, and so on). The reports indicate if the fund has any sales charges (load fees) and shows the annual expense ratios for the fund and the percentage of the fund's asset value represented by unrealized appreciation. For bond funds, Morningstar gives data on returns, effective maturity, quality of bonds held, and information on loads and expenses.

The Morningstar Service also utilizes a 5-star rating system. It rates past performance taking into account broad-market returns and the costs and risks associated with getting those returns. The top funds are given five stars—two more than Michelin assigns to the top restaurants in the world. The stars are useful in categorizing past performance. Unlike the Michelin stars that virtually guarantee the diner a meal of the designated quality, however, the Morningstar ratings do not guarantee an investor continued superior performance. Five-star funds will not dependably do better than three-star funds and the wise investor will look beyond the stars in making appropriate investment decisions. Of course, you might quite rationally decide to engage in the kind of mixed strategy undertaken by many institutional investors. Index some of your money and supplement your portfolio with one or more of the funds listed in my tables.

A Primer on Mutual-Fund Costs

We've talked about the magic of compound interest—how even modest rates of interest can compound to produce extraordinary investment results after a small number of years. After several years, even small differences in the interest rates you earn on your money will result in vast differences in the final sum of money you can accumulate for retirement or for other savings needs. For this reason, it is critically important that every investor understand how to measure both the explicit and the less transparent elements of investment transactions and management costs. Since many investors will be using mutual funds as their primary vehicle for buying stocks and bonds, they must be able to understand the facts and implications of mutual-fund costs. It is for this reason that the following "primer" is required reading for cost-conscious investors.

The mutual-fund industry has developed a system of charging expenses to investors that is as complicated as Internal Revenue Service income-tax regulations and equally unpleasant. There are two broad categories of mutual-fund costs: "load" fees charged when you buy or sell shares, and "expense charges" which are taken out of your investment returns each year.

Loading Fees

1. Front-end load. This is a commission charge that is paid when you purchase fund shares. Front-end loads are often as high as 8½ percent. That means that if you put $1,000 into a high-load mutual fund, you will have only $915 invested for you. You would need to earn 9.3 percent on your investment just to break even and get your investment back to $1,000. Not all fees are so excessive. So-called low-load funds charge only a 1 to 3 percent sales charge. Best of all are "no-load" funds, which have no front-end sales charges at all.

2. Back-end loads and exchange fees. Back-end loads are charges incurred when you redeem fund shares. The charge could be as much as 6 percent of the value of your redeemed shares if you sell out in the first year, with a declining percentage charge in subsequent years. Exchange fees are generally flat rate charges incurred when you exchange your fund shares for other funds within the same mutual-fund family.

Expense Charges

1. Operating and investment management expenses. A fund's "expense ratio" expresses the total operating and investment advisory fees incurred by the fund as a percentage of the fund's average net assets. These expense ratios range from a low of about ¼ of 1 percent per year to as much as 2 percent per year. (Note that the latter is eight times higher than the former—and that can make a huge difference over time.) Beware the loss leader come-on. Some new funds (especially money funds) *temporarily* waive all fees to enhance the advertised current yield. Investors should be alert to the fact that they will be socked for full expenses as soon as the introductory "come-on" period ends.

2. 12b-1 charges. These are fund distribution expenses charged not as a front-end load but rather as a continuing annual charge against fund assets. The "12b-1" refers to a Securities and Exchange Commission rule that permits these charges. As of 1989, over half of the publicly offered mutual funds had 12b-1 fees.

The important point to realize is that mutual-fund asset performance bears *no* relationship to the expenses charged. While you may "pay for what you get" in some products, you don't buy any better investment management by paying high fees. Quite the opposite—high fees lead to inferior investment performance.

How is the average investor to know what fees and charges he or she is paying? It's easy—just look at the weekly newspaper listings. There are usually two "prices" given for each mutual fund—a sell price (the net asset value you would receive if you redeemed your shares) and a buy price (the offering price, including sales charges, if you wished to buy into the fund). If the buy price is higher than the sell price, the fund charges a load. For example, suppose the buy price was $10 and the sell price (net asset value) was $9.15. This fund has an 8½ percent (85¢ divided by $10) load fee. Funds that do not have a load are indicated by *NL* ("no load") in the offering price column.

An "r" in newspaper listings denotes a redemption fee or deferred sales charge. Funds that have 12b-1 distribution charges are marked by a "p." A "t" indicates both redemption and 12b-1 fees.

Comparing Mutual-Fund Costs

The SEC enacted rules in 1988 that require funds to tabulate all fees and expenses in their prospectuses. This "fee table" must also show the cumulative expenses (expressed in dollars) paid on a $1,000 investment at the end of one-, three-, five-, and ten-year periods, assuming a 5 percent return on the fund's assets.

An SEC-required fee table for three representative mutual funds is shown in the exhibit on the next page. Note that Fund A has no loading or redemption charges and a modest operating expense ratio of 0.46 percent. While Fund B has no sales or redemption fees, it has a high operating expense ratio and a 12b-1 fee of ½ of 1 percent—bringing total fees to almost 2 percent annually. Fund C has a 7¼ percent load and "average" operating expenses of close to 1 percent per year. The bottom of the exhibit shows the total dollar costs per $1,000 of investment.

The annual percentage and dollar-cost differentials appear small but their impact can be substantial over time. The second exhibit, on page 454, entitled "The Impact of Mutual-Fund Costs," is based on a $10,000 initial investment in each of the funds and assumes each fund earns a gross return (before expenses) of 9 percent, similar to long-run historical returns. The exhibit shows that in twenty years the low-cost fund has far outdistanced its high-cost rivals. The low-cost fund produces more than $12,000 in returns compared with the high-cost fund. High fees are an important charge on investment results. Cost-conscious investors get the best investment results from no-load funds with low expense ratios.

A Sample Prospectus Fee Table

The following table illustrates *all* expenses and fees that a shareholder of three hypothetical mutual funds will incur. The purpose of this table is to assist the investor in understanding the various costs and expenses that a shareholder in the funds will bear directly or indirectly.

Shareholder Transaction Expenses	*Fund A*	*Fund B*	*Fund C*
Sales load imposed on purchases	None	None	7.25%
Sales load imposed on reinvested dividends	None	None	7.25
Redemption fees	None	None	None
Exchange fees	None	None	None

Annual Fund Operating Expenses	*Fund A*	*Fund B*	*Fund C*
Management expenses	0.13%	0.94%	0.70%
Investment advisory fees	0.20	—	—
Shareholder accounting costs	0.08	—	—
12b-1 fees	—	0.50	—
Distribution costs	0.02	—	—
Other expenses	0.03	0.46	0.25
Total operating expenses	**0.46%**	**1.90%**	**0.95%**

The following example illustrates the expenses that you would incur on a $1,000 investment over various time periods, assuming (1) a 5% annual rate of return and (2) redemption at the end of each period.

	Fund A	*Fund B*	*Fund C*
1 year	$ 5	$ 19	$ 82
3 years	15	59	101
5 years	26	99	121
10 years	58	207	181

Source: Vanguard Group of Investment Companies.

The Malkiel Step

   In previous editions, I highly recommended a strategy of buying shares in a special type of mutual fund called a closed-end fund (officially, a closed-end investment company). Closed-end funds differ from open-end mutual funds (the kind discussed in the previous section) in that they neither issue nor redeem shares after the initial offering. To buy or sell shares, you have to go to the market—generally the New York Stock Exchange.

The Impact of Mutual-Fund Costs[a]

	Fund A	Fund B	Fund C
Initial investment	$ 10,000	$ 10,000	$ 10,000
Day 1	10,000	10,000	9,275
5 years	15,064	14,091	13,660
10 years	22,693	19,856	20,117
15 years	34,186	27,980	29,627
20 years	51,499	39,427	43,632

[a]*This example is for illustration only; it does not imply the returns available on any particular investment made today.*

The price of the shares depends on what other investors are willing to pay for them and, unlike the price of shares in an open-end fund, is not necessarily related to net asset value. Thus, a closed-end fund can sell at a premium above or at a discount from its net asset value. During much of the 1970s and at the start of the 1980s, these funds were selling at substantial discounts from their net asset value. Closed-end funds hire professional managers, and their expenses are no higher than those of ordinary mutual funds. So for those who believe in professional investment management, here was a way to buy it at a discount and I told my readers so. One of the closed-end funds I recommended was run by John Neff.

A small proportion of the discounts on closed-end funds could be explained by rational considerations. Some funds had a substantial amount of unrealized capital gains in their portfolios that could affect the timing of an individual's tax liabilities. Other funds had substantial holdings of "letter stock," the sale of which was restricted and whose market prices might not have been accurate reflections of their true value. But these considerations could at best explain only a minor proportion of the discounts that ran as high as 40 percent during the late 1970s. My own explanation for the discounts ran in terms of an unexploited market inefficiency and I urged investors to take full advantage of the opportunity for as long as it lasted.

The beauty of buying these highly discounted closed-end funds was that, even if the discounts remained at high levels, investors would still reap extraordinary rewards from their purchase. If you could buy shares at a 25 percent discount, you would have $4 of asset value on which dividends could be earned for every $3 you invested. So even if the funds just equaled the market return, as believers in the random walk would expect, you would beat the averages.

It was like having a $100 savings account paying 5 percent interest. You deposit $100 and earn $5 interest each year. Only this savings account could be bought at a 25 percent discount— in other words, for $75. You still got $5 interest (5 percent of $100), but since you paid only $75 for the account, your rate of return was 6.67 percent (5 ÷ 75). Note that this increase in yield was in no way predicated on the discount narrowing. Even if you got only $75 back when you cashed in, you would still have received a big bonus in extra returns while holding the account. The discount on closed-end funds provided a similar bonus. You got your share of dividends from $1 worth of assets, even though you paid only 75¢.

I also recommended a number of special-purpose closed-end funds called the capital shares of dual-purpose funds. The details of these funds need not concern us here except to note that for these funds the discount was guaranteed to be eliminated at a specified maturity date during the early 1980s, when the shares could be either redeemed at net asset value or left invested with a regular open-end fund.

The strategy worked even better than expected. Discounts were eliminated for the special-purpose funds noted above and have narrowed significantly on the regular funds. While the publicity given closed-end funds in my books may have helped to close the discounts, I think the fundamental reason for the narrowing is that our capital markets are reasonably efficient. The market may misvalue assets from time to time, creating temporary inefficiencies. But if there is *truly* some area of pricing inefficiency that can be discovered by the market and dependably exploited, then value-seeking investors will take advantage of these opportunities and thereby eliminate them. Pricing irregularities may well exist and even persist for periods of time, but the financial laws of gravity will eventually take hold and true value will out.

I mentioned in previous editions that I gave my son, Jonathan, the royalties from the first edition of this book. Practicing what I preached, I invested them in a portfolio of closed-end and dual-purpose funds selling at substantial discounts. The investments were made mainly at the end of 1973 (near a peak in the market and thus a terrible time to invest) and near the end of 1974 (after the market had suffered a very sharp decline). The strategy has significantly outperformed the market and was an inflation beater even during the dismal markets of the 1970s. The narrowing of the discounts helped to produce quite spectacular returns. The strategy required courage, however. The 1973 investments, made when the market was very high, were under a good deal of water at the end of 1974.* Fortunately, new royalty checks came in at that time and more shares were bought for Jonathan, and the overall results have been more than satisfactory.

A Paradox

With their discounts for the most part dried up at the time this edition goes to press, most closed-end funds are no longer an especially attractive investment opportunity.† I have discussed them in some detail, however, because they illustrate an important paradox about investment advice, as well as the maxim that true values do eventually prevail in the market. There is a fundamental paradox about the usefulness of invest-

---

*According to my Rule 4, I might have switched to other closed-end funds to gain some tax advantages in 1974. However, Jonathan's tax situation did not warrant incurring the brokerage charges to effect such a switch.

†Indeed, when you buy a new closed-end fund at par value plus about 8 percent for underwriting commissions, not only do you get hit with the equivalent of a large loading fee but you also run the risk that the fund will sell at a discount at some time in the future. Never buy a closed-end fund at its initial offering price. It will almost invariably turn out to be a bad deal.

While most equity funds had relatively narrow discounts in 1994, the poor bond market, especially toward the end of the year, created some bargains in closed-end bond funds. Many bond funds sold at discounts of around 15 percent for a brief period late in 1994. Moreover, discounts widened on some equity funds during 1995. Tables of discounts appear weekly in the financial pages of many newspapers. It's worth checking these from time to time to see if discounts have temporarily widened. If so, closed-end funds can be a very good deal.

ment advice concerning specific securities. If the advice reaches enough people and they act on it, knowledge of the advice destroys its usefulness. If everyone knows about a "good buy" and they all rush in to buy, the price of the "good buy" will rise until it is no longer particularly attractive for investment. Indeed, there will be pressure on the price to rise as long as it is still a good buy.

This is the main logical pillar on which the efficient-market theory rests. If the spread of news is unimpeded, prices will react quickly so that they reflect all that is known about the particular situation. This led me to predict in the 1981 edition that such favorable discounts would not always be available. I wrote, "I would be very surprised to see the early-1980s levels of discounts perpetuate themselves indefinitely." For the same reason, I am skeptical that very simple currently popular rules such as "buy low P/E stocks" or "buy small company stocks" will perpetually produce unusually high risk-adjusted returns.

There is a well-known academic story about the random walk of a finance professor and two of his students. The finance professor, a proponent of the strongest form of the random-walk theory, was convinced that markets were always perfectly efficient. When he and the students spotted a $10 bill lying on the street, he told them to ignore it. "If it was really a $10 bill," he reasoned out loud, "someone would have already picked it up." Fortunately, the students were skeptical, not only of Wall Street professionals, but also of learned professors, and so they picked up the money.

Clearly, there is considerable logic to the finance professor's position. In markets where intelligent people are searching for value, it is unlikely that people will perpetually leave $10 bills around ready for the taking. But history tells us that unexploited opportunities do exist from time to time, as do periods of speculative excess pricing. We know of Dutchmen paying astronomical prices for tulip bulbs, of Englishmen splurging on the most improbable bubbles, and of modern institutional fund managers who convinced themselves that some stocks were so "nifty" and that the Japanese stock market was so unlike any other that any price was reasonable. And while investors were building castles in the air, real fundamental investment opportunities such as closed-end funds were passed by. Yet eventually excessive valuations were corrected and eventually investors did snatch up the bargain closed-end funds. Perhaps the finance professor's advice should have been, "You had better pick that $10 bill up quickly because if it's really there, someone else will surely take it." It is in this sense that I consider myself a random walker. I am convinced that true value will out, but from time to time it doesn't surprise me that anomalies do exist. There may be some $10 bills around at times and I'll certainly interrupt my random walk to purposefully stoop and pick them up.

Some Last Reflections on Our Walk

We are now at the end of our walk. Let's look back for a moment and see where we have been. It is clear that the ability to beat the average consistently is most rare. Neither fundamental analysis of a stock's firm foundation of value nor technical analysis of the market's propensity for building castles in the air can produce reliably superior results. Even the pros must hide their heads in shame when they compare their results with those obtained by the dart-board method of picking stocks. The only way to achieve above-average returns in an efficient market is to assume greater risk. But as Part Three showed, risk is far from a simple concept and neither beta nor any other single risk measure is likely to be adequate.

Sensible investment policies for individuals must then be developed in two steps. First, it is crucially important to understand the risk-return trade-offs that are available and to tailor your choice of securities to your temperament and requirements. Part Four provided a careful guide for this part of the walk, including a number of warm-up exercises concerning everything from tax planning to the management of reserve funds and a life-cycle guide to portfolio allocations. This chapter has covered the major part of our walk down Wall Street—three important steps for buying common stocks. I began by suggesting sensible strategies that are consistent with the existence of efficient markets. I recognized, however, that most investors will not be convinced that the random-walk theory is valid. Telling an investor there is no hope of beating the averages is like telling a six-year-old there is no Santa Claus. It takes the zing out of life.

For those of you incurably smitten with the speculative bug, who insist on picking individual stocks in an attempt to beat the market, I offered four rules. The odds are really stacked against you, but you may just get lucky and win big. I also suggested that you might want to place your bets on the few rare investment managers who, at least in the past, have shown some talent for finding those rare $10 bills lying around in the marketplace. The Random Walker's Address Book lists a number of funds with excellent long-term records and with moderate expenses. But never forget that past records are far from reliable guides to future performance.

Investing is a bit like lovemaking. Ultimately, it is really an art requiring a certain talent and the presence of a mysterious force called luck. Indeed, luck may be 99 percent responsible for the success of the very few people who have beaten the averages. "Although men flatter themselves with their great actions," La Rochefoucauld wrote, "they are not so often the result of great design as of chance."

The game of investing is like lovemaking in another important respect, too. It's much too much fun to give up. If you have the talent to recognize stocks that have good value, and the art to recognize a story that will catch the fancy of others, it's a great feeling to see the market vindicate you. Even if you are not so lucky, my rules will help you limit your risks and avoid much of the pain that is sometimes involved in the playing. If you know you will either win or at least not lose too much, you will be able to play the game with more satisfaction. At the very least, I hope this book makes the game all the more enjoyable.

A Random Walker's
Address Book and
Reference Guide to
Mutual Funds

Data on Selected Money-Market Funds

Fund Name	Year Organized	Minimum Initial Purchase ($)	Minimum Subsequent Purchase ($)	Minimum Amount for Check Withdrawal ($)	Net Assets ($millions)	7-Day Average Yield (%) (1995)	Average Maturity in Days (1995)	Recent Expense Ratio (%) (1994)
Vanguard Money Market Reserve (Prime Portfolio)[a] Vanguard Financial Center Valley Forge, PA 19482 800-662-7447	1975	3,000	50	250	15,927	5.79	39	0.32
Fidelity Spartan Money Market Fund 82 Devonshire St. Boston, MA 02109 800-544-8888	1989	20,000	1,000	1,000	7,600	5.66	34	0.44
Prudential Money Mart Assets[b] One Seaport Plaza New York, NY 10292 800-225-1852	1975	1,000	100	500	6,623	5.50	42	0.71
Dreyfus Basic Money Market Fund 144 Glenn Curtis Blvd. Uniondale, NY 11556 800-645-6561	1992	25,000 (5,000 for IRA)	1,000	1,000	1,704	5.76	53	0.65
Merrill Lynch CMA Money Market Fund 165 Broadway New York, NY 10080 800-221-7210	1979	20,000	None	500	28,653	5.39	61	0.55

Data on Selected Money-Market Funds *(Continued)*

Fund Name	Year Organized	Minimum Initial Purchase ($)	Minimum Subsequent Purchase ($)	Minimum Amount for Check Withdrawal ($)	Net Assets ($millions)	7-Day Average Yield (%) (1995)	Average Maturity in Days (1995)	Recent Expense Ratio (%) (1994)
USAA Money Market Fund USAA Building San Antonio, TX 78288 800-382-8722	1981	1,000	50	250	1,349	5.79	42	0.46
Smith Barney Cash Portfolio Class A (Available through local Smith Barney brokerage account only) 800-554-7835	1989	1,000	None	No direct checking from the fund	18,000	5.54	46	0.67
T. Rowe Price Prime Reserve Fund 100 East Pratt St. Baltimore, MD 21202 800-638-5660	1975	2,500 (1,000 for IRA)	100 (50 for IRA)	500	3,855	5.50	37	0.73

[a]I serve on the board of directors of this fund.
[b]I serve on the board of directors of Prudential Insurance Co.

Data on Selected Tax-Exempt Money-Market Funds

Fund Name	Year Organized	Minimum Initial Purchase ($)	Minimum Subsequent Purchase ($)	Minimum Amount for Check Withdrawal ($)	Net Assets ($millions)	7-Day Average Yield (%) (1995)	Average Maturity (in days) (1995)	Recent Expense Ratio (%) (1994)
Vanguard Municipal Bond/Money Market Portfolio[a] Vanguard Financial Center Valley Forge, PA 19482 800-662-7447	1980	3,000	50	250	4,180	3.64	42	0.20
Fidelity Spartan Municipal Money Market Fund	1991	25,000	1,000	1,000	2,200	3.65	77	0.33
Fidelity Tax Exempt Money Market Trust 82 Devonshire St. Boston, MA 02109 800-544-8888	1980	5,000	500	None	3,629	3.45	40	0.52
Prudential Tax-Free Money Market Fund[b] One Seaport Plaza New York, NY 10292 800-225-1852	1979	1,000	100	500	726	3.30	63	0.74
Dreyfus Basic Municipal Money Market Fund 144 Glenn Curtis Blvd. Uniondale, NY 11556 800-645-6561	1991	25,000	1,000	1,000	1,030	3.02	77	0.59
Merrill Lynch CMA Tax-Free Money Market Fund 165 Broadway New York, NY 10080 800-221-7210	1982	20,000	None	500	7,552	3.24	39	0.55

465

Data on Selected Tax-Exempt Money-Market Funds *(Continued)*

Fund Name	Year Organized	Minimum Initial Purchase ($)	Minimum Subsequent Purchase ($)	Minimum Amount for Check Withdrawal ($)	Net Assets ($millions)	7-Day Average Yield (%) (1995)	Average Maturity (in days) (1995)	Recent Expense Ratio (%) (1994)
Kemper Money Market Tax-Exempt Portfolio 12 South LaSalle St. Chicago, IL 60603 800-537-6001	1987	1,000	100	500	749	3.72	29	0.41
USAA Tax-Exempt Money Market Fund USAA Building San Antonio, TX 78288 800-382-8722	1984	3,000	50	250	1,478	3.56	55	0.40

[a]I serve on the board of directors of this fund.
[b]I serve on the board of directors of Prudential Insurance Co.

Data on Selected Long-Term Bond Funds

Fund Name	Maximum Initial Sales Charge (%)	Year Organized	Minimum Initial Purchase ($)	Minimum Subsequent Purchase ($)	Expense Ratio (%) (1994)	Net Assets ($millions)	5-Year Annualized Return (%) through 1994	Payroll Deduction or Bank Draft Plan Available	Keogh Plan Available	IRA Plan Available
Harbor Fund-Bond One Sea Gate Toledo, OH 43666 800-422-1050	None	1987	2,000	500	0.80	160	8.80	Yes	No	Yes
IDS Bond Fund American Express Financial Advisors 100 Roanoke Bldg. Minneapolis, MN 55402 800-328-8300	5.00	1974	2,000	100	0.68	2,134	9.07	Yes	Yes	Yes
Fidelity Investment Grade Bond Fund 82 Devonshire St. Boston, MA 02109 800-544-8888	None	1971	2,500	250	0.76	995	8.49	Yes	Yes	Yes
Vanguard Fixed Income (VFISF) Long-Term Corporate[a] Vanguard Financial Center Valley Forge, PA 19482 800-662-7447	None	1973	3,000	100	0.33	2,539	8.86	Yes	Yes	Yes

[a]I serve on the board of directors of this fund.

Data on Selected GNMA Bond Funds

Fund Name	Maximum Sales Charge (%)	Year Organized	Minimum Initial Purchase ($)	Minimum Subsequent Purchase ($)	Expense Ratio (%) (1994)	Net Assets ($millions)	Average Maturity (years) (1994)	5-Year Annualized Return (%) through 1994
Benham GNMA Income 1665 Charleston Rd. Mountain View, CA 94043 800-331-8331	None	1985	1,000	100	0.57	952	8.7	7.56
Dreyfus Investors GNMA 666 Old Country Road Garden City, NY 11530 800-645-6561	None	1987	2,500	100	0.95	1,459	NA	7.21
Fidelity Mortgage Securities 82 Devonshire St. Boston, MA 02109 800-544-8888	None	1984	2,500	250	0.79	349	8.7	7.41
T. Rowe Price GNMA 100 East Pratt St. Baltimore, MD 21202 800-638-5660	None	1985	2,500	100	0.77	758	8.3	7.06
Vanguard Fixed Income (VFISF) GNMA[a] Vanguard Financial Center Valley Forge, PA 19482 800-662-7447	None	1980	3,000	100	0.31	5,804	8.5	7.62

[a] I serve on the board of directors of this fund.

Data on Selected High-Yield Bond Funds

Fund Name	Maximum Sales Charge (%)	Year Organized	Minimum Initial Purchase ($)	Minimum Subsequent Purchase ($)	Expense Ratio (%) (1994)	Net Assets ($millions)	5-Year Annualized Return (%) through 1994	Payroll or Bank Plan Available	Keogh Plan Available	IRA Account Available
Advantage High-Yield Bond 280 Trumbull St. Hartford, CT 06103 800-241-2039	4.00	1986	500	250	1.35	136	13.17	Yes	No	No
Vanguard Fixed Income (VFISF) High-Yield Bond[a] Vanguard Financial Center Valley Forge, PA 19482 800-662-7447	None	1987	3,000	100	0.35	2,131	10.03	Yes	Yes	Yes
Paine Webber High-Income A 1285 Avenue of the Americas New York, NY 10019 800-647-1568	4.00	1984	1,000	100	0.90	269	12.58	Yes	No	Yes
Merrill Lynch Corporate Bond High-Income B 165 Broadway New York, NY 10000 800-637-3863	4.00	1988	1,000	100	1.28	2,274	11.84	Yes	Yes	Yes
Fidelity Capital & Income 82 Devonshire St. Boston, MA 02109 800-544-8888	None	1977	2,500	250	0.95	2,040	13.51	Yes	Yes	Yes

[a]I serve on the board of directors of this fund.

Data on Selected Bond Index Funds

Fund Name	Maximum Sales Charge (%)	Year Organized	Minimum Initial Purchase ($)	Minimum Subsequent Purchase ($)	Expense Ratio (%) (1994)	Net Assets ($millions)	Payroll or Bank Plan Available	Keogh Plan Available	IRA Account Available
Fidelity U.S. Bond Index[a] 82 Devonshire St. Boston, MA 02109 800-544-6666	None	1990	100,000	2,500	0.32	334	Yes	Yes	Yes
Portico Bond IMMDEX 207 East Buffalo St. Milwaukee, WI 53202 800-228-1024	None	1989	1,000	100	0.49	253	Yes	No	Yes
Vanguard Bond Index Fund: Total Bond[b] Vanguard Financial Center Valley Forge, PA 19482 800-662-7447	None	1986	3,000	100	0.18	1,728	Yes	Yes	Yes

[a] For institutional accounts only.
[b] I serve on the board of directors of this fund.

Data on Selected Tax-Exempt Bond Funds

Fund Name	Maximum Sales Charge (%)	Year Organized	Minimum Initial Purchase ($)	Minimum Subsequent Purchase ($)	Expense Ratio (%) (1994)	Net Assets ($millions)	5-Year Annualized Return (%) through 1994	Payroll or Bank Draft Plan Available
Dreyfus Municipal Bond 144 Glenn Curtis Blvd. Uniondale, NY 11556 800-645-6561	None	1976	2,500	100	0.68	3,496	6.27	Yes
Fidelity Municipal Bond 82 Devonshire St. Boston, MA 02109 800-544-8888	None	1976	2,500	250	0.54	1,006	6.09	Yes
Kemper Municipal Bond A 120 South LaSalle St. Chicago, IL 60603 800-621-1048	4.50	1976	1,000	100	0.57	3,403	6.73	Yes
Merrill Lynch Municipal Insured A 165 Broadway New York, NY 10080 800-637-3863	4.00	1977	1,000	50	0.42	1,692	6.62	Yes
T. Rowe Price Tax-Free Income 100 East Pratt St. Baltimore, MD 21202 800-683-5660	None	1976	2,500	100	0.59	1,233	6.73	Yes

Data on Selected Tax-Exempt Bond Funds *(Continued)*

Fund Name	Maximum Sales Charge (%)	Year Organized	Minimum Initial Purchase ($)	Minimum Subsequent Purchase ($)	Expense Ratio (%) (1994)	Net Assets ($millions)	5-Year Annualized Return (%) through 1994	Payroll or Bank Draft Plan Available
USAA Tax-Exempt Long-Term USAA Building San Antonio, TX 78288 800-382-8722	None	1981	3,000	50	0.39	1,661	6.45	Yes
Vanguard Municipal Insured Long-Term[a] Vanguard Financial Center Valley Forge, PA 19482 800-662-7447	None	1984	3,000 (500 for IRA)	100	0.20	1,743	7.01	Yes

[a]I serve on the board of directors of this fund.

Data on Selected Tax-Exempt High-Yield Bond Funds

Fund Name	Maximum Sales Charge (%)	Year Organized	Minimum Initial Purchase ($)	Minimum Subsequent Purchase ($)	Expense Ratio (%) (1994)	Net Assets ($millions)	5-Year Annualized Return (%) through 1994	Payroll or Bank Plan Available
Fidelity Aggressive Tax-Free Fund 82 Devonshire St. Boston, MA 02109 800-544-8888	None	1985	2,500	250	0.64	794	7.04	Yes
Franklin High-Yield Tax Free Income 777 Mariners Island Blvd. San Mateo, CA 94403 800-342-5236	4.30	1986	100	25	0.58	3,137	7.29	Yes
United Municipal High-Income 6300 Lamar Avenue P.O. Box 29217 Shawnee Mission, KS 66201 800-366-5465	4.30	1986	500	25	0.76	340	7.70	Yes
T. Rowe Price Tax Free High-Yield 100 East Pratt St. Baltimore, MD 21202 800-638-5660	None	1985	2,500	100	0.79	811	7.21	Yes
Vanguard Municipal High Yield[a] Vanguard Financial Center Valley Forge, PA 19482 800-662-7447	None	1978	3,000	100	0.20	1,585	7.39	Yes

[a]I serve on the board of directors of this fund.

Data on Selected "Index" Stock Funds

Fund Name	Maximum Sales Charge (%)	Year Organized	Minimum Initial Purchase ($)	Minimum Subsequent Purchase ($)	Expense Ratio (%) (1994)	Net Assets ($millions)	10-Year Annualized Return (%)	Portfolio Turnover Rate (%) (1994)	Payroll or Bank Plan Available	Keogh Plan Available	IRA Plan Available
Vanguard Index 500[a]	None	1976	3,000	100	0.19	9,204	14.05	7	Yes	Yes	Yes
Vanguard Index Extended Market	None	1987	3,000	100	0.20	957	NA	23	Yes	Yes	Yes
Vanguard Index Total Stock Market	None	1992	3,000	100	0.20	761	NA	3	Yes	Yes	Yes
Vanguard Index Small Cap Stock	None	1960	3,000	100	0.18	585	10.12	48	Yes	Yes	Yes
Vanguard International Equity European	None	1990	3,000	100	0.32	712	NA	5	Yes	Yes	Yes
Vanguard International Equity Pacific	None	1990	3,000	100	0.32	689	NA	3	Yes	Yes	Yes
Vanguard International Equity Emerging Market	None	1994	3,000	100	NA	94	NA	NA	Yes	Yes	Yes
Vanguard Financial Center Valley Forge, PA 19482 800-662-7447											
T. Rowe Price Equity Index 100 East Pratt St. Baltimore, MD 21202 800-638-5660	None	1990	2,500	100	0.45	266	NA	1	Yes	Yes	Yes

Data on Selected "Index" Stock Funds (Continued)

Fund Name	Maximum Sales Charge (%)	Year Organized	Minimum Initial Purchase ($)	Minimum Subsequent Purchase ($)	Expense Ratio (%) (1994)	Net Assets ($millions)	10-Year Annualized Return (%)	Portfolio Turnover Rate (%) (1994)	Payroll or Bank Plan Available	Keogh Plan Available	IRA Plan Available
Peoples S&P MidCap Index Dreyfus Corporation 144 Glenn Curtis Blvd. Uniondale, NY 11556 800-645-6561	None	1991	2,500	100	0.09	73	NA	16	Yes	Yes	Yes
Schwab 1,000 161 Montgomery St. San Francisco, CA 94104 800-526-8600	None	1991	1,000	NA	0.51	543	NA	3	Yes	Yes	Yes

aI serve on the board of directors of each of the Vanguard Index Funds.

475

Data on Selected "Equity-Income" Stock Funds

Fund Name	Maximum Sales Charge (%)	Year Organized	Minimum Initial Purchase ($)	Minimum Subsequent Purchase ($)	Expense Ratio (%) (1994)	Net Assets ($millions)	10-Year Annualized Return (%) through 1994	Portfolio Turnover Rate (%) (1994)	Risk Level (Beta)	Payroll or Bank Plan Available	Keogh Plan Available	IRA Plan Available
Prudential Equity-Income B[a] One Seaport Plaza New York, NY 10292 800-225-1852	5.00	1987	1,000	100	1.75	919	NA	57	0.83	Yes	No	Yes
Fidelity Equity-Income	2.00	1966	2,500	250	0.73	7,413	12.5	48	0.87	Yes	Yes	Yes
Fidelity Equity-Income II 82 Devonshire St. Boston, MA 02109 800-544-8888	None	1990	2,500	250	0.84	7,698	NA	81	0.82	Yes	Yes	Yes
T. Rowe Price Equity-Income 100 East Pratt St. Baltimore, MD 21202 800-638-5660	None	1985	2,500	100	0.91	3,144	NA	38	0.78	Yes	Yes	Yes
USAA Mutual Income Stock USAA Building San Antonio, TX 78228 800-382-8722	None	1987	1,000	50	0.73	1,172	NA	24	0.85	Yes	No	Yes

Data on Selected "Equity-Income" Stock Funds (Continued)

Fund Name	Maximum Sales Charge (%)	Year Organized	Minimum Initial Purchase ($)	Minimum Subsequent Purchase ($)	Expense Ratio (%) (1994)	Net Assets ($millions)	10-Year Annualized Return (%) through 1994	Portfolio Turnover Rate (%) (1994)	Risk Level (Beta)	Payroll or Bank Plan Available	Keogh Plan Available	IRA Plan Available
Vanguard Equity-Income[b] Vanguard Financial Center Valley Forge, PA 19482 800-662-7447	None	1988	3,000	100	0.43	869	NA	18	0.87	Yes	Yes	Yes

[a]I serve on the board of directors of Prudential Insurance Co.
[b]I serve on the board of directors of this fund.

Data on Selected "Growth and Income" Stock Funds

Fund Name	Maximum Sales Charge (%)	Year Organized	Minimum Initial Purchase ($)	Minimum Subsequent Purchase ($)	Expense Ratio (%) (1994)	Net Assets ($millions)	10-Year Annualized Return (%) through 1994	Portfolio Turnover Rate (%) (1994)	Risk Level (Beta)	Payroll or Bank Plan Available	Keogh Plan Available	IRA Plan Available
Mutual Beacon	None	1961	5,000	1,000	0.72	2,018	15.40	52	0.62	Yes	Yes	Yes
Mutual Shares	None	1949	5,000	100	0.73	3,713	14.77	48	0.72	Yes	Yes	Yes
Mutual Qualified 26 Broadway New York, NY 10004 800-553-3014	None	1980	1,000	50	0.76	1,776	15.13	56	0.69	Yes	Yes	Yes
Warburg Pincus Growth & Income 466 Lexington Avenue New York, NY 10017 800-257-5614	None	1988	1,000	500	1.28	628	NA	150	0.58	Yes	No	Yes
Safeco Equity Fund P.O. Box 36480 Seattle, WA 98124 800-426-6730	None	1932	1,000	100	0.85	438	16.16	33	1.15	Yes	Yes	Yes
Fidelity Growth & Income 82 Devonshire St. Boston, MA 02109 800-544-8888	3.00	1985	2,500	250	0.82	9,345	NA	92	0.80	Yes	Yes	Yes

Data on Selected "Growth and Income" Stock Funds (Continued)

Fund Name	Maximum Sales Charge (%)	Year Organized	Minimum Initial Purchase ($)	Minimum Subsequent Purchase ($)	Expense Ratio (%) (1994)	Net Assets ($millions)	10-Year Annualized Return (%) through 1994	Portfolio Turnover Rate (%) (1994)	Risk Level (Beta)	Payroll or Bank Plan Available	Keogh Plan Available	IRA Plan Available
Dodge & Cox Stock One Sansome St. San Francisco, CA 94104 800-621-3979	None	1965	2,500	100	0.61	524	15.41	15	1.02	Yes	No	Yes
Lexington Corporate Leaders Trust P.O. Box 1515 Park 80 West Plaza Two Saddlebrook, NJ 07662 800-526-0057	None	1935	1,000	50	0.62	155	14.86	NA	1.03	Yes	Yes	Yes
Vanguard Windsor II[a] Vanguard Financial Center Valley Forge, PA 19482 800-662-7447	None	1985	3,000	100	0.39	7,896	13.87	24	0.91	Yes	Yes	Yes

[a] I serve on the board of directors of this fund.

Data on Selected "Growth" Stock Funds

Fund Name	Maximum Sales Charge (%)	Year Organized	Minimum Initial Purchase ($)	Minimum Subsequent Purchase ($)	Expense Ratio (%) (1994)	Net Assets ($millions)	10-Year Annualized Return (%) through 1994	Portfolio Turnover Rate (%) (1994)	Risk Level (Beta)	Payroll or Bank Plan Available	Keogh Plan Available	IRA Plan Available
Crabbe Huson Special Fund	None	1987	2,000	500	1.48	346	NA	73	1.04	Yes	No	Yes
Crabbe Huson Equity Fund P.O. Box 6559 Portland, OR 97228 800-541-9732	None	1988	2,000	500	1.49	155	NA	114	0.88	Yes	No	Yes
Vanguard/Primecap[a] Vanguard Financial Center Valley Forge, PA 19482 800-662-7447	None	1984	3,000	100	0.68	1,472	15.54	8	1.10	Yes	Yes	Yes
Fidelity Blue Chip Growth	3.00	1987	2,500	250	1.22	3,287	NA	271	1.04	Yes	Yes	Yes
Fidelity Contrafund	3.00	1967	2,500	250	1.03	8,682	18.55	275	0.91	Yes	Yes	Yes
Fidelity Magellan 82 Devonshire St. Boston, MA 02109 800-544-8888	3.00	1963	2,500	250	0.96	36,442	17.95	137	1.01	Yes	Yes	Yes
Berger 100 210 University Blvd., Suite 900 Denver, CO 80602 800-333-1001	None	1966	250	50	1.70	2,113	19.14	64	1.10	Yes	Yes	Yes

Data on Selected "Growth" Stock Funds (Continued)

Fund Name	Maximum Sales Charge (%)	Year Organized	Minimum Initial Purchase ($)	Minimum Subsequent Purchase ($)	Expense Ratio (%) (1994)	Net Assets ($millions)	10-Year Annualized Return (%) through 1994	Portfolio Turnover Rate (%) (1994)	Risk Level (Beta)	Payroll or Bank Plan Available	Keogh Plan Available	IRA Plan Available
Prudential Equity B[b] One Seaport Plaza New York, NY 10292 800-225-1852	5.00	1982	1,000	100	1.66	1,891	14.25	21	0.92	Yes	No	Yes

[a]I serve on the board of directors of this fund. As of early 1995 this fund is temporarily closed.
[b]I serve on the board of directors of Prudential Insurance Co.

481

Data on Selected Small-Company Stock Funds

Fund Name	Maximum Sales Charge (%)	Year Organized	Minimum Initial Purchase ($)	Minimum Subsequent Purchase ($)	Expense Ratio (%) (1994)	Net Assets ($millions)	10-Year Annualized Return (%) through 1994	Portfolio Turnover Rate (%) (1994)	Risk Level (Beta)	Payroll or Bank Plan Available	Keogh Plan Available	IRA Plan Available
20th Century Giftrust Investors P.O. Box 419200 Kansas City, MO 64141–6200 800-345-2021	None	1983	250	25	1.00	274	25.58	101	1.32	No	No	No
MAS Small Cap Value One Tower Bridge #1150 P.O. Box 868 West Conshohocken, PA 19428 800-354-8185	None	1986	Closed	1,000	0.88	322	NA	162	0.89	No	No	No
PBHG Growth Fund 680 East Swedesford Rd. Wayne, PA 19087 800-433-0051	None	1985	1,000	None	1.40	658	NA	94	1.34	Yes	No	Yes
Regis ICM Small Company Fund One International Place, 44th Floor 100 Oliver St. Boston, MA 02110 800-638-7983	None	1989	100,000	1,000	0.95	126	NA	47	0.68	Yes	Yes	Yes

Data on Selected Small-Company Stock Funds (Continued)

Fund Name	Maximum Sales Charge (%)	Year Organized	Minimum Initial Purchase ($)	Minimum Subsequent Purchase ($)	Expense Ratio (%) (1994)	Net Assets ($millions)	10-Year Annualized Return (%) through 1994	Portfolio Turnover Rate (%) (1994)	Risk Level (Beta)	Payroll or Bank Plan Available	Keogh Plan Available	IRA Plan Available
Vanguard Explorer Fund[a] Vanguard Financial Center Valley Forge, PA 14982 800-662-7447	None	1967	3,000	100	0.70	1,093	10.11	76	0.82	Yes	Yes	Yes

[a]I serve on the board of directors of this fund.

Data on Selected International Stock Funds

Fund Name	Maximum Sales Charge (%)	Year Organized	Minimum Initial Purchase ($)	Minimum Subsequent Purchase ($)	Expense Ratio (%) (1994)	Net Assets ($millions)	10-Year Annualized Return (%) through 1994	Portfolio Turnover Rate (%) (1994)	Payroll or Bank Plan Available	Keogh Plan Available	IRA Plan Available
20th Century International Equity P.O. Box 419200 Kansas City, MO 64141–6200 800-345-2021	None	1991	2,500	25	1.90	1,272	NA	282	Yes	Yes	Yes
Janus Worldwide 100 Fillmore St., Suite 300 Denver, CO 80206 800-525-8983	None	1991	1,000	50	1.19	1,543	NA	141	Yes	Yes	Yes
Managers International Equity 40 Richards Avenue Norwalk, CT 06854 800-835-3879	None	1986	10,000	None	1.45	88	NA	26	Yes	Yes	Yes
USAA International Fund USAA Building San Antonio, TX 78288 800-382-8722	None	1988	1,000	50	1.31	338	NA	44	Yes	No	Yes
Vanguard Trustees' Equity International[a] Vanguard Financial Center Valley Forge, PA 19482 800-662-7447	None	1983	10,000	1,000	0.32	1,110	16.85	39	Yes	Yes	Yes

Data on Selected International Stock Funds *(Continued)*

Fund Name	Maximum Sales Charge (%)	Year Organized	Minimum Initial Purchase ($)	Minimum Subsequent Purchase ($)	Expense Ratio (%) (1994)	Net Assets ($millions)	10-Year Annualized Return (%) through 1994	Portfolio Turnover Rate (%) (1994)	Payroll or Bank Plan Available	Keogh Plan Available	IRA Plan Available
T. Rowe Price International Stock Fund 100 East Pratt St. Baltimore, MD 21202 800-638-5660	None	1980	2,500	100	0.96	5,982	18.00	22	Yes	Yes	Yes
Scudder International Fund Two International Plaza Boston, MA 02110 800-225-2470	None	1957	1,000	100	1.19	2,300	16.19	45	Yes	Yes	Yes

[a]I serve on the board of directors of this fund.

Data on Selected Emerging-Markets Stock Funds

Fund Name	Maximum Sales Charge (%)	Year Organized	Minimum Initial Purchase ($)	Minimum Subsequent Purchase ($)	Expense Ratio (%) (1994)	Net Assets ($millions)	10-Year Annualized Return (%) through 1994	Portfolio Turnover Rate (%) (1994)	Risk Level (Beta)	Payroll or Bank Plan Available	Keogh Plan Available	IRA Plan Available
Fidelity Emerging Markets 82 Devonshire St. Boston, MA 02109 800-544-8888	3.00	1990	2,500	250	1.55	1,508	NA	215	1.04	Yes	Yes	Yes
Newport Tiger Fund 1500 Forest Avenue, Suite 223 Richmond, VA 23229 800-776-5455	5.00	1989	1,000	100	1.56	445	NA	10	1.09	No	No	Yes
T. Rowe Price New Asia 100 East Pratt St. Baltimore, MD 21202 800-638-5660	None	1990	2,500	100	1.22	2,062	NA	63	1.12	Yes	Yes	Yes
Lexington Worldwide Emerging Market Fund P.O. Box 1515 Park 80 West Plaza Two Saddlebrook, NJ 07662 800-526-0057	None	1969	1,000	50	1.71	332	12.94	67	1.04	Yes	No	Yes

Data on Selected Emerging-Markets Stock Funds (Continued)

Fund Name	Maximum Sales Charge (%)	Year Organized	Minimum Initial Purchase ($)	Minimum Subsequent Purchase ($)	Expense Ratio (%) (1994)	Net Assets ($millions)	10-Year Annualized Return (%) through 1994	Portfolio Turnover Rate (%) (1994)	Risk Level (Beta)	Payroll or Bank Plan Available	Keogh Plan Available	IRA Plan Available
Vanguard International Equity Emerging Markets[a] Vanguard Financial Center Valley Forge, PA 19482 800-662-7447	None	1994	3,000	100	NA	94	NA	NA	NA	Yes	Yes	Yes

[a]I serve on the board of directors of this fund. This fund is an index fund.

Bibliography

I have suppressed my academic proclivity for sprinkling each page with footnotes to learned references showing who said what on particular issues. I do hope, however, that this bibliography indicates clearly the sources of the studies I have discussed and provides useful additional readings for those interested in particular points. The references are grouped by chapter, and in some cases (especially for Chapters Six and Seven), notation is made of what the sources contain. Where certain references are cited throughout this book, they are listed only in the first chapter for which they were used.

PART ONE

Chapter 1.

Bernard Baruch, *My Own Story*. Holt, 1957.

Jess H. Chua and Richard S. Woodward, "J. M. Keynes's Investment Performance: A Note." *The Journal of Finance,* March 1983.

Irving Fisher, *The Theory of Interest*. Kelley, 1961.

Benjamin Graham and David L. Dodd, *Security Analysis,* 1st ed. McGraw-Hill, 1934.

Samuel Eliot Guild, *Stock Growth and Discount Tables*. Financial Publishers, 1931.

John M. Keynes, *The General Theory of Employment, Interest and Money*. Harcourt, 1936.

Oskar Morgenstern and Clive William John Granger, *Predictability of Stock Market Prices*. Heath Lexington, 1970.

"Adam Smith," *The Money Game*. Random House, 1968.

John von Neuman and Oskar Morgenstern, *Theory of Games and Economic Behavior*. Princeton University Press, 1941.

John Burr Williams, *The Theory of Investment Value*. Harvard University Press, 1938.

Chapter 2.

Frederick L. Allen, *Only Yesterday.* Harper, 1931.

Edward Angly, *Oh Yeah?* Viking, 1931.

Walter Bagehot, *Lombard Street.* London: Murray, 1922.

Bruce Barton, *The Man Nobody Knows.* Bobbs-Merrill, 1925.

John N. Brooks, *Once in Golconda.* Harper & Row, 1969.

———, *The Seven Fat Years.* Harper, 1958.

John Carswell, *The South Sea Bubble.* London: Cresset Press, 1960.

Lester V. Chandler, *America's Greatest Depression 1929–1941.* Harper & Row, 1970.

William Cobbett, *The Parliamentary History of England,* Volume VII. London: Hansard, 1811.

Cedric B. Cowing, *Populists, Plungers, and Progressives.* Princeton University Press, 1965.

Charles Amos Dice, *New Levels in the Stock Market.* McGraw-Hill, 1929.

John Kenneth Galbraith, *The Great Crash, 1929.* Houghton Mifflin, 1955.

Peter M. Garber, "Tulipmania." Unpublished manuscript, Brown University, 1988.

Gustave Le Bon, *The Crowd: A Study of the Popular Mind.* Woking and London: Unwin Bros., 1895.

Charles Mackay, *Memoirs of Extraordinary Popular Delusions,* Volume I. Lindsay, 1850. (My discussions of the tulip-bulb craze and the South Sea Bubble rely heavily on Mackay's description.)

Cabell Phillips, *The New York Times Chronicle of American Life: From the Crash to the Blitz, 1929–1939.* Macmillan, 1969.

Nicolaas W. Posthumus, *Inquiry into the History of Prices in Holland.* Leiden: Brill, 1964.

Jelle C. Riemersma, *Religious Factors in Early Dutch Capitalism 1550–1650.* The Hague: Mouton, 1967.

Lionel Robbins, *The Great Depression.* London: Macmillan, 1935.

Robert Sobel, *Panic on Wall Street.* Macmillan, 1968.

Dana L. Thomas, *The Plungers and the Peacocks.* Putnam, 1967.

Twentieth Century Fund, *The Security Markets.* 1935.

Chapter 3.

Bill Adler, ed., *The Wall Street Reader.* World, 1970.

Daniel Akst, *Wonder Boy: Barry Minkow, the Kid Who Swindled Wall Street.* Charles Scribner's Sons, 1990.

David L. Babson and Company, Inc., "Wall Street 'Discovers' Investment Quality." *Weekly Staff Letter,* August 6, 1970.

Hurd Baruch, *Wall Street: Security Risk.* Acropolis, 1971.

Murray Teigh Bloom, *Rogues to Riches.* Putnam, 1971.

John Brooks, *Business Adventures.* Weybright and Talley, 1969.

McGeorge Bundy, President's Review in *The Ford Foundation Annual Report 1966.* February 1, 1967.

Joe Domanick, *Faking it in America: Barry Minkow and the Great ZZZZ Best Scam.* Contemporary Books, 1989.

Christopher Elias, *Fleecing the Lambs.* Regnery, 1971.

John G. Fuller, *The Money Changers.* Dial, 1962.

William W. Helman, *Conglomerates—What Happened?* Smith, Barney & Co., September 24, 1969.

Sidney K. Margolius, *The Innocent Investor and the Shaky Ground Floor.* Trident, 1971.

Martin Mayer, *New Breed on Wall Street.* Macmillan, 1969.

———, *Wall Street: Men and Money.* Harper, 1955.

Securities and Exchange Commission, *Special Study of the Securities Market.* House Document No. 95, 88th Congress. U.S. Government Printing Office, 1963.

Robert Sobel, *The Big Board.* Free Press, 1965.

"So Long as It's Electronic," *Forbes,* February 15, 1959.

Andrew Tobias, *The Funny Money Game.* Playboy Press, 1971.

John Wall, "Want to Get Rich Quick?" *Barron's,* February 5, 1968.

Chapter 4.

Burton G. Malkiel and John G. Cragg, "Expectations and the Structure of Share Prices." *American Economic Review,* September 1970. (This is a formal empirical study documenting the changing valuation standards of the market over time. It is the study referred to in the text.)

J. Peter Williamson, *Investments.* Praeger, 1971.

PART TWO

Chapter 5.

Benjamin Graham, *The Intelligent Investor.* Harper & Row, 1965.

Albert Haas, Jr., and Don D. Jackson, M.D., *Bulls, Bears and Dr. Freud.* World, 1967.

Gerald M. Loeb, *The Battle for Investment Survival.* Simon & Schuster, 1965.

John Magee and Robert Davis Edwards, *Technical Analysis of Stock Trends.* Stock Trend Service, 1954.

Fred Schwed, Jr., *Where Are the Customers' Yachts?* Simon & Schuster, 1940.

Chapter 6.

The following are general works summarizing parts of the academic literature on the efficacy of technical analysis:

Fischer Black, "Implications of the Random Walk Hypothesis for Portfolio Management." *Financial Analysts Journal,* March–April 1971.
   (A layman's survey of a number of studies.)

Richard A. Brealey, *An Introduction to Risk and Return from Common Stocks.* M.I.T. Press, 1969.
   (Only slightly mathematical.)

———, *Security Prices in a Competitive Market: More about Risk and Return from Common Stocks.* M.I.T. Press, 1971.
   (Only slightly mathematical.)

——— and Stewart Myers, *Principles of Corporate Finance.* McGraw-Hill, 1981.

Paul Cootner, ed., *The Random Character of Stock Market Prices.* M.I.T. Press, 1964.
   (A compendium of mathematical articles.)

Eugene F. Fama, "Efficient Capital Markets: A Review of Theory and Empirical Work," *Journal of Finance,* May 1970.
   (An excellent but highly mathematical summary of empirical research on the random-walk theory.)

James H. Lorie and Mary T. Hamilton, *The Stock Market: Theories and Evidence.* Irwin, 1975.
   (Only slightly mathematical.)

James H. Lorie and Richard A. Brealey, eds., *Modern Developments in Investment Management: A Book of Readings.* Praeger, 1972.

Specific studies of technical systems follow:

Sidney S. Alexander, "Price Movements in Speculative Markets: Trends or Random Walks." *Industrial Management Review,* May 1961.

Louis Bachelier, *Théorie de la Spéculation.* Paris: Gauthier-Villars, 1900.

Paul Cootner, "Stock Prices: Random vs. Systematic Changes." *Industrial Management Review,* Spring 1962.

John L. Evans, "The Random Walk Hypothesis, Portfolio Analysis and the Buy-and-Hold Criterion." *Journal of Financial and Quantitative Analysis,* September 1968.

Eugene F. Fama, "Mandelbrot and the Stable Paretian Hypothesis." *Journal of Business,* October 1963.

———, "Tomorrow on the New York Stock Exchange." *Journal of Business,* July 1965.

——— and Marshall E. Blume, "Filter Rules and Stock-Market Trading." *Journal of Business,* January 1966.

———, Lawrence Fisher, Michael C. Jensen, and Richard Roll, "The Adjustment of Stock Prices to New Information." *International Economic Review,* February 1969.

Michael D. Godfrey, C.W.J. Granger, and O. Morgenstern, "The Random-Walk Hypothesis of Stock Market Behavior." *Kyklos,* 1964.

C.W.J. Granger and O. Morgenstern, "Spectral Analysis of New York Stock Market Prices." *Kyklos,* 1963.

F.E. James, Jr., "Monthly Moving Averages—An Effective Investment Tool?" *Journal of Financial and Quantitative Analysis,* September 1968.

Michael C. Jensen, "Random Walks: Reality or Myth—Comment." *Financial Analysts Journal,* November–December 1967.

——— and George A. Benington, "Random Walks and Technical Theories: Some Additional Evidence." *Journal of Finance,* May 1970.

Charles P. Jones and Robert H. Litzenberger, "Quarterly Earnings Reports and Intermediate Stock Price Trends." *Journal of Finance,* March 1970.

Maurice G. Kendall, "The Analysis of Economic Time-Series, Part I: Prices." *Journal of the Royal Statistical Society,* 1953.

Thomas J. Kewley and Richard A. Stevenson, "The Odd-Lot Theory as Revealed by Purchase and Sale Statistics for Individual Stocks." *Financial Analysts Journal,* September–October 1967.

Robert A. Levy, "Random Walks: Reality or Myth." *Financial Analysts Journal,* November–December 1967.

———, "Relative Strength as a Criterion for Investment Selection." *Journal of Finance,* December 1967.

———, "The Predictive Significance of Five-Point Chart Patterns." *Journal of Business,* July 1971.

Benoit Mandelbrot, "Forecasts of Future Prices, Unbiased Markets, and 'Martingale' Models." *Journal of Business,* Special Supplement, January 1966.

——— and Howard M. Taylor, "On the Distribution of Stock Price Differences." *Operations Research,* November–December 1967.

Victor Niederhoffer and M.F.M. Osborne, "Market Making and Reversal on the Stock Exchange." *Journal of the American Statistical Association,* December 1966.

M.F.M. Osborne, "Brownian Motion in the Stock Market." *Operations Research,* March–April 1959.

———, "Periodic Structure in the Brownian Motion of Stock Prices." *Operations Research,* May–June 1962.

Harry V. Roberts, "Stock Market 'Patterns' and Financial Analysis: Methodological Suggestions." *Journal of Finance,* March 1959.

Paul A. Samuelson, "Proof that Properly Anticipated Prices Fluctuate Randomly." *Industrial Management Review,* Spring 1965.

Alan Seelenfreund, George G. C. Parker, and James C. Van Horne, "Stock Price Behavior and Trading." *Journal of Financial and Quantitative Analysis,* September 1968.

Seymour Smidt, "A New Look at the Random Walk Hypothesis." *Journal of Financial and Quantitative Analysis,* September 1968.

H. Theil and C. T. Leenders, "Tomorrow on the Amsterdam Stock Exchange." *Journal of Business,* July 1965.

James C. Van Horne and George G. C. Parker, "The Random-Walk Theory: An Empirical Test." *Financial Analysts Journal,* November–December 1967.

Charles C. Ying, "Stock Market Prices and Volumes of Sales." *Econometrica,* July 1966.

Alan J. Zakon and James C. Pennypacker, "An Analysis of the Advance Decline Line as a Stock Market Indicator." *Journal of Financial and Quantitative Analysis,* September 1968.

Other works cited:

Ira Cobleigh, *Happiness Is a Stock that Doubles in a Year.* Geis, 1967.

———, "Bull Markets and Bare Knees." In *The Wall Street Reader,* Bill Adler, ed. World, 1970.

Nicholas Darvas, *How I Made Two Million Dollars in the Stock Market.* American Research Council, 1960.

Garfield A. Drew, "The Misunderstood Odd-Lotter." *Barron's,* June 25, 1962.

———, "A Clarification of the Odd Lot Theory." *Financial Analysts Journal,* September–October 1967.

Thomas Gilovich, Robert Vallone, and Amos Tversky, "The Hot Hand in Basketball: On the Misperception of Random Sequences." *Cognitive Psychology,* July 1985.

Ralph A. Rotnem, "Measuring Mass Opinion in the Stock Market." *AIC* (American International College) *Journal,* Winter 1972.

Michael Sivvy, "Joe Granville: Messiah or Menace?" *Financial World,* June 15, 1980.

John Slatter, "Lambs in the Street." *Barron's,* January 31, 1966.

Edward O. Thorp, *Beat the Dealer.* Random House, 1966.

Chapter 7.

The following are general works summarizing parts of the academic literature on the efficacy of fundamental analysis:

Irwin Friend, Marshall Blume, and Jean Crockett, *Mutual Funds and Other Institutional Investors.* McGraw-Hill, 1970.
(A nonmathematical and very readable report on the performance of mutual funds.)

Michael C. Jensen, "Capital Markets: Theory and Evidence." *Bell Journal of Economics and Management Science,* Autumn 1972.
(An excellent but highly mathematical summary of findings on the broad form of the random-walk theory.)

Specific studies of fundamental analysis follow:

Fred D. Arditti, "Another Look at Mutual Fund Performance." *Journal of Financial and Quantitative Analysis,* June 1971.

Marshall E. Blume, "The Measurement of Investment Performance." *Wall Street Transcript,* July 26, 1971.

Robert S. Carlson, "Aggregate Performance of Mutual Funds, 1948–1967." *Journal of Financial and Quantitative Analysis,* March 1970.

Jess H. Chua and Richard S. Woodward, *Gains from Stock Market Timing.* Salomon Bros. Center, New York University, 1988.

Kalman J. Cohen and Jerry A. Pogue, "Some Comments concerning Mutual Fund versus Random Portfolio Performance." *Journal of Business,* April 1968.

Irwin Friend, F.E. Brown, Edward S. Herman, and Douglas Vickers, *A Study of Mutual Funds.* 87th Congress, House Report No. 2274. U.S. Government Printing Office, 1962.

Irwin Friend and Douglas Vickers, "Portfolio Selection and Investment Performance." *Journal of Finance,* September 1965.

Ira Horowitz, "The 'Reward-to-Variability' Ratio and Mutual Fund Performance." *Journal of Business,* October 1966.

———, "The Varying (?) Quality of Investment Trust Management." *Journal of the American Statistical Association,* December 1963.

Michael C. Jensen, "The Performance of Mutual Funds in the Period 1945–64." *Journal of Finance,* May 1968.

———, "Risk, the Pricing of Capital Assets, and the Evaluation of

Investment Portfolios." *Journal of Business,* April 1969.

Robert A. Levy, "Fund Managers Are Better than Dart Throwers." *Institutional Investor,* April 1971.

I.M.D. Little, "Higgledy Piggledy Growth." *Bulletin of the Oxford University Institute of Economics and Statistics,* November 1962.

Burton G. Malkiel and John G. Cragg, "Expectations and the Valuation of Shares." National Bureau of Economic Research, Working Paper No. 471, April 1980.

Harry Markowitz, *Portfolio Selection: Efficient Diversification of Investments.* Wiley, 1959.

Everett Mattlin, "Are the Days of the Numbers Games Numbered?" *Institutional Investor,* November 1971.

"Portfolio Management: U.S. Senate Style." *Institutional Investor,* October 1957.

D. L. Rosenhan, "On Being Sane in Insane Places." *Science,* January 1973.

Paul A. Samuelson, statement before *Committee on Banking and Currency,* U.S. Senate, August 2, 1967, re mutual fund legislation of 1967.

G. William Schwert, "Size and Stock Returns, and Other Empirical Regularities." *Journal of Financial Economics,* June 1983.

William F. Sharpe, "Mutual Fund Performance." *Journal of Business,* Special Supplement, January 1966.

———, *Portfolio Theory and Capital Markets.* McGraw-Hill, 1970.

———, "Risk-Aversion in the Stock Market: Some Empirical Evidence." *Journal of Finance,* September 1965.

John P. Shelton, "The Value Line Contest: A Test of the Predictability of Stock-Price Changes." *Journal of Business,* 1967.

Robert J. Shiller, "Do Stock Prices Move Too Much to be Justified by Subsequent Changes in Dividends?" *American Economic Review,* June 1981.

Jack L. Treymor, "How to Rate Management of Investment Funds." *Harvard Business Review,* January–February 1965.

Oldrich Vasicek and John A. McQuown, "The Efficient Market Model." *Financial Analysts Journal,* September–October 1972.

Henry C. Wallich, "What Really Is the Value of Investment Advice?" *Institutional Investor,* August 1967.

———, "What Does the Random Walk Hypothesis Mean to Security Analysts?" *Financial Analysts Journal,* March–April 1968.

Richard R. West, "Mutual Fund Performance and the Theory of Capital Asset Pricing: Some Comments." *Journal of Business,* April 1968.

Chapter 8.

Ray Ball, "Anomalies in Relationships between Securities' Yields and Yield-Surrogates." *Journal of Financial Economics*, June/September 1978.

Rolf Banz, "The Relationship between Return and Market Value of Common Stocks." *Journal of Financial Economics*, March 1981.

Sanjoy Basu, "The Relationship between Earnings' Yield, Market Value and the Return for NYSE Common Stocks: Further Evidence." *Journal of Financial Economics*, June 1983.

———, "Investment Performance of Common Stocks in Relation to Their Price-Earnings Ratios: A Test of the Efficient Market Hypothesis." *Journal of Finance*, June, 1977.

John Campbell, "Stock Returns and the Term Structure." *Journal of Financial Economics*, June 1987.

K. C. Chan, "On the Contrarian Investment Strategy." *Journal of Business*, April 1988.

Warner De Bondt and Richard Thaler, "Does the Stock Market Overreact?" *Journal of Finance*, July 1985.

Peter Dodd, *The Effect on Market Value of Transactions in the Market for Corporate Control.* Proceedings of Seminar on the Analysis of Security Prices, CRSP, University of Chicago, May 1981.

Eugene Fama, "The Behavior of Stock Market Prices." *Journal of Business*, January 1965.

———, "Efficient Capital Markets: II." *Journal of Finance*, December 1991.

———, Lawrence Fisher, Michael Jensen, and Richard Roll, "The Adjustment of Stock Prices to New Information." *International Economic Review*, February 1969.

——— and Kenneth French, "Permanent and Temporary Components of Stock Prices." *Journal of Political Economy*, April 1988.

Zsuzsanna Fluck, Burton G. Malkiel, and Richard E. Quandt, "The Predictability of Stock Returns and the Efficient Market Hypothesis." Financial Research Center Memorandum No. 139, Princeton University, 1993.

Kenneth French, "Stock Returns and the Weekend Effect." *Journal of Financial Economics*, March 1980.

——— and Richard Roll, "Stock Return Variances." *Journal of Financial Economics*, September 1986.

Ben Friedman and K. Kuttner, "Times Varying Risk Perceptions and the Pricing of Risky Assets." National Bureau of Economic Research, Working Paper No. 2694, 1988.

Mustafa N. Gultekin and N. Bulent Gultekin, "Stock Market Seasonality: International Evidence." *Journal of Financial Economics,* December 1983.

Robert A. Haugen, *The New Finance: The Case Against Efficient Markets.* Prentice-Hall, 1995.

Robert Haugen and Josef Lakonishok, *The Incredible January Effect.* Dow Jones-Irwin, 1988.

J. Jaffe and R. Westerfield, "The Week-End Effect in Common Stock Returns: The International Evidence." Unpublished manuscript, University of Pennsylvania, 1984.

Donald Keim, "Size Related Anomalies and Stock Return Seasonality: Further Empirical Evidence." *Journal of Financial Economics,* June 1983.

Alan Kleidon, "Variance Bounds Tests and Stock Price Valuation Models." *Journal of Political Economy,* October 1986.

———, "Bubbles, Fads and Stock Price Volatility Tests: A Partial Evaluation: Discussion." *Journal of Finance,* July, 1988.

Bruce Lehmann, "Fads, Martingales and Market Efficiency." Unpublished working paper, Hoover Institution, June 1988.

Andrew Lo and A. Craig MacKinlay, "Stock Market Prices Do Not Follow Random Walks." *Review of Financial Studies,* Spring 1988.

———, "When are Contrarian Profits Due to Stock Market Overreaction?" *Review of Financial Studies,* Vol. 3, No. 2, 1990.

Terry Marsh and Robert Merton, "Aggregate Dividend Behavior and Its Implications for Tests of Stock Market Rationality." Working Paper, Sloan School of Management, September 1983.

James Patell and Mark Wolfson, "The Intraday Speed of Adjustment of Stock Prices to Earnings and Dividend Announcements." *Journal of Financial Economics,* June 1984.

James Poterba and Lawrence Summers, "Mean Reversion in Stock Prices: Evidence and Implications." *Journal of Financial Economics,* October 1988.

R. Rendleman, C. Jones, and H. Latané, "Empirical Anomalies Based on Unexpected Earnings and the Importance of Risk Adjustments." *Journal of Financial Economics,* November 1982.

Richard Roll, "Orange Juice and Weather." *American Economic Review,* December 1984.

———, "R^2." *Journal of Finance,* July 1988.

———, "Comments: Symposium on Volatility in U.S. and Japanese Stock Markets." *Journal of Applied Corporate Finance,* Spring 1992.

PART THREE

Chapter 9.

The following are general discussions of capital-asset pricing theory arranged in increasing order of difficulty:

James H. Lorie and Mary T. Hamilton. *The Stock Market: Theories and Evidence.* Irwin, 1975, Chapters 10–12.

Franco Modigliani and Gerald A. Pogue, "An Introduction to Risk and Return, I." *Financial Analysts Journal,* March–April 1974.

———, "An Introduction to Risk and Return, II." *Financial Analysts Journal,* May–June 1974.

Michael C. Jensen, "Capital Markets, Theory and Evidence." *Bell Journal of Economics and Management Science,* Autumn 1972.

A number of more specific and technical studies follow:

William J. Baumol, "Mathematical Analysis of Portfolio Selection." *Financial Analysts Journal,* September-October 1966.

Fischer Black, Michael C. Jensen, and Myron Scholes, "The Capital Asset Pricing Model: Some Empirical Tests." In *Studies in the Theory of Capital Markets,* Michael C. Jensen. ed. Praeger, 1972.

Murray T. Bloom, *Rogues to Riches.* Putnam, 1971.

Eugene F. Fama and James D. MacBeth, "Risk, Return and Equilibrium: Empirical Tests." Unpublished Working Paper No. 7237, University of Chicago, Graduate School of Business, August 1972.

William L. Fouse, William W. Jahnke. and Barr Rosenberg, "Is Beta Phlogiston?" *Financial Analysts Journal,* January–February 1974.

Roger G. Ibbotson and Rex A. Sinquefield, *Stocks, Bonds, Bills, and Inflation: Historical Returns.* The Financial Analysts Research Foundation, University of Virginia, 1979, 1984.

Institutional Investors and Corporate Stock. U.S. Securities and Exchange Commission Institutional Investors Study Report, Raymond W. Goldsmith, ed. National Bureau of Economic Research, 1973.

Gerald D. Levitz, "Market Risk and the Management of Institutional Equity Portfolios." *Financial Analysts Journal,* January–February 1974.

Robert A. Levy, "Beta Coefficients as Predictors of Return." *Financial Analysts Journal,* January–February 1974.

Harry Markowitz, *Portfolio Selection: Efficient Diversification of Investments.* Wiley, 1959.

William F. Sharpe, *Portfolio Theory and Capital Markets.* McGraw-Hill, 1970.

————, "Risk, Market Sensitivity and Diversification." *Financial Analysts Journal,* January–February 1972.

———— and Guy M. Cooper, "Risk-Return Classes of New York Stock Exchange Common Stocks, 1931–1967." *Financial Analysts Journal,* March–April 1972.

Bruno H. Solnik, "The International Pricing of Risk: An Empirical Investigation of the World Capital Market Structure." *Journal of Finance,* May 1974.

"The Strange News about Risk and Return." *Fortune,* June 1973.

Chris Welles, "The Beta Revolution: Learning to Live with Risk." *Institutional Investor,* September 1971.

Chapter 10.

Marshall E. Blume, "On the Assessment of Risk." *Journal of Finance,* March 1971.

John G. Cragg and Burton G. Malkiel, *Expectations and the Structure of Share Prices.* University of Chicago Press, 1982.

Eugene F. Fama and Kenneth R. French, "The Cross-Section of Expected Stock Returns." *Journal of Finance*, June 1992.

Ravi Jagannathan and Zhenyu Wang, "The CAPM is Alive and Well." Unpublished Working Paper, University of Minnesota, 1993.

Richard Roll, "A Critique of the Asset Pricing Theory's Tests: Part 1: On Past and Potential Testability of the Theory." *Journal of Financial Economics,* March 1977.

S. A. Ross, "The Arbitrage Theory of Capital Asset Pricing." *Journal of Economic Theory,* December 1976.

Anise Wallace, "Is Beta Dead?" *Institutional Investor,* July 1980.

Chapter 11.

Zvi Bodie, Alex Kane, and Alan J. Marcus, *Essentials of Investments*, 2nd edition. Irwin, 1995.

Stephen Fay, *Beyond Greed.* Viking Press, 1982.

Options Exchanges, *Characteristics and Risks of Standardized Options.* 1994.

PART FOUR

Chapter 12.

David L. Babson and Company, Inc., *Weekly Staff Letter,* March 4, 1971.

Zvi Bodie, "Purchasing-Power Annuities: Financial Innovation for Stable Real Retirement Income in an Inflationary Environment." National Bureau of Economic Research, Working Paper No. 442, February 1980.

Vladimir P. Chernik, *The Consumer's Guide to Insurance Buying.* Sherbourne, 1970.

Max Fogiel, *How to Pay Lots Less for Life Insurance.* Research and Education Association, 1971.

Pennsylvania Insurance Department. *A Shoppers' Guide to Life Insurance.* 1972.

George E. Pinches, "The Random Walk Hypothesis and Technical Analysis." *Financial Analysts Journal,* March–April 1970.

Sylvia Porter, *Your Finances in the 1990s.* Prentice-Hall, 1990.

Jane Bryant Quinn, *Making the Most of Your Money.* Simon & Schuster, 1991.

Wiesenberger Financial Services, *Investment Companies and Their Securities.* 1980.

Chapter 13.

John C. Bogle, *Bogle on Mutual Funds: New Perspectives for the Intelligent Investor.* Irwin, 1994.

Lawrence Fisher, "Outcomes for 'Random' Investments in Common Stocks Listed on the New York Stock Exchange." *Journal of Business,* April 1965.

———— and James H. Lorie, "Rates of Return on Investments in Common Stocks." *Journal of Business,* January 1964.

Franco Modigliani and Richard Cohn, "Inflation and the Stock Market." *Financial Analysts Journal,* March–April 1979.

Chapter 14.

David Dreman, *The New Contrarian Investment Strategy.* Random House, 1982.

Barry Feldman. "An Economic Analysis of Constant Purchasing Power Bonds." Unpublished senior thesis, Princeton University, 1972.

Robert Frank, *Successful Investing through Mutual Funds.* Hart, 1969.

Burton G. Malkiel, "The Valuation of Closed-End Investment-Company Shares." *Journal of Finance,* June 1977.

Eugene Pratt, "Myths Associated with Closed-End Investment Company Discounts." *Financial Analysts Journal,* July–August, 1966.

Jeremy J. Siegel, *Stocks for the Long Run: A Guide to Selecting Markets for Long-Term Growth.* Irwin, 1994.

Ralph Lee Smith, *The Grim Truth about Mutual Funds.* Putnam, 1963.

John A. Straley, *What about Mutual Funds?* 2nd rev. ed. Harper & Row, 1967.

Rex Thompson, "Capital Market Efficiency and the Information Content of Discounts and Premiums on Closed-End Fund Shares: An Empirical Analysis." Graduate School of Industrial Administration, Carnegie-Mellon University, Working Paper No. 30, February 1978.

Chapter 15.

Joel M. Dickson and John B. Shoven, "Ranking Mutual Funds on an After-Tax Basis." Center for Economic Policy Research, Stanford University, Publication No. 344, April 1993.

Peter Lynch, *One Up on Wall Street.* Simon and Schuster, 1988.

Index